ENDURING ERASURES

RELIGION, CULTURE, AND PUBLIC LIFE

RELIGION, CULTURE, AND PUBLIC LIFE

··

Matthew Engelke, Founding Editor (2018–2024)
Seth Kimmel, Editor (2025–)

The Religion, Culture, and Public Life series is devoted to the study of religion in relation to social, cultural, and political dynamics, both contemporary and historical. It features work by scholars from a variety of disciplinary and methodological perspectives, including religious studies, anthropology, history, philosophy, political science, and sociology. The series is committed to deepening our critical understandings of the empirical and conceptual dimensions of religious thought and practice, as well as such related topics as secularism, pluralism, and political theology. The Religion, Culture, and Public Life series is sponsored by Columbia University's Institute for Religion, Culture, and Public Life.

For a complete list of books in the series, please see the Columbia University Press website.

ENDURING ERASURES

Afterlives of the

Armenian Genocide

HAKEM AMER AL-RUSTOM

Columbia University Press

New York

Publication of this book was made possible in part by funding from the Institute for Religion, Culture, and Public Life at Columbia University.

Columbia University Press

Publishers Since 1893

New York   Chichester, West Sussex

cup.columbia.edu

Library of Congress Cataloging-in-Publication Data

Names: Al-Rustom, Hakem Amer, author.

Title: Enduring erasures : afterlives of the Armenian genocide / Hakem Amer Al-Rustom.

Other titles: Afterlives of the Armenian genocide

Description: New York : Columbia University Press, [2025] | Series: Religion, culture, and public life | Includes bibliographical and index.

Identifiers: LCCN 2024033303 | ISBN 9780231213646 (hardback) | ISBN 9780231213653 (trade paperback) | ISBN 9780231559959 (ebook)

Subjects: LCSH: Armenian Genocide, 1915–1923. | Genocide survivors—Armenia—History—20th century. | Armenians—Turkey—History—20th century. | Armenians—France—History—20th century. | Armenian Church—Turkey. | Armenian diaspora.

Classification: LCC DS195.5 .A447 2025 | DDC 956.6/20154—dc23/eng/20241231

LC record available at https://lccn.loc.gov/2024033303

Cover design: Elliott S. Cairns

Cover image: Dominik Matus / Wikimedia Commons / CC BY 4.0

GPSR Authorized Representative: Easy Access System Europe, Mustamäe tee 50, 10621 Tallinn, Estonia, gpsr.requests@easproject.com *for Christine*

Hayatımla kaldım coğrafyamda
kendi tarihimi yazmaya.

I stayed in my geography with my life
To write my own history.

—Karin Karakaşlı, "Tarih-Coğrafya"/"History-Geography"

CONTENTS

BEGINNINGS

The idea for this book was born from a tragic event ignited by a historiographic intervention. In 2007, Istanbul witnessed the assassination of the Armenian journalist and editor Hrant Dink. His offense? An audacious challenge to the prevailing Turkish narratives concerning the Armenians, in which he hinted at the genocidal foundations of the Republic of Turkey. This tragic incident not only marked the loss of a prominent journalist and activist but also underscored the pivotal role that historiography plays in shaping and sustaining collective memory and national myths.

It was January 24, 2007—the day I returned to Paris and the day after I attended Hrant Dink's funeral in Istanbul. Pondering the funeral of the assassinated Armenian journalist, I thought: What does it mean for Turkey and for Armenians when some hundred thousand people march together in a four-mile funerary procession from Osmanbey to the Armenian cemetery in Kumkapı? The funeral procession was a political demonstration where, in the heart of Turkey's largest city, the crowd was shouting in Turkish, Kurdish, and Armenian, expressing solidarity with Dink and Armenians: "We are all Armenian! We are all Hrant Dink!" Surely there are not so many Armenians in Istanbul or in Turkey more generally, given that they amount to seventy thousand in Turkey's largest metropolis. Dink's death was unsettling for many in Turkey and in the Armenian diaspora—and for me. I was trying to make sense of this violent event and its contexts, which I did not know at the time.

Hrant Dink is a symbol for Armenian survivance in Turkey. He lived on the margins of the Turkish state and society as well as the Armenian diaspora, and therefore in multiple exiles. As an Armenian and a citizen of Turkey, a state whose constitution considers every citizen of the republic a Turk in the ethnic sense, he was an "other" both politically and socially. Dink was also an exile within the Armenian community.[1] For Armenians in Istanbul, Dink was an outcast, a secular person in a community that defines itself through belonging to the Armenian Apostolic Church. He was also an outspoken member of a community that deemed silence essential for its survival. In the Armenian diaspora outside Turkey, Dink was considered complicit with the Turkish state for refusing to center his activism on genocide recognition as many diasporic institutions wanted him to do.

Dink's exile was a product of his multiple refusals: on one hand, his refusal to assimilate and be silenced in Turkey, and on the other, his refusal to be tokenized as a victim for Armenian political activism. He believed that for there to be a future for the Armenians living in their homeland under the Turkish republican regime, or for there to be any Turkish–Armenian reconciliation, an engagement with Turkish civil society was key. He advocated for dialogue and political mobilization with communities like the Armenians, the Kurds, and other non-Muslim citizens of Turkey: these groups live on the society's margins, continue to be excluded, and face physical and institutional violence. Dink's exile was voluntary; as an Armenian born in Malatya who lived most of his life in Istanbul, he refused invitations to emigrate to Western Europe. Despite the repeated death threats that he received right up until his assassination, Dink chose to remain in Turkey rather than live as a privileged exile in a Western European capital.

Dink's death sparked a crisis that brought to the surface the ever-present, yet latent, history of violence against Armenians that continues to haunt Turkey to this day. His murder was dangerous to Turkey in the way it disrupted the official claim that Turkish history has evolved from its imperial origins toward the progress, modernity, and civility embodied in the secular republic that was established by Mustafa Kemal (Atatürk).[2] Before his assassination at the age of fifty-two, Dink questioned the foundational narratives and history of the Republic of Turkey. For his critiques, Dink was taken to court twice for "insulting Turkishness" under article 301 of the Turkish Penal Code,[3] which turned him into a public enemy. He brought Turkey's republican history under scrutiny when he suggested in a 2004 article that Sabiha Gökçen, a Turkish national hero and the world's first female combat pilot, was a Christian Armenian, a status that would render her a non-Turk. Dink's article was seen as a nail in the republic's coffin, because Gökçen was closely associated with the founder of the republic, Mustafa Kemal.[4] Speaking of Gökçen as an Armenian orphan also points to the systematic violence that destroyed the majority of Ottoman Armenians. It was upon this destruction of the Armenian population that the Republic of Turkey was founded, although the republican regime and its apologetic historians adamantly deny that a genocide ever took place. They downplay violence either as having been essential, blaming Armenians for it, or as an unintended consequence of war.[5] Dink's writings, activism, and assassination led—for perhaps the first time since the 1920s—to urgent public debates on Armenian history in Turkish civil society.

Dink's murder echoed throughout Armenian diasporic communities. Walking down the main street of Alfortville, a suburb (*banlieu*) of Paris, a few days later, I glimpsed many Armenian-owned coffeehouses, restaurants, and grocery stores with Dink's portrait in their windows. For many Armenians, the murder was not an isolated event, but rather a continuation of the efforts to annihilate Armenians that began in the late Ottoman period and that resulted in the killing of an estimated one million Armenians between 1915 and 1918. Some of the posters that hung on Armenian shops in Alfortville included a caption that read "1,500,000 + 1," placing the murder in a long timeline of events that constituted what Armenian activists in the diaspora describe as a "century of Turkish violence against Armenians." Before his death, Dink was criticized by some diasporic Armenians for not advancing the cause of genocide recognition in the way they wanted. After his killing, their position reversed almost overnight, as they turned Dink into a hero and a martyr. Armenian activists in France who had criticized Dink built an anti-Turkish campaign on his assassination. At the genocide memorial in Paris in April 2008, members of Dink's family and representatives of the Greek Cypriot community in France were staged side by side; the event simultaneously condemned Turkish aggression against Armenians in Turkey and the Turkish military occupation of northern Cyprus.

In another suburb of Paris, a large-scale memorial event for Dink took place in a hall named after the famous French-Armenian singer Charles Aznavour a few days after Dink's death. The flags of France and the Republic of Armenia decorated the center stage of the hall in the northern Parisian suburb of Arnouville-lès-Gonesse. The hostess welcomed people in French and asked the audience to sing the national anthem of Armenia. The remaining ceremony was largely in Turkish, featuring an interview that Dink gave to a Turkish television station before his assassination. I was surprised to see a three-hundred-strong Armenian audience addressed largely in Turkish rather than in Armenian or French. Despite the insistence of Armenian diasporic institutions in France on preserving the western Armenian language, one could explain the usage of French for the purpose of reaching out to a wider audience, given the political and cultural overtones of the event. But Turkish puzzled me, not only because it is still seen by many as the language of the perpetrator, but it does not advance the usage of western Armenian that many in the diaspora are struggling to preserve.

Following that event, I visited Krikor, who had emigrated from Istanbul to Paris in 1978, and shared with him my confusion as to why hundreds of Armenians in Arnouville-lès-Gonesse would be addressed in Turkish.

"Many Armenian migrants from Turkey speak Turkish as their first language—especially those migrants whose families came from different parts of Anatolia," Krikor explained.[6] "For example, Ara," nodding toward one of his friends, "his parents speak only Turkish." Krikor repeated my question to Ara in Armenian (although both speak Turkish), and Ara confirmed Krikor's statement, telling me in French: "We speak Turkish at home." He explained that his family comes from Everek, a village near Kayseri, and when the village school and church were closed after World War I, there was no place for them to learn Armenian. For this reason, the Armenians of this region mainly spoke Turkish. Krikor continued, "This was the fate of many Armenians who remained in Anatolia following the Lausanne Treaty. With only a few exceptions, most stopped speaking the local Armenian dialects. Those who stayed are likely now in Istanbul, or even here in France!" His comment ran contrary to a common view among many diasporic Armenians that Anatolia had been emptied of Armenians during the genocide. Because Krikor was born and raised in Istanbul, I asked him if he knew how Armenians survived in Anatolia decades after the genocide. "This is good question!" Krikor told me with an inquisitive smile. "I don't know the answer! I have always wondered about it. Perhaps you could try to find out yourself." This book is an attempt to answer this question.

Years later, I realized that this book was conceived at the instance of Dink's murder. On January 17, 2007, I was some two hundred meters away from Hrant Dink when he was shot dead upon entering the *Agos* office building in Istanbul. His death was revelatory. The sporadic encounters following Dink's funeral procession in Istanbul, the actual murder itself, the heroization of his killer in some Turkish media outlets and societal circles, and his memorialization among diasporic Armenians in France initiated my inquiries that led to this book. Yet it was that encounter with Krikor that provoked my curiosity about what happened to those who remained in their homeland and became Turkish citizens in the aftermath of the genocide and my interest in writing an investigative ethnography.

❧

As writers, we weave our narratives with the delicate threads of multiple beginnings. My journey through Armenian history finds yet another beginning, not in dusty archives or ancient landscapes, but in the intimate, the personal. For our work is often autobiographical. I cannot pinpoint the precise moment when the stories of Armenian suffering, annihilation, and forced exodus from

Anatolia first reached my ears, but neither can I recall a time when these stories were not engraved on my heart. They lived in the tales of my family and the bonds we shared with fellow Armenians in Cairo. I had heard from my maternal grandmother and my mother that my grandfather was an Armenian from Mardin—*Mardeen*, as we pronounce it in Arabic. When a listener did not know where that was, they would add, "It is a city near Diyarbakır, now in Turkey. The family came to Alexandria escaping from the Turks." These memories were etched into our very beings: for in Egypt, we bore the collective memory of a distant homeland. Like many, "I, too, live in the time of catastrophe, by which I mean I am living in the future created by it," to echo the words of Saidiya Hartman.[7] These words best capture how the Armenian past continues to sculpt not just my own existence but our shared present.

Everyone in the family knew of these events and yet rarely mentioned them because there was not much to talk about. What we possessed were mere fragments of this exodus: "Armenian . . . Mardin . . . near Diyarbakır . . ." These few syllables carried a heavy emptiness, whispering wind in the silence about what genocides inscribe on survivors—ruptures that leave survivors without kin, estranged from their homelands, and strangers everywhere they go. "Our heritage is unspoken," as Harry Harootunian aptly phrased it—he was referring to the ways in which his parents' silence about the genocide shaped his upbringing in the United States.[8]

As part Armenian, I grew up in Egypt assuming, like many diasporic Armenians, that Armenians were either killed in the genocide or survived in the diaspora. My "discovery" that Armenians remained and continue to live in what became the Republic of Turkey was like facing ghosts from a distant past. The Armenians who remained were othered by some Armenians in the diaspora: they were simultaneously seen as belonging to a shared Armenian past of the genocide and to the present of the perpetrator, because they lived in Turkey, spoke Turkish, and carried Turkish citizenship. I explore the traces of the Armenian survivors in Turkey through my own diasporic experience and within my Arab context. This book endeavors to *critically* understand how, unlike Armenians in the diaspora, Armenians in Turkey continued living in their homeland, yet under the same nationalist ideology that once sought their annihilation. They are citizens of a state that systematically attempted to erase their existence in Anatolia. It was with such complicated relationality to the Armenians of Turkey and in the midst of loss that my inquiry into the Armenian survival in Turkey began. And this was the very day Hrant Dink was assassinated.

While writing this book, I encountered Audre Lorde's 1977 essay "The Transformation of Silence into Language and Action."[9] My concern, which bore an existential weight, revolved around discovering my voice, a voice that would allow me to narrate stories in a manner that transcended recounting to include the journey that led me to these narratives. This challenge extends beyond the mechanics of writing to encompass a deeper question: How can I compassionately and honestly convey the stories entrusted to me? I have grappled with the responsibility of storytelling, particularly the delicate balance required to faithfully convey others' stories all the while recognizing that our interpretive lens is inevitably influenced by the gravity of power dynamics and our own predispositions. Mindful that our narratives are ultimately shaped by our own experiences that influence both the storyteller and the story being told, my concern has been further magnified by the awareness of the need to narrate without serving a nationalist view of the past, be it Armenian or Turkish, or promoting an agenda driven by blind allegiance to the communities with which I am associated.

Reflecting on the practice of ethnography, Ruth Behar states that "anthropology is about embarking on . . . a voyage."[10] In anthropology, Behar explains, this journey is not just geographic but also emotional. The journey is one of navigating through complex human experiences and histories of *loss* of people, cultures, and languages; one of *mourning*, as we witness people's emotional struggles with loss and displacement; and one of *longing*, as we struggle to capture and understand people and their histories, which continue to be altered or erased by state policies or simply by the natural cycle of time and people passing on.[11] Conducting historical ethnography has transported me across diverse geographies and through numerous epochs. My journey has sometimes involved physical travel, but it has always unfolded through the stories shared with me. While anthropologists are traditionally characterized as "participant observers," it is essential to recognize that we are ultimately receivers of stories. When individuals entrust us with intimate recounting of their pain, their remorse, and the contradictions of their lives, we become the dedicated recipients of their stories. This practice confronts the archetypal image of the dispassionate, objective observer and accepts that we are shaped by our own life stories, feelings, and susceptibilities. In embracing this reality, we become what Behar precisely terms "vulnerable observers."

In this light, Lorde's essay presented to me a methodological suggestion: "The transformation of silence into language and action is an act of self-revelation." Writers, therefore, must confront their own vulnerabilities. Lorde poses questions that I have tried to answer, and that thus have informed this book: "What are the words you do not yet have? What do you need to say? What are the tyrannies you swallow day by day and attempt to make your own?"[12] I paused upon reading two of Lorde's terms: self-revelation and tyranny. Lorde's concept of "self-revelation" involves a journey of self-discovery, wherein writers confront the muted and vulnerable aspects of their own lives. "Tyrannies" rightly describes what I and many others with marginalized status, silenced stories, and suppressed pasts feel. Just as the lack of a voice is a symptom of a lack of self-revelation, I felt the weight of these tyrannies without fully understanding what they were. I had not yet found the words for them.

This book is an attempt to uncover and find the language and courage to speak of the vulnerabilities of loss and alienation, a reality that we, as Armenians and Christians in and of the Middle East, continue to experience. Our communities have been diminished in numbers and political agency. This decline was markedly accelerated by the cataclysmic events of the early twentieth century, notably the Armenian genocide and the subsequent Lausanne Treaty of 1923, which institutionalized the forced exchange of populations between Greece and Turkey based on religious identity, expelling Orthodox Christians from Anatolia to Greece and Muslims from Greece to Anatolia. Additionally, the region has withstood a series of violent disruptions such as colonial interventions, the ascent of military and religious dictatorships, military occupations, and the exhortations from our diasporic communities to seek new horizons elsewhere. These disturbances have collectively fostered a significant rupture in the demographic and cultural tapestry of the Middle East from Turkey and Egypt to Palestine/Israel, Lebanon, Syria, and Iraq.

As members of these communities, we are constantly fixated on numbers and percentages: we inflate them when arguing for rights and diminish them when we feel helpless. I recall a conversation with an Armenian in Istanbul who asked me about the Christian population in Egypt. I told her that Christians make up around 10 percent of a population of eighty million, referring to the statistics in 2010. She was shocked to hear that we were talking about eight million Christians in Egypt. She thought that was too many, given that Armenians are only seventy thousand in Turkey and dwindling. She told me she had contemplated emigrating to Europe because "Christians don't have a future in Turkey." I told her that is what people say in other parts of the Middle East as well. In a poignant conversation with another Armenian in Turkey, he remarked with a sense of foreboding, "In a few years, we will be the subject of archaeological research!"—suggesting a future in which Armenians in Turkey might only be known through the remnants they leave behind, with no living voices to tell their stories. These exchanges not only reflect the varying perceptions and anxieties within these communities but also underscore a broader existential uncertainty that pervades minoritized communities in the region.

Anxieties about belonging also endure among Armenians in the diaspora. When I spoke with Armenian migrants from Turkey in France, they emphasized how when they left Turkey, they carried with them an identity deeply rooted in their Armenian culture and sense of belonging. Yet, upon setting foot in

Europe, they often found themselves cloaked in a blanket perception of Turkish nationality and culture—a label that diluted or even erased their distinct cultural specificities, sometimes even in the eyes of fellow Armenians in France. In the early days of my fieldwork, French Armenians relayed to me that they thought Armenians from Turkey acted like Muslims, because they opened their arms when they prayed and because women covered their hair when going into church. The assumption is, of course, one of an essentialized binary. Turkey and the Middle East are supposedly Muslim spaces, while Europe is Christian, so to have an eastern Christian with mannerisms similar to those of Muslims creates confusion: these eastern Christians are outliers from their common perceptions. In the same fashion, Muslims in Euro-American societies share the same burden of being othered by similar sets of assumptions.

Middle Eastern Christians navigate a world where they are perennially othered. On one side, they experience the same prejudiced brush that paints Muslims. These canvases are built upon their Middle Eastern or Arab origins as they emigrate to societies where white supremacy and Islamophobia are endemic. On the other hand, within their home societies, they are often perceived as outliers. They are discriminated against politically and legally, mistreated and referred to with racist slurs or as vestiges of Euro-American colonial legacies, and wrongly equated with Westerners, while sometimes even mistakenly labeled as their agents. This dichotomy leaves them doubly alienated: viewed as quasi-Westerners or inferior others at home but racialized in the same manner as their fellow Muslim citizens in the West. Their very existence often necessitates an explanation or qualification, as they are compelled to navigate identities that the postcolonial world order has deemed separate or even conflicting—be they Arab Christians, Christian Palestinians, Turkish Armenians, Coptic Egyptians, Syriac Christians, or others. In their predominantly Muslim home societies, these identities are marginalized and racialized as "other/s" by the mainstream majority.

Hyphenated or double identities represent more than just labels; they reflect the complex struggle of articulating a sense of belonging in a world that often seeks to simplify individual biographies and multiple allegiances into rigid, binary categories. As they attempt to reconcile these often-conflicted identities, Armenians and other Middle Eastern Christians frequently find themselves overly conscious of how they are perceived, both in their native societies and in their countries of migration. These communities often face the challenge of navigating between invisibility and assimilation, leading to the anxiety that many have about their future.

I am often asked why I chose to write about the Armenians in Turkey. What drives me to focus on a community that I do not belong to and that numbers less than seventy thousand in a country with a population of more than eighty million? What can the stories of these individuals, these members of a small community, tell us about survival, history, and the complexities of the nation-state world order? Ultimately, what do the stories tell us about being human? This book is therefore prompted by both personal and communal loss. The journey that we take in doing historical anthropology is not just to different times and places, but is also within our own selves, where we, in the words of T. S. Eliot, "arrive where we started. And know the place for the first time."[13] The loss I feel encompasses not only individuals I know but also reflects a broader communal context. The violence that accompanied the demise of the Ottoman Empire—whether through genocide and ethnic cleansing, or the rise of exclusionary ethnonationalisms, military dictatorships, and religiopolitical fundamentalism in the region—worked in tandem to displace populations, deny them rights, and erase traces of their histories. The Christians of the Middle East, like many minoritized communities around the world, have seen their numbers dwindle and living spaces diminish in the nation-state order that has emerged since imperial demise.

The destruction of Ottoman Armenians was, therefore, a predicament shared with other populations that bore the final cost of imperial demise, whose obliteration was necessary for the construction of ethnoracial states determined to exclude them. Yet the destruction of cities, buildings, and landscapes in the Middle East endures, either by war, national militaries, fundamentalisms, or through the neoliberal "developments" that one sees today all over the region. In the early years of my fieldwork, I traveled to Aleppo, seeking glimpses of a late Ottoman city that stood in remarkable contrast to cities in Turkey subjected to heavy-handed Turkification policies. Aleppo still retained many Ottoman elements in its social relations and neighborhoods; most importantly, it was not subjected to a top-down nationalist project as nearby Antakya was. Now, the Aleppo that provided a safe haven for genocide survivors during World War I lies in ruins, and its Armenians are scattered in Yerevan, Beirut, Istanbul, or New York. All this transpired within a mere hundred years since World War I, a period that shaped the face and historical direction of the region.

The loss that I continue to experience as a member of these minoritized Christian communities is ongoing and continuous, with everyday erasures that are slow and persistent. Seeing people emigrate—emptying neighborhoods, churches, and schools—signifies the fading away of lives, cultures, and modes of being right in front of my eyes, a reality that many of us have to confront. In the end, we are drawn to the stories that echo our deepest concerns, and I seek to tell those that weave these personal experiences of loss and displacement with the broader human condition. I see my role in writing this book not as one of claiming authority or authorized knowledge, but rather as a witness to stories that themselves speak of the ongoing personal and communal loss.

One of the difficulties this book grapples with is figuring out how to write with a critical lens that challenges hegemonic systems of representation. This critique is particularly focused on the portrayal of Armenians and Turkey and aims to unveil the dehumanizing effects of such representations. For example, the Turkish state often denies the Armenian genocide by highlighting the number of Muslims killed in the wake of the rise of Christian ethnonationalisms in the Balkans. As a result, those who advocate for the recognition of the Armenian genocide often shy away from mentioning the loss in life and properties as well as the displacement of Balkan Muslims. This continues to be a persistent trend even in some academic approaches to both histories.

In critiquing the representation of Armenians and Turkey, the book challenges the hegemonic systems that often dehumanize "other/s" in their portrayal. Such a stance necessitates a commitment to multiple refusals. One is a refusal to foreground the suffering of one group in order to deny violence against another. A second is a refusal of both the denialism of the Armenian genocide propagated by the Turkish state and its apologist intellectuals *and* the Orientalism and Islamophobia that pervade depictions of Muslims, Turkey, its citizens, and its history. To counter denialism and Orientalism simultaneously and to situate the predicament of Balkan Muslims as an important context for the Armenian genocide, we must transcend the confines of blind allegiances, whether rooted in nationalism, sectarianism, or racism.

Now, what does this mean for Armenians and Turkey? Turkey had been seen and read in ideologically contradictory terms: on the one hand as an anomaly in the Muslim world for its perceived secularity and European outlook, and on the other hand as a Muslim-majority country that has no place in Europe. Turkey is also positioned as a buffer zone between Europe and the Middle East, and so it has been presented in a framework that undermines the crimes of the state. In the last decade, the Turkish state has positioned itself as a voice against Islamophobia in Europe and in support of Palestinians living as noncitizens under Israeli military occupation. Turkey's position has been commended by many racialized and black populations in the Global North and South, Muslims and non-Muslims alike. But even while it has advocated for disenfranchised Palestinians and European Muslims, the Turkish state has often suppressed the violence that it has itself perpetrated. If one were to compile a nuanced inventory of actions by the Turkish state that are often sidelined in public discourses and media, it would include the violence against its Kurdish citizens as well as the Kurds of Iraq and Syria; the continuous military occupation of Cyprus (perhaps the second-longest occupation of this sort, after Israel's occupation of Palestinian and Syrian territories); the Turkish state's expansionist policies toward its southern Arab neighbors and Armenia; its support of the ethnic cleansing of the entire Armenian population of Artsakh; its long suppression and alienation of political dissent (which has targeted leftists, Islamists, and Kurds at different periods in Turkish history); the continuous denial of the Armenian genocide; and the everyday racism experienced by Turkey's Jewish and Christian citizens.

Can one genuinely address the Turkish government's anti-imperial rhetoric without rigorously scrutinizing its own oppressive, colonial-like actions, both domestically and regionally, and its selective advocacy for people of certain identities? The complexity of Turkey's history and geography necessitates the principle that we read and critique outside the binaries of admiration and vilification, civilization and barbarism. Like many states, Turkey legitimizes violence and excuses hypocrisy through the cunning art of making exceptions. One of the objectives of this book is to contribute to the critical practice of re-evaluating nation-states, like Turkey, that have long framed themselves within an anticolonial narrative. This re-evaluation involves recognizing their resistance against colonial powers while also acknowledging the destruction and violence they have caused and continue to perpetuate against populations that they racialized, marginalized, and inflicted violence upon. This approach requires us to read outside of binaries and enables us to launch multiple critiques of the nation-state and global politics, which tend to employ rules and standards with ideological, most often racist, selectivity. Thus, discourses and critiques of democracy and human rights or of racism and military occupation are often wielded selectively to serve power agendas, rather than applied consistently to defend those whose rights have been violated or whose lives and livelihoods have been compromised. The challenge, then, is not only to critique the nation-state but also to rethink the responsibilities of anthropologists and historians as public intellectuals, who are constantly confronting questions of power, injustice, and belonging.

As writers, we all have multiple belongings and allegiances, and it is important to acknowledge them, maintaining political consistency through critical analysis rather than succumbing to identity-based politics. Rigorously examining and questioning established narratives and ideologies requires challenging prevailing power structures, even when doing so might be unpopular or risky. This kind of examination is about prioritizing historical accountability over personal or institutional interests. As Edward W. Said aptly states in *Representations of the Intellectual*: "Never solidarity before criticism."[14] This stance highlights the tension between identity politics and the pursuit of a critical understanding of history and contemporary politics, often unsettling those who place allegiance above inquiry.

Grounded in the intellectual-political stance that resists the pull of belonging when it threatens critical engagement, my work as an anthropologist of history is driven by a commitment to interrogating the conditions under which certain narratives, communities, and people have been overlooked or silenced, and how these silences shape the production of historical knowledge. In doing so, it seeks not merely to acknowledge these absences but to destabilize the hegemonic narratives of history that render them marginal or nonexistent. My work does not begin from an obligation to a group, nation, or institution but from the imperative to ask difficult questions—even when those questions unsettle the very communities I belong to. This imperative pushes me to explore spaces beyond the margins of official archives and national histories, focusing on populations that have been racialized, erased, and cast into silence. My approach is embedded in a critical practice that refuses the false boundary between "pure" and political knowledge, a refusal that has been central to postcolonial critiques since the publication of Said's *Orientalism*. This refusal underscores that all acts of knowledge production are inherently political and intervene in the world accordingly. It is for this reason that I hyphenate intellectual-political: to reject the illusion that intellectual inquiry can ever be separate from the political, affirming instead that knowledge is always implicated in structures of power.

This book is born out of a dedication to refusing the constraints of colonial and ethnonationalist narratives, as well as religious and sectarian loyalties. Such frames have long shaped the study of Armenians, Turkey, and the wider Middle East and the Balkans. It underscores my belief that genuine solidarity must be rooted in critical thought and not in unquestioned loyalty to a group, a nation, a sect, or a religion. This work advocates for the principle that criticism is the lifeblood of intellectual-political consistency as well as an essential part of imagining and striving for different futures.[15] Said contended that our intellectual endeavors should never yield to the comfortable simplicity of blind allegiances, nor should our commitments be applied selectively. In this spirit, the book aims to ensure that solidarity is not a passive alignment or a blind endorsement, but an ongoing act of critical engagement and compassionate understanding. Being on the other side of power necessitates a deliberate commitment to the oppressed, the silenced, and the disenfranchised. It is my hope that readers will take this critical solidarity as a beginning for the book and find within its pages a shared commitment to rethinking history as a site of disruption and possibility for a more just and humane world.

APPRECIATION

I n the solitary endeavor of writing, we often forget that our thoughts are not entirely our own but are shaped and nurtured by a community of people who generously share their wisdom, critiques, and humor. This book is a testament to the collective effort of numerous individuals whose contributions, both big and small, have been instrumental in its fruition. While the limitations of memory may prevent me from acknowledging every person who has touched this journey, I endeavor to create a mosaic of gratitude for those who have left an indelible mark on the pages of this work. Their insights, encouragement, and companionship have been the guiding stars in the long and often winding road of research and writing that spanned more than a decade. In the following lines, I attempt to pay homage to the constellation of people who have made the realization of this book not just a possibility, but a reality.

I extend my deepest appreciation to my students at both the University of Michigan and the American University in Cairo. Embracing teaching as a vocation with profound responsibilities, I have been fortunate to engage with an audience that takes our classroom as a catalyst for change and critical engagement with the world. The opportunity to experiment with materials from my research in various courses has been invaluable. Through class discussions and insightful essays, my students have raised questions that have pushed me to think more critically and comparatively about the themes in this book. Teaching about the experiences and histories of Armenians in the shadow of the genocide within the context of the post-Ottoman Middle East, first in Egypt and then in the United States, has been particularly enriching. It has allowed me to understand the diverse perspectives of different audiences with their unique historical backgrounds and political commitments. I am especially grateful to my imaginative students in my Armenians in Turkey and the Diaspora class, as well as those in my seminars History, Memory, and Silence, Tracing the Ruins of Violent Pasts, and Violence and (De)colonization. Their curiosity and engagement have been constant sources of inspiration as I wrote this book. I hope that, in some small way, I have managed to answer their questions and make the story more accessible as well as contribute to their intellectual journeys as profoundly as they have contributed to mine.

At the University of Michigan, I have been fortunate to find myself at the intersection of intellectually stimulating communities that transcend departments, disciplines, and methods. The Doctoral Program in Anthropology and History has been a particularly enriching environment. I have always found willing interlocutors who have generously engaged with a diverse range of ideas and approaches. The vibrant intellectual culture of this program has been a constant source of inspiration and growth, for which I am grateful.

This book has benefited from the feedback received during a manuscript workshop organized by the History Department at Michigan. I am deeply grateful for the meticulous reading and insightful comments provided by the workshop participants, particularly David Kazanjian and Esra Özyürek. Additionally, I would like to thank all my colleagues who generously took time out of their midsummer schedules to offer their feedback, especially Joshua Cole, Reginald Jackson, Valerie Kivelson, and Ronald Suny. I am especially grateful for the unwavering support I received from Pamela Ballinger, Paul C. Johnson, Kenneth Mills, and Deborah Dash Moore, who were not only participants in the workshop but also served as invaluable intellectual interlocutors throughout the development of this project.

I am thankful to a number of individuals who generously read earlier drafts of this work. I would like to extend my heartfelt thanks to Magi Abdul-Masih, Ramy Aly, Özlem Biner, Tamar Boyadjian, Juan Cole, Webb Keane, Günay Kayarlar, Aram Kerovpyan, Gerard Libaridian, Helen Makhdoumian, Bedross Der Matossian, and Raya Naamneh for their contributions to the refinement of this manuscript. Additionally, I am thankful for the engaging discussions provided by the participants of the student-run Sociocultural Anthropology Workshop and the Multidisciplinary Workshop in Armenian Studies at Michigan.

Columbia University Press has been a supportive advocate for this project from our very first communication. I firmly believe that this book has found its rightful home within the Religion, Culture, and Public Life series, contributing to a rich, multidisciplinary, and multiregional conversation. I extend my gratitude to Matthew Engelke, the series editor, for his vision and guidance, and to the three reviewers for their incisive and thought-provoking queries. Their careful and engaged feedback challenged me to refine my arguments and clarify my intentions. Through their collective efforts, this work has been strengthened and made accessible to a broader audience, for which I am truly thankful. Additionally, my thanks go to Wendy Lochner, the publisher at the press, for her support in ensuring that this book appears in its present form. I express my appreciation to Alyssa Napier, Marisa Lastres, and Ben Kolstad whose meticulous attention to detail and dedication during the production process were indispensable.

For exceptional work on the manuscript, my heartfelt thanks go to Ellen Tilton-Cantrell, whose meticulous editing and empathetic reading have been nothing short of transformative. Ellen's keen eye and perceptive suggestions have not only polished the text but also deepened its substance, ensuring that every sentence resonates with clarity and purpose. While I am profoundly grateful to all those whose generous contributions have enriched and refined this book, ultimately the interpretations, perspectives, and decisions reflected in these pages remain my own. Any shortcomings, oversights, or errors are solely my responsibility.

The Center for Armenian Studies at Michigan has been a space where I intersected with people from diverse places and disciplines. I am thankful for the opportunity to work closely with scholars who have enriched my understanding and expanded my disciplinary horizons. I would like to extend my gratitude to the center's postdoctoral fellows: Cevat Dargin, Matthew Ghazarian, and Helen Makhdoumian with whom I explored the concepts of dispossession and critical indigenous studies. Karen Jallatyan and Anoush Suni provided invaluable insights into the analytical framework of afterlives, while Maral Aktokmakyan introduced me, through her sensitive reading, to the world of Zabel Yessayan.

I extend my heartfelt thanks to my colleagues at Michigan for their invaluable camaraderie: Samer Ali, Ruth Behar, Michèle Hannoosh, Murad Idris, Yanay Israeli, Leila Kawar, Nancy Khalil, Michael Lempert, Amir Marshi, Yasmin Moll, Rebekah Modrak, Ekaterina Olson Shipyatsky, Andrew Shryock, and Mrinalini Sinha.

The American University in Cairo holds a special place in my academic journey as the first institution where I developed and taught my courses. These courses have profoundly shaped me as both a teacher and a thinker, laying the foundation upon which my courses at Michigan have been built. I am deeply grateful to Soraya Altorki, Ramy Aly, Mariam Ayad, Amina Elbendary, Salima Ikram, Ian Morrison, Helen Rizzo, Hanan Sabea, and Adam Talib. Ultimately, the engagement with the students in the Graduate Program in Sociology–Anthropology has been an incredibly humbling experience. Their intellectual brilliance and insatiable curiosity have not only challenged me but also enhanced my abilities as both a reader and a mentor.

As I reflect on my journey through graduate training, I am filled with immense gratitude for the teachers and thinkers who helped shape my intellectual path. Their wisdom, support, and guidance have been foundational to my academic and personal growth. I would like to extend my heartfelt thanks to Rita Astuti, Maurice Bloch, the late Peter Loizos, Martha Mundy, Johnathan Parry, and the late Peter Gow at the London School of Economics, and Yael Navaro at the University of Cambridge.

I am particularly grateful for the chance to participate in the graduate seminars of Nadia Abu El-Haj and Audra Simpson at Columbia University. They have each been exceptionally welcoming in their respective seminars, providing me with insights that have been crucial in the development of the arguments that shaped my work.

I owe a debt of gratitude to those who have enriched my thinking with their ideas. Foremost, I would like to express my profound thanks to Edward W. Said and Patrick Wolfe, both of whom are dearly missed. Their contributions continue to resonate deeply, influencing my work even though our conversations could not continue. I am also grateful to Gil Anidjar, David Kazanjian, Michael Löwy, Marc Nichanian, and Ella Shohat, who have significantly shaped my intellectual landscape. And to Sami Khatib, with whom I read the work of Walter Benjamin and organized a series of workshops titled Walter Benjamin and the Non-European in Cairo, Ann Arbor, and Beirut that enriched my engagement with Benjamin's work on history and its intersections with postcolonial writings.

Some of the key ideas in this book grew through the stimulating conversations with colleagues who have offered their insights. I am grateful for Sinem Adar, Sebouh Aslanian, Anny Bakalian, Rana Barakat, Stephen Berrey, Melissa Bilal, Ayşe Buğra, Deanna Cachoian-Schanz, Girish Daswani, Ankur Datta, Vazken Khatchig Davidian, Lerna Ekmekçioğlu, Aslı Iğsız, Ardi Imseis, Adel Iskandar, Sossie Kasbarian, Nora Mildanoğlu Kayaer, the late Vangelis Kechriotis, Vahakn Keshishian, Kéram Kévonian, Çağlar Keyder, Ohannes Kiliçdağı, Ayşenur Korkmaz, Maud Mandel, Susan Pattie, Helmut Puff, Chandan Reddy, Ara Sanjian, Ara Sarafian, Nükhet Sirman, Talin Suciyan, Khachig Tölölyan, Fatma Ülgen, Uğur Ümit Üngör, Onur Yıldırım, and Altuğ Yılmaz.

I owe a special thanks to Bashir Bashir for inviting me to participate in the Arab-Jewish Engagement Working Group at the Bruno Kreisky Forum in Vienna. Over the course of six years, engaging with fellow scholars and the rich debates we shared was pivotal in enabling me to think comparatively about Armenian history alongside the Jewish and Palestinian experiences in the aftermath of the Holocaust. These sustained interactions have profoundly influenced the interventions I have adopted in this book, fostering an understanding of history that transcends both identity politics and the selective focus on suffering in some historical narratives of political violence.

My utmost gratitude goes to the many Armenians in and from Turkey who generously shared their stories and experiences with me. While I do not name them here to protect their privacy, each of their contributions has been invaluable in shaping this book. Their openness and trust have allowed me to explore and present a narrative that is both personal and historical. It is my sincere hope that this work has been honest in translating their experiences and stories, even if partially, to wider publics and constituencies.

The Hrant Dink Foundation and *Agos* were cornerstones for my fieldwork in Istanbul, helping me navigate the nuances and complexities of the Armenian community and the city itself—nuances that anthropologists often miss in the early days of fieldwork. This community became my anchor in the city, providing a vital space for engagement and connection. Hrant Dink himself sparked my interest in this book. While I missed meeting him by days, perhaps even hours, but his tragic death and the collective mourning ignited a wave of political participation and activism. His assassination brought people together across divides, fostering solidarity and a shared commitment to justice. This collective response shaped my understanding of his enduring impact and inspired me to engage with the questions and struggles that his work illuminated.

I am deeply grateful to Karin Karakaşlı for the opportunity to engage with her poem "History-Geography," which resonates profoundly with the themes of this book. My thanks also go to Erica Hesketh, director of The Poetry Translation Centre in London, for facilitating its inclusion in both Turkish and its English translation.

To my own Armenian community in Cairo, where I first learned about our family history, where we came from, and why—my deepest gratitude. It was within the Armenian Catholic Church of St. Thérèse in Heliopolis that I first encountered the varied rhythms of Armenian life. There, Armenian was sung and spoken, mingling seamlessly with Turkish-accented Arabic and Armenian-accented French, creating a layered linguistic and cultural tapestry that shaped my earliest understanding of identity, belonging, and exile. Language and place, as I experienced them, were never simple or fixed. Instead, they were complex and fraught, bearing the weight of histories of violence, displacement, and survival. This complexity was further heightened by the dissonance between places of origin and the places where we lived—spaces that carried memories of what was left behind and the realities of new beginnings. These layers of geography and memory intertwined, shaping an existence that was as much about loss as it was about adaptation and resilience. It is this community that provided the foundation for my connection to the larger questions this book seeks to explore. The stories I heard and lived, often shared in fragments over gatherings or through whispered recollections, kindled my curiosity about the broader Armenian experience and its resonance beyond Cairo. I hope this book, in some small way, honors both the people and their stories and illuminates the enduring legacies of displacement, survival, and hope that they carry.

There are rare individuals whose support transcends the professional realm, touching our lives so profoundly that they come to be counted as family. To these cherished people, I extend my deepest gratitude. Allison Alexy and Reginald Jackson have provided constant solidarity. Anne and Budge Gere have graciously adopted us into their lives, becoming not just friends but family, and lovingly assuming the role of our children's "grandparents in the Western Hemisphere." To Magi Abdul-Masih, Najib and Nelly Coutya, Aram and Virginia Kerovpyan, Gerard Libaridian, Michelle Obeid, and Behzad Yaghmaian, I am deeply grateful for their friendship, their steady presence, and their boundless generosity. Whether through offering sage advice, a word of encouragement, or simply the comfort of knowing they are always there.

I am deeply grateful to the Moughalians, who became family almost instantly upon entering my life in the middle of my writing this book. They have extended their love and support in countless ways and added so much joy and warmth to this journey.

My parents, Amer and Marianne, have been the firm foundation upon which I stand. Alongside them, my brother Bassel and my sister Layal have also been integral to my journey. Their sacrifices and love have not only supported me but have made the very writing of this book possible. They have instilled in me the values of justice and consistency, and it is our family's survivance that has informed my inclination to pursue and write this work. This book, then, is an attempt to channel and make sense of the heavy heritage and unreconciled memories of violence that have been passed down to us.

To Lara Maria and Elie Jean, your beautiful entry into my life has given birth to me as a father, adding hope and faith that different futures are indeed possible. Your laughter and curiosity are the light in my days and the inspiration for my aspirations. Christine, my unwavering companion on this often-solitary journey of writing: she has been my rock. The sacrifices she has made, the patience she has shown, and the support she has provided have allowed me the time and space to pour myself into this work. She has made writing not just bearable, but meaningful. It is to Christine that I dedicate this book.

ENDURING ERASURES

INTRODUCTION

"**I** want you to meet our new friend, Hakem. He is from Mardin," Mary said when she was introducing me at a gathering at her place in Paris. Her comment "he is from Mardin" came to me as a shock, because I had never thought of myself as being from a place that I had never visited and could not even locate on a map. This connection was solely based on my maternal family's roots. Although I knew the name "Mardin" from family conversations, it was not a place that I ever would have described myself as being from. This, however, changed during the time I spent in Paris and Istanbul tracing the stories of Armenians who survived in Turkey and, at the same time, tracing the Armenian in me.

Krikor and Mary were the first Armenians I met in Paris in 2006. Krikor was an active leftist in Turkey at the peak of the anti-communist strife in the 1970s. Krikor once told me that it was difficult being both a leftist and an Armenian in Turkey back then, as this made him a double target for the Turkish state. This vulnerability prompted his migration to France in 1978, where Krikor and Mary formed a group dedicated to Armenian music. I met them for the first time after a concert they gave at the chapel of the St. Louis Hospital in the Tenth District of Paris. The church was built in 1611 and had a dozen pews that were mostly filled for the concert, which was dedicated to Armenian Christmas hymns.[1] After the concert, I waited until Krikor came from backstage. I introduced myself and told him in Turkish that the concert was *lokum gibi*—as sweet as Turkish delight, words I had picked up during my first visit to Istanbul a year earlier. He laughed. In retrospect, it was a loaded move on my part to speak to an Armenian from Istanbul whom I was meeting for the first time in Turkish, given the history (which I did not yet know in the early days of my fieldwork). Mary joined us, and

I later complimented her on her singing. They invited me to their apartment, where a few of their friends were going for a drink after the concert.

Chatting at their place, Mary was interested in hearing about where I came from and about my family background. I told her that I was born and raised in Egypt, as was my mother, whose father was an Armenian from Mardin. My father is from Syria. When I mentioned Syria, she said enthusiastically that her mother was from Kessab. "Do you know it?" she asked. "It is a mountainous Armenian village, very beautiful, and a popular summer destination in Syria. It is right on the Turkish border." She continued, with regret: "In fact, the Armenians of the village lost the majority of their fertile lands to Turkey. They can see the fruits ripen on their trees, but they cannot touch them. They are now on the other side of a border." Mary was referring to the Sanjak of Alexandretta that the French colonial government carved out of Syria and ceded to Turkey in 1938. When I asked Mary if her father was also an Armenian, she said, "No, he was French." Our non-Armenian fathers and the places of our birth and upbringing would not occupy any significant part of any of our conversations in the following years. She was mostly *from* Kessab and I, *from* Mardin—places we had barely visited and that no longer exist the way we imagine them, except in the stories we tell about them.

This encounter with Mary that made me *from* Mardin was not a onetime occurrence. It was repeated every time I was introduced to someone new. If the Armenians I knew did not volunteer the Mardin connection, people I met would keep asking me where—in pre-genocide Anatolia—I came *from*. During my time in Paris and Istanbul, I met Armenians *from* Sivas, Kayseri, Van, Harput, etc. And I have adopted the same outlook myself: whenever I meet new Armenians, I now speak of Mardin as ours, as mine. And indeed, although it is frequently mentioned in my family that my grandfather came *from* Mardin, he was not born there; he was born in Egypt. It was his father who escaped to Egypt in the early days of World War I, specifically in 1914, as documented in the archives of the Armenian Catholic Church in Alexandria. We all place ourselves and each other on a map of Ottoman Anatolia before the Armenian catastrophe—the genocide—using the names of cities and villages that predated their destruction and Turkification by the republican regime. In some instances, places like Everek and Kharpert/Harput no longer exist as separate entities, as they were annexed to cities that carried the Turkish names Develi and Elazığ, respectively. Such places continue to exist through the stories that Armenians share with one another.

It was through this encounter with Mary that I became someone *from* Mardin; and with my new affiliation, I started my fieldwork. A pressing question that emerged during this period and that continues to inform this book is what it means for people to say that they come *from* places that they have little or no physical connection to. Or to rephrase the question: What is the significance for people of speaking about belonging through the telling of stories? What is notable is that these places are important constituents of self-identification, regardless of how the places exist today or the physical connections one actually has with them. Armenians, myself included, assert their survivance in the shadow of the genocide by articulating their presence through the practice of telling a *from* story, which provides a way to speak of their self-identification in the present through their family histories. Such histories—selective, imagined, and fragmented as they may be—forge common diasporic kinships among Armenians, kinships that are not framed with the logic of the nation-state that dispossessed them from the locales that their parents and grandparents called home.

This act of narrating belonging through storytelling, rather than through physical presence, underscores the many ways Armenians assert their "survivance"—a term that, as in Native American studies, invokes both survival and resistance in the face of historical erasure. While much of the existing scholarship on the Armenians in Turkey has either focused on Armenian history in the formative years of the republic or examined how the Armenian genocide persists in the present through memory and material traces, the stories of those who remained in Anatolia—where their presence continues to be actively erased—require a different analytical lens. In bridging these two scholarly trajectories, *Enduring Erasures* examines how Armenians were dispossessed in the early republican period and how traces of their presence continue to surface in the present. To do so, I introduce the concept of "denativization" to capture the enduring consequences of violence, dispossession, and erasure, highlighting how these historical forces continue to shape Armenian experiences today. In recent years, anthropologists and historians have increasingly studied these afterlives of violence, particularly in the wake of Hrant Dink's assassination in 2007, which catalyzed renewed critical inquiries into Armenian presence in Turkey.[2] *Enduring Erasures* builds on and extends this emerging body of work by centering histories that lie outside conventional archives and must be pieced together from a constellation of sources that includes oral narratives, refusals, silences, contested memories, and literary texts. In doing so, it argues that absence itself is a historical force, not only shaping Armenians' lived experiences but also structuring the ways their presence, despite systematic erasure, persists over time.

Living and experiencing the afterlives of the catastrophe means being perpetually in the shadow of loss, destruction, and dispossession. The homeland, cities, and villages that have been materially lost continue, in their absence, to invoke people's emotions and to shape their sense of belonging and the relationships they forge with others.[3] For example, the Armenian American author William Saroyan, who was born in Fresno, California, often referred to himself in Armenian as *Bitlistsi*, that is, as being "of" or "from" Bitlis, the city from which his parents came before the genocide.[4] Such a practice is not unique to Armenians. Leslie Marmon Silko, a Native American writer whose people survived annihilation and dispossession, once noted that in the Pueblo culture to which she belongs, people construct identities through storytelling.[5] For Pueblo people, individual identity is expressed by telling stories—both of pride and shame—about what is important to the family to which they belong.

Such relational belonging is also practiced by many Armenians when they express their belonging by telling the stories of their parents' and grandparents' villages as their own, regardless of their distance from those places temporally and geographically. Using the present tense and the plural—"we are from Mardin"—makes the statement always true and makes it speak of the present. Armenians speak of affiliation, identification, and belonging as articulated, experienced, communicated, and shared through stories. Such stories, Silko writes, "are always bringing us together, keeping this whole together, keeping this family together, keeping this clan together." When one Armenian tells another that they belong to the group of Armenians who came from this or that specific Anatolian locale, the listener reciprocates by telling their own *from* story. Through this exchange, they cumulatively create a larger story about a common origin and the shared experience of loss, despite the fact they come *from* different Anatolian locales. It is in such differences that the common Armenian experience is told. Relatedness as well as similarities and differences are woven through the process of telling stories about being an Armenian *from* a specific locale in Anatolia. Storytelling in this context is not about communicating facts and exchanging information.[6] Rather, through the sharing of experiences, storytelling creates meaning about one's present by detouring to the past and becoming a path to survivance in the midst of the loss and destruction that many Armenians continue to bear.[7]

BOTH REFUGEES AND REFUSE

Ottoman Armenians were estranged from their Anatolian homeland multiple times. Many were killed or left to die in the Syrian Desert during the mass deportations that turned into death marches, which started in the spring and continued through the hot summer of 1915. The majority of the Ottoman Armenian population perished in the genocide. Those who survived hid or were left to the mercy of those among the Kurds, Turks, and Arabs who offered them protection; many of those who survived were abused as they made their way into the Syrian Desert and from there to cities in Syria and Iraq.

Between 1914 and 1918, an estimated one million Armenians were murdered in the Ottoman Empire.[8] The Young Turk regime orchestrated this atrocity, justifying it through a complex combination of factors. Key among these was the perception of Armenians as internal adversaries during a period when the empire faced existential threats from the Balkan Wars (1912–1913) and World War I (1914–1918). In response to these conflicts, the Young Turk regime pursued a policy aimed at creating a homogeneous Muslim (and later Turkish) state. The support extended by European powers to non-Muslims in the Balkans and later to Armenians was perceived as a direct challenge to the Ottoman state's territorial integrity and survival. Driven by a desire to preserve the empire and fueled by burgeoning nationalist sentiments, the Young Turk government increasingly saw Armenians as an internal threat that had to be eradicated to secure the empire's future. This led to the systematic disarming, deportation, and mass killing of Armenians, rationalized as essential for the defense of the empire and the Turkish nation. The genocide represented the tragic climax of radical political ideologies and the intense pressures of global conflict during World War I.[9] The group of Young Turks responsible for the Armenian genocide were not motivated by religious fanaticism or ethnonationalism. Creating an ethnonationalist state was not yet on the horizon. Instead, they were Ottoman modernizers focused on preserving the Ottoman state.[10]

Armenian displacement continued after World War I ended, when many survivors, numbers unknown, returned to their cities and villages in Anatolia. Following the signing of the Treaty of Ankara in 1921 with France, the Ankara government (the precursor to the Turkish republican regime) gained control over the French-occupied parts of southern Anatolia bordering Syria. This transfer of control forced as many as two hundred thousand Armenians to leave southern Anatolia, including Cilicia; those who remained were eventually forced out by the Kemalist forces to places such as Syria (which included Lebanon), Egypt, Greece, and France.[11] Those who arrived in France did so with French travel documents indicating that they could not go back to their homeland.[12] By 1923, the Republic of Turkey, under the leadership of Mustafa Kemal (later Atatürk), was established throughout what had been Ottoman Anatolia, becoming a state with a clear confessional ethnicity; the diverse Ottoman Muslims were made to constitute the Turkish majority. The Armenians, with their deep-rooted cultural and linguistic ties to Anatolia or western Armenia, have historically regarded themselves as belonging to the region. Yet they were consequently redefined as foreign and racialized as one of Turkey's non-Muslim "minorities" in the aftermath of the Lausanne Treaty of 1923.

These new political realities turned the Armenians, who had been citizens of the Ottoman Empire, into a foreign minority within Turkey and a stateless (*apatride*) refugee population outside Turkey. Describing the state of refugees after World War II, Hannah Arendt observes that they were left without a government to represent or protect them, a comment that also reflects the state that Armenians were in after World War I.[13] Additionally, Armenian refugees did not have a country to return to, making their exile and dispossession permanent. These refugees eventually formed Armenian diasporic communities wherever they settled. Within the borders of what became Turkey after the Ottoman demise and without counting the thousands of hidden and Islamized Armenians,[14] some seventy thousand Armenians officially became Turkish citizens when the republic was declared in October 1923. The majority of these seventy thousand Armenians remained in Istanbul; far fewer remained in Anatolia.[15] This book focuses on the Armenians who remained in Anatolia after 1923.

I refer to the Armenian survivors in Turkey, outside of Istanbul, as Anatolian Armenians, a term that many Armenians also use. This term distinguishes them from both the Armenians of Istanbul and the converted or Islamized Armenians in Turkey, as well as from the Armenians living in diasporic communities outside the borders of Turkey.[16] Such a distinction is important for two reasons. First, unlike the Armenians of Istanbul, who were under the legal protection of the Lausanne Treaty (chapter 2), the Anatolian Armenians lost the markers of their communal life, as the majority of Armenian churches and schools were gradually closed and many were confiscated, and therefore lacked the institutional basis to maintain the cultural reproduction of their language, history, and community. Second, the converted Armenians, mostly women and their descendants, went through a process of assimilation in line with the state's nationalist ideology, which sees in Turkish-speaking Sunni Muslims its nationalist majoritarian population—at least as far as their official religious affiliation is concerned, because the state keeps data on the descendants of converts. By examining the lives of the descendants of the residual genocide survivors outside of Istanbul, chapter 3 brings to the foreground the lives of those who have lived without (or with a very minimal) social and institutional Armenian framework and who have not adopted the racialized religious identity of the Turkish majority in whose name the state rules.

Use of the label "Anatolian Armenian," however, runs the risk of assuming that this population is homogeneous and, like most labels, conceals the diversity and even contradictions lurking beneath it. We can trace the diversity among

Anatolian Armenians in the language(s) they speak, as many Armenian communities speak Kurdish and Turkish as their first language; in their family and social histories, including the details of where they came from, to whom they were married, and what occupation and education they had; in the means by which their parents or grandparents survived the genocide, as some survived by hiding on mountains, others by conversion, and others by managing to stay alive during deportation routes into Syrian and Iraqi cities; and in their regional self-identification, because Armenians in Anatolia had region-specific identities, dialects, and local customs. In other words, Anatolian Armenians are far from homogeneous, and in many instances, such regional and local specificities have been important in their everyday lives as Armenians. Their shared Armenianness is lived, experienced, and remembered through specific, and therefore different, local places and social contexts. The coming chapters map the structure and overarching experiences that Armenians share as a population living under the very regime that once sought their annihilation and encouraged their expulsion throughout the life of the Kemalist republic. The Anatolian Armenians were neither totally assimilated nor Islamized.

It was my understanding, as well as the assumption of many Armenians in the diaspora, that Armenians were either killed in the genocide or survived as refugees. Before beginning my research for this book, I was not aware of the survivors who stayed in Anatolia after the genocide. As I came to understand through my fieldwork, the survivors who stayed—who only left their homelands decades later—became the *refuse* of Turkish society and history and were also *refused* recognition by many Armenians in Istanbul and the diaspora because of their Turkified or Kurdified cultures. Considered the "leftovers of the sword" (*kılıç artığı*) in Turkey, Armenians were seen as scraps, residue, surplus, waste, remnants, remainders, discarded, and refuse, as the Turkish word for leftovers (*artık*) denotes. As the leftovers and refuse of Turkish society, the Armenians who continued living in their homelands as Turkish citizens went largely silenced in Turkish historiography. Armenian survival in Turkey was ignored and largely unaccepted by Armenians in the diaspora as well. As Madame Shushan, a French-Armenian woman in Alfortville, conveyed to me, "For a long time we did not know that they [Armenians in Turkey] existed." As a result, their Armenianness was questioned and sometimes even denied by many in the Armenian diasporic world. Shushan explained that Armenians from Turkey came to France without speaking Armenian and did not know anything about the genocide. I noticed that for some Armenians in France, Armenians in Turkey were unnoticed, on one hand, and regarded with suspicion, on the other, for having continued to live within the perpetrator state and society. It is within the perspective of refuse and the refused that this book traces the ways in which Armenians remained in Turkey, especially Anatolia, and examines how denativization unfolded as they emigrated out of Anatolia to Istanbul in the 1950s and 1960s and to France in the 1970s and 1980s.

THE RACIALIZATION OF CONFESSIONAL BELONGING

Although Armenians were granted Turkish citizenship in the early years of the Turkish republic, their non-Muslim status reflected their racialization as non-Turks. This categorization, which continues today, means that one cannot be simultaneously a non-Muslim and a Turk, a formula that positions Armenians and other non-Muslims as foreign to "Turkishness," the forged demographic majority of the newly formed Turkey.[17] To understand the origins of such racialization, it is essential to grasp the Ottoman concept and practice of *millet*, which shaped the organization and classification of communities within the empire based on their confessional affiliation, ultimately laying the groundwork for the Turkish state's classification of its citizens. The Ottoman Empire's understanding of millet emphasized religious and confessional affiliations, and the empire divided its population into four millet communities: Muslims, Armenians, Jews, and Rūm-Orthodox ("Greeks").[18] The linguistically diverse Muslim populations within the empire, regardless of their sect or confession, were unified under the umbrella of the "ruling millet" (*milleti hakime*). Notably, Sunni Islam, particularly of the Hanafi school of Islamic jurisprudence, effectively absorbed various Muslim sects, including the Shi'is and Alevis, becoming the ruling religious community (millet) that dominated power and governed the state. Non-Muslims were divided into three distinct millets: the Jewish millet, the Rūm-Orthodox millet (or simply Rūm, commonly known as the "Greeks," encompassing the linguistically diverse Eastern Orthodox Christians),[19] and the Armenian millet (encompassing the adherents of all non-Chalcedonian "Oriental Orthodox" churches).[20] Significantly, the two Christian communities, the Armenians and the Rūms, were separated by confession, emphasizing the doctrinal differences that made them into two distinct Christian millets within Ottoman administration and society.

Starting in the nineteenth century, ethnicity and race became dominant means of classifying people and also became internalized in people's self-identification. Race and ethnicity slowly became the primary constituents of confessional belonging in the Ottoman context. The transformation of religious and confessional affiliations into racialized categories was a complex process that can be traced to the rise of nationalist movements in the Ottoman Balkans seeking independence from the empire. Confessionalism and religion were not the only factors in shaping ethnic identities; language also played a crucial role, where nationalist movements used the local language as a marker of ethnicity. For example, populations that the Ottoman state considered part of the Rūm-Orthodox millet because of their Orthodox Christian faith, such as Romanians and Serbs, began to see in their spoken Romanian or Serbian languages, respectively, a feature of a cultural community distinct from that of the Greek-speaking Orthodox, who represented the hegemonic group within the Rūm millet.[21] Several Balkan states, notably Greece, Romania, and Serbia, gained independence and were established in the nineteenth century based on a confessional ethnicity, wherein belonging to a local Orthodox church and identifying with the spoken language became markers of ethnicity, laying the foundation for ethnonationalist states in the Balkans.

With the emergence of such confessional ethnicities, Muslims in much of the Balkans, as well as in Anatolia, were eventually racialized as "Turks." Non-Muslims retained their Ottoman millet confessional labels, but these labels took on racialized meanings.[22] A designation as Armenian, Rūm, or Jewish was transformed into an essentialized identity in the ethnic and racial sense rather than merely reflecting religious confession and faith.[23] Two illustrative cases that shed light on these transformations are the experiences of the Dönme, descendants of Ottoman Jews who converted to Islam, and the experiences of Muslim migrants from Bulgaria. These examples help us understand the intricate and shifting dynamics of religion as race during the transition from the Ottoman Empire to the Republic of Turkey.

In his study of the Dönme (literally, "converts" in Turkish), descendants of Ottoman Jews who converted to Islam in the seventeenth century, Marc David Baer explores how religion and race intersect in shaping identities during the transition from the late Ottoman Empire to the Republic of Turkey. For two centuries, the Dönme identified themselves as Muslims and were accepted as such by broader society. They also played a pivotal role in the 1908 Young Turk revolution that set the stage for a secular ethnonationalist republic. With the establishment of the republic, the Dönme faced exclusion and racism, primarily due to two factors that ultimately denied them full inclusion in the secular Republic of Turkey: "ethnicized religion," which equated Turkish identity with being Muslim, and "racialized nationalism," which emphasized the importance of having "Turkish blood" to being fully accepted as Turks.[24] Given these factors, for the Dönme to be accepted in secular Turkey, they had to undergo a two-step conversion. Initially, they had to be recognized as genuinely Muslim, and then they had to relinquish that religious identity for a secular Turkish one. Baer describes this as a "double-blind" process, which was hypothetical, because the Dönme, despite their efforts, encountered obstacles in being fully accepted as Muslims to begin with, and therefore their second conversion to secular Turkishness was never fully realized.[25] In this context, Jewishness underwent a transformation from being a religious identity in the Ottoman Empire to a racialized identity removed from its religious connotations in Turkey. This explains why even undergoing conversion to Islam two centuries earlier did not secure the Dönme community full acceptance in the secular republic.

In her study on Bulgarian Muslim immigrants to Turkey, Ayşe Parla reveals that these migrants were embraced in the country as *soydaş* to highlight the kinship relations that Turks and Bulgarian Muslims have by virtue of being Muslim. Although *soydaş* is commonly translated as "ethnic kin" in Turkey, Parla contends that "racial kin" is a more appropriate translation, as it emphasizes the nationalist notion that "sharing the same blood" is crucial for inclusion in Turkish citizenship. This example illuminates how Turkish citizenship, both in theory and practice, is based on "ethnoracial" theories that dictate who is included or excluded based on a secularized confessional belonging that crosses borders and languages.[26]

Analysis of the racialization of the Dönme and the Bulgarian Muslim migrants in Turkey offers a key insight into how non-Muslims were racialized in the country. These examples point to the shift toward an identity framework in which a religious label is transformed into a racialized one, disconnected from its confessional meaning, whereby religion becomes race in a secularized context. This process, which has been described as "deconfessionalization," was observed with Ottoman Armenians in the nineteenth century; similarly, the reduction of Jewishness to a secular, racialized category in Nazi Germany has been referred to as "detheologization."[27] This shift to a new conception of collective identity and confessional belonging mirrors the wider process of racialization within the Ottoman Empire. In other words, "Armenianness" was no longer strictly defined by adherence to the confessional formula of the Armenian Apostolic Church, and thus in effect included Armenian Catholics and Protestants. Such a process of deconfessionalization brought about a modern reconceptualization of Armenian belonging, in which elements such as ethnicity, race, and vernacular language took precedence over the doctrinal and theological formulae of the church.[28] Despite this shift, the Armenian Apostolic Church remained central to the lives of Armenian citizens in Turkey, even after the church was stripped of its political and judicial authority, its role reduced solely to religious functions. This continued centrality was due in part to the Lausanne Treaty, which minoritized Armenians based on their confessional affiliation.[29]

Within this wider historical context, in speaking of racialization in Turkey, I follow Paul Silverstein's definition, wherein "race" is "a cultural category of difference that is contextually constructed as essential and natural—as residing within the very body of the individual—and is thus generally tied, in scientific theory and popular understanding, to a set of somatic, physiognomic, and even genetic character traits." Silverstein maintains that racialization is the process through which social and cultural distinguishing features—including class, ethnicity, generation, and kinship/affinity—are essentialized, naturalized, and/or given a biological interpretation.[30] Discussing racialization as a process rather than as a fixed category highlights the inherent instability of "race" and the ongoing process of constructing hierarchical otherness within societies. In North America and Europe, populations are often racialized based on physiognomic and somatic traits. However, in Turkey and the wider Balkans and Middle East, such visible distinctions do not significantly contribute to the racialization of people. In this context, confessional affiliation and the language spoken play a crucial role in the racialization of populations and consequently determine the inclusion and exclusion of groups by the Turkish state.

In the context of this study, the term "deconfessionalization" refers to the broadening of what it means to be Armenian to incorporate all Armenians and not just those who practice strict adherence to the Armenian Apostolic Church. However, this broadening does not imply the complete erasure of confessional identity. Instead, it marks a shift in its significance within the broader context of Armenian identity, whereby the perception of one's confessional affiliation (similar to the perception of biological difference) became an ethnic and racial marker.[31] In this light, I coined the term "confessional ethnicity" to capture the late Ottoman period's nuanced resurgence of confessionalism, now imbued with racial significance in post-Ottoman Turkey.[32] This choice of words precisely delineates the subtle distinctions between the two Christian communities, the Rūms and the Armenians, who continue to be seen as distinct racial and ethnic minorities in Turkey. The commonly used "ethnoreligious" label risks homogenizing the Armenians and Rūms as simply being Christian groups, obscuring their distinct racialized and ethicized identities. Additionally, the term "confessional ethnicity" helps to disentangle the complex hierarchies among the diverse Muslim populations, recognizing the historical and ongoing privileged status of Sunni Islam of the Hanafi jurisprudence in both the Ottoman and post-Ottoman Turkish contexts. By conceptualizing Turkey as a nation that organizes and differentiates its citizenry along lines of confessional ethnicities, we acknowledge both the categorization of Sunnis, Shi'is, and Alevis collectively as Muslims integral to Turkish identity in a racialized sense, and the contrasting categorization of non-Muslim communities as distinct confessional ethnicities.

It is within the context of the racialization of confessional belonging that this ethnography understands religion and religious belonging as a lens through which to situate Armenian political exclusion and belonging, with Armenian Christianity in its deconfessionalized, that is, secularized form being central to Armenians' racialization as non-Turks. Religion in its racialized and ethnicized form frames the social and political exclusion of Armenians as a confessional ethnicity in the secular republic. The transformation of "being Armenian" from a confessional identity to a racial marker sheds light on the broader cultural, social, and political belonging of Armenians as citizens of the perpetrator state. Such a transformation was anchored administratively within the wider legal framework of the minority protection articles of the Lausanne Treaty of 1923 (chapter 2).

It is important to highlight that being an Armenian in this context is not just about belonging to the Armenian church or belonging to a Christian minority in a Muslim-majority society. The situation is more complex. Armenians were not killed in the genocide because they were Christians, but rather, because their Christianity marked them racially as non-Turks. As this ethnography demonstrates, Armenians could not become Turks, even if they converted to Islam; this is because Turkishness was also racially conceived, as Baer and Parla demonstrate.[33] Moreover, when Armenians (and other non-Muslims) are labeled as *gavur*, meaning infidel or unbeliever, this label does not merely pertain to religious or confessional differences. Derived from the Qur'anic Arabic word *kāfir*, which refers to those who reject or obscure the truth about faith, *gavur* has historically functioned as a derogatory term for Christians and Jews in Turkey. In the secularized Turkish context, it signifies a racialized form of othering that renders the "othered" inferior. This distinction reflects the complex interplay of racial and confessional identities within the post-Ottoman Turkish context that the term "confessional ethnicity" seeks to depict.

In taking this racialized foreignness as a marker of the Armenians' denativization, I read the experiences of Armenians in Turkey as a continuous process of erasure and elimination that is not limited to the genocidal violence that took place during World War I. Nor is this a matter that can be resolved through the granting of rights based on minority status, as denativization operates beyond legal recognition, embedded in the very structures that render Armenians foreign in their own homeland. Instead, this process has been sustained throughout the life of the Republic of Turkey and continues into the present, even after the vast majority of Armenians left Anatolia, leaving behind small numbers of

Armenians that, in most cases, also lacked means for sustainable communal life. While the genocide is often perceived as the end of the Armenian presence in Ottoman Anatolia, this book takes the genocide during World War I as persisting through its afterlives. Rather than a closed chapter, I position the genocide as a temporal beginning for retelling the Armenian story as one of survivance in the face of their ongoing denativization.

THE CATASTROPHIC HISTORY OF
THE ARMENIANS' DENATIVIZATION

During World War I, Armenians faced premeditated mass annihilation, deportations, and death marches in the Syrian Desert that led to the killing of some one million Ottoman Armenians. Historical catastrophes such as this did not at first have a name. Early on, and before the coinage of the term "genocide" and its criminalization in international law in 1948, Armenians referred to these events using the term *Yeghern*, meaning a crime or pogrom, a term also used to refer to earlier violent events such as the Hamidian massacres (1894-1896) and the Adana massacres (1909).[34] Perhaps the most commonly used word by Armenians was *Ak'sor*, meaning exile or deportation.[35] In an interview conducted in Cyprus in 1931, the novelist and literary critic Hagop Oshagan used the term *Aghed*, Catastrophe, which he capitalized. Referred to as *Aghed*, a proper name, the genocide became a designated, known, and knowable event.[36]

The events were later called a genocide after the lawyer Raphael Lemkin coined the term during the annihilation of European Jewry by the German state, the Holocaust, to describe the collective murder of a population with specific traits, such as race or ethnicity, with the goal of total annihilation.[37] Lemkin cited the case of Ottoman Armenians in coining the term and in helping to criminalize genocide in international law.[38] Before Lemkin, however, Armenians coined and used an Armenian equivalent to genocide to describe the mass annihilation of Armenians. Mardiros Ananikian (1875–1924) used the term *tseghasbanutyun* in an article published in November 1915.[39] It was not until the usage of the term by Mardiros Sarian (1872–1954), a genocide survivor and an activist in the Armenian Revolutionary Federation, that *tseghasbanutyun* became popular; Sarian used the term in a publication in 1918 and later in a book that he published in 1933.[40] The term combines the word *tsegh*, meaning "tribe or race," and *sbanutyun*, meaning "killing and murder," and later became the Armenian translation of Lemkin's legal term "genocide."

In his critique of genocide historiography, the Armenian literary critic Marc Nichanian calls these events a catastrophe (*aghed*), following Oshagan.[41] For Nichanian, the term "genocide" comes with limitations. Nichanian distinguishes between catastrophe and genocide, asserting that "there is no genocide without denial," because the perpetrators often "erase every trace of their act." In his seminal dialogue with David Kazanjian, Nichanian argues that the survivors ultimately have to resort to the archives of the perpetrator to prove the crimes they were subjected to took place.[42] He emphasizes that the perpetrator, whom he calls the executioner, seeks not only to kill, eliminate, and exterminate, but above all, to force the victim to continually prove the atrocity occurred.[43] While genocide can be an accurate term to describe the events from a legal perspective and for comparative studies of mass violence, it remains focused on the crimes of the perpetrators. By embracing the modern concept of proof and evidence, which is often rooted in archival documentation, the perpetrator is able to destroy evidence and trap survivors in a continuous cycle of needing to prove the crime occurred. For Nichanian, this reliance on proof only reinforces the perpetrator's denialism.[44] Furthermore, as genocide is framed within the legal framework of evidence and facts, it risks silencing what lies outside legible evidence, such as the lives and patterns of Armenian survival, and limits our understanding of the suffering of the largely undocumented and unarchived Armenians who survived and remained in Anatolia as Turkish citizens. Yet in the context of the persistent denial of the Turkish state and its apologetic intellectuals, avoiding the word "genocide," employing Armenian terms such as *aghed* (catastrophe), and mistranslating the term *yeghern* to mean "catastrophe" instead of "crime" risk diluting the criminality of mass annihilation and removing the perpetrators' responsibility, as there could be no perpetrator without a crime. And indeed, although Nichanian himself used the term "catastrophe" to critique genocide historiography, many Turkish intellectuals have adopted this term to evade the designation of genocide and thereby implicitly deny the crime of genocide.[45]

Against this background of genocide denialism of the state-centric narratives that omit the destructive aspects of state building, I employ the term "denativization" to describe the ongoing process of dispossession, erasure, and elimination experienced by Armenians in Turkey. Denativization is a process through which Armenians were turned into a foreign minority in Turkey, even while some continued to live in their villages, cities, and lands. It is a process through which Armenians have been silenced in historiography to serve nationalist narratives and their built environment has been and continues to be removed from the Anatolian landscape or renovated in ways that divorce it from the history of violence committed against Armenians. And it is the process through which Armenians have lost or become estranged from their homelands, livelihoods, traditions, histories, experiences, languages, and cultural belonging. The process of denativization continues through the present constituting the ongoing afterlives of the Armenian genocide.[46]

The framework of denativization intervenes in historiography in three ways. First, the framework shows that the Armenian genocide was one part of a longer history of dispossession, erasure, and elimination that is ongoing—a catastrophe of denativization. The framework thus regards the genocide as ongoing through its afterlives and moves us away from understanding it as consisting of only empirically provable or deniable events with a clearly demarcated beginning and end. Within this context, the book moves away from historiography that is defined by a single event of destruction, such as a war or a genocide, to narrate the denativization of Armenians as an ongoing process. It is notable that most historians, until recently, have ended the history of Ottoman Armenians with the genocide, exile, and the formation of diasporic communities and have remained largely silent about those who remained and became Turkish citizens. By portraying the Armenian existence in Anatolia as ending with the genocide, Armenian historiography has compartmentalized the narrative into three periods: the period before the genocide (when Armenians were a part of the Ottoman Empire), the genocide, and the period after the genocide (when Armenians primarily resettled in diasporic communities—a point explored in chapter 1). Denativization, therefore, extends the temporality of the violence and destruction Armenians were subjected to as starting before the genocide and continuing through the Republic of Turkey until the present, even after the majority of Armenians left Anatolia. In the framework of denativization, all of this belongs to a single catastrophic history that both cleansed Armenians from Anatolia and is cleansing Anatolia of traces that they ever existed on the land. This erasure is not only reflected in policies, narratives, and demographics, but also in the destruction of the material remnants of Armenian presence.

The cover of this book features the Church of Surp (Saint) Sargis, an 11th-century structure and the only remaining church of the Khtzkonk Monastery, located today in the Kars province of Turkey. Once part of a larger monastic complex, five churches survived the genocide, yet the state continued its campaign of erasure by demolishing them one by one. Now, only one church remains—partially standing, a haunting remnant of what once was. Its image encapsulates the ongoing destruction of Armenian history and presence in Anatolia, demonstrating that the erasure of Armenians did not end with the genocide or their forced migration during the republican period. Rather, it endures through the continuous dismantling of their physical and historical traces, ultimately erasing even the markers of their past existence.[47]

This gradual destruction of Armenian historical sites, long after the genocide, underscores how erasure is not confined to a single event in history but continues through deliberate state actions. This framework allows us to move away from the centrality of an event-based history that positions the genocide as a dominant historiographic framework and that consequently bifurcates Armenian history between the diaspora framework for Armenian diasporic communities and minority status for those who remained in Turkey.

This book contends that comprehending the Armenian predicament requires more than analyzing it solely through the lens of genocidal violence, forced displacement, property confiscation, competing nationalist narratives, denial of genocidal violence, and the experience of exclusion as minoritized citizens in Turkey. Instead, it necessitates an understanding of the overarching structure facilitating the continuous erasure and silencing of Armenians from Anatolian history. This book contributes to such an understanding by exploring how the Armenians continued to be displaced after the genocide and by showing that such displacement goes beyond the physical realm, enduring on the level of discourse surrounding history and memory. It emphasizes understanding the structural mechanisms that continually erase Armenians from Anatolia's history and silence their presence. These mechanisms, sometimes seemingly positive—as in the case of site renovations, tourism initiatives, and apology campaigns—all contribute to the ongoing erasure and denativization that persist in the present as facets of the genocidal structure upon which Turkey was founded (chapter 6). This book emphasizes that the process of Turkish nation-state formation in Anatolia is far from settled; the state continually asserts its sovereignty by simultaneously erasing the physical and narrative connections between Armenians and Anatolia. This erasure occurs as the state invents its own nativist discourse to advance its claims on the history and geography of Anatolia, with the aim of excluding all non-Turkish and therefore non-Muslim inhabitants from the land.

Denativization therefore challenges a genocide-centered historiography that regards violence as a finality to allow space for the numerous afterlives of the genocide, tracing the lives created in the shadow of violence through the stories of those who remained.[48] Speaking of the endurance of erasures points to its twofold meaning: erasures that continue unabated—endure—yet is also something Armenians must themselves endure, requiring agency and the assertion of presence in the face of ongoing uprooting. *Enduring Erasures* is concerned with the *survivors*, as well as their *survivance*. Survivors live in the afterlife of the genocide: those who have lived in the shadow of the killings and who have borne unmeasurable losses in lives, social relations, family networks, language and culture, built environment, or the simple feeling of security while still living in their neighborhoods, villages, and cities. The coming chapters trace the afterlives of the catastrophe in the lives of surviving Armenians, examining the ongoing process of denativization in their lives. I draw on a constellation of sources— ethnography, life stories, international treaties, and literary works—in writing about those afterlives.

Second, denativization foregrounds not only the actions of the state but also the experiences of the people who have been denativized: the largely undocumented and unarchived Armenians who remained in Anatolia as Turkish citizens and their descendants. Denativization here speaks of the experiences of populations such as post-Ottoman Armenians who continue to have physical relationships with the specific geographies from which they were dispossessed. Denativization speaks to the experiences of those who were transformed into a foreign minority while still living on lands that many considered their homeland when a nation-state claimed sovereignty in the name of a national collective that persistently excluded them. The concept of denativization expands on Edward W. Said's framework in *The Question of Palestine*, which underscores the influence of interpretation in narrating realities that diverge from the actual demographic conditions on the ground. The concept highlights how Armenians, despite their personal, communal, and historical connections to Anatolia, undergo displacement in the realm of narrative, which reinterprets the history and geography from the Turkish nationalist vantage point. Thus, denativization is not only a physical displacement but also a set of discursive practices, illustrating the intricate ways in which interpretation shapes and distorts history and denies the actual presence of a population.[49] Denativization therefore expands the concept of cleansing to include not only genocide, expulsion, forced migration, and assimilation, but also the reinterpreting of Anatolia as a Turkish homeland through efforts to discursively sever Armenians' historical connection to the land. Such discursive efforts include retelling the population's history from the vantage point of the nation-state and altering the significance of places and buildings by imposing alternative narratives, names, and histories, thus severing the Armenian connection to the past so as to exclude Armenians from the present and future of Anatolia, now a Turkified and Islamized nationalist space.

Third, by allowing for an understanding of the Armenian predicament as contextual and shared with multiple peoples of Anatolia, the framework of denativization challenges both insular ethnocentric approaches and the nationalist binaries central to much historiographic work, including the moralist identitarian binaries of victim versus victimizer. Examining this history under the framework of denativization follows Said's methodological call for the "integration and connections between the past and the present ... to speak of overlapping territories, intertwined histories."[50] This framework allows us to critically understand the Armenian experience as contextual and as shared with the multiple peoples who make claims or have connections to Anatolia as a homeland— the Rūms, the Kurds, Syriac Christians, Jews, and the Alevis, among others. Such communities continue to be excluded and suppressed by the Turkish republican regime in different ways and for different reasons. In speaking of the denativization of Armenians, the book writes against the nationalist order of demographic categorization in an effort to represent a complex historical understanding that insular ethnocentric accounts fail to provide. To this end, the coming chapters read the denativization of Armenian as intertwined with the experience of the Alevi Kurds of Dersim (chapter 1), with the Rūm experience during the Lausanne conference (chapter 2), and with the experience of the Kurds and Balkan Muslim refugees in Anatolia (chapter 3). All these populations share overlapping territories, homelands, cities, and neighborhoods, and their histories' violence and dispossession are intertwined with those of Armenians and other minoritized communities, such as Syriac Christians and Jews.

This approach also challenges the common tendency to analyze the Armenian genocide and the violence against other populations separately, instead examining their interdependence. In this regard, this book resonates with studies that similarly trace the entangled nature of violence, memory, and dispossession across different communities in Anatolia. Zerrin Özlem Biner's ethnography on southeastern Anatolia highlights how violence is not confined to discrete historical moments but unfolds as a protracted process that implicates multiple communities—Syriacs, Kurds, and Armenians—through dispossession. Similarly, as David Leupold demonstrates, the Armenian genocide not only erased Armenians from eastern Anatolia but also concentrated Kurdish populations in their former lands, shaping new territorial claims and political struggles as Armenians, Kurds, and Turks continue to construct and contest historical legitimacy through competing national narratives.[51] These overlapping histories complicate nationalist binaries and ethnic boundaries requiring new approaches to understanding historical displacement and erasure. Writing outside the logic of the nation-state advances the decolonization of Armenian and post-Ottoman histories by moving beyond the binary categories established by colonial and nationalist regimes and by presenting the complex, diverse, and sometimes contradictory realities within and between the different communities of Ottoman and post-Ottoman Anatolia.[52]

Furthermore, the book pulls against the gravity of reductive narratives by showing that the denativization of Armenians has multiple actors and is not solely a direct result of the Turkish nationalist policies of dispossession, cleansing, and erasure. European colonial interests in the Ottoman Empire (chapter 2) and Armenian institutions in Istanbul and France (chapters 4 and 5) have also led to Armenian denativization. In this light, the book considers both Turkish and Armenian erasure of Anatolian Armenians as belonging to the same history of denativization, yet it positions them as occurring in historical and political terrains that, while parallel, are not identical. The denativization of Anatolian Armenians therefore takes place in multiple stages and through different political actors and settings. Although this approach writes against the nationalist order that continues to inform both Armenian and Turkish histories, it is important to note that it does not equate the systematic annihilation policies of the Young Turk regime of the Ottoman Empire and the denialism of the Turkish state with the Armenian diasporic project of homogenizing Armenian history and culture. Furthermore, chapter 6 grapples with the ways in which Armenians in Turkey articulate counterclaims to the nativist discourse of the Turkish state in the face of the state's denial of the genocide and its erasure of traces of Armenian presence from the land.

Speaking of the denativization of Armenians does not essentialize Armenians by presupposing that they are empirically or authentically a population "native" to Anatolia by virtue of having cultural and historical connections to Anatolia or western Armenia. Denativization is an attempt to move Armenian historiography away from the framework of the genocide as an event with a punctual beginning and end; it is therefore a historiographic prism that speaks about the genocide's afterlives. It does not endorse national nativism that views Armenians as a self-evident, contained, and homogeneous ethnonational group with unique or exclusive claims to Anatolia, a construction put forth by nineteenth-century Armenian intellectuals and critiqued by Marc Nichanian.[53] Rather, speaking of the denativization of Armenians is to critique the Turkish state's own invention of the "Turk" as native in the wake of Turkish nationalism and in the formative years of the Republic of Turkey.

Denativization as a historiographic intervention in Armenian history draws attention to a longer process of erasure and elimination, one that is larger than any particular instance of murder or removal. While denativization intersects with Patrick Wolfe's "logic of elimination" as it operates in settler colonial contexts, it differs in key ways. Wolfe's framework primarily theorizes settler colonialism as a structure that seeks to replace native societies through land dispossession and assimilation. However, denativization operates within a distinct historical and geopolitical context—shaped by genocide, international treaties, and diaspora—where dispossession extends beyond state-driven erasure to encompass multiple forces that continue to displace Anatolian Armenians beyond the moment of genocide. Unlike settler colonialism, where the goal is to eliminate and replace native peoples with settlers, denativization does not necessarily require the introduction of a settler population. Instead, it functions through nationalist state-building projects that racialize Armenians as foreign in their own homeland. Furthermore, denativization extends beyond territorial dispossession to include discursive and cultural displacement, making it distinct from the settler-colonial drive for territorial replacement that Wolfe describes.[54]

The book does not limit denativization to the massacres and the genocide and does not position them in a cause-and-effect timeline or in a teleological sequence of events that starts with the Hamidian (1894–1896) and Adana massacres (1909), leading to the genocide (1915–1918).[55] This historiographic framing sets the genocide within a linear timeline of violence, thus reading the massacres as making the genocide teleologically inevitable.[56] This approach is problematic, because it does not account for the complex and intersecting factors as well as the rapid changes that took place in the political and socioeconomic contexts of specific Anatolian locales as well as those of the wider Ottoman Balkans.[57] Furthermore, commencing the history of the genocide with the Hamidian massacres limits the genocide to the violence perpetrated by the Ottoman state and does not account for other factors, such as European colonial interventions in Ottoman territories and the shifts in Ottoman institutions and political culture due to Europeanization policies.

The historiographic intervention in this book aims to bring in multifaceted factors that lead to the denativization of Armenians—not merely as a consequence of violence but as an enduring process that extends far beyond the genocide itself. Denativization describes a broader ontological and epistemic transformation, whereby Armenians are not just dispossessed of land or rights but are also rendered foreign in their own homeland. The book moves beyond material loss to examine how Armenians have been expelled from historiography, public space, and political legitimacy for over a century, making denativization a persistent historical structure rather than a contemporary strategy of governance. This catastrophe accounts for the genocide and erasures that took place in its wake, including the minoritization of Armenians and the denial of Armenian sovereignty and equal citizenship rights in republican Turkey through the Lausanne Treaty of 1923 as well as the policies to empty Anatolia of the remaining Armenians throughout the republic's life—whether through forced migration, assimilation, or the destruction and repurposing of Armenian-built environments and heritage sites.

WHO AND WHAT REMAINS?

In her acclaimed *Aweraknerun mēj* (*In the Ruins*),[58] the Armenian writer Zabel Yessayan documented her visit to Adana in the aftermath of the 1909 massacres perpetrated against the Armenians. Yessayan went on a "reconnaissance voyage," especially seeking the orphaned Armenians of Adana.[59] She then recounted what she had seen and heard after the fact. Because she was not a witness to the actual massacres, the book was not an "attempt to reconstitute the facts"[60] about the killing of some thirty thousand Armenians, but rather to recount her experiences witnessing the ruins and the incalculable consequences of the destruction where survivors continued to live among those ruins. Yessayan wrote in her preface:

> Those who had not been massacred were blamed for surviving; those who had taken up arms to defend their homes and besieged villages were condemned to death or long periods of detention . . . Before us was a province ravaged by fire and bloodshed, and we had a small army of widows and orphans on our already weak hands. There was no end to the misery, the consequences were incalculable, and there was not the slightest prospect of a new spiritual beginning.[61]

Yessayan's words paint an image of the survivors and what remained: the enduring suffering felt in the memories and on the bodies of those who "survived" and who had to bury corpses, live their lives face to face with the destroyed cities and buildings, and mourn the loss of family, neighbors, and friends. The survivors bore the burden of living in the aftermath of the massacres, where caring for the vulnerable became a necessity, as the Armenian population had been reduced to a "small army of widows and orphans."

While the text speaks of the destruction that the Adana massacres of 1909 left behind, it could have been an account of the Armenians in any Ottoman province during or after the genocide that started merely four years after the publication of Yessayan's book. It could also have depicted the residents of Dersim or any of the Kurdish villages in southeastern Anatolia that were emptied and destroyed by the Turkish state in the 1930s and 1940s; state violence endures in Turkey. Armenians initially saw the 1908 revolution as a positive step toward constitutional rule, which would grant them equality and rights in the empire.[62] As violence against Armenians continued in different forms throughout the foundation of the Kemalist republic, the Adana massacres constituted a watershed moment for Armenians in the Ottoman Empire because, as Bedross Der Matossian argues, it "shattered" their hopes for inclusion, citizenship, and equal rights following the Ottoman revolution of 1908.[63] Denativization is a perpetual process, and Armenians were not the only target. The conquest of Anatolia, the erasure of its diverse cultures, and the dispossession of its populations continues in the state's violence against Kurds and Syriac Christians, among others. Yet it was not only the loss of life and destruction of cities that Armenians bore; the massacres also meant that Armenians were denied a role as citizens or as political agents in the future of the republic. Following the massacres, even though the Ottoman state promised to implement reforms, Armenians were excluded from the political life of the Ottoman Empire and eventually became a target of genocide when World War I started. This paved the way for the Turkish nationalism that was about to build an ethnonational Turkish state where Armenians would have no place.[64] Therefore, the massacres committed against Armenians in Adana remained unpunished.[65]

In light of this, I write the story of the Armenian survival in Turkey as the *destruction* that accompanied the *construction* of the Turkish nation-state.[66] The neglect of destructive components of state formation may be symptomatic of the post-1648 Westphalian nation-state system, which promotes a political order dominated by nation-states that are expected to be tolerant of minorities.[67] The nation-state continues to be seen as inevitable, even as the desired outcome of progressing from empire to the modern state, particularly with the rise of nationalism based on confessional ethnicities in the nineteenth century in the Ottoman Balkans. Such an order has allowed certain populations—defined on the basis of ethnicity, religion, confession, and/or language—to declare sovereignty in the name of an imagined collective and to deny it to all those who do not satisfy the criteria of belonging. Populations such as the Palestinians, the indigenous populations in the Americas and Australasia, Kurds, Assyrians, Tibetans, Berbers, and Armenians, to name but a few, are excluded and denied civil, political, and/or cultural rights and are sometimes also denied sovereignty.[68] Such populations are racialized, minoritized, or erased through assimilation or forced migration, and such violence continues to shape the lives of the displaced and their descendants. Nation-states—even when they claim progress, universality, tolerance, and the rule of law for their citizens—have not only denied such promises to the excluded populations but have systematically endeavored to erase, eliminate, and kill these populations within their borders.[69] Genocide does not mean total annihilation of a population, it kills many and then strips the survivors of their political, social, and cultural lives; survivors live with the long-term consequences of the violence.[70]

Taking inspiration from Hannah Arendt's perspective on the challenges faced by Jews after the Holocaust and Saidiya Hartman's insights on the legacy of slavery, I approach the Armenian experience in a broader "multidirectional" context.

This is not to equate or flatten the differences between such horrific experiences, to diminish the unique histories of these different historical catastrophes, or to create hierarchies among such catastrophes. It is critical to understand each catastrophe on its own terms, yet without understanding them competitively, as Michael Rothberg advocates.[71] Such as an approach allows us to situate the Armenian genocide and its afterlives within a larger historical framework, highlighting how historical catastrophes illuminate other histories of violence and the enduring structures they leave behind—structures that persist in shaping the conditions, experiences, and possibilities of those who live under their shadow, as Yessayan, Arendt, and Hartman articulated. Drawing on the historical continuities between the Armenian genocide and the Jewish post-Holocaust predicament, as well as the enduring legacy of slavery for Black Americans, I highlight the common thread of structural violence that persists long after the initial acts of violence have ceased. These communities have navigated the legacies of trauma, displacement, and marginalization, with their lives fashioned by the gravity of continuous erasure and the struggle for recognition and justice.

In the words of Hannah Arendt, the state of the refugees after World War II "meant the loss of the entire social texture into which they were born and in which they established for themselves a distinct place in the world."[72] Similarly, Saidiya Hartman speaks of the ways in which each enslaved person was "torn from kin and community, exiled from one's country, dishonored and violated."[73] Long after the official end of slavery in the United States, African Americans continue to face "skewed life chances, limited access to health and education, premature death, incarceration, and impoverishment," a situation that speaks to the afterlives of slavery.[74] The concept of "afterlives" resonates with the enduring struggles of Armenians: survivors have been described as "walking corpses" when they survived physically yet were subjected to the intense emotional and physical violence of rape,[75] and when they found themselves without family, kin, and properties in a world where their previous existence was no longer recognizable. In essence, Arendt's and Hartman's perspectives on their respective histories shed light on the profound and lasting impact of traumatic events and historical injustices on many Armenians who may have survived but who bore genocidal violence on their bodies, in their memories, and through their enduring displacement.

Loss is knowable by what it leaves behind:[76] the debris of buildings and the stories that Yessayan collected from the "stricken" Armenians (Yessayan's description of the survivors), who, in the words of Marc Nichanian, were "invaded by horror, incapable of detaching themselves from it."[77] Yessayan was a witness not only for what she saw, but also to the Armenian experience of the catastrophe;[78]

not to what was lost, but what remained.[79] In her second chapter, "In the Ruins" ("*Aweraknerun mēj*" in Armenian), which holds the same title as the book, she observes: "Ruins everywhere . . . Nothing has been spared; all the churches, schools, and dwellings have been reduced to formless piles of charred stone . . . Draped in rags stained with blood and tears, a crowd of widows, orphans, and old people presents itself to us. This is all that is left of Adana's Armenian population." Yessayan's usage of *mēj* in the title could mean being *in* but also *among* the ruins. The latter suggests that ruins could be the people, whose lives were ruined as they survive the massacres. In fact, the word for ruins, *awerak*, speaks of both the destroyed buildings and ruined people; the word is used figuratively to describe someone who has lost their vigor, youth, freshness, and strength.[80] Yessayan therefore invites us to extend the understanding of ruins and the ruined to focus on *who*, and not only *what*, remains (a shift also encouraged by Ann Stoler's work on ruination as discussed below). A focus on the people who remain allows us to understand historical catastrophes through survivance instead of through the physical objects that have been destroyed or lost.[81] In this sense, the Turkish national narrative rendered Armenian survivors as "leftovers of the sword," the undesired surplus who lingered and survived despite the systematic policy of annihilation they experienced. The perpetrator state implemented a policy whereby Armenians had to be erased and forgotten so that the Kemalist republic could emerge as a triumphant project of rationality, modernity, and secularity that the Turkish nationalists and Europeans would hail as an anomaly in the Muslim world.[82]

Orlando Patterson refers to people's physical survival after they have lost the social context in which they once lived as "social death." Patterson describes this process as one of "social negation," involving the desocialization and depersonalization of the people.[83] The effects of social death can indeed have long-term implications, not only for the individuals directly subjected to slavery but also for their descendants. The legacy of slavery, Patterson argues, including the social death experienced by the enslaved, can perpetuate systemic inequalities, racial discrimination, and social stigma that affect subsequent generations. Thus, the impact of social death can extend far beyond the immediate context of slavery, shaping the experiences of future generations.

In this context, the Armenian experience in Turkey serves as a reminder of the destructive consequences of nation-state construction. It underscores the need to critically examine and challenge the existing state-centric global order that perpetuates the exclusion and erasure of certain populations. The concept of social death, which is associated with "Afro-pessimism" as an intervention, sheds light on the multifaceted dimensions of this exclusion, extending beyond physical harm to include the erasure of the social context that constitutes the event's afterlives. In his critique of Afro-Pessimism, however, Jared Sexton warns against oversimplifying Black lives and struggles. Sexton maintains that the emphasis on the ontological position of blackness as social death risks reducing the complex experiences and historical agency of Black people to a singular narrative of victimhood and negation.[84]

Sexton's critique is particularly relevant when considering the Armenian context; the concept of social death helps us understand the destruction of society, kin and social relations, neighborhoods, and the wider social context within which people lived, all conditions that Armenian survivors had to bear after the genocide. Just as Sexton cautions against oversimplifying Black experiences, it is crucial to avoid reducing Armenian experiences to a singular narrative of victimhood. By challenging this tendency, this work presents the genocide not as an endpoint but as leading to the formation of new lives and counternarratives as well as continuing to tell stories that assert presence. Therefore, following Gerald Vizenor, I speak of Armenian "survivance," rather than mere survival, to recognize an active assertion of presence, a stance that is proactive rather than merely reactive, and an identity that endures beyond merely surviving. Native survivance narratives are declarations that repudiate subjugation, catastrophe, and the perception that survivors are limited to a tragic plot of victimhood.[85] In Vizenor's words, "The character of survivance creates a sense of native presence and actuality over absence, nihility, and victimry; survivance is the continuance of stories, not a mere reaction, however pertinent."[86] Following the example of such narratives, I speak about genocide, destruction, and social death without reducing the Armenian experience to a history of victimhood. Building on the application of Vizenor's survivance to the Armenian context— through an examination of memory activism and the refusal to disappear—this ethnography foregrounds the struggle against social death and the assertion of presence through the reconstruction of life in the face of denativization. Survivance, therefore, is an ongoing negotiation of agency in the face of state denial and historical erasure.[87]

Furthermore, Vizenor extends survivance to mean "an active sense of presence over absence, deracination, and oblivion."[88] Essentially, this encapsulates what I mean by denativization. It frames the Armenian catastrophe as an ongoing process that transcends scattered, violent events, including genocide. Denativization traces loss in the aftermath of destruction through what remains[89] and shifts the narrative subject to Armenian survivance. It is not just what Armenians are subjected to, but also what they endure as they make life in spite of it. Therefore, the book traces the genocide through its afterlives to uncover the agency of Armenians in the face of violence and its denial, highlighting how they have navigated and reconstructed their lives and communities in the aftermath of the catastrophe in the midst of the social and political pressures in Turkey and France. The book also traces how the Turkish state maintains its denialism through continuous policies of erasure that Armenians continuously challenge.

The ruins left behind by political violence have been a defining feature in recent ethnographies on post-Ottoman spaces. This approach was inaugurated by the Yael Navaro's ethnography on the abandoned Greek-Cypriot houses and villages following the Turkish invasion of northern Cyprus in 1974.[90] The theme of "ruins" has systematically been shaping the scholarly debates on the ever-present discourse on the Armenian genocide in contemporary Turkey. Such works have focused on material cultural artifacts that remained, as well as emptied landscapes, destroyed cities and cemeteries, and abandoned buildings.[91]

This book builds on Ann Stoler's work, which shifts the concept of ruins from the physical remains of the past to ruination as a continuous process in the present.[92] Such a process, Stoler suggests, includes people who were abandoned by states, who are themselves "the embodied ruins" of racialized empires and states.[93] Following Yessayan and Stoler, this book extends the reading of the past in the aftermath of destruction to *who* remains, rather than focusing only on *what* remains. This approach recognizes Armenian survivors not merely as remnants of the past, but as living testimonies to and survivors of multiple displacements and violent episodes. These survivors, who lived under the continuous efforts of the Turkish state to uproot those who remained in Anatolia and erase traces of their livelihoods from the landscape, experienced and continue to experience the afterlives of the genocide.

Through the concept of denativization, this book reads the Turkish nation-state formation not through the lens of anti-imperial national independence, as the official narrative sustains, but by bringing the destruction it caused to the center of the narrative. In this context, this book scrutinizes the way we understand and theorize nation-state projects and asks how we can read national independence projects from the standpoint of survivors without falling into the discourses embedded within identarian binarism of victimhood and triumphalism that are inherent in nationalist projects. To answer this question, I draw on the remnants of past catastrophes: the unarchived lives and stories of Armenians who remained in Anatolia and became Turkish citizens, as traced through historical, anthropological, and literary sources. These fragmented narratives, often excluded from official archives, reveal how the Turkish nation-state was constructed as a project of erasure and exclusion, realizing the vision of its founders at the expense of the populations it destroyed. *Enduring Erasures* reassembles these stories to critique the methodological assumptions of nationalist historiography and offer a critical lens through which to examine the processes of state formation and survival.

However, framing the elimination of Armenians as an ongoing process requires careful attention to avoid reinforcing Orientalist discourses that essentialize "Turks" as an inherently genocidal nation that throughout its history has wanted to kill Armenians.[94] Rather, doing so situates the violence against Armenians historically with the rise of nationalism in the late Ottoman Empire and contextually with the violence perpetrated against other populations by the Kemalist republic and its predecessor, the regime of the Young Turks. Recognizing this broader historical context necessitates moving beyond viewing genocide as a singular, bounded event and instead understanding its enduring structures. The afterlives of the Armenian genocide are not a chain of episodic events; rather, they constitute the catastrophe of denativization. This catastrophe is not insular but is connected to the catastrophes of other populations of Anatolia as well as to the global history of populations who continue to face annihilation, dispossession, destruction, and erasure. Many states were founded on the destruction of populations already living on the claimed territories. Overall, denativization reads the Armenian catastrophe as ongoing and as larger than a collection of scattered violent events that include the genocide.

AFTERLIVES AS AN ANALYTICAL FRAMEWORK

Writing on the eve of the German occupation of Paris in 1940, Walter Benjamin sees in Paul Klee's 1920 painting *Angelus Novus* a metaphor for history. Benjamin sees the angel as turned toward the past: "Where we perceive a chain of events, he sees one single catastrophe which keeps piling wreckage upon wreckage and hurls it in front of his feet."[95] The angel invites us to confront the multiple ghosts of historical catastrophes—settler colonization, slavery, massacres, genocides or other events of invasion, violence, and violation—as not just being separate incidents. Rather, these catastrophes inaugurate and propagate violent structures to ensure that the violated remain dominated.[96] The Armenian genocide therefore continues into the present through its multifaceted afterlives. Benjamin's metaphor runs against the grain of the scholarly work done on Ottoman Armenians and in modern Armenian history. Such scholarly work largely privileges the genocide over the experiences of those who survived and continued to live with the consequences of the violent erasure policies of the Turkish republican regime.

If one reads *Angelus Novus* through the lens of Walter Benjamin's historical method, it becomes clear that the angel is not merely gazing backward at the past as a sequence of events but also looking downward, gathering the wreckage of who "falls down, [is] left behind, [and] is trampled under foot, forgotten and forsaken."[97] Benjamin's reading of history challenges linear narratives of progress and instead compels us to recognize history's debris—the lives and struggles buried under dominant accounts. By assembling such wreckages of the shattered lives of survivors, this book disrupts the claims to progress, order, and democracy that the republican regime presumably brought after the demise of the Ottoman Empire and World War I. In employing Benjamin's method of compiling the wreckage, the fragments, and the disjointed lives, one starts to understand the denativization of Armenian survivors in Turkey not merely as a confessional ethnic minority citizens, as the Turkish state does. One comes to understand the survivors' predicament as a population whose very destruction and the ongoing denial of the violence committed against them are cornerstones of the republican regime and its institutions, economy, self-perception, historiography, and nationalist self-imagination.[98] The genocide therefore continues into the present through its afterlives, which the descendants of the survivors continue to be impacted by.

Although I use the word "genocide" to refer to temporally delineated genocidal violence ("the genocide during World War I"), historical catastrophes such as the Armenian genocide have perpetual lives; they are not confined to a temporally delineated destructive event. Marc Nichanian sees the Armenian catastrophe not just as a past event but as a continuing process that is still unfolding and continues to shape the future.[99] Populations targeted for annihilation and erasure often, if not always, leave members and traces behind; not everyone is killed and not everyone leaves. Just as Yessayan depicted the lives of the survivors of the Adana massacres, Armenian survivors of the genocide also lost family, community, and homes. Their predicament is shared by other populations whose lives continue to be informed by historical catastrophes, such as Jewish refugees during and after the Holocaust (whose situation is discussed in the work of Hannah Arendt) and Black Americans, who have navigated the enduring legacy of slavery in the United States (demonstrated by Saidiya Hartman).[100] Following Arendt and Hartman, I pursue the Armenian genocide through its multiple and ongoing afterlives among survivors, first in Turkey and then in France after their migration in the 1970s and 1980s. Under the Kemalist republican regime in Turkey, where their lives were fashioned by the gravity of continuous erasure, this population had and has continued to have their lives shaped and skewed by the genocide. While the mass killings have officially ended, denativization endures.

As the coming chapters will demonstrate, the estrangement of Anatolian Armenians is multiple and not limited to Turkey, as Anatolian Armenians do not fit the idealized image that some diasporic Armenians want all Armenians to fit.

As an analytical framework, the concept of afterlives breaks through the barriers of temporality, allowing us to grasp the present in its multiple complexities. It reveals that despite breaks and events that seem neatly confined to the past, the influence of what has gone before remains active in our present. This concept encourages us to move beyond a reductive view of history as a series of ruptures and continuities. It invites us to explore the murky and often indistinct traces of the past, uncovering how historical events, ideologies, and even long-gone individuals continue to mold and haunt our contemporary political, cultural, and social landscapes. The concept of afterlives challenges us to expand our understanding of what and who is considered to be alive. It prompts us to rethink the traditional boundaries between life and death, presence and absence, suggesting that the influence and presence of entities or individuals can extend beyond their physical existence.[101] By employing the concept of afterlives, we gain a deeper insight into the enduring impacts of the past and the intricate ways it continues to influence our present. The concept of afterlives provides a framework through which to explore and articulate what Avery Gordon refers to as the "ghostly aspects of life"—those elements of our past that, while seemingly concluded, continue to influence and shape our present. By focusing on afterlives, we can trace the enduring presence of what Gordon describes as the "endings that are not over," and attend to how they manifest in our current reality and finding the language to describe their impact.[102]

The term "afterlives" is being increasingly employed by historians and historical anthropologists to explore the lasting effects of phenomena such as empires, slavery, genocides, destruction, environmental disasters, wars, and revolutions, among others.[103] This perspective goes beyond simply creating a historical account that details events, losses, deaths, or changes in power. Instead, it aims to trace the past through its ongoing presence—focusing on who and what continues to shape and inform our current realities. By investigating the afterlives of these significant historical events, we navigate how they persist in collective memories, influence people's sense of belonging and emotions, and impact social and political lives. And we highlight the interconnectedness and interdependence of the past and present.

In his ethnography on the afterlives of destruction in Argentina, Gastón Gordillo builds upon Walter Benjamin's essay "The Task of the Translator," which speaks of "life" that should not be confined to organic corporeality but extended to anything with its own history.[104] Gordillo illustrates this with the example of rubble, which can have an afterlife determined by its historical context and the constellations of events and interactions that have shaped it and which challenges the notion of ruins as mere relics of a distant past. Gordillo's perspective on afterlives thus encourages us to reconsider the temporal and material boundaries of what is considered "alive," recognizing the enduring presence and impact of historical artifacts and sites in shaping present realities.

Speaking of the afterlives of genocide emphasizes the many ways the genocide continues to inform the lives of survivors and their descendants as well as society at large in Turkey and the diaspora. The phrase "afterlives of genocide" refers to how the power structure that annihilated Armenians, destroyed their cities, and confiscated their properties was foundational for the Republic of Turkey—and how these structures continue to persist in shaping the present. Such a power structure endures in the ways in which Armenians in Turkey continue to face erasure and exclusion in their everyday lives as barely tolerated citizens who are racialized as a "foreign minority" and blamed for the violence they endured. The legacy of trauma and displacement continues to inform the lives of Armenians, both in Turkey and the diaspora, long after the violence occurred. Understanding the genocide through its afterlives draws attention to denativization as an ongoing structure of the Armenian genocide.

The intent of the genocide was to annihilate Armenians, and denativization has continued as the genocide's afterlives. As a concept, the idea of the genocide's afterlives—which refers to the genocide as a structure with multiple ongoing consequences for Armenians—is broader and more encompassing than that of denativization, which is specifically about the ways in which Armenians in Turkey have been turned into a foreign minority in their homeland. Overall, this book emphasizes the enduring influence of historical events and structures beyond their immediate occurrence. While Gordillo focuses on the material afterlives of objects and sites, this ethnography explores the social, cultural, and political afterlives of a genocidal event as active forces that continue to exert influence on the present.

The book does not attempt to construct a historical account about what was lost, who was killed, and what was destroyed. Instead it traces the past through its afterlives—who and what remained—with the aim of retelling the story of Armenian survivance in Turkey as one of ongoing denativization. This approach uncovers the unspoken and overlooked, challenging the neat nationalist narratives that erased the foundational violence upon which the Turkish state was founded (chapter 1) and thus shaped our understanding of the past. This reading questions the assumptions upon which Turkish and Armenian histories have been written to map the ideological underpinnings that produced narratives that excluded the Armenian survivors in Turkey. It amplifies the muted voices and silenced experiences marginalized by state power, revealing the complex layers of history that have been systematically erased (chapter 3). Rather than viewing erasure and dispossession as isolated incidents that span post-Ottoman Armenian history, this analysis frames them as ongoing structures, perpetuated through the Turkish state since its inception by the legal framework of the Lausanne Treaty of 1923 (chapter 2) and through the state's policies toward Armenians and Armenian landscapes and heritage sites in Anatolia (chapter 6). Furthermore, it acknowledges the diversity within Armenian communities, illustrating the varied and sometimes conflicting experiences of being Armenian that challenge the notion of a homogeneous Armenian experience (chapters 3 and 4). Moreover, these afterlives make it evident that the exclusion and erasure of Armenians extend beyond the actions of the Turkish state. They point to the significant role of French colonial policies in Anatolia (chapter 2) and the political dynamics within the diaspora, both of which played a role in severing Armenians from Anatolia (chapter 5). The retelling of the past here traces the genocide through its afterlives as an open-ended set of often unreconcilable plurals.

As the stories in the coming chapters demonstrate, Armenians who remained in Turkey were not meant to survive, and those who survived were not meant to become Turkish citizens. The Armenian survival in Turkey, therefore, was undesirable for the founders of the new republic, and "unthinkable" for many Armenians in the diaspora. For many Armenians living in the diaspora, Armenians were either killed in the genocide or survived in the diaspora, rendering their survival in Turkey unthinkable in a perspective that regards genocide as total annihilation without survivors.[105] In Turkey, Armenians were largely seen as traitors to the Ottoman state for allegedly collaborating with its enemies and were therefore seen as deserving their fate.[106] Even today, Armenians are sometimes referred to in Turkey as the "leftovers of the sword," a derogatory expression that humiliates the survivors for not dying.[107] This term presents a paradox: even though the Turkish state officially denies the genocide, the term indicates that violence has been committed against Armenians. Meanwhile, it boasts of the killing of Armenians as essential, excusable, and even heroic.[108] The paradox of this expression connotes that Armenian survival in Turkey is far from being totally absent from national consciousness; rather, it rests in multiple silences that are maintained through the production of historical narratives, as the next chapter discusses.[109]

This book, of course, focuses on the Armenian experience of survival in Anatolia as a set of continuous displacements and erasures. This survival is considered unthinkable by most Armenians, because of their assumption that Armenians were either killed in the genocide or survived in the diaspora; it is considered undesirable by Turks, whose nationalist movement implemented policies of violent assimilation to create a homogeneous confessional ethnicity based on Sunni Muslim identity for its citizenry. The book interjects this history of survival in order to understand genocide not as finality, and survival not as passive, but as a process involving the active, creative, and determined agency to affirm a presence that transcends victimhood. This approach recasts survival not as mere continuation to live but as active "survivance."[110]

TRACING AFTERLIVES

This historical ethnography traces the ways in which Armenians survived in Turkey years after the genocide and the reasons that prompted them to migrate from their villages and cities in Anatolia to Istanbul and later to France. It tells stories of Armenian survivance that fell between the cracks of both Armenian and Turkish historiographies. Armenian survivors who remained as Turkish citizens were rendered impossible in the nationalist view of their respective communities. To explain these multiple silences and displacements, this book traces their experiences, which are not part of any archive, yet are traceable through multiple genres of storytelling. In addition to ethnographic encounters in Paris and Istanbul, this book considers the telling of stories about Armenian survivance from a constellation of sources, such as novels, oral histories, and testimonies, and reflects on "surviving objects," such as destroyed and renovated Armenian buildings.[111] Such sources bring together Armenian undocumented and fragmented pasts to tell of how Armenians continued to live in the shadow of the genocide, how they survived, what prompted them to leave Anatolia for Istanbul, what led to their eventual migration to France, and how their lives continue to be silenced in Turkey and within parts of the Armenian diaspora. These sources emphasize that the erasure of Armenians is not an event of the past, but an ongoing process in the present, perpetuated by the genocidal structure upon which the Turkish state was founded, which continues to permeate every aspect of the social and political lives of Armenian citizens in Turkey.

The silences I encountered in tracing the Armenian past in Turkey were not merely in archives, statistical tables, and historiography; they also registered in oral encounters during my fieldwork. One episode is worth mentioning in this context. Many of the people I met in Istanbul told me, "If you are interested in Armenians in Anatolia, you must meet Kaspar. He was born and raised in Diyarbakır and has many stories to share." I met Kaspar, accompanied by a mutual friend. After short introductions, he offered me a faint smile—a gesture that seemed to acknowledge my curiosity, while making it clear he had no intention of answering my questions—as he kept his gaze on the papers on his desk:

KASPAR: So what do you want to know?

HAKEM: I have a few questions about how Armenians continued living in Anatolia after 1915. How did . . .

KASPAR: [Abruptly interrupting] You know, when you are chasing dogs or cats, after a while you will lose track of some of them; some are going to hide, others will escape. But you cannot kill every single one of them.

HAKEM: But can I ask you specific questions about Anatolia and your experience in Diyarbakır?

KASPAR: No, you can't! If you want to know about Armenians in Diyarbakır, read Mıgırdiç Margosyan's novels, he is from the city, and says everything in his books. Start with *Gavur Mahallesi*.

Kaspar was referring me to Margosyan's 1992 novel, named after the Armenian quarter of the city known as the *mahalle* (neighborhood) where the *gavur* live. This term not only carries religious connotations but also serves as a racialized marker, categorizing non-Muslims as "others" in a complex interplay of racial and confessional identities within the post-Ottoman Turkish context, as argued earlier. *Gavur* is usually translated into English as "infidels" or "unbelievers." The novel's title could be translated as "The Neighborhood Where the Infidels Live" or "The Infidel's Quarter," as the English translation is titled.

Kaspar's refusal to answer my questions was not what I had hoped for; his straightforward and firm refusal surprised and frustrated me. As an anthropologist investigating the past in the shadow of violence, I was seeking a narrative of personal or family survival, a story with a beginning and an end that I could scribble in my field notes, analyze, theorize, and turn into a story so that I could ultimately claim to have documented the unwritten history of forgotten Armenians. My assumptions back then were still positivist in the sense that I went to meet Kaspar to collect "data." This was not to be the case. My *failed* conversation with Kaspar, which failed for reasons he never explained and should not be required to explain, taught me to abandon the idea of pursuing orders and structures that ethnographers and historians often seek and led me to follow instead the randomness and surprises from the field, to listen to silences and take refusals not as failure but rather as a starting point. After all, the very idea of "failure" in this context rests on the assumption that successful ethnography is defined by the collection and analysis of data as a form of empirical authority. The conversation also taught me the humility necessary to empathize with Kaspar's right to refuse to speak, be researched, or give testimony as an exercise of sovereignty.[112]

Audra Simpson illuminates the centrality of refusal in ethnographic practice, presenting it not merely as negation but as a deliberate, active stance of asserting sovereignty and autonomy. In her view, "refusal" allows indigenous peoples to withhold participation or information from ethnographic research, challenging colonial knowledge production and resisting the traditional power dynamics in which they are seen merely as subjects rather than active agents in their narratives and representation.[113]

This book builds on Simpson's concept, exploring various expressions of "ethnographic refusal." There is Hrant Dink's refusal to assimilate, be silenced, or tokenized as he struggled to maintain his voice in the face of systemic pressures to conform or be marginalized. There is my own refusal to propagate nationalist narratives or to write about violence as the monopoly of one group, a refusal I am making in order to challenge the simplification and the tribalization of history. There is the refusal to show solidarity with the group with which one has associated out of loyalty. Finally, there is the refusal of my interlocutors to speak as witnesses when I so much want to listen to their stories in order to collect information for my "research." In this context, Simpson's concept of refusal as an expression of sovereignty is a methodological intervention in this book. Emphasizing the inherent right of individuals and communities to define their own narratives and assert their agency and autonomy, she views refusal as a mechanism of sovereignty—one that actively resists the state's terms of recognition, colonial narratives, and the anthropological expectation that the people and the field are always obliged to speak to us. Refusal asserts a people's right to withhold, to set the conditions of their engagement, and to determine what is shared and what remains unsaid.[114]

Building on this critical foundation, the book engages with the concept of "counter-histories" to challenge prevailing historical narratives that have long dictated the boundaries of what is remembered and erased. Rather than merely rejecting history as fixed and authoritative, counter-histories expose the mechanisms through which historical knowledge is produced, legitimized, and sustained. However, this is not an effort to simply "give voice" to Armenians—a framing that risks reproducing colonial power dynamics by positioning the scholar as a mediator for the silenced. As I explore further in chapter 1, counter-histories critique the liberal impulse of inclusive histories that place marginalized narratives alongside dominant ones without dismantling the structures of power that sustain them. They also reject the very claim to "recover" lost voices, resisting efforts to restore what was erased without confronting the systems that enabled their erasure. Rather than merely supplementing the master narrative, counter-histories seek to disrupt it by exposing its omissions, contradictions, and ideological foundations.

In conversation with Audra Simpson's critique of ethnographic "voice," counter-histories offers a methodological challenge to dominant narratives—not only by recognizing the sovereignty of interlocutors, including their right to refuse participation, withhold aspects of their history, and reject imposed representations, but also by actively unsettling the very structures that produce historical erasure. In this way, counter-histories and Simpson's critique converge in their refusal to assimilative and extractive approaches to historical narration, rejecting the mere insertion of silenced voices into preexisting frameworks and instead demanding a fundamental reconfiguration of how history is written.[115]

By applying this approach, the book exposes the limitations and biases inherent in nationalist historiographies. It specifically highlights how Armenians were systematically reduced to a foreign minority in Turkey despite being Turkish citizens. This transformation involves more than just physical displacement and exclusion as a minority. It encompasses the ongoing process of "denativization," which strips Armenians of their status and belonging to Anatolia politically, socially, and historically, as well as in the narratives of the official and societal discourses of Turkey (chapters 2 and 6).

I therefore resorted to observing rather than asking questions in my first year in the field. I relied mainly on the scattered fragments that appeared randomly through images, events, and memoirs that continue to emerge in the present,[116] which are the main sources of knowledge in this book. It was only toward the end of my fieldwork period that I managed to have longer conversations with people I had known for at least two years. These conversations offered more detailed glimpses of Armenian lives in different parts of Anatolia since 1923—or, to be accurate, what my interlocutors retained about those years from the stories they heard from their parents about the early republic and from what they personally experienced in Turkey since their birth in the 1950s.

I realized that, as frustrating as the encounter was, both my *failure* to get Kaspar to speak and the few words he uttered proved revelatory. After three years of fieldwork in France and Turkey, Kaspar's few words summarized the Armenian experience in Turkey that I encountered in the field. His analogy— comparing Armenian endurance amid the policies of annihilation to the elusive nature of cats and dogs—offered a crucial insight into Armenian survivance. By employing the metaphor of animals commonly chased away, he highlighted the dehumanizing aspect of the genocide, which enabled such widespread destruction. Indeed, in the racist language that preceded the genocide, the Young

Turks referred to Armenians as "dogs." The dehumanization was not only a tool for extermination, but an ironic testament to the Armenians' adaptability and resourcefulness, traits that propelled their survivance. In this context, the derogatory comparison is inverted, portraying Armenians not as mere passive victims but as active agents of their own history. This resilience resonates with Jacques Derrida's concept of "afterlife [survivance]," where survival signifies not the spectral return from death, but the persistence of a life force that defies obliteration—in Derrida's words, "an excess of life which resists annihilation."[117] In this reading, Armenians are the unwanted surplus embodying an agency that challenges their imposed marginality.

Furthermore, Kaspar pointed me to Margosyan's autobiographical literary works, which opened a venue to search for knowledge that goes beyond the ethnographic and the archival, into the literary and the autobiographical. Finally, and most importantly, Kaspar abdicated his role as a witness to violence that was expected from him—by me and perhaps by other Armenians in the diaspora. Although he declined the Turkish state's efforts to assimilate him, at that moment, he also refused to speak. My "failed" encounter with Kaspar and his refusal to describe what life was like for survivors in Anatolia after the genocide revealed the ways that knowledge about denativized Armenians has become nearly impossible for outsiders since the 1920s. What I considered at the time to be a "failed" encounter, I now understand as Kaspar's exercise of epistemic sovereignty and my learning of epistemic humility.

Amidst the ruins of the past, historians and ethnographers resemble Walter Benjamin's storytellers, who borrow their authority to narrate from death—from that which "is-not."[118] To understand the concept of the ruin, Gastón Gordillo, following Theodor Adorno, sees in the "critical power of negativity" a twofold potential: to "disintegrate the positivity of the given" and to subvert the fantasy that recovering the past could ever be complete or represent a whole.[119] Gordillo critiques the practice of anthropology that assumes that any locale is inherently researchable as the "phantasmagoria of positivity."[120] This critique represents an epistemic shift from the empirical authority of "being-there" (in field sites or archives) to the storyteller's "hauntological authority" of the negative.[121] Belonging to Anatolia therefore emerges through the collective act of storytelling that takes place amidst absences, where Armenians together extend the lives of their long-gone dead ancestors, destroyed cities, and lost homelands.[122] Recent historical ethnographies that study the aftermath of violence have shifted from documenting what is present to grappling with what has been erased, misappropriated, or made inaccessible—a move that Yael Navaro calls "negative methodology."[123] This approach does not treat archival absence as a mere void; rather, it engages erasure as an active force—one that structures memory, shapes historical consciousness, and dictates the terms of what can and cannot be known. By foregrounding denial, refusal, and silence, it reveals how power operates not only through what is recorded but through what is systematically withheld, distorted, or made to disappear.

The genocide was the watershed event for Armenians in Turkey and the wider diaspora that continues to shape many aspects of their lives. It has also been the vantage point from which to conceive and write Armenian history. Genocide history continues to oscillate between the denial and affirmation of the violent events. Such an approach assumes that genocidal events are facts that can be proven or denied. Marc Nichanian brings the debate out of the binary of asserting and denying facts by speaking of the "nothingness of the archive." Nichanian speaks about the negativity of the fact; the only "true 'fact'" for him is in the negative—that is, the destruction of the archive, because the perpetrators of the genocide did not leave a trace for their crime. The "will to exterminate" Armenians, which is a prerequisite for a crime to be designated as genocide in international law, cannot be proven legally or historically.[124] Through the negativity of the fact, Nichanian scrutinizes the empirical authority of the archives, thus rendering the discipline of history "perfectly powerless."[125]

While Nichanian exposes the limits of historical empiricism, this book extends this critique into ethnographic practice, refusing to construct a linear historical recovery. Instead, it follows dispersed lives, tracking the residual effects of denativization as they unfold in the present. In light of Kaspar's refusal, this book aims to trace the history of the denativization of Armenians through the life stories of the survivors I met in Paris and Istanbul. My intention here was not to write an alternative history; I also do not claim have written a corrective history of Turkey or of Armenians. Rather the book is a counter-history that unsettles dominant narratives by exposing their omissions, silences, and the structures of power that sustain them. It is anchored in my refusal to propagate the exceptionalism inherent in the ways that both Turks and Armenians perceive themselves. Such exceptionalism is manifested both in the way that Turkey denies the genocide and in the way that Armenians emphasize their victimhood as survivors of mass annihilation, both when recounting the experience of the genocide and when describing their self-perception. My approach here is to write the lives of Armenians, including the violence they have been subjected to, without limiting Armenians to their victimhood and their history to violence alone. This stance may prompt the question of why an anthropologist or a historian would be drawn to narrating stories that uncover silences. One compelling motivation for undertaking this endeavor is the drive to challenge the prevailing dominance of nationalist narratives and nation-state paradigms that are often centered on the genocide and victimhood of Armenians, pervasively influencing both political discourses and academic research in Armenian and related area studies. Because tragedy is a dominant genre in Armenian studies, this book disrupts this status quo by foregrounding the complex lives of surviving Armenians as survivance and by mapping the conflicting powers that acted upon them, starting with the Lausanne Treaty of 1923 that codified the minority status of Armenians.

Similarly, ethnography on Armenians in Turkey poses challenges because of their demographic dispersal across multiple locales—each generation often born and die in a different place. This precludes any attempt for a more "holistic" ethnography of a single community and, crucially, is not a multi-sited ethnography, where researchers typically follow tangible flows or linkages across well-defined "sites." Instead, I trace fragmented connections among dispersed Anatolian Armenians—recovering only partial stories, rumors, and refusals in the midst of ongoing erasures in Istanbul and Paris. In keeping with a negative methodology, I do not presume historical data to be readily retrievable or verifiable. Rather, the book foregrounds silences, absences, rumors, and dispersions as meaningful in themselves, reflecting how denativization unfolds across time and space under conditions of perpetual violence. Resisting the positivist demand for conclusive proof and archived visibility, this methodological approach recognizes that fragmentation—and the impossibility of a unified ethnographic field—are integral facets of Armenians' lived realities.

Through this framework, I revisit the Armenian survivors in Anatolia and their migration to Istanbul and Paris. I aim not to return to the past as an end in itself,[126] but to capture Armenians in this present historical juncture, marked by their absence from Anatolia, where traces of their past still surface through stories despite their physical absence. This book therefore detours to the Armenian past not to reconstruct a stable historical narrative but to trace the wreckages that the destructive forces embedded in nationalist projects—be they the Turkish state, Armenian diaspora institutions, or European imperialism—and their enduring afterlives. These forces have shaped censored archives, displaced communities, and the persistent silences surrounding Armenian presence in Turkey. It is within this framework that I read the unwritten past of Armenians in Anatolia as the wreckage excluded from official archives, challenging the sanitized archives of civility through the experiences of Armenian survivors in Turkey. This book is therefore anchored on that which lies outside the archives and a population that is external to the nation-state project by focusing on the mostly unarchived Anatolian Armenian past in post-Ottoman Turkey.

UNPLANNED ENCOUNTERS

Ethnographic fieldwork is sustained by one's initial surprises in the field. The people we meet, the words we hear, and our unplanned encounters all have a vital say in how we see, what we trace, and who we follow. During my fieldwork in France, I initially intended to study the formation of the Armenian diaspora in France. I was particularly interested in migration into Europe, especially France, given the ongoing debates and incidents in the country surrounding anti-Semitism, Islamophobia, and the recent expulsions of Roma communities. Meanwhile, France is a prime destination for the so-called *sans papier* ("without [residency] papers" in French) from Egypt and the rest of Africa. Just as my research in France evolved in response to unfolding encounters and political contexts, my fieldwork took an unexpected turn when Krikor suggested I travel to Istanbul to meet Hrant Dink. By then, however, Dink had already been assassinated, and what began as an attempt to meet him turned instead into an effort to understand why he was killed—what forces made his murder possible, what anxieties he provoked, and how his critiques unsettled the dominant political stances of both Turkey and the Armenian diaspora. The encounter I had hoped for never took place, yet the attempt itself redirected my ethnography in ways I had not foreseen, shaping how I came to think about the entanglements of the Armenian diaspora, genocide history, and the political struggles that the Armenian citizens of Turkey continue to face.

My ethnographic inquiry remained anchored in the Paris suburb of Alfortville. Between 2007–2009 and 2011–2012, I conducted ethnographic fieldwork there, and every year from 2007–2013, I spent around three months in Istanbul tracing the places and people that my interlocutors in France evoked. France represented an intriguing starting point for this story, because—since at least the second half of the nineteenth century—it has been the destination for migrants from elsewhere in Europe, from the colonies both before and after their independence, and (in smaller numbers) from elsewhere in the world. This includes migration in the wake of labor exploitation and land expropriation, as was the case with Algeria. While France perpetrated horrendous violence in its colonies, it was also where many refugees settled following catastrophic events such as the Armenian genocide, the Holocaust, and the Spanish Civil War. I was predominantly interested in the Armenian migration to France given the long-standing French colonial interests in the Ottoman Empire and the post-Ottoman Middle East. The French government welcomed Christian and Jewish migrations from its ex-colonies, such as Armenians from Ottoman Cilicia, Christians from Lebanon, and Jews from Algeria. When it came to Armenians leaving Anatolia during and after the genocide, France received the largest number of refugees: sixty-five thousand Armenian refugees, around 30 percent of all Armenian refugees in the Near East and Europe.[127] This is because France was occupying the provinces to which Armenians returned after the genocide, and therefore the majority of the Armenians became refugees in France after France ceded these ex-Ottoman provinces to the Turkish revolutionaries under the Treaty of Ankara of 1921. Alfortville was an obvious choice for fieldwork, given that it has been a destination for Armenians for more a century: refugees in the aftermath of World War I and then Armenians from Lebanon in the wake of the civil war, from Turkey since the 1960s, and from post-Soviet Armenia since independence.

In Alfortville, I sought to meet Anatolian Armenians. I spent Sundays and several other days each week there, eating in their restaurants, frequenting their cafes and doing my grocery shopping, attending church services every Sunday and on special religious holidays, and participating in public events at the Armenian school and cultural center as well as events relevant to Armenians organized by the city hall, the Mairie d'Alfortville. I quickly discovered that many of the Armenians I met were "from Turkey": teachers in the local Armenian school; priests, deacons, and choir members at the church; the owners of the two main grocery stores; and the owners of the popular kebab restaurant in the neighborhood. This ethnography became historical in the field, where the people I met were more interested in speaking with me about their past in Istanbul and their family villages of origin in Anatolia than about their lives after migrating to France. As is the case with many diasporic and exilic individuals, their present lives in France evoked the past in Turkey, often with nostalgia and longing, even though they rarely contemplated a return, some not even for a short visit.

This prompted me to ask what Turkish history would look like from the standpoint of Armenian survivors. I continued to frequently visit Istanbul and to make short visits to some of the places they invoked in Anatolia, such as Diyarbakır and Mardin in 2008, as well as Antakya, As-Suwaydiyah/Samandağ, and Vakıf/Vakıflıköy in 2009. Vakıf/Vakıflıköy is known for being the last remaining Armenian village in Turkey, because it has some two hundred Armenians and a functioning church.[128]

Interviews, even casual conversations with Armenians from Turkey in Alfortville and Istanbul, were kept short at the beginning; some Armenians even ended them abruptly. But it was even more difficult to speak to French Armenians. I was asked, "Why would they speak to a stranger, an 'Arab' with a Turkish-sounding name?" "Armenians of Alfortville will think you are an informant for the Turkish state!" a politically active French-Armenian woman commented when I told her that I sought to speak with Armenians from Turkey. I often invoked my

Armenian grandfather and our family connection to Mardin in conversation to assure Armenians of my good intentions, but this rarely came to my aid when I was talking with those in nationalist Armenian circles. I remained an "Arab" to many Armenians and to Turks, and my motivations for tracing the Armenians in Turkey were often questioned and doubted, or at best not taken seriously. Missed appointments were another way to evade me in Paris and Alfortville, along with telling me generic statements about how I should not make distinctions between Armenians from Turkey and those born and raised in France. "We have no Turkish-speaking Armenians here, we have only Armenians who are well assimilated in France," I was once told by an Istanbul Armenian whom I often heard speaking in Turkish throughout Alfortville.

Yet in less nationalist Armenian circles, having one Armenian grandfather was enough for me to be accepted as an Armenian. I was placed on the pre-genocide map of Ottoman Anatolia as coming *from* Mardin, the city from which my grandfather's family came when they escaped the genocide. This was not the case in Istanbul. People there did not readily accept me as Armenian. When I complained about this to an Armenian in Istanbul, she insisted that Armenians in Turkey do not readily speak to outsiders, even Armenians from Europe or elsewhere, due to the fear of exposing themselves or the community in a social and political context dominated by genocide denialism and anti-Armenian racism. Like other Armenians, I found that my Armenianness was both forged and denied, depending on the context, the people, and the situation.

TRACING DENATIVIZATION

Enduring Erasures tells the Armenian experiences of displacement, erasure, and survivance, taking post–World War I diplomacy (1919–1923) and the assassination of Hrant Dink in Istanbul (2007) as starting points for understanding the Armenian experience as demonstrating various stages of denativization. In speaking of stages, the book considers both the state's explicitly planned policies as well as stages that were part of the aftermath of genocide and elimination policies, but not specifically planned. The book reads denativization as a process that is multiple and open-ended; that happens at different stops in the experience of Armenians, from Anatolia to the Lausanne Treaty to their migration to Istanbul and then to France; and that is ongoing. The book focuses on specific events that tell the story of denativization—how and when it occurred and who the actors were—events that do not represent a comprehensive history.

As Armenians survived in Turkey as a population unwanted by the Turkish nation-state builders, chapter 1 looks at denativization in historiography, where the Armenians in Turkey were excluded from both Turkish nationalist and Armenian diasporic histories. The Armenian survivors therefore constitute counter-histories for both narratives. This chapter juxtaposes the lives of Hrant Dink and Sabiha Gökçen, a Turkish national hero who became the world's first female combat pilot, as representatives of different, even opposite, strands of being an Armenian survivor in Turkey. Because of this violence and the persistent denial that it occurred, the Armenian past in Turkey survives in the unverifiable medium of storytelling that this chapter presents. It is notable that historiographical erasures have created sanitized "histories of civilization" that justify the national project and the nation-state. The chapter shows that strategic erasures have been key to creating stark divisions between those who are a "part of Turkish national history" and those "external to that history." The retelling of the stories of Hrant Dink and Sabiha Gökçen is a lens into these erasures—and into the reasons why some people would see any challenges to these erasures as an existential threat to the Turkish state.

Understanding the Turkish state formation as one built on the destruction of the prior populations, chapter 2 rereads the Treaty of Lausanne of 1923 as a key historical document, demonstrating that the treaty not only secured Turkish sovereignty but also denied sovereignty and political agency to surviving Armenians and other non-Muslims. Post–World War I international diplomacy maps the ways in which Turkish nationalists and European imperial powers legally rendered the Armenians who remained both "foreign" and a "minority" in their homeland. Rather than serving merely as a historical marker for denativization, Lausanne operates as a methodological lens through which to examine how the treaty ensured that Armenian citizens of Turkey would remain politically marginalized, legally constrained, and structurally unequal by instituting their racialization as a minority. The text of the treaty became the regime with which the Turkish state managed Armenians and ignored past violence perpetrated against them.

This reading of the treaty brings into question the Armenian focus on the 1915 genocide as the end of their history in Anatolia and the Turkish focus on Lausanne as the starting point for Turkish history. Thus, the silence about Anatolian Armenians was produced not in the absence of facts about them, but rather by concentrating on other events in the historiography of this treaty. Chapter 2 also uncovers the process by which the diverse Ottoman Muslims in Anatolia, as well as Balkan Muslim refugees to Anatolia, were made to constitute a demographic majority under the label "Turk," rendering non-Muslim citizens—the Armenians, Jews, and Rūm-Orthodox (Greeks)—as being governed under a regime protected by the League of Nations as minorities. While non-Muslims were included as foreign minorities, Muslims such as Kurds, Alevis, and Alevi-Kurds were subjected to assimilation into Turkish Sunni Muslim majoritarianism.

Chapter 3 considers the aftermath of postwar diplomacy by presenting the lives of ordinary and unnoticed Armenians who continued living in Anatolia after the genocide and exploring the reasons that prompted them to leave Anatolia beginning in the 1940s. The chapter shows the necessity of looking beyond the archive to the personal narratives of individual survivors to uncover silences in the dominant historiographical narrative, and it shows as well that the knowledge and understanding gained will always be partial. It tells the stories of Armenians from three Anatolian towns—Everek (in Kayseri province), Sasun (Batman), and Arapgir (Malatya)—who became Turkish citizens when the republic was founded. Their stories point to the diversity of the experiences of people who were pushed out of Anatolia. And although the survivors' specific reasons for leaving vary, their stories collectively point to explicit efforts by the state to push the remaining Armenian population out of Anatolia.

The experiences of Anatolian Armenians often have not fit into the simplified narratives and rigid understandings of Armenianness and Armenian history that are widespread in Istanbul and the Armenian diaspora in France. Many cultural practices of Anatolian Armenians overlap to some degree with those of their non-Armenian neighbors. Furthermore, the relations between Anatolian Armenians and their non-Armenian neighbors also have been complex: just as Turks and Kurds massacred Armenians, they also helped Armenians survive. When Anatolian Armenians emigrated to Istanbul, or later to Europe, their locally inflected Armenianness was often not understood or valued by the Armenians in their new communities. Chapter 4 highlights the fact that there have been multiple and contradictory forms of Armenianness, including Islamized ones, as well as multiple and contradictory sorts of relations between Anatolian Armenians and their neighbors. It also suggests that the dismissive response to Anatolian Armenians on the part of Armenians already living in Istanbul or France is itself denativizing. By denying Anatolian Armenians the space to articulate an experience of being Armenian that is different from the one institutionalized in Istanbul or France, Armenians in Istanbul and France have contributed to the sense of rupture and estrangement experienced by Anatolian Armenians. This denial has thus played a role in the loss of cultural identity and feeling of cultural belonging experienced by Anatolian Armenians.

In contrast to those who survived in Anatolia, the Armenians in the diaspora (the descendants of the refugees) established roots in the countries to which they emigrated, including France. Chapter 5 demonstrates that ways in which the Armenian diaspora institutions have tried to maintain Armenian identity in the diaspora in France, while working within the constraints of French republicanism. In trying to resist one sort of "homogenization" (full assimilation into the host culture), diasporic institutions have contributed to the denativization of Armenians from Anatolia in two ways. First, they have imposed a narrower and more rigid sense of Armenian identity and affiliation, whereby homogenization here implies cultural loss. Second, they forged a new link with the Republic of Armenia, the new homeland that came to replace Anatolia in the diaspora.

This book reads the afterlives of the Armenian genocide in Turkey and France as encompassing multiple stages of denativization. Throughout these stages, we find the Armenian predicament to be intertwined with those of other populations whose destruction was central to building nation-states and who continue to live on the margins of the nation-state order of the world. Nation-states annihilate, expel, and assimilate those populations that do not fit the vision of demographic homogeneity imagined by the nationalist bourgeoisie. Chapter 6 looks at the contemporary discourses in Turkey to demonstrate how denativization endures, not only through policies and legal frameworks but through cultural narratives that reshape the very meaning of presence. Such discourses are present in a wide variety of places, from political speech and media representation to renovations of ancient Armenian religious sites in Anatolia—renovations that have systematically divorced the buildings from the histories of violence to which Armenians have been subjected. Denativization, then, is not merely historical but an ongoing process that unfolds in the realm of discourse, narration, and memory. Yet, against this enduring erasure, we also find an enduring presence—a refusal to be fully displaced, a commitment to assert presence, and an insistence on belonging. Understanding the Armenian predicament as denativization means also recognizing the ways in which Armenians continue to inscribe themselves on the land they collectively lost, not as a longing for a lost past, but as a claim to presence—one that resists and unsettles the logic of erasure itself.

CHAPTER 1

KILLING THE INFIDEL

Armenian Erasures as Turkey's Counter-Histories

On Friday, January 19, 2007, I was trying to set up a meeting with Hrant Dink at the very moment his body was lying on an Istanbul sidewalk with blood streaming from it. I had arranged to meet Selim, a translator and civil rights activist, in the central Taksim Square of Istanbul that day to try the food at a newly opened Armenian restaurant in Kurtuluş. This neighborhood—along with Kumkapı, where the Armenian Patriarchate is located—is one of the neighborhoods with a large concentration of Armenians. Kurtuluş, I was told, is known to have been established by Greek-speaking migrants from the island of Chios who settled in Istanbul in the sixteenth century. Until the late 1960s, Kurtuluş was predominantly inhabited by Greek-speaking Rūm-Orthodox Christian citizens of Turkey and was known by its Greek name Tatavla ("horse stable"). The Turkish state then changed the neighborhood's name to Kurtuluş ("independence"), a name that staved off the view of Istanbul as foreign and undermined the predominance of Greek, which was spoken by its local population until recently. The name also evokes the Turkish War of Independence (*Kurtuluş Savaşı*), embedding it within a nationalist framework that casts the war as an anti-imperial struggle. Within this narrative, non-Muslims are often depicted as remnants or agents of colonialism, and the renaming of the neighborhood serves as both a symbolic and linguistic act of erasure: asserting Turkish sovereignty on the urban space while marginalizing the historical presence of its Rūm and other non-Muslim residents. Yet, despite this erasure, traces of the past remain: the Rūm-Orthodox presence is still visible in the many churches and large cemetery that dominate its landscape.

Walking in Kurtuluş, I could see a few shops with small Armenian script written on their windows. Some were selling books to teach the Armenian alphabet to children, religious items such as icons of Christ and plastic statues of the Virgin Mary, and albums of Armenian folk and liturgical songs. These touches of Armenianness were visible but not salient; one had to look carefully to notice them, and I did. Nothing in the faces, attitude, or language of the people working in those "Armenian" shops was different from those in any "Turkish" one. While I had been intending to write on the Armenians of France before going to Istanbul that January, Krikor had suggested that I might want to speak to his Turkish friend Selim during my short stay in the city.

Selim and I arrived at the Armenian restaurant Hamov ("delicious" in Armenian) around 2:30 pm, after the lunch hour rush had ended. The owners greeted Selim warmly. Selim explained to them that I was a friend of Krikor's from Paris and that I was doing research on the Armenians in France. They told us that they would prepare a plate of *meze* (appetizers) for each of us, so that we could sample the variety of their Armenian food. When two big and colorful dishes subsequently landed on the table, the salads and dishes all looked "Turkish" to me. "Of course, it is the same cuisine," Selim asserted. "You will find a difference in the taste though. People differentiate between a dish cooked by an Armenian or a Turk by the number of onions used in the food! The joke goes as follows: when they see the digit 2 next to 'onion' in a recipe text, a Turk understands it as two onions, while an Armenian as two kilograms of onions!" I tried the *yaprak sarma*, spiced rice rolled in vine leaves; it was indeed sweeter than the Turkish version, with hints of cinnamon. Another dish was a puree of chickpeas and potatoes mixed with tahini and spices presented on a small plate and covered with cinnamon powder and olive oil. While the other dishes were common, I was told that this dish, *topik*, was exclusively Armenian. Krikor had once wondered aloud about why Turks did not claim the dish as Turkish, like they claimed other Armenian things in Turkey. "It seems they didn't like its taste!" he said jokingly.

I told Selim about my interest in the Armenian diaspora in France and said that I had a few questions to ask him about Armenians in Istanbul. Selim was keen to highlight the difference between the two communities before we continued: "If there is one place where Armenians do not constitute a diaspora, it is here in Istanbul, and in fact all over Turkey." He explained that there has been a continuous presence of Armenians within the borders of contemporary Turkey for more two millennia and that parts of eastern Turkey are also western Armenia. "If you meet Hrant, he can tell you more about it," Selim continued. "He is an Armenian who is very keen on calling Turkey his country despite what the Armenian diasporic leaders think. He even refuses to leave the country despite the death threats he has been receiving in Turkey, and the opportunities he has been offered to emigrate to Europe." I replied, "You are the third person to mention his name to me. Will it be possible to meet him?" "Yes, of course," said Selim, "he is a good friend of mine, and I will arrange this for you."

Selim's mobile phone rang while we were eating. As he listened to the person on the other end, his face became pale. I only heard Selim's words—"*Efendim* . . . *ne zaman?*" (Hello, yes . . . when?)—and the phone conversation quickly came to an end. For a few moments, he was silent, and his eyes turned red and shone with restrained tears. I realized that something had happened, but it did not seem to be too serious due to his restrained reaction. "We were just talking about Hrant Dink," Selim said with a faint, grief-laden smile, his reddened eyes brimming with unshed tears. "He was just shot in front of the newspaper's office."

Selim did not yet know whether Dink had survived the shooting. I dared to eat one more spoonful of food but soon realized the seriousness of the situation and the emotions involved. Selim left to join his friends at the *Agos* office. I started making my way out after him, while the Armenian family who owned the restaurant continued speaking to me with a smiling politeness divorced from emotion. How could they be calm when a fellow Armenian was shot just around the corner? I was scared and uncomfortable, especially because I did not know what I should say, think, or even feel. The owners refused to let me pay for the meal, because it was my first visit. I thanked them and left. Scared, I took side streets until I arrived back in Taksim Square, only to find people gathering with handwritten posters in solidarity with Turkey's Armenians. I saw scores of candles on the ground as people started to mourn. Dink was officially declared dead. News outlets in Turkey uncovered details of the assassination, showing that at the crime scene, after shooting him three times in the back of his neck, his assassin ran away and shouted with triumph, "I killed the infidel" (*gavuru öldürdüm*). The label "*gavur*" (infidel) has assumed a racialized undertone in Turkey and is reserved for non-Muslim individuals, but since all Muslims are assumed to be racially and ethnically Turks, an Armenian (including an Armenian who converted to Islam) is rendered a *gavur.* The label carries within itself the "other/s" of the Turkish confessional ethnic nationalism. Dink was therefore killed as an infidel in the racialized sense of the term.

꒰꒱

Dink's funeral was on January 24, five days after his assassination. The procession started in front of the *Agos* offices in Osmanbey and continued in a four-mile march to the Armenian patriarchal church in Kumkapı. The marchers were accompanied by a car equipped with loudspeakers and carrying musicians playing tunes of lamentation on the duduk, the traditional Armenian wooden flute-like instrument. Between the intervals of duduk improvisation, the musicians played an Armenian folk song from eastern Anatolia, "Sari Gyalin," sung in Armenian, as well as its Turkish version, "Sarı Gelin." Selim told me during the funeral procession that the song, which speaks of the common heritage of Armenians and Turks in Anatolia, had been dear to Dink. With this music, the solemn march became a political statement and civil rights demonstration in which people expressed solidarity with Dink and Turkey's many minority groups. The demonstrators included Kurds, anti-establishment Turks, and many of Turkey's non-Muslims, all of them accusing the state—or to be precise, the *Derin Devlet* (the "Deep State")—for orchestrating, or at least being complicit in, Dink's assassination.

The term *"Derin Devlet"* was among the very first Turkish phrases I learned. During the funeral, Selim explained to me that the Deep State is a shadowy body within the visible state that comprises conservative and ultranationalist actors in the military and state intelligence who claim to act as custodians of the Kemalist ethic of secularity and independence from foreign intervention.[1] To the Deep State, the two main perceived threats to Kemalist republicanism are political Islam and the "foreign" elements within Turkey, which include Kurds and the non-Muslim communities of Armenians, Jews, and Rūm-Orthodox. Unexplained and untraceable crimes such as the September 1955 pogroms against non-Muslims in Istanbul and Dink's assassination are often blamed on this body.[2]

Dink's funeral brought up political concerns beyond those specific to Armenians. Showing solidarity with Dink and with Turkey's Armenian citizens, the crowd shouted in Kurdish, Greek, Armenian, and Turkish, all the languages native to Turkey: "We are all Armenians" and "We are all Hrant Dink." The funeral was a political demonstration where citizens issued a demand that the state grant civil rights to all citizens of the republic. The demonstrators echoed concerns Dink had expressed in the last article he wrote for *Agos*, where he mentioned that he had reported death threats to the police and received no response. "To what extent are these threats real?" he asked in his last article.[3] The irony is that his question was answered mere hours after the publication of the article, when he was interred in the Balıklı Armenian cemetery. Yet in his death, Dink brought the city's commercial center to a standstill and caused memories of past violence to "flash up" in the city's present.[4]

Standing in front of the building where the *Agos* offices are, with tens of thousands of demonstrators, Selim showed me a number of Turkish flags hanging from the windows of apartments known to him to be owned by Armenians. I was surprised that Armenians would fly Turkish flags in the wake of Dink's assassination, a crime that seemed to be perpetrated in the name of or by the Turkish state. Selim explained to me that "during the September 1955 riots against non-Muslims in Istanbul, many Armenians and Rūms hung Turkish flags on their shops, businesses, and homes in the hope that they would be spared." He explained that at such vulnerable times, non-Muslims feel the need to demonstrate their loyalty to the state to prevent potential retribution.

News outlets in Turkey uncovered details of the assassination, revealing that the killer was a sixteen-year-old boy from Trabzon, a Black Sea coastal city.[5] A few days following the assassination, photographs of Dink's murderer were made public, showing him receiving a hero's welcome in a police station in the city of Samsun, where he was caught the following day. The pictures, taken from a mobile phone in the police station, showed the assassin standing proudly with police officers, holding a Turkish flag with his two hands. Behind him was a poster with a quote from Mustafa Kemal: "The nation's land is sacred. It cannot be left to fate" (Vatan toprağı kutsaldır, kaderine terk edilemez).[6] Kemal's "apparition"—through his words glued to a Turkish flag—emphasize that he continues to intervene to save the nation from its internal enemies.[7]

What was Hrant Dink's crime that led to his tragic fate? And what was the daring challenge to the Turkish state and society that provoked an outcry from the republic's founder about the sacredness of the land? This chapter reflects on these questions by navigating the silences within Turkish historiography, shedding light on the deliberate omissions and manipulations that have shaped the nationalist historical narrative. It juxtaposes the lives of Dink and Sabiha Gökçen (Turkey's celebrated female combat pilot) as symbols of silenced Armenian narratives. By retelling their stories as intertwined, this chapter exposes the intricacies of denativization in historiography, illustrating how these stories embody "counter-histories" that subvert dominant historical accounts by centering the experiences and voices of those who have been marginalized, silenced, or erased in nationalist histories.

Drawing on the work of literary critics Catherine Gallagher and Stephen Greenblatt, counter-histories are more than alternative narratives; they represent "a spectrum of assaults on the grands récits [master narratives]," actively critiquing dominant historical frameworks and methodologically challenge the structures of power underpinning those frameworks.[8] By bringing omitted aspects of "barbarism"—invoking Benjamin's use of the term to challenge claims of civilization—to the center of historical conceptualization, counter-histories disrupt the coherence and authority of nationalist histories. The retelling of the overlapping and intertwined lives of Dink and Gökçen serves as counter-histories of Turkey,[9] revealing why breaking established silences is perceived as an existential threat to the Turkish state. To this end, this chapter narrates the denativization of Armenians as a counter-history that disrupts the nationalist assumptions that sustain dominant historiographies of the Turkish nation-state and exposes the silences they seek to preserve.

It is notable that the history of Armenians in Turkey has been silenced through self-censorship and through omissions in oral transmission, in addition to being silenced in historiography. Their lives represent several aspects of denativization that Armenians experienced in Turkey: the outright violence experienced by Dink, the alleged conversion and assimilation by Gökçen, and (as a consequence of both violence and assimilation) the denial of violence against Armenians in Turkish nationalist history. This chapter navigates the denativization of Armenians in historiography, reading beyond the nationalist binaries (such as Armenian/Turkish and civilization/barbarism) that dominate the writing of both histories. To refuse such binaries is to employ counter-histories as a methodological intervention that actively disrupts the frameworks of ethnic nationalisms, nation-states, and the claims of moral superiority and triumphalism embedded in them.

REVEALING SABIHA GÖKÇEN'S SECRET

In an article published in the Turkish-Armenian weekly *Agos* on February 6, 2004, three years before his assassination, Hrant Dink embarked on a daring endeavor that ultimately sealed his fate. In his article titled "The Secret of Sabiha Hatun," Dink challenged the prevailing aura surrounding a national figure, Sabiha Gökçen (1913–2001), by revealing a hidden truth: she was, in fact, an Armenian orphan. This revelation acted as a catalyst to expose the anxieties within Turkish society about confronting the multifaceted nature of the country's history, especially around the Armenian predicament in the final years of the Ottoman Empire. The article was a testament to Dink's unwavering commitment to exposing the silenced Armenian narratives in Turkey: making them visible and, in doing so, challenging the established story that had been woven into the fabric of the nation. Dink's article about Sabiha Gökçen's true identity was just one instance in a series of his historical interventions, and in the years that followed, it would set the stage for his tragic assassination. His slaying was a consequence of his relentless pursuit of a future based on equal citizenship rights, a future that does not grant privileges to the bearers of a certain confessional ethnicity. Dink saw a historiography critical of state-sanctioned nationalist narratives as one means to achieve such an endeavor.

The official story runs as follows: Gökçen was born in 1913 in the city of Bursa and was the daughter of Hafız Mustafa İzzet, a Young Turk who was a provincial (*vilayet*) secretary. Gökçen was orphaned when her father died. She was still going to primary school at the time and continued living with her siblings.[10] Gökçen's life took a different turn after she met Mustafa Kemal, the founder of the republic. During Kemal's visit to Bursa in 1924, Gökçen had a great desire to meet him but was unable to do so. When he visited again in the following year, Kemal stayed in a mansion next to where Gökçen lived, enabling her to see him from her window. One day she decided to jump over the fence to meet him, and when the guards stopped her, she expressed her desire to meet *Gazi* Paşa (a reference to Mustafa Kemal) and to kiss his hand.[11] Upon hearing this, Kemal asked her to draw near him, and she then expressed her desire to continue her education without leaning on her siblings. Being an orphan, she told Kemal, she did not want to remain a burden on them by pursuing her education. Kemal then offered to have Gökçen to live with him in Ankara and become his adopted daughter. The offer was one she could not refuse, and so she gladly accepted, making Gökçen one of the three adopted daughters of the republic's founding father.[12]

This close association with Kemal was later solidified when Gökçen became a pilot and participated in the third military operation that bombarded the Kurdish city of Dersim (Turkified as "Tunceli") in August 1938, turning Gökçen into Turkey's, and the world's, first female combat pilot. Just like her adoptive father the Gazi, she became a warrior for the new republic. As a national hero, Sabiha Gökçen embodied Kemal's vision of the "myth of the military nation," which considers every Turk as being born a soldier,[13] prompting Kemal to praise Gökçen with the following words:

> I am proud of you, Gökçen! And not just me, the whole Turkish nation that has been following this incident very closely is proud of you . . . You should be proud of yourself for showing to the whole world, once again, what our young girls can do. We are a military nation. From ages seven to seventy, women and men alike, we have been created as soldiers.[14]

In his article, Hrant Dink brought Gökçen back to a different life. He narrated another story of the heroic persona known to the Turkish public. Dink quoted Hripsime Sebilciyan—an Armenian woman from the Anatolian city of Gaziantep who later immigrated to Soviet Armenia—as saying that she was Gökçen's niece and that Gökçen was not a Turkish orphan, but an Armenian one. In revealing a "secret" about a national icon, the article infuriated the Turkish public and stirred a public debate in the media. The Turkish daily *Hürriyet* discussed

Dink's article,[15] which prompted no less than the office of the chief of staff of the Turkish armed forces to issue the following statement in defense of the official Turkish version of Gökçen's life:

> She [Gökçen] is a Turk and the first war pilot of the Turkish Armed Forces, is an honorary member of the Turkish air force. Sabiha Gökçen is also a valuable and a strong symbol of Turkish women, and she represents Atatürk's vision of the ideal place of Turkish women in modern Turkish society. Opening such a figure to debate, for whatever purpose, makes no contribution to national integrity and social peace. It is unacceptable to qualify a claim, which is published in an abusive discourse against national sentiments and values, as "newsmaking." These days, when we are in need of very strong national solidarity, the majority of our people understand the purpose of such news stories that are against our national integrity, solidarity and national values and follow these publications with concern.[16]

The chief of staff strongly asserted that Dink's article endangered "national integrity" and "social peace." This was due to the article's potential to ignite divisive discussions about Gökçen's status as a national symbol and her connection to Mustafa Kemal. The suggestion that Gökçen was an Armenian orphan evoked connections to the genocidal violence against Armenians. Clearly, the chief of staff deemed associating someone with being Armenian as negative and derogatory, considering such an association to be an attack on Gökçen and, by extension, on Kemal's legacy. The strong reaction stems from the fact that it challenges the established narrative of Turkish national history. Later, another of Kemal's adoptive daughters, Gökçen's "sister," responded to Dink's article, asserting the details of the official narratives and reiterating that her real parents were Muslim Bosnian migrants to Turkey. The statement that Gökçen was the daughter of Muslim immigrants from the Balkans stayed within a narrative that was known and acceptable within the framework of confessional ethnicities of Turkey. Being the daughter of Bosnian parents who immigrated to Anatolia would not, in this case, contradict the fact that she was a Turk. In Turkey, the "Turk" in the social, historical, and political context of late and post-Ottoman societies was a racialized umbrella category for the diverse ethnic and linguistic Muslim population of the Ottoman Empire. Ottoman Muslims would become racialized as ethnic "Turks" following the nation-state projects in the Balkans, which took Christianity as an essential component of their nationalisms. Equating Islam with Turkishness to constitute the nation's official confessional ethnicity later gained a legal dimension in the Treaty of Lausanne of 1923, a point to which I return in chapter 2.

But why would an article by one Armenian about the parentage of one woman carry such heavy political weight? In Turkey, saying that someone is Armenian is seen as an insult or defamation. For example, in 2010, Cem Büyükçakır, a Turkish journalist, received an eleven-month prison sentence for publishing a comment by a reader saying that the then-president of the republic, Abdullah Gül, was Armenian. This comment was taken as an insult to the president, leading to an official complaint to be filed by the presidential office.[17] Another example is when the then prime minister, Recep Tayyip Erdoğan, was a presidential candidate in 2014 and responded to claims that he was not a Turk by saying on a TV program, "Some have called me a Georgian. Others have called me—I beg your pardon with a much uglier thing—an Armenian [*afedersin çok daha çirkin şeyler Ermeni diyen oldu*]. I am a Turk!" It was not enough for Erdoğan to assert his Turkish identity; he also had to deny any claim that he was an Armenian, describing Armenianness as ugly. For Erdoğan, being called an Armenian was also an insult. Thus, in the middle of his sentence, he said *"afedersin"*—a polite expression in Turkish, equivalent to the English "I beg your pardon" or "Please excuse me"—to apologize to the listener before saying something potentially rude or insulting.[18] In Turkey, calling somebody an "Armenian" is also used as a slur, and being "Armenian" carries the stigma of being *gavur* (infidel), a racist slur used for Jews and Christians. The state keeps records of citizens with Armenian ancestry that could hinder their promotion within civil and military institutional structures.[19] Being an Armenian in Turkey carries an inherent stigma; even if one's grandparents converted to Islam, one would still be racialized as *gavur*, as Ara's story in chapter 3 demonstrates.

Against this background, it was not Gökçen's "foreign" parentage that disturbed the Turkish establishment and public opinion, but rather the possibility that she might have been a local Armenian: even though she was from Anatolia, being Armenian would mean that she remained external to the state's official confessional ethnicity. Gökçen's alleged Armenianness touches a sensitive chord that goes, to quote the chief of staff of the Turkish military, "against our national integrity, solidarity, and national values." Claiming that Gökçen is an Armenian orphan is an invitation to revisit the foundational history of the republic, including the thorny topic of what happened to Armenians during World War I. Were they the unintended victims of war, as the Turkish official claim says, or were they subjected to a centralized systemic policy of annihilation?[20]

The importance of this discussion stems from the fact that it was a rare moment in the history of the republic for the predicament of Ottoman Armenians during World War I to be discussed in relation to the tightly protected memory and legacy of Mustafa Kemal. After all, the genocide that took place during World War I and the foundation of the republic in 1923 occurred within a fairly short period of time; thus the Turkish denial of the Armenian genocide was always key to the Turkish narrative of the republic's founding.[21] Gökçen's life has been seen as intertwined with Kemal's, especially because the Turkish state has boasted of Gökçen as a heroic citizen and an iconic figure of modern womanhood. Proven or not, the suggestion that a national figure closely associated with Kemal was an Armenian orphan breached the acceptable limits of political discourse in Turkey. Before publishing the article, Dink had already been prosecuted twice for "insulting Turkishness" under Article 301 of the Turkish Penal Code, which made him a target for further prosecution. This article punishes any person who is perceived as "publicly insulting" the Turkish nation, the state, parliament, judicial institutions, military, or police organizations with imprisonment for six months to two years.

CRITICAL APPROACHES TO NATIONALIST HISTORIES

Nation-states have secrets, and often they are lethal ones. Nationalists create teleological histories where the past is narrated in a linear timeline of progress originating in antiquity and encompassing past greatness as well as histories of trauma and victimization.[22] Through erasures, silences, and omissions, they sanitize their histories by obscuring the violence committed in the name of the national project. In Turkish history, Fatma Müge Göçek situates the mechanisms of denial of violence against Armenians as an interplay of silence, secrecy, and subversion. Silence manifests as a public and personal refusal to acknowledge uncomfortable histories, often enforced through legal threats and self-censorship. Secrecy involves the powerful controlling the flow of information, leading to forced ignorance and the inability to speak out. Subversion is the active distortion of truth through the production of texts that manipulate narratives, employing tactics such as selective omission, fabrication, and exaggeration. Each mechanism contributes to the suppression and distortion of history, serving to maintain power structures and, most importantly, avoid accountability.[23]

The transformation of Sabiha Gökçen into a symbol of Turkish womanhood involves a deeply paradoxical notion. The Turkish nationalist narrative suggests that she had to suppress or deny her Armenianness to be perceived as a true Turk and embody the ideal of Turkish womanhood. Building on Göçek's analysis, Gökçen's Armenian secret, therefore, is muted to maintain the legitimacy of the state, making such secrets to be heavily guarded by the state. When we consider historiography as being subject to the gravity of power, as Michel-Rolph Trouillot aptly demonstrates,[24] it becomes apparent that historical accounts significantly alter our understanding of a nation-state's practices, not just by what they encompass in their narratives but also by whom they exclude, appease, and blame. This understanding of the political dimension of historiography is central to understanding the ways in which nationalist historiography silences its victims by erasing them completely, denying the violence they perpetrated, or by blaming them for the very violence to which they were subjected as Göçek demonstrates.

In his seminal text "Theses on the Philosophy of History," Walter Benjamin declares that "there is no document of civilization which is not at the same time a document of barbarism."[25] Writing in 1940 as German fascist ethnonationalism was expanding in Europe, Benjamin was confronting the Nazi claims of progress that concealed the barbarism of labor camps, military invasion, occupation, and the impending genocidal violence that would kill eleven million Europeans, six million of whom were Jewish. Benjamin therefore invites us to think that assertions of civilization are never devoid of barbarism; the "barbaric" is intrinsic to high culture and counters any claim to civilization. In a commentary on Benjamin's text, Michael Löwy sees Benjamin as pressing us to recognize that it is through the anonymous labor of the exploited slaves, peasants, and workers that high culture exists and its triumphal monuments are erected. Such forms of exploitation are therefore "document[s] of barbarism," because they are by-products of class injustice, social and political oppression, and inequalities and because such monuments of high culture are transmitted and sustained through the violence of wars and invasions.[26]

In thesis VII, Benjamin goes on to say, "And just as such a document is not free of barbarism, barbarism taints also the manner in which it was transmitted from one owner to another."[27] Benjamin's dictum not only refers to the transfer and theft of cultural assets or to the way such assets are weaponized to become a symbol of the victor's dominance in wartime. He also points to the ways in which stories about the past, including written traditions, are narrated and transmitted from one owner to another, securing the civilizational claims of the victors.[28]

The histories of nation-state projects are also often narrated from the perspectives of their founders, who articulate the raisons d'être of their political projects. Their histories therefore are written from the vantage points of founder-victors and their beneficiaries. Writing in the late 1970s, when Palestinian history was largely unknown to Euro-American readers, Edward W. Said saw the urgency of articulating the silenced Palestinian experience.[29] In an essay titled "Zionism from the Standpoint of Its Victims,"[30] Said writes into the history of

European Zionism what the Palestinians had to bear and the unacknowledged human cost of the Zionist colonization of Palestine that led to the foundation of Israel through the ethnic cleansing and dispossession of Palestinians.[31] Yet the victimhood of nation-states is rarely singular. In a response to Said's work, Ella Shohat argues that Palestinians were not the only victims of European Zionism and that one must also consider "the negative consequences of Zionism" on Arab Jews, the Mizrahim, throughout the region.[32] Said and Shohat therefore point to the fact that nationalisms have multiple victims. They shed light on the darker aspects of nation-states, often celebrated and shielded by officially sanctioned historiographies. By foregrounding the narratives of the nation-states' victims, they unveil the suppressed stories that constitute counter-histories, disrupting the officially celebrated histories of these nation-states. In doing so, they remind us that any critique of state violence should be relational and contextual—based on scrutinizing state power and nationalist ideology—rather than identity-based.

Following this line of thought, populations such as the Armenians in Turkey, whose destruction was foundational to a nation-state project, were also effaced from the national narrative. This effacement would resemble a conception of German history that did not include the destruction of European Jewry or an understanding of U.S. history that did not include the annihilation of indigenous populations.[33] The Armenians were annihilated, their built environment was destroyed or converted, and they were left without a community—only a small number of churches that eventually closed under the Kemalist republican regime and the eventual emigration of almost all Armenians from Anatolia to Istanbul.

Such acts of destruction and dispossession have been concealed or excused by nation-states, as well as by historiographies written from their vantage point, in order to present their projects as progressing from chaos to civilization and from premodern empires to modern nation-states. Benjamin's philosophy of history invites us to think of history as encompassing both civilization and barbarism. In this light, it was not just that the violence against Armenians was omitted; rather, forging narratives about Armenian survivors as foreigners and as the enemy within Turkey has enabled Turkish national historiography to appear to be a "document of civilization" with claims to progress, democracy, and secularism: a Europe-facing project. The stories compiled in this and the coming chapters were not simply omitted but actively silenced to reinforce the legitimacy of the nation-state as a "document of civilization." Since the two are inseparable, Benjamin speaks of just a single document: when a document narrates history as one of civilization, it already carries within itself the silenced barbaric episodes that would eventually come to question the official narrative, as was the case with

Dink's article on Gökçen. This chapter focuses on these silences. For without the erasure of the barbaric, it would be difficult for nationalists to present their national project and their nation-state as an outpost of progress.[34] Yet these erasures are never absolute; the very silences that sustain the nation-state's claims to civilization also create the conditions for their undoing, as what resurfaces from these silences becomes the counter-histories that expose what has been suppressed.

Because Armenian genocide survivors in Turkey generally, and those in Anatolia specifically, were conceptually unthinkable to the majority of both Turks and Armenians, they were silenced in the majority of Armenian and Turkish historical narratives, as I will demonstrate later in this chapter. In these narratives, they were silenced not through mere omission but through the process of historical production described by Michel-Rolph Trouillot, where silence is not an absence but an active presence—embedded in the ways Armenians were selectively narrated into Turkish history, marginalized and distorted rather than completely erased.[35] Those who are excluded from the archives tend to be silenced in historiography, as Trouillot argues, and whoever is excluded from the national project is also excluded from the archives of the state. For the archives are an important determinant of how the present will be officially remembered in the future.[36] The remains of the past that are not preserved in institutional or personal archives have been largely dumped, for "the refuse is what the archive refuses."[37] In this sense, what is preserved in archives and what was turned into refuse are dialectically interdependent, because they are determined by what is and is not considered to be of value.

Walter Benjamin's critique of historicism problematizes the archive by considering what is omitted from it as sources of knowledge that have the potential to disrupt existing master narratives. Central to Benjamin's method is the image of the ragpicker, a figure who collects the discarded remnants of the past. In the context of nineteenth-century France, the ragpicker, considered the refuse of society, becomes an apt metaphor for the historian who assembles and reinterprets what has been overlooked or discarded.[38] As a philosopher of ruins, Benjamin emphasizes that out of destruction, these remnants—the rags and the forgotten—can expose, unsettle, and challenge the status quo. The approach of viewing history as a form of ragpicking brings the discarded and the trashed to a new center, from which we can reframe the past and write counter-histories.

This necessity of creating new centers for our historical imagination—centers that do not merely add to dominant narratives but fundamentally reshape the terrain of historical knowledge—is best articulated by Toni Morrison's literary vision in narrating the African-American experience. Morrison famously stated, "I stood at the border, stood at the edge and claimed it as central and let the rest of the world move over."[39] Like Benjamin's historian who retrieves history from the ruins, Morrison insists on reclaiming space not as an act of inclusion, but as a radical repositioning. When asked why she did not include white characters in her novels, she responded, "I wanted to feel free not to have the white gaze in this place that was so precious to me." She further argued that writers are not obligated to write for or about all people, rejecting the expectation that marginalized people must always be framed in relation to dominant narratives. This approach aims not to simply enhance or enrich the dominant narrative by including other voices but to confront and deconstruct it entirely. Rather than assuming that histories or narratives gain legitimacy when they enter the existing canon, this methodological intervention insists on a transformation of perspective—on redefining whose experiences shape the center. By elevating these overlooked aspects, counter-histories aim to disrupt and dismantle the overarching narrative structure and the fundamental assumptions that uphold it. Their intent is to challenge the accepted historical discourse by making visible what has long been marginalized, silenced, or omitted, thereby unsettling the established historical canon.

Counter-histories represent a departure from dominant narratives—even those that focus on minoritized populations or racialized groups. Histories of minoritized and racialized populations are often positioned to complicate the master narrative by providing differing angles or new layers, but without fundamentally challenging the central assumptions of the master narrative. In this sense, they exist in a symbiotic relationship with the master narrative, functioning as supplements or as tangential accounts that orbit its dominant assumptions and privileged actors. Such approaches also tend to be identity based and can inadvertently reaffirm identitarian politics, where people are included based on the (mostly visible) identities that they are assumed to represent. Counter-histories, in contrast, seek to dismantle the very framework of identitarian politics and the master narrative itself. They endeavor to reconstruct history from the ground up, privileging the perspectives of those who have been historically marginalized or silenced. Because they are centered on the experiences and narratives of these groups, counter-histories challenge the hierarchical structures that have traditionally shaped historical discourse. This approach aligns with Benjamin's notion of history as a constellation of moments, wherein each moment is a potential site for revolutionary change. In this way, counter-histories not only offer alternative narratives but also serve as a form of resistance, aiming to transform the way history is conceived and written. They are a call to action, urging us to reconsider the past in order to envision a radically reimagined future. Counter-histories, therefore, challenge us to go beyond the calls for inclusive histories—which aim to incorporate diverse voices, perspectives, and identities—demanding instead a shift toward disruptive histories that actively destabilize the narratives and structures of power that underpin historical discourses and not just widen them.

DEFYING HOMOGENIZED PERSPECTIVES

Armenian survival in Turkey disrupts both Armenian and Turkish ethnocentric and nationalist narratives. On one hand, Armenian diasporic historians see Ottoman Armenians as either having been killed in the genocide or as surviving in the diaspora. On the other, the Turkish state denies the violence against them while also racializing them as "foreign" to Turkishness and as a "minority" for being non-Muslims. Being Armenians, they cannot be Turks; even those who converted to Sunni Islam have borne their Armenianness as a racial mark, both socially and when interacting with state institutions, as recent oral historical accounts demonstrate.[40] They were therefore regarded and treated as unwanted and unclaimed by the postimperial nationalist projects. Houri, an Anatolian Armenian, once told me that she left her village of Sasun as an Armenian and was received by the Armenians of Istanbul as a Kurd because she spoke a local dialect of Armenian and Kurdish. Similarly, migrants to France often emphasized that they left Turkey as Armenians only to arrive to France as Turks, referring to the way French Armenians perceived them. Neither fully embraced by Armenians nor Turks, Anatolian Armenians exist in a perpetual displacement, in a liminal space between the cracks of Armenian and Turkish societies. Refused by both societies, they survive as the refuse of both nations—a position that unsettles the rigid national categories through which history is conventionally written. Their survival defies the dominant historiographical frameworks that either erase them or force them into nationalist binaries. Such survival demands, instead, a historical approach that neither marginalizes them as exceptions nor assimilates them into pre-existing narratives. In doing so, their survival calls for a historical engagement that resists absorption into dominant narratives and insists on reframing the terms of historical knowledge production.

When speaking of trash or refuse, I do not mean "trash" in the sense of a littered slum. Rather, I borrow the Japanese artist Tetsuo Kogawa's metaphor of trash that "would resemble a city after a nuclear attack, a ruin in which even the 'details' cannot be discerned." In this metaphoric sense, Armenians become the scattered ruins, waste, or debris that unexpectedly remained in the aftermath of violent catastrophes.[41] Surviving despite being considered the unwanted trash of nationalist histories, the Armenians in Turkey unsettle the perceived purity of both societies as they defy the homogenized nationalist perspective. The survivors challenge the definition of the Armenian experience as being reducible to the genocide/diaspora binary and trouble the imagined "racial" purity of Turkey's citizenry. They bear the imprint of genocidal violence in their lives, disrupting the coherence of dominant historical narratives. In this way, Armenians in Turkey do not merely exist at the margins of history; they generate counter-histories against Turkish and Armenian historiographies, unsettling the foundational assumptions of both.

Armenians in Turkey—who have survived as the unwanted refuse of both the Turkish and Armenian post-Ottoman societies—lie outside the narrative plots of both Turkish and Armenian collective histories. Their presence unsettles Turkish claims of innocence and complicates the Armenian understanding of genocide as total annihilation. Centering their stories within historical narratives opposes the validation and perpetuation of nationalist interpretations of history. Yet disturbing the nationalist historiographies—presented as documents of civilization—is not to claim a truth or legible evidence in the court of history, but an attempt to retrieve the scattered and undocumented experiences of ordinary and forgotten Armenians. In this sense, writing the experiences of Anatolian Armenians does not constitute a minority or ethnocentric history in contrast to hegemonic histories; rather, it represents counter-histories that are already embedded within both pasts but that have been undermined and silenced. Bringing their life stories to the surface counters official histories to challenge communal belonging and nationalist narratives by exposing the suppressed, barbaric elements that underpin both histories.

Dink's murder was prompted by a historiographic intervention, and he was killed as an enemy of the nation and the state. Just as with the perpetrators of the Adana massacres of 1909 and the Armenian genocide, Dink's murder continues to go unpunished.[42] Both the official narrative and Dink's agree that Sabiha Gökçen was an orphan and that she was born in 1913, and they align on most of the remaining details of her life. It is her parents' religious affiliation, and therefore her ethnicity, that is the bone of contention in this scandal, as this affiliation determines whether she is included—or not—within the Turkish nation-state. She was born around a year prior to the beginning of the systematic mass annihilation and deportation of Armenians by the Young Turk regime of the Ottoman Empire. In Dink's version, Gökçen shared the predicament of hundreds of thousands of Armenian children who were orphaned during the war when their fathers were targeted to be killed and mothers were either raped or joined local households as wives or slaves. For the Armenian genocide was gendered: women and children were spared, following the patriarchal perception that one's race and ethnicity were determined through a patrilineal line, and that Armenian women could not produce Armenian children without Armenian fathers.[43] Women suffered sexual violence, rape, and forced marriages into Kurdish, Turkish, and Arab Bedouin families, all of which constituted the afterlives of the genocide for the first generation of the survivors.[44]

Because of this background, Gökçen could only be historicized, written about, and remembered if she was part of the Turkish national history; if she was Armenian, she would be external to that history and might call attention to the genocide that turned thousands into orphans who were raised as Turks or Kurds. On the other hand, even if Gökçen's Armenianness was proven, she would not likely be claimed by Armenians. For many Armenians she was a convert who became a Turkish national figure through her association with Mustafa Kamal and her participation in the military campaign that bombarded Dersim in 1937–1938. It is notable that Dersim was mostly populated by Alevi Kurds, many of whom could have been Armenians who had converted to Islam during and after the genocide.[45]

An aspect of the Turkish nationalist myth is the assumption that every Turk is a soldier who fights for Turkish causes, even if violence is inflicted on the internal "enemies" of the state and nation.[46] This includes the Kurds, who, after the elimination of Armenians, inherited the Armenian predicament as internal enemies and were violently targeted by the state. Indeed, the bombardment of Dersim that cost the lives of more than thirteen thousand Alevi Kurds was normalized and undermined by Gökçen. In a 1987 interview, Gökçen was asked about the civilian casualties in Dersim. She replied that there were no casualties and that "it was just a reconnaissance campaign, the army had intelligence as well. They knew where these bad people were hiding. It would be inhuman to destroy places where there would be children."[47] Gökçen denied the violence committed on the people of Dersim and insinuated that even if there had been violence, it was targeted against "bad people," suggesting that such violence was necessary and legitimate. In these contexts, Gökçen's Armenianness and her bombardment of the Kurdish population of Dersim bring forth the "barbarism" that lie within the sanitized Turkish history and shed light on the multiple ways that Armenian survivors in Turkey have been silenced in Turkish and Armenian historiographies.[48]

PARALLEL SILENCES IN HISTORIOGRAPHIES
THAT REIFY THE NATION-STATE

For many scholars of Armenia and Armenians, the genocide represents a finality and marks the end of the Armenian presence in Anatolia. The majority of historical studies on the late Ottoman Armenians have focused on the genocide, following a linear sequence from the late Ottoman Empire to the genocide, and then to the formation of the diaspora and Soviet Armenia, and finally to the independence of the Republic of Armenia.[49] Until recently, there has been a dearth in the literature on those who remained in Turkey, with even less attention given to Armenians in Anatolia.[50] Additionally, Armenian historians have also excluded Muslim Armenians and those Armenians born of mixed parentage, as they have viewed conversion as representing a finality much like the genocide.[51] Their historiographical approaches have produced narratives that reify the separation between communities and focus on conflict.[52] By centering identity-based categories between populations, such approaches risk producing reductive representations of society that homogenize populations as well as ignore cultural and historical connections between racialized populations. Such approaches therefore may reflect the influence of a nation-state logic, wherein being without a titular ethnic state strips one of a recognized national history.

In the nation-state-centric readings of history by diasporic Armenians, Armenians were subjected to total annihilation. A belief in total annihilation narrows the possibility of Armenian survival in Turkey, the reality of multiple and contradictory forms of Armenianness such as the Islamized ones, or the possibility that—just as Turks and Kurds massacred Armenians—they also helped Armenians survive by either hiding them or incorporating them into their families and tribal structures. In these narratives, such contradictions would go against the dominant understanding of Armenian history propagated by many diasporic institutions, intellectuals, and activists, which positions Armenians as victims who were either killed in the genocide or who survived the massacres in the diaspora. This reading does not conceive of Armenians surviving in their homeland as citizens of the perpetrator state. It is notable that until Dink's assassination, this reading largely excluded Armenians in Turkey, but after his murder, they slowly came to occupy a central place in the attention of diasporic institutions and activism.

In the Turkish nationalist narrative of history, non-Muslims—including Armenians—supported Russia, France, and other European imperial powers during World War I and sided with Greece during its invasion of Anatolia, which ended with Turkey's victory under Mustafa Kemal.[53] In this view, the War of Independence (1919–1923) led by Kemal not only opposed the Greek invasion and challenged European colonial interests in Anatolia, but also liberated the Ottoman Empire from what the nationalists perceived as "foreign" and "disloyal" elements within: the non-Muslim Ottomans. Such narratives depict non-Muslims as being co-opted by European imperial powers and blame them for their own predicament. The historiography of the War of Independence has largely been written as a Turkish triumphalist story over foreign imperialism as well as over local communities who were made foreign, such as the Armenians. In this Turkish revisionist narrative, the new state of Turkey became a country for Ottoman Muslims (who were racialized as "Turks"), and non-Muslims (who were also "non-Turks") were made to have no future.[54]

Armenian and Turkish historiographies share a common silence about the Armenian genocide survivors who remained in Turkey. These silences in historiography aim to produce Turkish and Armenian narratives that depict both communities as homogeneous; in doing so, they silence individuals, communities, and episodes that challenge their nationalist perceptions of the self and other. When Trouillot explains in his seminal *Silencing the Past* that silence is an important ingredient in the production of history, he emphasizes that "not all silences are equal." He notes that they therefore "cannot be addressed—or redressed—in the same manner."[55] Even though Armenian and Turkish historiographies share a silence about the Armenians who remain in Turkey, they differ in the kind of silence they continue to produce. In the Armenian narrative, silence is absence about and a refusal of those who remained in Turkey. This view reflects an assumption that Armenians were either killed during the genocide or survived in the diaspora or Soviet Armenia, but not in Turkey—as survival in Turkey would contradict the understanding of genocide as total annihilation.[56]

The silence in Turkish historiography is more complex, because such silence is not mere absence, but rather an ongoing process that continues to be reproduced in the very act of making Turkish history. As Trouillot demonstrates in his chapter on "Sans Souci," silence is produced through the alteration of meaning, interpretation, and significance assigned to events.[57] Therefore, to uncover a silence, one needs to understand the powers that both bury the story and offer a new reading of it. Following this line of thought, Armenians are not only present in the Turkish nationalist narrative, but central to its construction. And indeed, Fatma Ulgen succinctly demonstrates this centrality in a discourse analysis of the *Nutuk*, the "Great Speech" that Mustafa Kemal delivered in 1927.[58]

Ulgen reads Kemal's speech as a foundational text for the republic and its historiography, and Kemal himself as the mythmaker of Turkish history. The six-hundred-page *Nutuk* mentions the Armenian deportations early in the text, which Ulgen reads as a testimony to the centrality of the Armenian genocide to

Turkey's foundation.[59] The text thus indicates what should be remembered and forgotten about Armenians in the nation's own history.[60] In the *Nutuk*, Kemal blames the "Christian elements," namely the Armenians and the Rūms (Greeks), for the devastation that took place during the war. Kemal presents Armenians as disloyal and murderous; the Turks emerge in his story as the oppressed (*mazlum*) side in that conflict. He says, "Making common cause with the foreign troops, the Armenians completely destroyed an old Mohamedan [Muslim] town, Maras, with their artillery and machinegun fire. They annihilated thousands of innocent and defenseless women and children. The Armenians were the instigators of this savagery, unique in history."[61]

The Turkish official narrative silences the genocidal intent by justifying the Armenian deportations as self-defense, as a necessary measure during war, or by blaming the Armenians for the violence that they allegedly instigated. Furthermore, the Turkish narrative is framed within an anti-imperial framework as countering European interests in Ottoman territories. Such framing is evident in the historiography of the War of Independence. The silence about the genocide is not absence; rather, it constitutes the production of knowledge through an interpretation of the events that displaces responsibility for the Armenian annihilation, an interpretation that has been foundational to Turkish historiography.[62] A parallel silence about those who remained runs in the Armenian reading of the genocide as being total and final. But the Turkish official narrative uses the Armenian presence as a token to silence the genocidal intent and to engender a Turkish humanitarian narrative around the ways in which the surviving Armenian women and children were incorporated into Turkish and Kurdish families in Anatolia.[63] Armenian survival in Turkey—to draw on Trouillot's description of the Haitian Revolution—became "unthinkable" to both Turkish and Armenian state-centric narratives, because it went against the established assumptions and plots of the nationalist narratives. In both narratives, Armenians were not meant to survive the genocide, and if they survived, they were not meant to remain in Turkey.

This unthinkability parallels Michel-Rolph Trouillot's description of the Haitian Revolution as "unthinkable," a term he used to highlight its defiance of the dominant Eurocentric worldview. The idea that enslaved Africans could successfully rebel, defeat European colonial powers, and establish an independent nation was beyond the conceptual possibilities of prevailing ideological frameworks. This exclusion from what could be imagined also meant silence in historiography, as such events could not be adequately recognized or narrated within existing historical paradigms. However, Trouillot's argument has been critiqued for its focus on the European male–centered paradigm of the Enlightenment.

For the enslaved people and leaders of the revolution, the uprising was neither unimaginable nor impossible—it was a deliberate and strategically planned endeavor that directly challenged colonial and racial hierarchies. Similarly, while the survival of Armenians in Turkey was deemed unthinkable within the nationalist frameworks of both Turkish and Armenian historiographies, it was not unthinkable for those who endured and rebuilt their lives in Anatolia. Their continued presence constitutes a counter-history, disrupting assumptions of total annihilation or erasure and asserting agency that challenges the deterministic logic and triumphalist claims embedded in these narratives.[64]

The writing of Armenian history was until recently dominated by two opposing poles: Armenian narratives that assert the genocide as total annihilation and narratives (such as those embraced by the Turkish state) that deny the genocide. The problematic of Armenian history is not just this binary, but the assumption upon which this binary rests: the nation-state. Historiographies of post-Ottoman societies have taken the nation-state project as a given; therefore, their histories have been written teleologically to justify the nation-state. Such framing naturalizes the rupture between empire and nation-state, obscuring the persistence of imperial formations and intercommunal histories that do not conform to nationalist teleologies.

In a state-centered world order, the nation-state is seen as a triumph and a goal, to which all political struggles must graduate, and the majority of the research and publications in Armenian history reflect this logic. Produced largely under the auspices of state-centric approaches from disciplines ranging from history to genocide studies, these approaches that tend to focus on the violence committed against Armenians during the genocide. Thus, they tend to bring Armenian history in Anatolia to an end with the genocide, ignoring Armenian survivors in Turkey.[65] While such works were groundbreaking because they highlighted the centrality of the genocide for post-Ottoman Armenians and for the writing of modern Armenian history, they tell us more about the perpetrators' policies to kill Armenians than they do about Armenian survival—about the struggles, adaptations, and compromises that Armenians make as survivors under the republican regime. Since Hrant Dink's assassination, more work has emerged on those who remained in Turkey, thus breaking the silence around the Armenians who survived as Turkish citizens after the genocide had ended.[66] Until the publication of these works, the historiography of post-Ottoman societies, including those of Turkey and of the Armenians, often narrate the past as leading to the nation-state, as if the occurrence of the nation-state was inevitable.[67] Such teleological presentations render what came before as leading to either a successful state project (as in the case of Turkey) or to a genocide (as in the case of Armenians in Anatolia). Nation-state projects are also framed within the anti-colonial and anti-imperial struggle for independence, often described in positive terms as processes of "formation" and "building" that "rise" out of the ashes of imperial and colonial rule to join the orderly regimes of the postwar world. Such framing presents the triumphalism of the nation-state as inevitable or desirable, even when the destruction it causes is acknowledged. This phenomenon is apparent in the narratives of Turkish history presented by widely read authors of Turkish history survey texts such as Bernard Lewis (who denies the Armenian genocide) and Erik Zürcher (who acknowledges the genocide).[68] Furthermore, nationalist historiographies often erase the violence and destruction committed in the process of establishing the nation-state in their endeavor to forge a sanitized version of history. The Turkish nationalist narrative, for example, positions the Turks as the victims (*mazlum*) of Armenians, claiming that Armenians betrayed their Ottoman compatriots and therefore deserve their predicament.[69]

The post-Ottoman framework offers a way out of these entrenched nationalist narratives by challenging the assumption that the nation-state was the inevitable successor to empire. Instead of treating intercommunal coexistence as an archaic or failed model, post-Ottoman studies foreground the ways in which pluralistic pasts persist, sometimes as contested memories, and sometimes as lived experiences beneath the surface of nationalist teleologies.[70] In the case of Armenian history, this means moving beyond a framework that sees the genocide as an absolute rupture, instead attending to the ways in which Armenians continued to exist, adapt, and negotiate their survival in Turkey since 1923. This approach complicates the binary of total annihilation vs. denial, highlighting how memory, identity, and historical continuity remain dynamic in post-Ottoman spaces.

However, if the post-Ottoman framework foregrounds the persistence of plural pasts, it also forces us to confront the mechanisms through which these pasts are actively erased or distorted. The modern nation-state does not simply inherit history—it reshapes it, silencing those who challenge its legitimacy. The Armenian historian Talin Suciyan warns against the framework of nationalism to understand genocide and mass atrocities, because it shifts attention away from the state's decision to commit genocide, instead blaming the nationalism that the victims (ideologically or nominally) affiliated with for the state to maintain its legitimacy. Because the crime of genocide ultimately calls the legitimacy of the perpetrator state into question, the state actively obstructs any efforts to uncover its criminal foundations. Therefore, those in power have a vested interest in concealing the state's own role as perpetrator behind a façade of benevolent nationalism.[71]

Building on this critique, nationalist historiographies further obscure violence by erasing victims from historical narratives and framing nationalist projects as orderly progressions from chaos to civilization, from premodern empires to modern nation-states. To write outside the gravity of the nation-state-centric approaches, this book builds on critical works that position destruction at the core of nation-state building and unsettle the historiography of the nation-state by writing back into history the violence that had either been omitted or that had been excused as necessary or inevitable.[72]

This tendency to contain violence holds true of some historians of Turkey, whether the historian is a genocide denier like Bernard Lewis or one who acknowledges it like Erik Zürcher, to take two examples of widely discussed surveys of Turkish republican history. We find that the final outcome of both narratives represents nationalists as having worked against all odds to establish the awaited birth of the nation-state.[73] It is notable that genocide deniers, such as the Orientalist historian Bernard Lewis, are able to deny the genocide while simultaneously speaking of the Armenian predicament as "a horrible human tragedy." Lewis goes so far as to say that the Armenian "tragedy" had an effect on Armenians similar to that of the Holocaust on the Jews. Yet for Lewis, in contrast to the Holocaust, there is "no serious proof of a decision or of a plan on the part of the Ottoman government regarding the extermination of the Armenian nation."[74] Consequently, Lewis's framing minimizes the violence against Armenians as the unintended consequences of the deportations. In casting the Armenian predicament not as a crime or an intentional historical catastrophe, Lewis reduces it to a natural catastrophe without intention or perpetrators: for him, it was merely a set of deportations and relocations that came to a bad end.[75] Lewis therefore denies the intention of the crime even as he speaks about it as a tragedy akin to the Holocaust.

Narratives that acknowledge the genocide also reify the nation-state, as we see in Erik Zürcher's *Turkey: A Modern History*. Zürcher frames the genocide as an event with a particular contextual logic; the Armenians make a short appearance in the narrative of the genocide and only reemerge in the context of being one of the country's non-Muslim minorities when the republic was established.[76] Representing Armenians as minority is symptomatic of the nation-state-centric worldview. Toward the end of his book, Zürcher's conclusion amounts to an apologetic stance toward the genocide when he writes:

> Like all modern states, whether national or colonial, it has very dark pages in its recent history and these should be recognized. But at the same time the achievements of the founders of modern Turkey should receive due recognition.

Kemalism as a model for development belongs firmly to the period of the inter-bellum. It would be wrong to see in Kemalism a recipe for solving Turkey's prob-lems in the twenty-first century, but in searching for the roots of modern Turkey every historian has to keep turning back to that remarkable generation of people born around 1880, without whom Turkey would probably not have survived.[77]

Zürcher normalizes genocidal violence by saying that "like all modern states" Turkey has "dark pages," but that for him what redeems those dark pages is the "survival" of the Turkish state. This framing reduces genocide to a regrettable but incidental aspect of a broader, ultimately redeemable project, rather than recog-nizing it as the foundational violence upon which the very structure of the state lies. Furthermore, speaking of the "Turkish state" is anachronistic, because he conflates the Ottoman with the Turkish state. He attributes this survival to the "remarkable generation," many of whom were involved in or oversaw the annihi-lation policies against the empire's Armenian population.

We must therefore take the discussion of the Armenian genocide beyond the futile debate between denialism and anti-denialism and put the logic of the nation-state itself under scrutiny. We can do so by looking at the counter-history of Turkey from the standpoint of Armenians as one of the defeated populations of the Ottoman imperial demise that was not totally annihilated. This examina-tion sheds light on the dark side of national independence, an ideology that even those who acknowledge the genocide ascribe to because violence is considered a rite of passage for the desired nation-state order. Shedding light on the violence and destruction committed in the name of nation-states ultimately complicates the state's "document of civilization" by bringing in the silenced chapters of barbarism. In these chapters, the Turkish nation-state foundation was not only a struggle against European colonial interests in the region, an effort to bring political order and modernity in the wake of imperial collapse, or even the result of competing nationalisms. It also meant the destruction of the Armenians, the dispossession of their property, and the erasure of their (im)material culture in Anatolia. Furthermore, such violence by the republican regime has persisted up to the present, targeting the Kurdish population. Even though Zürcher acknowl-edges that the killing of Armenians was premeditated, and therefore a genocide, he silences the genocide in his book by justifying it and rendering it redeem-able by the triumph of the Kemalist republic. However, on the centennial of the Armenian genocide, Zürcher addressed the role of Ottoman and Turkish histo-rians in perpetuating the silence around the genocide. He acknowledged the fail-ure of earlier historians, including himself, to confront its significance in shaping Turkey and advocated for its recognition.[78]

RUPTURES IN THE TRANSMISSION OF KNOWLEDGE

In the decades following the genocide, knowledge about Anatolian Armenians has been fractured by silence and erasure on multiple fronts. The Turkish state's official historiography has long suppressed any public reckoning with this past, while many Armenians have likewise self-censored out of fear of retribution. As a result, the stories of those who remained in Anatolia have been left in limbo—caught between the absence of recorded testimony, the politicization of formal archives, and an official and self-imposed culture of silence. This section explores how these forces have ruptured the transmission of knowledge and considers the impact of archival gaps on understanding the history of Armenians in Turkey.

If historians have silenced the genocide in their respective narratives of Turkish history, Anatolian Armenians and other witnesses to Anatolia's unrecorded past have also self-censored their own stories. The reasons for this vary—from a refusal to speak, as in my encounter with Kaspar, to fears of retribution by the Turkish state. While this book focuses on the experiences of Armenians, many hidden Armenians or non-Armenians also witnessed scenes from the unrecorded past of Turkey. During his travels, the Turkish writer and novelist Kemal Yalçın sought to find out what happened to non-Muslim citizens of Turkey when they were sent to labor camps in Aşkale in 1942–1943. This eastern Anatolian town was the site of a work camp for Christians and Jews who were unable to pay the Varlık Vergisi, an extremely high wealth tax imposed on minorities in 1942.[79] Yalçın approached a group of elderly men sitting in a teahouse in Aşkale. They did not agree to let him record their accounts, except for one man named Baba Yusuf, who expressed the urgency of documenting such stories:

It's a shame what happened to those [non-Muslim] men! Everyone knows what was done to them. There's not a soul in Aşkale who doesn't know. But they won't open their mouths out of fear. We've all been silent, haven't said a word. We've made it until now in that way. But how long should we remain silent? We don't have much longer to live. We may be gone tomorrow. What you'd like to know, ask! Turn on your tape recorder, take a picture of me. Even write down my name![80]

Being elderly and aware of his impending death, Baba Yusuf broke his long silence about the violence experienced by Armenians and other non-Muslims. His long silence is typical; many witnesses—and especially Armenians themselves—were afraid to speak publicly about this violence. When Yalçın was touring Anatolia in the late 1990s in search of residual Armenians, he had difficulty finding and speaking with Armenians. In Amasya, his first stop on the journey, Master Ali (whose help he sought) explained to him the difficulties of tracing Anatolian Armenians and highlighted the issues of trust: "You can't go just anywhere to look for [Armenians who became Muslims to survive]. Let's say, for instance, that you find one. Do you think he'll trust you enough to speak with you? Remember: these people have been rescued from the jaws of death. Fear has worked its way into their very bones!"[81]

By turning Armenians into a vulnerable population in Turkey, the Turkish state created the conditions that prevented everyone, including the Armenians themselves, from transmitting what happened to them. The Armenian past therefore hangs between two silences: one imposed by the Turkish state and its institutions, and the other self-imposed, as Armenians self-censored to avoid stigma and social and political repercussions. Many Armenians told me that the older generation did not speak about the genocide in front of their children for fear of social repercussions. Knowledge by and about Armenians was sanctioned as they entered a new reality after the genocide. In his preface to the first volume of *Sessizliğin Sesi* (*Sounds of Silence*), a series of books that collects oral testimonies and documents the experiences of the Armenians in various Turkish cities, Ali Bayramoğlu describes the difficulties in transmitting knowledge by and about Armenians in Turkey:

> The story of a community which has kept silent, which has not told its story, which for years has considered that remembering and recounting was a dangerous act. The Armenians of Turkey are stricken by a voluntary amnesia . . . Even if they knew, they did not remember, even if they remembered, they did not want to speak. They strove to protect future generations by hiding their story, by hiding themselves. What they did not speak of was not only suffering, they did not even speak of their Armenian-ness, of what being Armenian means, they could not.[82]

Such ruptures rendered stories of violence, extermination, and survival of Armenians not only taboo in the official Turkish historiography but also as Melisa Bilal says, "marginalized in the collective memory of Armenians."[83]

Given such absences and silences in historiographic knowledge, I have sometimes contemplated what an archive for the Armenians in Antolia might look like if one existed. The first set of documents that often exists for Turkish citizens—the Turkish state's civil registries and national statistics—poses its own challenges. While the population in Anatolia was classified in state records by religious belonging and mother tongue, Armenians may have feared revealing their affiliation and therefore not reported their Armenian identity to the state. This classification also presents a series of complications. For example, is the child of an Armenian mother and a Kurdish father Armenian? Is the child's mother Armenian if she converts to Islam? How should people who lived in the Armenian villages that converted to Islam, yet who continued to speak a dialect of Armenian, be classified? The second set of documents, church archives, usually holds information about the three central rites of passage for Armenians: marriages, baptisms, and funerals. There were a handful of functioning churches in Anatolia between 1923 and the 1980s, such as in Diyarbakır, Kayseri, Sivas, and a few other places, but when those churches eventually shut down, their records disappeared or were made unavailable by the Armenian Patriarchate in Istanbul. The third set of documents—Armenian school registries—tells us about the number of students attending the schools and, by extension, the size of the Armenian community in a particular city. But after 1923, no Armenian schools continued to function outside Istanbul.

Some information is available in the functioning churches and schools in Istanbul, but I was denied access to data about the number of students in Istanbul who were born in Anatolia. I heard rumors that the Armenian Patriarchate had transferred its important documents to the Patriarchate of Jerusalem or to the Mother See of Etchmiadzin, Armenia. Scholars have speculated about whether further archives exist, and if so, where. If they do exist, who are the gatekeepers, and who can access them? Questions about Armenian archives in Turkey, as well as Turkish archives on Armenians, continue to be heavily politicized and contested.

Yet even if any archives were available for Armenians in Anatolia, they would not be able to tell us about the lives of the small group of ordinary and unwanted Armenians who remained in Anatolia after 1923 and are the main focus of this book. For these Armenians are unclaimed by both Turkish and Armenian nationalist collectives. Carolyn Steedman likens the partialities of knowledge preserved in archives to the knowledge kept in memory, pointing out that both are "made from selected and consciously chosen documentation and also from the made fragmentations that no one intended to preserve and that just ended up there."[84] As with memory, archives lack systematization and are subject to a degree of randomness. Given this, the function of the *archons* (the guardians of documents) is critical, because they are also entrusted with the hermeneutic right of interpreting the documents and giving them relevance and meaning.[85] Archons interpret documents at the moment they archive them, for they must generate a law, a regime, and a system for ordering and classifying those documents. In ordering documents, archons reflect the perceptions and dynamics of the institution of power that has entrusted them with the task. The documents, therefore, mirror the regime that created them and are meant to perpetuate the regime's legitimacy and continuation. For this reason, Derrida asserts, "There is no political power without control of the archive, if not of memory,"[86] while Trouillot takes this further, stating that "history is a story about power."[87]

The absence of such archives, as is the case for the Armenians in Anatolia, is indicative of the way power functions. As Gil Anidjar underscores, the archive is itself a site of erasure where what is excluded from archives is rendered non-existent. These archival gaps are not mere historical oversights; they are essentially political and intentional. By controlling or erasing records, the state and its institutions shape legal outcomes, influence public opinion, and perpetuate the marginalization of communities whose histories remain unarchived. Because of the systemic silence and imposed amnesia about Armenians, knowledge about Armenians resides in silences and gaps. Such silences and imposed censorship continue to be broken by people like Hrant Dink and Kemal Yalçın, providing a possibility for creating counter-histories in the face of silences imposed by the state, even when self-censorship has been a powerful force as well.

This absence of accessible Armenian archives has propelled me to pursue knowledge beyond conventional archives, searching in literary texts and travel accounts—together forming the constellation of sources, through which I reconstruct complementary traces of the past about Armenians. These become sources for knowledge amidst the silence of statistics, archives, and historiographies. It is notable that literary works and oral histories since the 1990s have started to break the silence that has overshadowed Armenians in Turkey since the 1920s. This phenomenon has been attributed to the opening of political spaces coupled with economic liberalization, as well as the escalation of violence against the Kurds in the country's southeast.[88] Furthermore, the cultural changes in the aftermath of the September 1980 coup, with liberalization policies that took place since 1989, allowed for a space where sanctioned discussions on Turkey's multiethnic and diverse confessional past became possible.[89]

In the absence of archives and historical accounts about the Armenian survivors in Anatolia, knowledge has been produced in other genres of representation. The autobiographical novel by the Armenian novelist Mıgırdıç Margosyan, titled *Gavur Mahallesi* (1992), was one of the first of such eruptions pertaining to the lost linguistic and confessional diversity that Anatolia once possessed. The novel narrates episodes from lives of Armenians in Diyarbakır, channeled through the author's own experience. In the 1990s, cultural production started to reflect Turkey's suppressed diverse past in the form of music albums that feature non-Muslim musicians and composers of the Ottoman Empire and the early years of the republic. Some examples that I often encountered during my fieldwork in Istanbul were: books and collections of historical photographs were published that focused on the curbed population diversity in Turkey, village-specific books and multilingual song albums were produced, and the folkloric band Kardeş Türküler (Sibling Folksongs) formed in 1993 to perform shared Anatolian folksongs in banned languages such as Armenian and Kurdish. Yet many such endeavors took place within the wider context of ongoing violence and a neoliberal government policy that silences violence, past and present, even as they celebrated multiculturalism.[90]

It was also in the same decade that Hrant Dink established the Armenian-Turkish bilingual newspaper *Agos* in 1996, opening a critical space to voice the concerns of Armenians in Turkey. *Agos* additionally became a platform for Armenians in Turkey and the diaspora to reconnect and find their lost relatives, as was the case for Fethiye Çetin, who later became Dink's lawyer and friend. Other notable works include Kemal Yalçın's *You Rejoice My Heart* (2003) and autobiographies such as Fathiye Çetin's own family story, published in *My Grandmother* (2004). Following Dink's assassination in 2007, collections of oral historical testimonies emerged, most notably Fethiye Çetin and Ayşe Gül Altınay's *Torunlar* (*The Grandchildren*, 2009), with stories of the grandchildren of converted Armenians in Turkey, and a series of oral histories published by the Hrant Dink Foundation titled *Sessizliğin Sesi* (*Sounds of Silence*), of which the first volume was published in 2011.[91] A few historiographical works have emerged since 2015, focusing on the Istanbul population and basing their inquiries on archival research, most notably Talin Suciyan and Lerna Ekmekçioğlu.[92]

Tracing the silences about Armenian survival in Turkey challenges the perceived purity of collective historiographies and the embedded moralism in both. Moralism is embedded in Turkish historiographies, because they blame the Armenians and emphasize their successful establishment of a nation-state, and in Armenian historiographies, because their victimhood was at the hands of Turkish despotism and ruthless violence. In constructing linear ethnocentric views of their pasts, both historiographies legitimize ethnic purity and assert a moralistic binary of one group over another. Reading the assumptions behind both Turkish and Armenian historiographies is not to undermine the power discrepancy between Armenians and Turks that led to the genocide and destruction that made way for Turkey to be established, but rather is to re-center the gravity of nationalism in the construction of the historical narrative.

READING DINK AND GÖKÇEN
OUTSIDE THE RHETORIC OF THE NATION-STATE

Dink's daring exposure of Gökçen's Armenian parents and the subsequent criminal act of his assassination brought the violence that established and maintains the
Turkish state to the surface. The near apparition of the republic's founder during
this historical juncture signified a stark realization that the forces behind the assassination sought more than the mere silencing of an individual. Mustafa Kemal's
celebrated words depicted on the Turkish flag in the aftermath of the tragic event
hinted at a deliberate intervention in the shaping of the nation's future, suggesting
a forceful hand in the determination of its future direction rather than leaving it
to the uncertainty of rumor or the unpredictability of dissenting memory.

Here we return to Dink and Gökçen as representatives of different, even
opposite, strands of being Armenian "survivors" in Turkey in order to understand
the destruction upon which the republic was founded. Both Dink and Gökçen
started their lives as orphans, and Dink's life intersected with that of Gökçen's
when he attempted to reveal her Armenian "secret." Gökçen's early life as an
Armenian orphan, who was assimilated through adoption and later as a Turkish
fighter pilot, exposes the foundational violence of the nation-state project and,
with it, the nationalism embedded in Turkish and Armenian historiographies.

But to what extent was the claim that Gökçen was Hripsime Sebilciyan's aunt
true? The day after discussing Dink's article on Gökçen, the Turkish daily *Hürriyet* published an article based on an interview with Pars Tuğlacı, an Armenian
historian and a close friend of Gökçen's.[93] Tuğlacı dismissed the claims in Dink's
article that Gökçen was an Armenian from Antep and her relationship to Sebilciyan. Instead, he said Gökçen was born in Bursa (in line with the official narrative) and was in fact an Armenian orphan, affirming the remaining details about
her life from meeting Mustafa Kemal onward. Tuğlacı said that Gökçen knew
that she was Armenian after her relatives in Beirut reached out to her and later
visited them. In the article, Tuğlacı dismissed the question of whether Kemal
knew that she was Armenian, saying that "nothing would change" if he did. The
article was adamant to preclude any association being made between Gökçen
being an Armenian orphan and Kemal's legacy. It quoted Tuğlacı saying that
Kemal was a humanist and that he never sought to "separate people according
to their nationality," a doubtful claim given that Kemal was vested in building an
ethnonationalist state and adamant about the exclusion of Armenians and others
from his project.[94]

Regardless of what we think about who Sabiha Gökçen was, that history is not
knowable through a conventional fact-based history. Writing in the aftermath

of the catastrophe, as Marc Nichanian argues, resides in the realm of specula-
tion, as these crimes went unarchived, unpunished, and denied. It is a kind of
history that, unlike that of the nation-state's, is not presented as facts. Gökçen's
secret past makes her a sharer of the predicament of other Armenian survivors;
their history remains in the realm of ambiguity, rumors, and speculations. Dink
challenged the fact-based history of the state, which is not only seem knowable
but goes unquestioned because the state propagates it as uncontested facts to
the extent that they become part of the national and nationalist psyche. Here,
Nichanian's distinction between genocide and catastrophe becomes important.
Given that "[t]here is no genocide without denial," he highlights how the act
of proving genocide becomes a perpetual process entrenched in denial, differ-
entiating it from catastrophe, which does not come with the same burden of
proof. This brings to light the critical role of state-supported archives in shaping
historiography; these archives produce the so-called verified facts. Catastrophe,
on the other hand, remains unknowable by the state-centric logic and the positivist methods of knowledge production.[95]

The rumors around Gökçen's origin are symptomatic of the writing of both
Turkish and Armenian post-Ottoman histories in the shadow of the genocide.
While both histories differ in telling what happened to Armenians during World
War I, both agree on silencing the Armenian survivors in Turkey who became
Turkish citizens from their narratives. Just as Turkish nationalist historiography
made it impossible for Gökçen to be Armenian, Armenian post-genocide history
has made it impossible for both Gökçen and Dink (until his assassination) to be
fully Armenian. For a good Armenian either died in the genocide or survived in
the diaspora, working on national causes rather than remaining in Turkey.[96]

Dink challenged the official narrative by presenting Gökçen's Armenian
past, which fits within the parameters of the biographies of other survivors
of the genocide: orphanhood, having relatives scattered, not being able to
find relatives, and antecedents that remains in the realm of speculations. Such
knowledge—based on oral histories, family networks, and other forms of tracing the pasts of unnoticed people—is not consumed and digested as fact, in
contrast to the Turkish state's presentation of Gökçen's life. Killing Dink was
meant to silence such knowledge, and in doing so, to silence those in solidarity with him: those who found in Dink's voice an articulation of their silenced
narratives. This includes Turkey's Armenians but also Kurds and antiestablish-
ment Turks, among many other marginalized citizens of the republican regime.
Furthermore, Dink was never widely claimed by Armenians until his death, as
his death allowed Armenians to place him in a nationalist narrative of Armenian victimhood at the hands of the Turks. Dink and those who support him

do not fit in nationalist binaries; rather, they lie outside the hegemonic narratives, except, perhaps, in their recycling of the mainstream anti-Jewish racist rhetoric that dominates Turkish society and politics. In his nuanced yet contentious efforts to forge reconciliation between Muslims and Christians, Turks and Armenians and in Turkey, Dink, along with other political figures, including the Kurdish leader Abdullah Öcalan, has invoked racist narratives that scapegoat the Jews. Such narratives employed anti-Semitic tropes, suggesting that Jews were to blame for the Armenian genocide. By portraying Turks and Kurds as mere pawns in this purported plot, this rhetoric sought to absolve Muslims of direct responsibility, thereby facilitating a conceptual space where Armenians might forgive the deeds committed against them.[97]

The nation-state-centric approach means that each side is an owner of a chapter in the same history but focuses on certain events with a different interpretation of what each event signifies. When we read Dink's and Gökçen's lives as intertwined, we move away from the binaries established by nation-state narratives. Doing so allows us the space to write about the complex experiences of survival. Abandoning the nation-state-centric narratives, we are able to read both Dink's and Gökçen's lives as belonging to both Turkey and Armenians. Additionally, this approach allows us to transcend traditional historiographic plots: the Armenian emphasis on victimhood and the Turkish claim to innocence.

The attitude of Turkish society toward Dink's politics had varied. While he was a hero for many leftists, Kurds, and those who advocated demilitarizing Turkish society and politics, the leadership of the Armenian church and institutions in Istanbul saw him as exposing the community to public scrutiny, which they feared could rebound on them. Many Turkish nationalists regarded him as a threat to the foundational principles of the republic, and some state institutions and media surprised many when they blamed Dink for his assassination. In this sense, Dink's life is representative of the Armenians in Turkey who were silenced in both Turkish and Armenian histories. The silence in historiography and rejection of Dink are both symptomatic of the binary-based mindset of nation-states.

Rebuffing Dink's claims, the chief of staff asserted that Gökçen "is a Turk," denying the possibility that she could have been an Armenian orphan. Through this denial, he was preventing a discussion of the events that took place during World War I, leading to the foundation of the republic. Dink's claims about Gökçen opened the foundational years of the republic to scrutiny; the reaction of the chief of staff and the heroic reception of the assassin in the police station show that such claims continue to have implications for Turkey's present. Dink's retelling of Gökçen's story presents the counter-histories of the Turkish nation-state. Echoing Saidiya Hartman, such histories have "always been inseparable from writing a history of present."[98] And indeed, Dink meant to reopen the past to change perceptions of the present while aspiring to a more just and rights-based future. Dink's assassination was meant to hinder such a catalyst of change and thus propagates the genocidal structure that permeates the life of the Kemalist republic.

Gökçen's early life as an Armenian orphan and later life as a Turkish pilot fighter open the foundational violence of the nation-state project to scrutiny. In response to Dink's claims, his assassin killed him as an "infidel," a racialized Armenian who refused erasure through silence, assimilation, or emigration. Dink had brought the silenced "document of barbarism" in to disrupt the republican regime's claims of progress and civilization. For this reason, killing him was seen as a service to the nation; the assassin heroically shouted that he killed the "infidel" and police officers posed in front of the camera with the assassin-hero. Gökçen herself had achieved her fame through the operation that she conducted in Dersim, which killed thousands of Kurdish-Alevi civilians, many of whom may have been Armenian converts. She also saw her mission as a service to the nation in the name of progress. The irony is that Dink's assassin and Gökçen both justified their acts of murder in the name of progress and service to the nation-state. Both lives point to the violence in the name of progress that lies at the foundation of the Kemalist republic, a violence continues to be inflicted on Armenians, Kurds, and other marginalized groups.

Both Turks and Armenians had a vested interest in maintaining and reproducing the silence around the Armenians in Turkey in order to preserve their own perceived purity and protect the civility of their community. Maintaining this silence has been essential to claiming the moral high ground, whether through moral triumphalism (in the case of the Turks) or through moral victimhood (in the case of the Armenians). While Turkish historiography serves the interests of the state, the fear instilled in the Armenians who survived and remained in Anatolia—manifested in self-censorship—reveals both the extent of state control and its limitations in shaping how Armenians understand who they are as citizens of the perpetrator state. Through the lives of Dink and Gökçen, this chapter located both the absences and the production of silence about Armenians in both histories, demonstrating how counter-histories emerge within these silences—not simply as acts of recovery, but as disruptions that unsettle the dominant historical frameworks. After Dink revealed the violent chapters of Turkish history, he was assassinated and the Turkish armed forces came to defend Gökçen's heroic memory and to protect the foundation of the republic. And yet, while barbarism may be suppressed and silenced for some time, Dink's life is a fine example of Walter Benjamin's assertion that ultimately nothing is totally lost to history and that the silenced will eventually "[flash] up at a moment of danger."[99] For it is the political present that ignites the relevance of the past, and history remains a catalyst for contemporary contests over recognition and memory. It is within this context that Dink challenged such neat narratives of Turkish and Armenian historiographies through Gökçen's life. Gökçen's assimilation and Dink's assassination represent distinct yet intertwined ways in which Armenians were subjected to denativization, persisting as traces in the archive of barbarism at the heart of the Republic of Turkey.

CHAPTER 2

MINORITIZED BY LAW

Lausanne as a Treaty of Counter-Sovereignty

During the period from the end of World War I in November 1918 through the founding of the Republic of Turkey in October 1923, Armenian political rights and sovereignty over their territories eroded as the Turkish nationalist project was triumphant both in its War of Independence and in postwar diplomacy. Turkish and Armenian historiographies alike have created narratives of rupture, positioning this period as either an end or a beginning. Ever since Turkey won the War of Independence (1919–1923), Turkish historiography has marked this period as a new beginning for the Turkish nation-state.[1] In contrast, the genocide-centric Armenian reading sees this period as marking an end in Armenian historiography, where "the Armenian question was put to rest by both East and West."[2] After all, the Lausanne Treaty marks the end to Armenian political aspirations in a post-Ottoman order that became dominated by nation-states; therefore, for stateless Armenians, who were also denied representation in the proceedings of the conference, Lausanne was a failure.[3]

By the end of World War I, around one million Armenians had perished. Yet the efforts to eliminate the remaining Armenians through expulsion and assimilation continued after the war. Such efforts were enshrined in the legal structure of the Republic of Turkey through the Treaty of Lausanne, which was signed in July 1923. Through a rereading of the treaty from an Armenian vantage point, this chapter understands these five years within a framework of continuity: as neither a beginning nor an end, but rather as part of the genocide's afterlives that furthered the Armenians' denativization and consolidated the Turkish nationalists' conquest of Anatolia, turning it into a Turkish ethnonational space.

The Armenian catastrophe continued after the war through the shattered and ruptured lives of the survivors. Armenians were living in the shadow of the genocide that had brought an end to their communal and social existence in Anatolia. Men were killed and women were sexually abused and abducted, the population reduced to one largely made up of religious converts, orphaned children, and women working in prostitution to survive.[4] The consequences of the genocide were, to borrow a word from Zabel Yasseyan's description of the earlier 1909 Adana massacres, incalculable.[5] The nation-state-centric order that emerged after the war denied Armenians and many other stateless populations sovereignty over the territories in which they lived and left them with diminished political rights and little agency to determine their destiny. Armenians were turned into fragmented populations of people. Despite having survived, they lost "the entire social texture into which they were born":[6] their kin, social networks, homes, and properties.

While the Lausanne Treaty granted minoritized populations certain rights, it altered Armenians' legal presence on their lands by reducing their status to that of a minority subsumed under Turkish national sovereignty. With the creation of a Muslim majority in what became Turkey, the legal and numerical status of non-Muslims—who were to be governed through the minority protection regime of the Treaty of Lausanne—was reduced. Like many other communities in the world, Armenians were eliminated from their lands through genocide, wars, dispossession, and forced removal. Additionally, they were denied sovereignty over the land through the legal mechanisms of the nation-state. For when the Turkish nationalists claimed sovereignty in the name of Ottoman Muslims, who would later constitute the Turkish majority, they simultaneously denied the sovereignty of Armenians, Kurds, Jews, Rūm-Orthodox (Greeks), and other populations living in Anatolia, as well as any form of territorial aspiration on the part of these populations. This assertion of Turkish sovereignty, which is continuously practiced through the denial of Armenian sovereignty, is a process that Manu Vimalassery (now Karuka) calls the "counter-sovereignty" practiced by the founders of the Turkish republic.[7] By depicting the War of Independence as a victory over imperialism, the Turkish historiographical narrative obscured the history of the nation-state as a project built on the destruction of populations that existed before the establishment of the Turkish confessional ethnic state.[8]

This chapter rereads the Lausanne Treaty as a counter-history to its conventional framing as a diplomatic triumph that restored peace after World War I. Rather than focusing on Lausanne as a document that officially ended World War I in the Ottoman Empire and secured Turkish sovereignty in the face of European imperial interests in the Ottoman provinces, this reading approaches the treaty as an exercise of counter-sovereignty by the Turkish nationalists—a strategy that has preempted all other political claims, including those of Armenians, to Anatolia.[9] By centering the Armenian predicament, this reading resists nationalist and state-centered historiographies that present Lausanne as a moment of resolution, instead foregrounding its role in legitimizing Armenian erasure. Such a process is intrinsic to denativization, as the Turkish state has built its legitimacy on the rejection of Armenian sovereignty or any territorial claim in Anatolia as well as the denial and justification of the violence against them.

The Lausanne Treaty—whose final text says nothing about the Armenians— was not merely a diplomatic accord but a defining moment Armenian history, legally formalizing their denativization from their Anatolian homelands. It also created the legal mechanism by which they became Turkish citizens, but only on the condition of their minoritization. Although the treaty nominally granted Armenians Turkish citizenship, it did so by reinforcing their minoritized and subordinate position. This process—marking Armenians as legally included but structurally excluded—became a foundational mechanism of Turkish sovereignty. Reading Lausanne as a document of counter-sovereignty reveals how nation-states selectively extend rights and protections, not to ensure equality but to consolidate power. The treaty's long-term consequences for Armenians and other minoritized populations in post-Ottoman Turkey illustrate how its legal ambiguities became mechanisms of exclusion that endured far beyond its immediate geopolitical context.

THE MINORITIZATION OF NON-MUSLIM COMMUNITIES

Following the establishment of the short-lived Democratic Republic of Armenia and the end of World War I, a Turkish diplomat made the following remark about Anatolian Armenians to an American counterpart:

> One hundred years ago we had a Greek question and a Serbian question and a Wallachian question. The result was Greece, Serbia and Romania. Fifty years ago we had a Bulgarian question. The Result was Bulgaria. In 1910 we had an Albanian question. The result was Albania. Today we have an Armenian question—but we will have no Armenia. We are going to scatter the Armenians, dismember their cities and there will be no Armenian nation. Armenia will be part of the Turkish Empire.[10]

This comment is representative of the official Turkish nationalist approach to post–World War I diplomacy. The Armenian population had two important attributes that motivated the policies of mass extermination during World War I: they were non-Muslims and they inhabited Anatolia. These two attributes—in a context in which the Balkan Ottoman provinces had achieved independence as Christian-majority confessional ethnic states—created a predicament for the Armenians and the Rūm-Orthodox, as well as Jews. As non-Muslims, these communities were racialized as "non-Turks," and their existence challenged the presumed Ottoman Muslim (later "Turkish") national sovereignty for two reasons. First, these communities might give the European powers reasons to intervene in the empire's affairs, as they had before. Second, if Armenians were left to achieve national sovereignty or autonomy in Anatolia, following the example of the Christian Balkan ethnonational states, they might threaten what the Turkish nationalists considered the Ottoman heartland, which had a Muslim demographic majority, just as Balkan states had expelled as many as 5.5 million Muslims between 1821 and 1923.[11]

The Turkish nationalists were therefore keen to articulate their aims and motivations in the period that led to the establishment of the Republic of Turkey, especially in the period between the Greek invasion of Smyrna/İzmir on May 15, 1919, which instigated the War of Independence, and the signing of the Lausanne Treaty on July 24, 1923, which was foundational for the Republic of Turkey. The Turkish revolutionaries and nationalists, who were led by Mustafa Kemal and who had made up the provisional Ankara government since the establishment of the Grand National Assembly of Turkey in April 1920, were determined to reject territorial sovereignty, nationhood, or autonomy claimed by any non-Muslim community in Anatolia.[12] To them, foreign intervention often took place under the guise of protecting non-Muslim communities, and such intervention did in fact occur in different periods of Ottoman history. Following Kemal's landing in Samsun on May 19, 1919, four days after the Greek invasion, they took several measures to unify Anatolia's Muslims under their leadership and to turn regional organizations in Anatolia into a pan-Muslim (i.e., Turkish) national organization.[13] After the end of the Balkan Wars (1912–1913), the Turkish nationalist movement directed its efforts toward preserving the Ottoman provinces of Anatolia from European and Russian expansion or claims by Armenians.[14] This chapter focuses on such efforts between 1919 and 1923.

On June 22, 1919, the Turkish nationalists Küsrev, Kâzim Karabekir, Ali Fuat (Cebesoy), Hüseyin Rauf (Orbay), and Mustafa Kemal (Atatürk) issued the Amasya Circular, a document that was distributed across Anatolia. The document stated in its first article that the integrity of the country and independence of the nation were in danger and that the central government in Istanbul was incapable of fulfilling its responsibilities, given that it remained under the control of the Allied Forces. The Amasya Circular indicated the necessity of forming an independent national council, called for convening a national congress in Sivas, and reaffirmed the Erzurum Congress that was already planned for July 10 for the "defense" of the six eastern provinces of Anatolia, which had a significant Armenian population.[15] In the document's preamble, the Erzurum Congress (August 7, 1919) expressed fear of national disintegration, of partition of the homeland through Armenian expansion in the Caucasus region, and of the possible realization of the Greek national dream in Pontus, the Black Sea region. It therefore asserted in its article 1 the indivisible unity of the six eastern provinces and the brotherhood of all the Muslim elements (*anasır-ı İslamiye*) in those provinces. In article 3, the text asserted that the nationalists considered European interference to be aimed at creating Rūm (Greek) and Armenian territorial entities (*Rūmluk ve Ermenilik*) in Anatolia. The text further asserted that the nationalists rejected any European mandate in Anatolia and any special privileges (*imtiyazat*) being granted to Ottoman Christians.[16]

The Sivas Congress (September 11, 1919) also asserted the brotherhood of all the Muslims of Anatolia (article 1) and emphasized the principle of a united resistance against foreign intervention and occupation, and especially against any activity that called for the establishment of "Greek or Armenian entities" (*Rūmluk ve Ermenilik*) in Anatolia.[17] Following the congresses, the Ankara government signed the Amasya Protocol (October 22, 1919) with the Ottoman government in Istanbul to integrate their efforts to protect national unity. The protocol had the Istanbul government agreeing to adopt the nationalist program as stated in the Erzurum and Sivas Congresses; in return, the nationalists acknowledged the authority of the imperial government in Istanbul.[18] The articles of the protocol do not seem to have been made public; its content, however, is traceable through one of Mustafa Kemal's speeches, wherein Kemal resolved, yet again, that "granting privileges to non-Muslim elements [*anasır-ı gayrimüslime*] in a manner that would violate our political sovereignty . . . would not be accepted."[19]

All the effort put into the unification of Anatolian Muslims and the rejection of foreign meddling in Anatolia were consolidated in the text of the National Pact (Misak-ı Milli), agreed upon during the last session of the Ottoman Parliament on January 28, 1920, and made public three weeks later, on February 17. This pact was foundational in defining the borders and population of what was to become the Republic of Turkey three years later. Article 1 states that all territories with Ottoman Muslim majority populations living inside the armistice line of October 30, 1918 (Mudros), united in religion, race, and descent, constitute an indivisible whole.[20] It is notable that the nationalists advocated not a "Turkish" national sovereignty but rather an "Ottoman Muslim" one.[21] The war that the nationalists led, subsequently called the *Turkish* War of Independence, was not Turkish in the ethnic sense, but rather included diverse Ottoman Muslims.[22] While the nationalists included diverse Muslim ethnolinguistic groups such as Turks, Kurds, and others, the National Pact was clear in excluding Ottoman Arabs from its project. Article 1 also states "the fate of the territories inhabited by an Arab majority which were under foreign occupation should be determined by plebiscite."[23]

The meeting of parliamentarians in Ankara on April 23, 1920, held to confront the anticipated British occupation of Istanbul, became the foundation of the Grand National Assembly (Büyük Millet Meclisi), which was transformed into an interim Ankara government and later became the parliament of the Republic of Turkey. With the aim of unifying the diverse Ottoman Muslim populations, Mustafa Kemal spoke of his vision for Turkey in a speech delivered before parliament in the same year. He asserted the national aim of unifying all Ottoman Muslims—Turks, Kurds, Laz, Circassians, and others—whom he referred to collectively as "Muslim elements" (*anasır-ı İslamiye*) and whom he saw as constituting "sibling nations" (*kardeş milletler*). For Kemal, it was these elements living within the national borders (*hududu milli*) whom the parliament represented and whom the nationalists aimed to defend.[24] The War of Independence became a rite of passage not only for the Republic of Turkey but also for its Muslim citizens, who were invented as Turks.[25] The war initiated these diverse communities into a national kinship. Those who shed blood for the fatherland became "brothers" and those who did not, mainly the non-Muslims, were rendered "step-brothers if not 'foreigners.'"[26] Such inclusion of the various Muslim elements came with limitations, as the case of the Dönme—Jewish converts to Islam—reveals. Despite their conversion, the Dönme were excluded from the nationalist vision of "Muslim elements" and "sibling nations" because their Jewish origins remained a racial marker that overshadowed their Muslim identity.[27]

The aftermath of World War I—when Kemal articulated this vision of the nation to be—was the moment that turned many Ottoman non-Muslim communities into minorities or refugees on the margins of nation-states. These states defined themselves through a trinitarian vision of the nation as comprising racial, social and geographic rights, as Kemal states. Religion and language were constituents of confessional ethnicities; the racialized religious identity of a specific national population. Nationalism in Europe paved the way for the designation of a segment of the population as a minority or as refugees, because almost none of these nation-states achieved the desired demographic homogeneity in practice. Large populations were minoritized, as they did not fit the criteria of belonging imposed by the nation-state regimes. The Treaty of Versailles, for example,

gave sixty million people a state and turned twenty-five million into minorities.[28] Debate over minority populations was of importance in the treaties signed
during the Paris Peace Conference: in particular, the Treaty of Versailles with
Germany (June 28, 1919) and the Treaty of Sèvres with the Ottoman Empire
(August 10, 1920). Both treaties bore the seeds of future conflicts because they
were largely imposed and meant to punish the powers that had lost the war.

Newly established states with significant minority populations perceived
minorities as a potential source of tension and a pretext for conflict.[29] Jane
Cowan emphasizes the fact that the states bound by treaties for the protection
of minority populations within their borders carried one or more of the following characteristics: they were newly established, significantly expanded, or allied
with the losing side. Most importantly, they did not include any of the Great
Powers, which the Turkish delegation at Lausanne challenged (as discussed
later). These minority protection agreements guaranteed civil and political
rights for members of "racial, linguistic and religious minorities" in addition to a
degree of autonomy in terms of education and the usage of the minority's native
language. Upon signing minority protection treaties, the signatory states came
under the supervision of the League of Nations as the guarantors of those treaties.[30] It is within this context that the Turkish delegation viewed the privileges
granted to minorities as a direct threat to Turkey's stability. They therefore considered a compulsory population exchange necessary to prevent minorities from
becoming tools of foreign influence. İsmet Paşa, the head of the Turkish delegation, argued that as long as large, influential non-Muslim communities remained
within Turkey's borders, capable of aiding foreign powers, the country could neither secure internal stability nor contribute effectively to regional peace.[31]

The mechanism by which the League could investigate the infraction of treaties was through the use of minority petitions,[32] in which only a member of the
League—that is, another state—had the right to submit a petition or to protest
the treatment of a minority living in another state. Non-state actors, such as the
Armenians and other minoritized groups and their representative bodies, were
unable to communicate directly with the League or submit petitions; they could,
however, submit information and evidence to the League against the accused
state.[33] This minority protection regime had two consequences: it gave states
precedence over minority groups and granted minorities "no legal personality."[34]
Yet it restricted the sovereignty of the signatory states, because the League of
Nations could intervene to ensure the implementation of the minority treaties.[35] This minority protection regime had vital consequences for the Armenian predicament in the aftermath of the genocide. Even though the Ottoman
Empire lost the war as a member of the Central Powers (with Germany and

Austria-Hungary), it was the Turkish national movement represented by the Ankara government that gained international recognition over the Istanbul imperial government.[36] This situation left the Armenians and other communities stateless, preventing their representatives from entering into negotiation with other states and empires.

By surveying postwar international diplomacy, the remainder of the chapter demonstrates the ways that Turkish nationalists and the state-centric international order denied stateless Armenians sovereignty and territorial rights over Anatolia in favor of the Turkish nationalist movement, treating these denials as another aspect of the Armenians' denativization. Leading up to the discussion of the Armenian question during the Lausanne negotiations, the next section examines the diplomacy that took place prior to Lausanne and its effect on turning Ottoman Armenians into refugees and minorities in the 1920s.

TWO PRE-LAUSANNE TREATIES
THAT LED ARMENIANS TO FLEE ANATOLIA

Following the defeat of Germany and its Ottoman ally in World War I, the winning powers forced the Ottoman Empire to sign the Treaty of Sèvres in August 1920. Sèvres saw the realization of a long-held European imperial dream of dividing Ottoman territories among the Great Powers. Greece was given all of Thrace and the western Anatolian coast around Smyrna/İzmir, reinforcing the Greek occupation of the city that took place a year earlier with British backing.[37] The remainder of Anatolia was divided into spheres of influence allocated to Italy, France, and Britain, in addition to the establishment of an Armenian state in the provinces of Van, Erzurum, and the Black Sea port of Trabzon. Istanbul, the Ottoman capital, and the Bosphorus and the Dardanelles Straits were to be put under international administration. The only regions not claimed by foreign powers under Sèvres were northern and central Anatolia, including the cities of Ankara, Bursa, Samsun, and the western half of the Black Sea coastal area.

Turkey marks Mustafa Kemal's landing in Samsun in 1919 as the beginning of its War of Independence, which enabled Turkish nationalists to claim for their nationalist project the Ottoman lands occupied during the Greek invasion and nominally lost under Sèvres. For Ottoman Armenians and Rūms, the war proved to be one of conquest that ensured their displacement and dispossession from Anatolia. After the Turkish victory over the Greek army in Anatolia (1919–1920), many Rūms and Armenians who were evacuated from or fled Smyrna/

İzmir ended up going to Greece.[38] The Turkish military at the time did not differentiate between the Rūm and the Armenians: they were both "Christians," or simply non-Muslims, and thus non-Turks. Meanwhile the Greek government extended its relief efforts to Armenians and other Christians who were escaping Anatolia.[39] This was evident in oral history accounts. For example, in July 2008, I visited the mountainous village of Avcılar close to İznik with a Turkish friend who was raised in this region. When we stopped at a coffeehouse (*kahvehane*), my friend asked the four elderly men sitting there about the village, and one of them told us the following: "Ours is an Armenian village [*Ermeni köyü*]. The original name was Merdigöz and was changed in the early 1980s to Avcılar. Look at this building; it used to be the Armenian school of the village, now it is used by the local municipality [*belediye*] for some educational purposes. We have no schools here; our children go to schools in the neighboring villages." When we asked him about what happened to the Armenians of the village, he said, "They all left in 1921–22," which was also when the Greek army retreated to Greece and when many Rūms and Armenians fled to Greece with them. And this exodos was not limited to the Aegean coast of Anatolia; Greek ships were also transporting both Greeks and Armenians from the Black Sea ports of Anatolia.[40]

To reverse the territorial concessions and borders stipulated in the Treaty of Sèvres and signed by the Istanbul Ottoman government, the Ankara government signed two treaties. The first, the Treaty of Alexandropol (now Gyumri, Armenia), was signed on December 2, 1920, with the Democratic Republic of Armenia, which determined the borders between Turkey and Armenia (article 2). The treaty also renounced, under Turkish pressure, the territories that Sèvres had given to the Armenian state (article 10).[41] The second was the Moscow Treaty of Brotherhood with Russia (March 16, 1921), in which article 1 explicitly defined the borders of what would become Turkey as those outlined in the National Pact (Misak-ı Milli) of January 28, 1920, thus also rejecting the borders drawn up at Sèvres. The Moscow Treaty also reflected an anti-Western and anti-colonial position; its preamble stated that the two governments, Ankara and Moscow, shared "the principles of the brotherhood of nations and of the right of peoples of self-determination, acknowledging their solidarity in the struggle against imperialism."[42] This friendship treaty determined the fate of the eastern borders of what became Turkey. In addition, it helped to prevent the government of Soviet Armenia from supporting any Armenian territorial claims in Anatolia, allowing the Ankara government to oversee the southern and western borders.

The Treaty of Sèvres was never ratified or implemented by either Greece or the Ottoman state or enforced by European powers. Nor was it ever officially nullified by its European signatories, a fact that led some Armenians activists

I met in France to continue to refer to its provisions in making territorial claims from Turkey in favor of the Republic of Armenia.[43] Following successful Turkish resistance against the invading Greek forces in Anatolia, Sèvres was ignored. The Lausanne Treaty of 1923 became the new foundation for defining Turkey's borders as well as for managing its relationship with its neighbors and the minoritized communities that remained within its borders.

Another important move that challenged the Sèvres borders was the signing of the Treaty of Ankara with France, whose army occupied Syria and neighboring parts of southern Anatolia. Article 3 of the treaty stated that France and the Ankara government agreed to withdraw their forces to a border defined in article 8.[44] As France signed on behalf of Ottoman Syria, the agreement effectively meant that the Ankara government acknowledged French rule over Syria and that the French colonial claims over Ottoman Syria would not be challenged by the Turkish nationalists. The agreement was in accordance with the National Pact, which excluded the Arabic-speaking provinces. Ceding these territories occupied by France to the Ankara government resulted in the expulsion or voluntary migration of the majority of the Armenian population of the region that had survived the genocide, creating the Armenian refugee crisis.

During the Lausanne Conference, the British foreign minister Lord Curzon commented retrospectively on the Armenian exodus following the Treaty of Ankara, saying: "When the French evacuated Cilicia, the Armenian population of that province followed panic-stricken in their wake, and is now strewn in the towns of Alexandretta, Aleppo, Beirout [Beirut] and the Syrian border. There only remain, I believe, about 130,000 Armenians in Turkish Asiatic territory [Anatolia] out of a population which once numbered over 3 million. Hundreds of thousands of them are scattered about as refugees in the Caucasus, Russia, Persia and adjacent countries." Lord Curzon asked the Turkish delegation to encourage the Armenians to return to Anatolia and to designate part of the region for their resettlement.[45] However, Curzon's request was met with stubborn resistance from the Turkish delegation, as I will discuss later.

It was reported that more than fifty thousand Armenians fled French-controlled Cilicia by the time the Treaty of Ankara was concluded.[46] Armenians who were expelled or fled arrived in France or French-controlled Syria, among other destinations. Those who arrived in France entered with a document stating: "Reason of his travel: He cannot return" (But de son voyage: il ne peut pas retourner). This travel document reflected the legal reality that obligated Armenians to stay in France: they could not go back to their home country, which was now defunct, and the provisional Ankara government prevented their return.

The deportees were resettled as refugees in France, first in camps in the coastal city of Marseilles and then in other areas, such as Lyon and Alfortville.[47]

The Armenian refugees who crossed the newly drawn border into Syria, defined by the Treaty of Ankara, were granted citizenship of the Mandate of Syria and Lebanon by France.[48] The mass movement of Armenians into Syria and Lebanon initially met with objection from the French, who feared that it might disturb the ethnoreligious balance of French-controlled Syria. However, when France saw that the fleeing Armenians would remain on the border, which was a no-man's-land, it allowed their entry into Syria and Lebanon (which were under French mandate) and settled them in farmlands away from the Turkish border, as agreed with the Turkish nationalists.[49] France extended citizenship rights to Armenians living under the Mandate in 1926, making Armenian Christians one of the officially recognized sects in Lebanon.[50] These international contexts worked in favor of the Turkish nationalists' aspirations for demographic homogeneity in Anatolia and facilitated the expulsion of people and the expropriation of the property of the large majority of the Armenian population of southern Anatolia who survived the genocide.

EXPELLED AND EXEMPTED POPULATIONS UNDER THE LAUSANNE TREATY

Before the Lausanne Conference started, the Ankara government had gained some international recognition and had solidified its eastern borders with Soviet Russia and its southern borders with France, with the exception of what would become the Turkey–Iraq border. In addition, the defeat of the Greek army secured Turkish sovereignty over Istanbul and the straits under the Armistice of Mudanya of October 11, 1922. The final act of post–World War I diplomacy took place at the Lausanne Conference, which was concluded by an international treaty signed on July 24, 1923.

Under this treaty, the Greek government and the Turkish nationalists (the Ankara government), orchestrated the first major forced population exchange in modern history, whereby the Rūm-Orthodox Christians were forced to move from Turkey to Greece as "Greeks," and Muslims from Greece to Turkey as "Turks." The extensive work on Lausanne by the historian Onur Yıldırım shows that previous studies of the conference have focused on either British and American interests in the Near East, or the demographic homogeneity and territorial sovereignty of Greece and Turkey. These approaches have left the exchanged population of close to 1.5 million minoritized communities across the newly forged Turkish–Greek border marginal both in historiography and in the political debate of the time.[51]

Discussion of the Armenian predicament after the war was central to debates over the fate of the surviving Armenians at the Lausanne Conference, although the Turkish delegation prevented their formal participation in the conference and the final text of the treaty does not mention them. Yet the Armenian question has been largely ignored in many subsequent historical and academic studies on the Armenian citizens of Turkey and the conference itself. What must be highlighted is the fact that the Armenians who remained in Turkey after the conclusion of the conference started to be governed according to a treaty negotiated by the Greek and Turkish states, each of which sought to defend its respective confessional ethnicity, now a "minority" within the borders of the other. The Armenians, who were denied representation in the official proceedings, had no say in their future in the newly founded state in which they began to be governed. It is therefore important to write Armenians into the history of the conference. Their exclusion from the articles of the treaty sheds light on the predicament of stateless populations in the world order of a time in which nation-states were central.

This new international order that was in place following the Paris Peace Conference had important ramifications for the Armenian question in Lausanne. First, as states, Turkey and Greece had exclusive rights to decide on the fate of their coreligionists without granting any say to the population involved. Second, Armenians and other stateless populations were not allowed representation in the official proceedings of the conference. Third, although the imperial powers pressed the Turkish delegation to accept a minority protection treaty, the Turkish delegation vehemently resisted, as it considered the acceptance of such a treaty as limiting its sovereignty and sowing the seeds of future conflicts.

In the end, the treaty exempted roughly 120,000 persons on both sides of the Turkish–Greek border from being exchanged: the Rūm population of Istanbul and the islands of Imbros (Gökceada) and Tenedos (Bozcaada) in Turkey and the Muslim population of western Thrace in Greece. The remainder of the Muslims in Greece and the Rūm Christians in Turkey—including the Karamanli Rūms—were subjected to a forced population exchange. Under Lausanne, as many as 350,000 Muslims, many of whom were Greek speakers, were forced into Turkey as "Turks" simply because they were Muslims. (The population of Turkey was 13.5 million at the time.) And around 1.2 million Rūms, many of whom were Turkish speakers, were forced into Greece as "Greeks" because

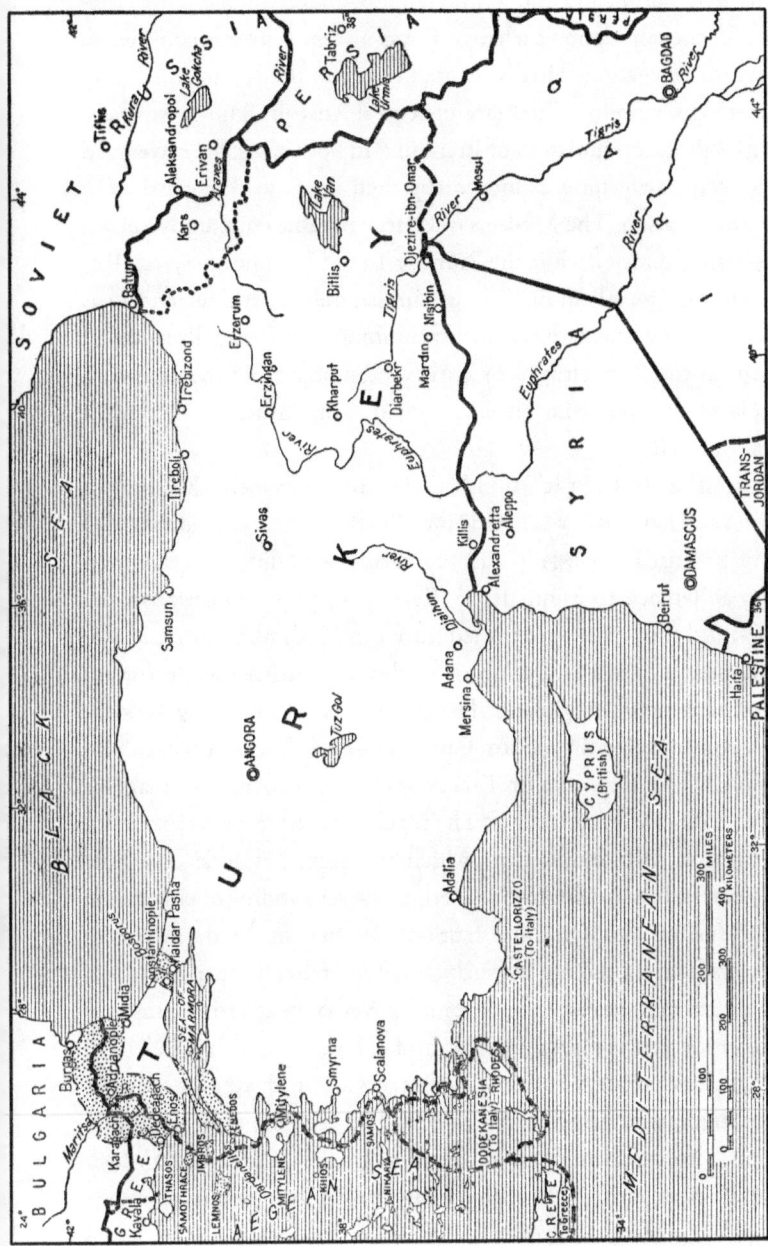

FIGURE 2.1 Territorial boundaries of the Republic of Turkey as established by the Lausanne Treaty in 1923. The borders delineated largely remain unchanged, except for the Sanjak of Alexandretta (in northwestern Syria), which was initially part of the Ottoman province of Aleppo before falling within the French Mandate over Syria. In 1939, following a questionable referendum organized by Turkey, the region was annexed to Turkey and renamed the Hatay Province.

Source: Lawrence Martin, *The Treaties of Peace, 1919–1923: Maps Compiled Especially for This Edition and a Summary of the Legal Basis of the New Boundaries* (New York: Carnegie Endowment for International Peace, 1924).

they were Orthodox Christians.[52] (The population of Greece was 4.5 million at the time.) Consequently, the criteria for the exchange were largely based on religious terms, as religion was a marker of one's ethnicity; language and cultural affiliations were hardly a factor. While religion ended up being the criterion considered for the population exchange, it was not the only one considered, because the Turkish delegation initially wanted to retain the Karamanli Rūms, the Turkish-speaking Orthodox Christians in central Anatolia, and to expel the Greek-speaking Orthodox population of Istanbul.[53] In both cases, the exchanged persons were looked down upon as inferior by their supposed compatriots in their country of destination. The Muslims of Greece became commonly known as Greece's "Turkish" minority, while the Rūms of Turkey became known as Turkey's "Greek" minority (mostly in English; in Turkish they are still referred to as Rūms). The Armenians, along with the Jewish community, were legally regarded as being the same as the Rūm citizens of Turkey, exempted from the exchange. Thus, whatever laws applied to Rūm citizens applied to the Armenian and Jewish citizens of Turkey as well.[54]

In keeping with the aims of the Turkish nationalist movement, Muslims of various ethnicities and languages were made into "Turks." This exchange allowed Turkish identity to exist both legally and practically according to a common denominator of adherence to Sunni Islam. The remaining populations—the Armenians, Jews, and the Rūms were turned into non-Muslim minorities. Likewise, Greece adopted a Hellenized form of Orthodox Christianity to form a homogeneous citizenry within its borders by systematically assimilating Turkish-speaking and Slavic-speaking Orthodox Christians into Greek language and self-identification.[55] The Republic of Turkey was fashioned in the image of Greece and other Balkan Christian states. The republic based its own citizenship on religious affiliation with Sunni Islam, which also served as an as an ethnic marker of Turkishness. It is this confessional ethnic understanding of citizenship that turned non-Muslims into non-Turkish minorities. In contrast, the Ottoman state, ruling a diverse empire, did not use such ethnic and religious markers as prerequisites for political membership, yet Ottoman governance at various stages of its history had considered the millets in a pyramid of hierarchy, with the Muslim one at the top. Scholars have argued that such markers are products of modernity and nation-state building in the age of nationalism.[56] In fact, the 1908 revolution aimed to create an Ottoman identity under the umbrella of Ottomanism, in which all were going to be equal citizens, an identity that the Turkish nationalist movement and the republic adamantly reversed.[57]

While Lausanne offered a legal framework for Greece and Turkey to protect minoritized populations as their own coreligionists in each other's countries, the conference did not consider the pleas of the other non-Muslim communities that would remain in Turkey, especially the Armenians. These residual populations—all labeled "non-Muslim minorities" in the text of the treaty—were automatically administered under the articles of the Lausanne Treaty, so that whatever applied to the Rūms would also apply to them. More specifically, the Armenian demands at Lausanne were ignored due to the fact that the Armenian representatives and lobbyists were prevented from being involved in the official proceedings at the request of the Turkish delegation. For the purposes of this argument, I limit the discussion on the Lausanne Conference to three main themes surrounding the Armenians during the negotiations: Armenian representation at the conference; the debate regarding the fate of Armenians in what would become the Republic of Turkey; and obligatory military service for Armenians who were to become citizens of Turkey.

THE TURKISH DELEGATION'S EFFORTS
TO REDEFINE "MINORITIES"

The Turkish delegation at Lausanne was headed by İsmet Paşa (İnönü) and his associate Rıza Nur, neither of whom was a professional diplomat. İsmet was an army general and a close friend of Mustafa Kemal, while Nur was a medical doctor and served as the minister of health. It is notable that the Turkish delegation was not homogeneous, and indeed, there were disagreements between İsmet Paşa and Nur, especially regarding the former's friendship with Mustafa Kemal. (Nur was delegated to represent the anti-Kemal faction in the Ankara government.[58]) Because of the many disagreements between the two, the delegation communicated regularly with the government before making decisions, as is evident from the frequent telegrams that the delegates sent to Ankara.[59] Despite the disagreements and negotiations, the delegation was strictly instructed not to deviate from the borders drawn in the 1920 National Pact (Misak-ı Milli), which had been agreed upon during the last session of the Ottoman parliament.[60] The National Pact imagined Turkey as a state for non-Arabic-speaking Ottoman Muslims, who were made to constitute a demographic majority.

The classification of the diverse Ottoman population was deliberated in the conference proceedings. Rıza Nur would later note in his memoirs how the French delegation defined minorities in Turkey according to three categories: race, language, and religion. Nur regarded this as a "conspiracy" by the European powers to divide what he perceived as the "Turkish" population, saying:

> This is very bad, a big danger, those men who are against us, how deeply and well they are thinking! With their reference to race, they are going to define Çerkes [Circassians], Abaza [an ethno-linguistic population from the Caucasus], Boşnak [Bosniaks], Kürt [Kurds] … etc. in addition to Rūms [Orthodox Christians] and Armenians as minorities. With their reference to language, they are going to define those Muslims who speak a language other than Turkish as minorities. With their reference to religion, they are going to turn two million Kızılbaş [Alevi] who are pure Turks into minorities. In other words, they are going to scatter us like cotton. The minute I heard this, my skin shivered, and I dedicated myself to the removal of these definitions. I worked hard, and at the end I achieved it.[61]

This text reflects the same view of the "Turkish" population that the Turkish nationalists upheld and expressed in their pre-Lausanne meetings in 1919 and 1920. Mustafa Kemal had repeatedly referred to Ottoman Muslims as the "Muslim elements" (*anasır-ı İslamiye*) that the Grand National Assembly represented. Furthermore, the 1920 National Pact was clear in seeing the diverse Muslim populations as constituting an "indivisible whole." In the Lausanne negotiations, both the Turkish delegation and European powers contested the definition of minority populations in what was to become Turkey. Both the Turkish delegation and the Europeans viewed Ottoman Christians as "minorities," but the former refused to apply the same criteria to the diverse Muslim ethnolinguistic groups. The reasons for this refusal were twofold. First, the Turkish delegation was working within the Ottoman understanding of *millet* as a religiously defined community, whereby all Muslims, regardless of language and sect, constituted one community, the "ruling millet" (*milleti hakime*) that rules the empire. Second, if the diverse Muslim populations were considered minorities along with the three traditional non-Muslim millets (Armenians, Jews, and Rūms), it would have been difficult to make the case that the Turkish delegation represented a working demographic majority within the territories they were negotiating to secure.

Yet in practice, the Turkish nationalists who founded the republic did not consider Islam to be the only criterion for "real" Turkish citizens. By examining parliamentary debates in the formative years of the republic, Lerna Ekmekçioğlu demonstrates that the criteria were even more specific. The ideal citizen for the nationalists was a Sunni Muslim who spoke Turkish and who was of the Hanafi school of Muslim jurisprudence. This naturally excluded Kurds for not speaking Turkish, Alevis for not being Sunni Muslim, and Alevi Kurds for both.[62] As Nur's comment and Kemal's speech (where Kemal referred to Muslims as collectively as "Muslim elements" (*anasır-ı İslamiye*) show, Muslim populations in Anatolia were eventually racialized and considered "Turks," and once the republic was established, those who were not Turkish speakers were subjected to centralized policies of Turkification. The Ottoman understanding of the millet, in which populations were to be distinguished by their religious affiliation, was thus influential in defining the ethnic categorization of the population to be exchanged and the population that would become citizens of Turkey. The Muslim millet, as the ruling millet of the empire, were made to constitute the Turkish majority of the state, while members of the confessional ethnic communities—the Armenian, Rūm, and Jewish millets—were turned into non-Muslim minoritized citizens of the republic.[63]

THE ARMENIAN DELEGATION'S EXCLUSION AT LAUSANNE

The Armenian delegation in Lausanne—which was headed by Gabriel Noradunghian, an Armenian who served as the minister of foreign affairs of the Ottoman Empire until the eve of the genocide—was excluded from all formal negotiations. The goal of the delegation was to designate an unspecified territory in Anatolia upon which the remaining Armenians and seven hundred thousand Armenian refugees could be settled.[64]

For this reason, between the signing of the Treaty of Ankara with France in October 1921 and the declaration of the Republic of Turkey in October 1923, the Ankara government took systematic measures to radically reduce the demographic presence of Armenians and other Christians in Anatolia by issuing laws to prevent Armenians from returning and by confiscating their vacated properties, rendering the Armenian exile permanent and forming the widely scattered Armenian diaspora.[65] Before signing the Lausanne Treaty and before declaring the foundation of the Republic of Turkey on October 29, 1923, the parliament of the Ankara government issued the following laws, which cemented the permanent dispossession of Armenians. It issued the law of April 20, 1922, which allowed for the confiscation of property belonging to the Armenians who left the Cilicia region, and the law of April 1923, which extended this confiscation to the property of any Armenians, whatever the date of or motives for their departure from Anatolia. After the conclusion of the Lausanne Conference in

July, a third law that prohibited the return of Armenians to Cilicia and the eastern provinces.[66] Furthermore, upon establishment of the Republic of Turkey, the citizenship law did not allow those Armenians who were outside Turkey to return and become citizens of the republic.[67] The granting of citizenship and refugee status to Armenians in France and the mandate of Syria and Lebanon—and the prohibitions against their return to Anatolia—had obliged Armenians to settle elsewhere because they were stripped of the opportunity to return and claim rights to the properties they had left behind.

The Turkish delegation repeatedly protested the inclusion of the Armenian representative in the minorities subcommission. Nevertheless, the European Allies tried to bring the Armenian and Bulgarian representatives to present their cases in front of the delegates. In a letter to the minority subcomission dated December 26, 1922, Rıza Nur strongly protested the inclusion of Armenian representatives in minority discussions, arguing that they were merely private individuals with no official mandate from the Armenian government. The Turkish delegation contended that engaging with them would be akin to using the subjects of one state against that same state, violating Turkey's sovereignty. The delegation further insisted that if such non-state delegates were heard, Turkey should have the right to introduce representatives from various Muslim populations under Allied rule. Furthermore, to put pressure on the British representatives, the Turkish delegation advocated for the inclusion of an Irish representative.[68] Consequently, the Turkish delegation refused to recognize any session where Armenians were included as an official minority of Turkey, considering such meetings null and void.

The Turkish delegation here invoked the international order of the time, which held that treaties were to be negotiated between states as the holders of sovereignty who had the right for self-determination. This order rendered Armenians, and other minoritized populations, non-state actors and thus allowed Nur to contest the participation of the Armenian delegation. This placed the Armenians in an ambiguous situation: on one hand, they were external to the Turkish nationalist project by virtue of their confessional ethnicity, and on the other, they were considered a domestic matter for the Turkish delegation. Such ambiguity stemmed from the Armenian predicament of denativization. While they were now spoken about as a minority and as external to the Turkish national project, they were still living on their lands that the Turkish delegation was claiming. For the Turkish delegation, Armenians were treated as a domestic matter, in order to avoid European interference on one hand, yet treated as foreign and disposable on the other.

As a result, Armenians were not represented by any state in these negotiations. The only existing Armenian state was Soviet, and the Treaty of Kars defined its relationship with the Ankara government. The role of Soviet Armenia was therefore neutralized, and its government was unable to mobilize on behalf of the remaining Armenians in Anatolia, even had it wanted to do so. İsmet Paşa himself said that speaking with the Armenian delegation would jeopardize Turkish relations with the Armenian state and the Soviet Union at large.

At a more general level, the Great Powers wanted to manipulate the internal affairs of newly established states or those that had been on the losing side in the war, but they were not willing to discuss the issue of minorities in their own countries and colonies.[69] The British vetoed including an Irish delegation at the conference, which the Turkish delegation had requested. The Turkish delegation's insistence that, if Armenians were allowed to participate, representatives from Ireland—then a British colony—and other minority groups should also be heard, coupled with its firm refusal to recognize the Armenian delegation, placed Lord Curzon in a difficult position. Given that Ireland's status as a British colony made its inclusion politically problematic for the British, Curzon ultimately refrained from further advocating for the Armenian delegation's participation, acknowledging that its members were private individuals rather than official state representatives, and allowed the debate to conclude.[70] According to Mark Mazower, these minority treaties in interwar Europe need to be understood in the context of power relations between the Great Powers and others. He argues that they "were a way of educating less civilized nations in international deportment" and were hence seen as inapplicable to the European powers—something that the Turkish delegates were conscious of and challenged when they demanded the inclusion of an Irish representative if Armenians were to be included.[71]

THE QUESTION OF WHETHER TO DEPORT
OR RETAIN ARMENIANS

The Turkish delegation aimed to expel the Armenians and to prevent the refugees from returning by negotiating an exchange of populations similar to the exchange involving the Rūms.[72] The delegation was under strong international pressure not to deport Armenians, and thus sought an international legal framework through which to accomplish its goal. The efforts to cleanse Anatolia of its remaining Armenians and confiscate their properties reached a peak in the fall of 1922, just about when the contested topic of minority protection was about to be discussed at the Lausanne Conference.[73] In a telegram sent by İsmet Paşa to Ankara on November 25, 1922, he explained to the government in Ankara why increased deportation of Armenians was not a viable option, saying, "In my opinion, it is impossible to justify the deportation of Armenians from the country to the world. However, we can talk about the exchange of Rūms [Greeks]. As for the expulsion of Turkish Orthodox Christians, discussing such a matter is fundamentally unacceptable. From this perspective, I am awaiting by the telegram machine for the approval of my views...I also firmly request that *no new deportations or forced resettlements be carried out from Anatolia at this time*."[74]

This telegram demonstrates that the Ankara government continued to deport Christians—Rūms and Armenians—from the shores of the Black Sea even while the Lausanne Conference was deciding the destiny of the region's non-Muslim populations.[75] The Turkish delegation feared that news of further deportations would jeopardize the Turkish position within the international arena.[76] In fact, in the two years preceding the Lausanne Conference, Armenians experienced repeated persecution and deportation, especially in the Cilicia region ceded by France under the Ankara Treaty.[77] The telegram also reveals that the Turkish government was considering how to find a legal framework to expel the remaining Armenians. However, the Turkish delegation wanted this expulsion to be in the form of a negotiated "exchange" similar to the one negotiated with Greece, because more deportations would not have been acceptable for Europeans given the pressure from the major powers on the Ankara government at the time.[78]

For a short while, the Turkish delegation entertained the idea of exchanging Anatolian Armenians with a Turkish population in Soviet Armenia. In a telegram dated December 6, 1922, İsmet Paşa highlighted an important point to Ankara: "With whom shall I negotiate the exchange of local Armenians [*yerli Ermeniler*] with the Turks in Armenia?"[79] He went on to explain why such an exchange could not be discussed with the government of Armenia: three years earlier, the Ankara government had signed the Treaty of Alexandropol with the Democratic Republic of Armenia, in which the Armenian government recognized the Ankara government and renounced territorial claims in Turkey, including claims to lands granted to an Armenian state under the Treaty of Sèvres.[80] Consequently, new negotiations over populations might have created a refugee problem similar to that of the Rūms[81] and led to a redrawing of the previously agreed-upon borders. For example, if the exchange were to be discussed with Soviet Russia, the Turkish nationalists feared jeopardizing the Moscow Treaty of Brotherhood between the Ankara government and Soviet Russia as well as the Treaty of Kars with Soviet Armenia, Georgia, and Azerbaijan, both signed in 1921.

Given these complexities, İsmet concluded in the same telegram of December 6 that "this is why there is no one with whom we can discuss the exchange of Armenians . . . and there is no way other than accepting those whom we choose to [have] stay in our land . . . [and] to treat them as citizens [*onlara vatandaşyüzü göstermektedir*]. I am aiming, if possible, to make them refute the idea of an Armenian homeland [*Ermeni yurdu*] [in Anatolia] as well as the idea of a legal framework for minorities and also to make them declare this refutation."[82] As stated earlier, Armenians were unofficially expelled or enticed to leave Anatolia throughout the negotiations at Lausanne in order to reduce their numbers and therefore scale down the responsibility that the new Turkish state would have toward them as a minority. The refutation of an Armenian homeland— or any form of communal sovereignty—in Anatolia reaffirms the declaration of Turkish nationalists at the Sivas Congress. To reinforce this position, the Turkish delegation pursued another strategy: reframing the Armenian issue as one of reciprocal population exchange rather than forced expulsion. This approach sought to preempt any potential claims by international actors that Turkey was unilaterally removing Armenians in violation of minority protections.

The following day, Hüseyin Rauf in Ankara conveyed this shift in a telegram to İsmet, confirming that the Turkish Council of Ministers had formally decided on an exchange policy: "Regarding the exchange of Armenians with Turks in Armenia, the decision of the Council of Ministers has been received. I agree with His Excellency and with the states involved. Today, in the Council of Ministers meeting, I will bring up the matter again and present the results of the discussions immediately."[83] Rather than acknowledging outright expulsion, the Turkish government framed the measure as a negotiated exchange, providing diplomatic cover while advancing its long-term goal of minimizing its Armenian population. Later that day, however, a telegram affirmed İsmet's plan of retaining the Armenians to avoid potentially unwanted political complications should an exchange be proposed.

THE SENSITIVE TOPIC OF PROTECTING MINORITIES

The protection of minorities was considered a hurdle for national sovereignty and therefore was not welcomed by delegates who wanted to build nation-states without foreign intervention.[84] Furthermore, this issue was sensitive for Turkish nationalists, because Europeans had sought to intervene in Ottoman social and economic affairs since the 1600s under the pretext of "protecting" Ottoman Christians. The dominant ideology of the early republic demanded unity among its citizens; thus, the Lausanne Treaty posed two challenges to Turkish nationalists. First, the nationalists perceived minorities as a handicap to the goals of social homogenization and Turkish nation-building. Second, they feared the treaty would foster enmity toward minorities and give Europeans a pretext to intervene, especially because some Christians had sought protection from, and collaborated with, European forces occupying Ottoman territory after World War I. For Turkish nationalists, Lausanne also granted Europeans a pretext for future intervention in Turkish affairs. Article 44 of the treaty supported this view, as it stipulated that "Turkey agrees that any Member of the Council of the League of Nations shall have the right to bring to the attention of the Council any infraction or danger of infraction of any of these obligations [toward non-Muslim minorities]." For these reasons, the Turkish delegation initially sought an unconditional exchange of the non-Muslims.[85] Nationalists especially wanted the exchange to target those communities who would demand political and/or territorial concessions or would be a cause for future European interventions in Turkish affairs.

When all the efforts exerted by the European allies to include the Armenian delegation in the conference and to grant autonomy for Armenians in Anatolia failed, Lord Curzon put pressure on the Turkish delegation to exempt non-Muslims from obligatory military service in Turkey.[86] This suggestion was also firmly rejected by the Turkish delegation on the grounds that it would give one segment of the population privileges that would not be enjoyed by the majority of citizens.[87] The Turkish delegation gave other economic and demographic reasons for this refutation: while Muslim Turks would be going to war risking their lives and businesses for the sake of the nation, non-Muslims would prosper exponentially; similarly, Muslim Turks might die in combat and thus not raise many children, such that the Turkish population would not increase as quickly as the population of non-Muslims. However, Nur mentions other reasons in his self-congratulatory memoirs that are worth quoting here:

> It seems that if they [non-Muslims] are obliged to military conscription, youth would escape to Greece, when it is time to do military service ... This means that military conscription is an obstacle for Christians. Through this, we can get rid of those Christians whom we could not get rid of through the exchange in the period of thirty years. Therefore, military conscription will put an end to Christian existence in Turkey in forty to fifty years. This is my calculation; this is why I insisted on military conscription. I was never hesitant, and they were not able to convince me otherwise, and finally I succeeded. The experience of the first five years after the peace proved me right that Rūms, Armenians, and Jews who reached the age of military service mostly escaped [by leaving the country], and of course whoever escaped military service is not able to come back without fear of punishment. Thousand thanks [for this]! I am very pleased from my achievement.[88]

It is important to contextualize this statement by looking into Nur's motivation. Upon the establishment of the republic, Mustafa Kemal credited his friend İsmet for the success of the delegation at Lausanne, while Nur's input was ignored and undermined.[89] Nur became an outcast and was self-exiled in Egypt and France; thus, in his memoirs, he tried to document his contribution to the establishment of Turkey. Yet his statement demonstrates that his contribution to Turkish nationalist causes was predicated on a premeditated plan to empty Turkey of non-Muslims; he credited this contribution to his shrewdness in the negotiations. He expected that such a contribution would be well received by his readers and that he would thus be recognized as a visionary who endeavored to work for Turkey's long-term interests.

The Turkish delegation succeeded in limiting Turkey's responsibilities toward minorities. As an outcome of Turkish state policies over the first six decades of the republic, the size of the minority population that remained in Turkey was greatly reduced, until it was only a small fraction of the population that the Turkish delegation had initially wanted to expel through a negotiated exchange.

THE AFTERMATH OF LAUSANNE

After the signing of the Lausanne Treaty and the establishment of the Republic of Turkey, Armenians found themselves foreigners while continuing to live in their homelands as the republican regime settled over their territories. Neither the Turkish delegation nor the European powers considered the Armenian question at Lausanne with the aim of achieving justice.[90] Instead, the Armenian question was a bargaining card: on the one hand, it was employed by the British to punish the Turks[91] and to pressure them for concessions; on the other hand, the Ankara government asserted its sovereignty over Anatolia by challenging the minority protections articles, which it saw as disguising European interventions.[92] The cumulative end result was the denial of Armenian sovereignty over Anatolia, reducing the Armenians to a "foreign" minority governed by a treaty negotiated with Greece and the European imperial powers. By ignoring Armenian representation and demands, the treaties of Ankara and Lausanne absolved the founders of the republican regime from responsibility for the genocidal violence and ethnic cleansing they and their predecessors perpetrated against Armenians. The treaties also prevented Armenians from returning to Anatolia, reclaiming the properties they left behind, or seeking compensation for those properties. Meanwhile, it was also impossible for Armenians to pursue territorial claims in Anatolia, given that the world order was centered around nation-states.

The position taken by the Turkish delegation at the Lausanne negotiations was either to blame the Western powers, who they claimed had manipulated the Armenians, or to blame the victims themselves for committing treason against the Ottoman state. The Turkish state refused to be held accountable for Anatolian Armenians and refused even to permit them to return to their Anatolian cities and villages in what became Turkey. On many occasions, the Turkish delegation urged Western powers that they should solve the Armenian refugee problem themselves. The refusal to permit the return of the refugees, coupled with the arguments presented by the Turkish delegation in Lausanne, supports the view that the Ankara government wanted to begin the new republic with as few Armenians in its territory as possible[93] and with a clean record regarding both the killings during the genocide and the claiming of properties belonging to Armenians. Creating new demographic and social realities and rewriting late Ottoman history from the vantage point of Turkish nationalism helped the Ankara government legitimize Turkish nationalist sovereignty over Anatolia.

On the eve of World War I, 20 percent of the population of the area that later became Turkey was Christian. After the Ottoman state under the government of the Young Turks massacred close to a million Ottoman Armenians, deported Armenians to France after the Ankara Treaty, and finally exchanged 1.2 million Rūm-Orthodox for the Muslims in Greece, the Christian population dropped to 2.5 percent, which was lower than the 5 percent target that the nationalists were hoping to achieve.[94] By 1923, Anatolia had been a battlefield of military conflicts for nine years, and was depopulated and impoverished. At the same time, the region was mythologized by the Turkish nationalists—the majority of whom were not Anatolian, but rather Muslims from the European Ottoman provinces—as a homeland for Ottoman Muslims, who constituted what became a Turkish majority.[95]

The treaty left three distinct legacies—beyond the legacy of further denativizing Anatolia's Armenian population—for Turkey, Greece, and the wider region. The first legacy was to legalize all the forced migrations that occurred in previous wars in the region, especially the Balkans. The second was to establish the possibility of compulsory migration (i.e., deportations) under international law. And the third was to institute religious affiliation as a building block of national identity and a marker of ethnicity, a process that had started with the rise of nationalism in the Balkan Ottoman provinces.[96] The Ottoman millet administration of non-Muslims did not entirely disappear in the new republic; rather, the understanding of millet was transformed from being a community defined by religious affiliation into a minority defined by a confessional ethnicity and governed by the articles of the Lausanne Treaty. Such a transformation in the power regime was manifested in the Turkish bureaucratic language. For example, in the pre-republican political discourse, the Turkish nationalist leaders used the term "elements" (*anasır* in Ottoman, translated as *öğeler* in Turkish) to refer to non-Muslims, which is the same word they used to refer to the diverse Muslim populations.[97] After the Lausanne Treaty (1923), the Turkish state referred to them as "minorities" (*ekalliyetler* in Ottoman, later *azınlıklar* in Turkish). Meanwhile, by not applying the same understanding to the diverse Muslim populations, the state removed their ethnic and linguistic specificities as Muslims were forced to become legally and administratively "Turks."

This transformation in how minority populations were conceptualized reflects the dual forces at work during the negotiations at Lausanne, where both technocratic and ethno-nationalist approaches shaped the population exchange. Ethno-nationalism was central to the process and conclusion of the Lausanne Conference, particularly in the compulsory population exchange, which legal historian Umut Özsu analyzes through the dual roles of technocracy and ethno-nationalism. Technocracy framed the exchange as a rational, managerial solution to demographic and territorial conflicts, while ethno-nationalism pursued the homogenization of nation-states, treating minorities as obstacles to sovereignty and stability. Özsu argues that these two approaches worked in tandem: technocracy provided a façade of neutrality, legitimizing the exchange as a "scientific" and humanitarian effort, while ethno-nationalism drove the ideological goal of reshaping populations to align with nationalistic visions. This interplay also created ambiguity, as the exchange was presented as a pragmatic solution to ethnic tensions but simultaneously entrenched the very nationalist ideologies it sought to mitigate.[98]

The consequences of the Lausanne Treaty extended beyond the immediate population exchange and the redefinition of minority identities, leaving other long-lasting impacts. It burdened the receiving governments with efforts to resettle refugees and created many legal and social challenges concerning the properties that were involuntarily abandoned by the refugees.[99] The Lausanne settlement left disputes over refugees' involuntarily abandoned property unresolved, straining Greek–Turkish relations for years.[100] This dispute had graver consequences for Greece than for Turkey due to the disproportionate number of refugees that the Greek government had to resettle,[101] yet Greece received foreign assistance to help settling refugees in Anatolia and Turkey did not.[102] Turkey, on other hand, lost its entrepreneurial class in the fields of finance, industry, and commerce, which was largely composed of Rūms and Armenians.[103] The appropriation of Armenian properties and capital played a pivotal role in the emergence of a Turkish

Muslim bourgeoise.[104] In Turkey, the abandoned properties that were not seized by local power brokers reverted to the state[105] and were also used as resources to finance political and military campaigns committed to the Turkish nationalist cause.[106] Consequently, Çağlar Keyder described the abandoned properties of the exchanged and eliminated non-Muslims of Anatolia as the "dowry" of the new Turkish state, as these properties were distributed to the Muslim population to create a local Muslim bourgeoisie to replace the non-Muslim one that had existed during the late Ottoman and early republican periods.[107]

IMPLEMENTING THE LAUSANNE TREATY

An Istanbulite Rūm who was living in Switzerland when I met him in Paris in 2008 and who lamented having to leave Istanbul once told me that he considers "the Lausanne Treaty [to be] the first legal document of ethnic cleansing in modern history." In fact, according to contemporary international law, any forced expulsion with the aim of establishing a homogeneous demographic makeup in a designated area is defined as ethnic cleansing.[108] These policies created a large social and political predicament for the Armenians who continued to live in Anatolia.

Under the Lausanne Treaty, non-Muslims were governed by articles 37–44. Article 39 specifically granted them equal citizenship, but only after designating them as "minorities" in their homeland:

> Turkish nationals belonging to *non-Moslem minorities* will enjoy the same civil and political rights as Muslims. All the inhabitants of Turkey, without distinction of religion, shall be equal before the law. Differences of religion, creed or confession shall not prejudice any Turkish national in matters relating to the enjoyment of civil or political rights . . . No restrictions shall be imposed on the free use by any Turkish national of any language in private intercourse, in commerce, religion, in the press, or in publications of any kind or at public meetings.[109]

The Lausanne Treaty provided a legal framework for the treatment of minorities in Turkey, but the reality diverged far from this ideal. According to Rıfat Bali, an independent scholar and archivist, discriminatory acts against non-Muslims in Turkey were performed with the intention of "Turkifying" the economy and society. He affirms that Turkification aimed to replace non-Muslims with Muslims; a Turk in essence must be "Muslim." While many of the laws did not necessarily advocate discrimination against non-Muslims, the degree of arbitrariness in their application shows that they were designed to single out non-Muslim citizens.[110] For example, a study by Dilek Güven based on U.S. embassy archives (now in Washington, D.C.) discusses the violent attacks against non-Muslims on September 6 and 7, 1955, known as the 1955 Pogroms.[111] The archives contain reports on anti-Christian discrimination and the active efforts to remove Armenians from Anatolia, a process not resolved in Lausanne through "legal" deportations. The 1930s witnessed forced Armenian migration from Anatolia to the French Mandates of Syria and Lebanon, as well as to Istanbul, where two camps were established for internally displaced Armenians who arrived during the resettlement of Balkan Muslim refugees and migrants.[112] Later, as Güven points out, Armenians were encouraged to leave Turkey in the 1940s. The United States requested that the Turkish government prohibit them from going to Soviet Armenia in response to Stalin's invitation to do so, and to instead advise them to move to the United States or France.

Ultimately, Lausanne presents a contradiction: the treaty granted equal citizenship rights to the remaining non-Muslims in Turkey but based this equality on their minoritized otherness to the Turkish nation.[113] This international order has allowed nation-states to be legally founded on a presumed homogeneous demographic composition that forms a country's majority, yet that definition has also been used against those belonging to other ethnic, confessional, or "racial" groups, who were classified as "minorities." The minority protection regime therefore deepened the political and social exclusion of minority populations through the very same mechanism that granted them the provisions of equal citizenship.[114]

The denativization of Anatolian Armenians goes beyond granting or denying them citizenship rights, for it means that their exclusion and destruction were foundational for the republican regime economically and politically, as was the denial of violence against them.[115] Mustafa Kemal, the founder of the republic, was uncompromising when he stated in a speech that he delivered in Adana in 1923 that the "Armenians have no rights at all in this prosperous country. The country is ours, the country belongs to the Turks. In history this country was Turkish, therefore it is Turkish and will remain Turkish forever. The country has finally been returned to its rightful owners. The Armenians and the others have no rights at all here. These fertile regions are the country of the real Turks."[116] Kemal later emphasized this in his 1927 *Nutuk* (Great Speech), which became the foundational text of the official Turkish historiography.[117] In the *Nutuk*, Kemal spoke of Armenians as being disloyal and murderous, making the case for the necessity of deporting them during World War I. Fatma Ulgen argues that by invoking the Armenians early on in the text, Kemal positioned the Armenian genocide as a cornerstone in the edifice of Turkish national perception of itself, of both its past and future.[118] The destruction of Ottoman Armenians was therefore the foundation of Turkey both economically and ideologically.

The Lausanne Treaty brought about a profound and enduring silence about the very existence of Armenians in post-Ottoman Turkey. Armenians were systematically excluded from the negotiations, their demands were used as bargaining chips between the Turkish delegation and the European empires, and the text of the treaty made no mention of them. The postwar power struggle between the Turkish nationalists and European empires further denativized Armenians legally and structurally by granting the Turkish nationalists uncontested sovereignty under the treaty. By recognizing Turkish sovereignty alone, the treaty entrenched Armenian exclusion, subsuming them (and other non-Muslims) under the Turkish ethnonational state as a minoritized confessional ethnicity rather than citizens with political rights and historical claims. The treaty was therefore a document of counter-sovereignty, the very structure that denied Armenians sovereignty, prevented refugees from returning to their lands, and stripped them of the ability to reclaim their properties.

The Armenian "displacement" under Lausanne was not purely physical, as those who became citizens were still living on their lands, but was rather a legal displacement that transformed them into internal foreigners within the new Turkish state. The treaty initiated them into their new status as minorities with reduced political rights as citizens, marking their inclusion through the very framework that rendered them subordinate. Yet, the silence enshrined in Lausanne has not erased the traces of those excluded from it. Reading Lausanne from the vantage point of those it marginalized offers a counter-history—one that reveals how sovereignty was secured through the denial of equal citizenship rights to Armenians. It also demonstrates how the afterlives of this legal displacement continue to shape the lives of the Armenian citizens of Turkey. This process of denativization did not end with Lausanne but continued under the republican regime, as the state sought to further erase the remaining Armenians from Anatolia—an ongoing reality that the next chapter explores through the lives of three Anatolian Armenians.

CHAPTER 3

ANATOLIAN FRAGMENTS

The Life Stories of Three Survivors

Walking through the old quarter of the southeastern Anatolian city of Diyarbakır on a very warm afternoon in August 2007, my eyes were transfixed by the dark basalt city walls, houses, churches, and mosques, that loomed above me. The buildings speak of a different past—one that is more diverse and beautiful than the past depicted in Turkish and global media, where this region is presented as the locus of violence and conflict between the Turkish army and the Kurdistan Workers' Party (Partiya Karkerên Kurdistan, or PKK). The demography of the region has changed drastically since World War I, due to the Turkish state's decades-long forced migration policies, intended to disperse Kurdish villages and tribes throughout the country. In many parts of Anatolia's east and southeast, Kurds who have been displaced by the state have replaced Armenians and Syriac Christians (Süryanis). Kurdish is now widely spoken in the winding streets of the city. Children are everywhere in Diyarbakır: some walk in groups or play football, while others attempt to sell cheap products—sweets, paper tissues, bottles of cold water—to passing pedestrians or the motorists stopped at red lights.

After visiting Benûsen, one of the poorest districts in Diyarbakır, which houses forced migrants from Kurdish villages and the families of those killed in conflicts with the Turkish state, Kurdish acquaintances guided me around that neighborhood. In doing so, they were showing me the aftereffects of the displacement of hundreds of thousands of Kurds during the decades since the Turkish republic was founded. I commented to my Kurdish acquaintance on the large number of children in the streets, remarking that the children were beautiful—a common Arabic compliment, and one that we often give parents when we meet their children. My comment triggered an immediate reaction from one of the Kurdish men, who worked in development projects on the internally displaced Kurds. He said in Turkish: "Their fathers *were* beautiful; their brothers *were* also beautiful." (*Babaları güzeldi; kardeşleri de güzeldi*). From the way he emphasized the past tense and his angry stare at me, I understood that many of those children had lost their fathers, brothers, or relatives through the violence inflicted by the Turkish state. I confronted the fact that he was addressing me—as somebody who had come from Istanbul and who spoke in Turkish—as a person who embodied the state's view of the Kurds, who saw the Kurds as violent and rebellious and blamed them for the lack of order and development in the country's east and southeast. I came to Diyarbakır tracing Armenian ruins, only to confront the ongoing Kurdish catastrophe.[1] It was clear to me at that moment that the republican regime rests not only on the destruction of Armenians, but also on the subsequent displacement and violence against Kurds.

After leaving that neighborhood, my friends and I asked for directions to the Armenian church, Surp Giragos. With its seven altars, Surp Giragos was known to be the largest Armenian church in the Middle East. Having been warned by people in Istanbul of the risk of being mugged in the dense maze of backstreets, we put our wallets in our front pockets, the women held their bags tightly to their chests, and we all attempted to walk with that special form of confidence available only to people who are familiar with a place. On a half-closed metal door, we found a small, rusted sign that read Surp Giragos Ermeni Kilisesi (Saint Giragos Armenian Church).[2] I squeezed through the narrow entrance, calling in Turkish "*Merhaba*" (hello) as I entered. There were two children playing in the church's courtyard. A member of our group went to speak to a woman who seemed to be living in a small room to one side. He said in Turkish, "We were hoping to see the church from inside. We come from Istanbul, and he [i.e., me] is from Egypt." Nodding her head in agreement, the woman called her husband, who was the caretaker, from inside the room. We walked across the courtyard to the church, and as I drew closer to the shattered windows to get a glimpse of the church's interior, I was met by a surprising sight. "There is no church!" I explained. "Look! It's in ruins—there is no ceiling and nothing remains from the interiors! Only the main pillars and the arches survive." The caretaker unlocked the small side door of the church, or what remained of it, and we entered slowly. As the others moved farther into building, I stood by the door, trying to make sense of the space. Where was the main entrance? Where was the altar? Which direction did people face during the liturgy?

It seemed that either the construction of the church had never been completed, or else that the building had been abandoned for a few hundred years. The church was disfigured, and the ceiling was completely destroyed.[3] When

FIGURE 3.1 Surp Giragos church exterior (2007, pre-renovation). The main entrance is visible on the right side of the image, offering a glimpse of the structure's condition before restoration efforts began.

FIGURE 3.2 The interior of Surp Giragos Church, showcasing the nave with the primary altar in the center. The church, known as the largest Armenian church in the Middle East, contains seven altars. This figure provides insight into the architectural and cultural significance of Surp Giragos, highlighting its role as a prominent structure in the region.

we inquired about the history of the building, the caretaker volunteered his own story to us:

> I am of Armenian background. My grandfather was around twelve years old during the genocide [*soykırım*]. He was adopted by a Kurdish family and was raised as a Muslim. When he grew up, he asked his adopted family if he could go back to his village. They agreed, and he returned, but since he did not change his official documents, he remained officially a Muslim. He continued to speak [to various people] about his Armenian background. We [likewise] tell people that we are Armenians. There is one man I know—a member of one of the three remaining Armenian families in this city—who hides his Armenian identity. I tell him, "Why do you hide it? I openly speak about it." He replies, saying, "You can afford to, since at the end of the day, you are registered as a Muslim. I am not." Even now, though, whenever I get into a fight or an argument with someone in the neighborhood, people rebuke me, saying, "After all, you are Armenian [*zaten Ermenisin!*]!"

I was surprised by the caretaker's candor, mainly because such tales are taboo in Turkey, and the usage of the term "genocide" could be punishable by law under article 301 of the Turkish Penal Code under the rubric of insulting Turkishness. It was evident that Diyarbakır follows different rules than Ankara and Istanbul. The city challenges many aspects of the Turkish state ideology and is regarded as the heart of Kurdish nationalism. Taking a taxi from Diyarbakır airport, the driver, upon hearing that we had just arrived from Istanbul, looked at us through the mirror and told us in Turkish, "Welcome to the nation's capital!" (*Ülkenin başkentine hoş geldiniz!*) implying an independent Kurdistan with Diyarbakır as its capital. In our encounters with people from different backgrounds, we were introduced as "coming from Turkey" (*Türkiye'den geliyorlar*). Furthermore, Kurdish is the de facto language of the city.

Curious about the history of the Surp Giragos church, I asked the caretaker when it had been abandoned. He replied:

> This church used to be completely full until 1982–83; on certain religious days, there wouldn't be place for people even to stand. Folks started migrating to Istanbul after that; many migrated from Istanbul to Europe, a few continued living in Istanbul. The majority of people went to the Netherlands, others to France and America. It was completely closed in the early 1990s, when the few remaining families left. Now there are around three families, and they're very discreet about their Armenian identity.

Surprisingly, the church's seemingly ancient desecration had in fact occurred only in the last two decades. I asked about the ceiling: could it really have decayed so rapidly? Has it not been destroyed intentionally? He replied:

The wooden ceiling was destroyed because of rain and climatic factors. Before they left, Armenians faced much harassment. You can see how the windows around the church all are blocked with red bricks and cement to avoid harassment. This aggravation was not instigated by the government, but by ordinary people living nearby. It became very difficult for Armenians to continue to live here.

I turned again to the caretaker. "What would bring a Kurdish Muslim with an Armenian background to a deserted Armenian church in the heart of the city?" I asked him. He replied:

When the person responsible for the church decided to leave, like the rest of the Armenians, for Istanbul in the early 1990s, he called me. I was still living in my village. He asked me to come and take his place, to become the caretaker of the church. The [Armenian] Patriarchate in Istanbul agreed that I could live in the room in this courtyard because, after all, I had an Armenian background. Ever since, I have been living here and taking care of the church. Whenever I visit Istanbul, I visit the Patriarchate and some of the Armenian families who used to be here.

As we left the Armenian church, three children assumed the duty as our tourist guides. Because my companions, some of whom were Turkish, and I were communicating with a mix of English and Turkish, we were all tourists in their eyes. The children did not simply take us from one historic site to another; they offered us their own brief histories of the area. As we were leaving the Ulu Camii (Grand Mosque), we were met by more children, who told us, "This mosque used to be a cathedral. You can see at this entrance the drawings of vine leaves. Christians used wine inside." "How do you know this story? Did you learn this at school?" I asked. He replied, "No, there are many guides who bring tourists here, and I listen to them when they explain to tourists." The conversion of Christian places of worship did not begin with the Armenian genocide. The Ulu Camii, which was converted from a cathedral to a mosque before the genocide—part of a pattern dating back to the Muslim conquest of the region—speaks to a much longer history of erasure of the Christian presence in southern Anatolia.

Surp Giragos was later renovated; it reopened for worship in October 2011 and was hailed as "Turkey's first church to be revived as a permanent place of worship." The church was damaged again in 2015 and then reopened in 2022. The damage was blamed on the Kurdish PKK, and the Turkish minister of culture attended the reopening in 2022.[4]

❧

Diyarbakır is one microcosm of the Armenian predicament in Anatolia since World War I. Armenians in Diyarbakır experienced massacres, forced migration, life with discrete and double identities, and eventual migration to Istanbul and Europe—and, more recently, their buildings have become relics for tourist attraction. All represent stages in the process of denativization. Following the signing of the Lausanne Treaty, the republican regime was obliged to retain the remaining Armenians of Anatolia and grant them Turkish citizenship. The Turkish state consolidated its conquest of Anatolia through a mix of formal, informal, and semiformal, mostly violent, policies that ranged from forced expulsion to heavy-handed assimilation, designed to alter the demographic makeup of the territory, especially given that the territory was largely inhabited by Kurds. Such measures were designed both to entice Armenians to move to Istanbul and to crush Kurdish solidarity by dismantling relations within families, villages, and tribes. I take such measures as further denativizing steps through which the Turkish state sought to manage an initially unwanted population in Anatolia that the regime was obliged to retain under the Treaty of Lausanne. Like many cities and villages of Anatolia, Diyarbakır manifested the afterlives of the Armenian genocide as it became a center of the Kurdish resistance to the Turkish republican regime, which continues to seek the subjugation, confinement, assimilation, and erasure of Kurds.

Turkish and Armenian post-Ottoman historical accounts concur in obliterating the lives of ordinary Armenians in Turkey from the narratives. These multiple silences point to the fact that what is conceptually unthinkable is historiographically impossible. Nationalist historiographies such as the Turkish and Armenian ones are collectivist in scope. And collectivist historiographies are potentially also totalitarian, as Hannah Arendt argues.[5] As Arendt points out, a denial of human life is common to different forms of totalitarianism (such as Nazism and Stalinism). To Arendt, an "eyewitness account of an historical experience"[6] disturbs the silence imposed on and constructed around those whose lives have been denied by the ideologies of collectivist regimes. Narration can also redeem the life denied, because "all sorrows can be borne if you put them into a story or tell a story about them."[7]

This chapter seeks to circumvent the limitations of collective histories and gaps in the archives by using *personal* narratives as a source of knowledge about past events, focusing on narratives from three ordinary Anatolian Armenians. Through the lives of these three individuals, the chapter traces some of the reasons behind the multiple waves of Armenian emigration from Anatolia to Istanbul between the 1930s and 1970s. The personal narratives explored here provide a counterpoint to the stories of Hrant Dink and Sabiha Gökçen, the two public figures discussed in chapter 1. This chapter endeavors to document the process by which Armenians were dispersed within and beyond Anatolia, living as Turkish citizens in the shadow of the Lausanne Treaty. Personal stories illuminate an era that was intentionally erased from Turkish and Armenian historiographies: the lives of Armenians who continued to inhabit Anatolia, the very landscape of the genocide, and whose existence became intertwined with those of the Kurds, some of whom had been complicit in the Armenian massacres. These life stories are not exhaustive or comprehensive; rather, they capture fragments of lives that critique the dominant narratives in Armenian and Turkish histories.

Violence against Armenians is not confined to major disruptive events such as genocide, mass displacement, or singular acts of violence; rather, it permeates the fabric of everyday life, forming the very order of existence for Armenians under the Turkish republic. As Veena Das argues in her exploration of critical events, these moments are not merely ruptures in the social fabric but also catalysts that redefine moral and cultural frameworks.[8] However, in the case of Armenians, violence operates not only through these critical moments but as a persistent, normalized reality embedded in the structures of daily life. Here, I draw on Walter Benjamin's "Theses on the Philosophy of History," particularly his assertion that "the tradition of the oppressed teaches us that the 'state of emergency' in which we live is not the exception but the rule."[9] In this sense, the daily lived experience of Armenians in Anatolia reflects a protracted "state of emergency," wherein violence is normalized and woven into the fabric of their lives, making survival itself a form of survivance. By presenting these life stories, this chapter seeks to challenge the reduction of Armenian suffering to singular, critical events, highlighting instead the enduring processes of erasure, marginalization, and violence.

Yet such stories would not be found in archives. The narratives presented here emerge from silences in dominant historiographical accounts and must be sought in personal stories that fall outside the document-based frameworks of history. As this chapter demonstrates, uncovering silences in the dominant historiographical narratives, it is necessary to look beyond the archive to the lived experiences—though the knowledge they provide will always be partial, shaped by positionality and context. This reflects what Donna Haraway calls—in the plural—"situated knowledges": forms of knowledges that are always produced from experiences specific to a particular history and geography, rather than from an illusion of relativism or assumed objectivity.[10] These narratives are not simply an "Armenian view" on history; rather, they challenge dominant historiographies by exposing the limits of state-centered accounts and revealing the power structures that shape historical erasure. In doing so, they also disrupt the claims for an inclusive history that while accommodating multiple perspectives, it ultimately reinforces the epistemic authority of the state and maintains the foundational exclusions upon which nationalist historiographies are built. Collecting knowledge that is specific, "partial,"[11] and "situated"[12] allows us to conceive of "more adequate, sustained, objective, transforming accounts of the world."[13] Rather than merely offering an alternative perspective, the narratives presented here actively counter state-centered historiographies by foregrounding the lived experiences of ordinary Armenians, whose histories have been silenced within nationalist and collective memory.

It is notable that some anthropologists tend to write of life *stories* instead of life *histories*, as the interpretation of those histories will depend on present politics and realities.[14] Given the physical and cultural annihilation, multiple migrations, and ruptured lives of Armenians, we are left with random individuals and communities. Hence, we cannot know to what extent these three life stories are representative of Anatolian Armenians; indeed, we can never reclaim the Anatolian whole[15] nor recover its past as it was. Amidst absences and silences, these life stories give us glimpses of the experiences of some Armenians in Anatolia and demonstrate the ways in which "Anatolia" remains in multiple fragments traceable through storytelling that continue to be made available in the present.[16]

The life stories of members of a denativized group, however, can "show the variety of forms life histories can take within a single region" or community, city, or social entity.[17] Such personal accounts show differences in the manner an event or a period of history has been experienced, internalized, and remembered by different groups, depending on their position vis-à-vis the state.[18] Life stories demonstrate ethnographically how Turkish, Armenian, and Kurdish societies in Anatolia are complex and interconnected and far from monolithic. The chapter therefore runs against the multilayered silences that surround the historiography of Anatolian Armenians by showing that not all Armenians were killed or had to convert to stay in Turkey and that the Turkish state continued its efforts to push Armenians out of Anatolia following the Lausanne Treaty. Consequently, stories of the Armenian survivors in Anatolia shed light on the power dynamics that forced them to emigrate and overshadowed the silences surrounding their past. In this regard, the stories are autobiographical for their narrators. The stories are also histories, insofar as the narrators are "contemplating the past and producing knowledge about it," thus opening a small window on an undocumented and fragmented past.[19] These narratives therefore blend the personal with the historical, unfolding the life of one individual that is deeply rooted in a particular historical context and geographic locale.[20]

NARRATING SILENCED LIVES

As in the counter-histories traced earlier, what follows collects partial fragments that surface beyond the sanctioned archive, reflecting Benjamin's sense of flashes and fragments that interrupt the linear narratives of official history. The three stories discussed here focus on the ways that Anatolia continued to be emptied of its Armenians after 1923. I treat these narratives as fragments of the unwritten experiences of Anatolian Armenians.[21] The fragments collected here raise questions about the premises of official history, allowing us to reevaluate the past.[22] They help us to bring the debate on the Armenian predicament in Turkey out of the archives. And these fragments expand our understanding of the Armenian predicament in the formative years of the Republic of Turkey beyond what was retained in the archives of the Turkish state and the Armenian church.

Ara's Everek

Ara and I met through Krikor in 2006, and we became well acquainted during the two years I spent in Paris between the autumn of 2006 and the spring of 2009. We saw each other at least three times a week: twice a week at an Armenian music workshop and once a week on Sundays in the Armenian church of Alfortville where he had recently been ordained as a deacon. We once met by coincidence in October 2008 in Alfortville at a kebab restaurant owned by Agop and his wife, another Armenian migrant from Istanbul, which I frequented almost every day. We both ordered an Iskender kebab, and Agop gave us much more than the usual portion, Ara being an old friend and his brother's classmate in Istanbul and me being an almost a daily customer for more than two years. So, Ara and I being together brought us exceptionally generous hospitality from Agop.

    Ara was born in Istanbul in 1955, a year after his family had to leave their village near Kayseri. He then went to study at the Armenian theological seminary in Jerusalem in 1969 and returned to Istanbul in 1973. Upon finishing his obligatory military service in Turkey in 1977, he emigrated to France. During lunch, Ara updated me on his project of opening a baklava shop in Alfortville, which he had told me about on earlier occasions. Our conversation continued on the variety of cuisines in Anatolia, which led me to ask him about his family's village in Anatolia. Ara narrates:

> We come from the village of Everek, close to Kayseri.[23] There used to be a lot of Armenians there, as the city expanded and became divided into higher Everek on the mountain and lower Everek. Each had its own church. Besides Everek, the nearby village of Talas was also Armenian. They both had Armenian schools until I think 1918 or 1919, when they were stopped by Atatürk during the war in Anatolia. That is why Armenians in Everek and Talas knew Armenian, while those from the city of Kayseri did not.
>
> My grandfather had six brothers. As they left during the war and settled in Deir Zor [Syria], he returned to Everek in 1919 to find no one remaining from his family. It was a very big family. Later he knew that one of his brothers was in Marseille and another in Los Angeles. The other four were never found. I still have family in Marseille, who are the descendants of my grandfather's brother. The one in Los Angeles had no children. My grandfather got married in 1922 and had four sons and two daughters. So, my father had three brothers and two sisters. A brother remained in Istanbul and one moved to Marseille.

Like Ara's family, almost all Ottoman Armenian families were dispersed during and after World War I, forming what is now known as the "Armenian diaspora." Few people remained, sometimes only one member of each family to protect the family property in the hope that they would be able to come back. In the case of Everek, some of the Armenians—such as Ara's father, who had fled to Syria—were able to return right after World War I had ended. They returned to their village to find destruction and no family, as the majority were killed or had converted or escaped.

The majority of Armenians repressed stories of violence that occurred during the genocide. Yet unlike the Armenian diaspora in France, which had the social and political capacity to mobilize around spreading awareness about the genocide (chapter 5), Armenians who remained in Turkey faced social and political censorship that prevented them from doing so. Many Armenian migrants from Turkey in France commented that they began to learn about the genocide after they left Turkey. Ara said, "The elder generation did not speak about the genocide. Only among themselves did they speak, but with the younger, they didn't. I don't know why, but they didn't speak about it in front of us." Another Armenian once explained this by saying that members of the older generation feared that their children would bring the genocide up in schools or in public if they spoke about it in front of them. By not discussing the genocide in their children's presence, they believed that they would protect their children from potential problems in schools with teachers or classmates. As expressed by Harry Harootunian in his recent work discussing his parents' reluctance to discuss the genocide after relocating to the United States, Armenians possess an unarticulated legacy. The memory of their past suffering persists in silence, unexpressed and unshared, even though speaking about this suffering was not as restricted in the diaspora as it was in Turkey.[24]

Although some Armenian families remained in Anatolia during the first three decades of the republic, many of them started migrating to Istanbul in the 1950s. Many interlocutors have attributed this to conflicts with Kurdish landlords in Anatolia, to the aftermath of the violent attacks on non-Muslims in Istanbul on September 6 and 7, 1955, or to the desire to attend Armenian schools in Istanbul. For example, Ara's family experienced the following:

> Back in 1954 [one year before Ara's birth in Istanbul], an Armenian girl from the village, related to the family, was kidnapped by the Kurds for marriage. These kidnappings were common. See, Kurds do not like to intermarry from within the tribe/village/family because if they do so, they might have diseases . . . etc. so they kidnap girls who are considered outsiders in order to "change the blood," which means that they mix their blood with outsiders through marrying an outsider. So, this Armenian girl was kidnapped.
>
> My uncle, Harut, fought to bring back the abducted girl. He ended up killing the man who kidnapped her and brought back the girl to the family. After this incident, the *ağa*, village head, told him that his safety could not be guaranteed, and all the family had to leave. So, my father with the rest of the family moved to Ankara for a while as we had some relatives there and then to Istanbul; shortly afterwards, I was born in Istanbul. That was 1955.

Stories about abducting Armenian girls for marriage frequently emerged when I spoke with Armenians from Anatolia. These stories draw attention to the ways in which power dynamics between Kurds and Armenians—both communities suppressed under the Turkish state—shifted after World War I and to the ways that Armenians experienced these shifts in their everyday encounters with Kurds.

Ara himself was not raised in Anatolia, and his knowledge about Kurdish kinship practices seems blurred for a number of reasons. First, an ideal marriage in the Kurdish tribal system would be with cousins and not outsiders. Second, marriage has economic and political considerations and is usually negotiated between the groom and the bride's father or male guardian. It is noteworthy that abduction of Armenian women was employed as a strategy during the Hamid-ian massacres as a policy of "institutionalized rape," euphemized as marriage.[25] Abduction was also a policy used during the genocide itself as part of the anni-hilation of Armenians. Those who were able to transmit Armenianness to their children (i.e., adult men) were killed, and those who were unable to do so (i.e., women and children) were spared and "put to good use": children were Turkified and Armenian women were made to give birth to non-Armenian children (i.e., children fathered by non-Armenian men).[26]

Ara's story tells us that the abduction of Armenians in Anatolia continued through the republican period. While not new, these abductions speak to the weakening of the already vulnerable situation of Anatolian Armenians. And such abductions, which undermine the male authority of the bride's family or tribe, speak to an expression of gendered power that goes against the social customs of Kurds and Armenians.[27] Abduction is also economically desirable, because it absolves the groom's family of financial commitments toward the Armenian bride.[28] The kidnapping of Armenians in Anatolia can be explained as part of the dispersal and weakening of their social networks after the genocide. This dis-persal is manifested in Ara's story, when the family had to leave because his uncle killed the man who abducted one of his family members.

Other stories I heard from migrants from the southeastern provinces speak about conflict with Kurdish landlords over land. All of these stories emphasize the refusal of the police to interfere in conflicts between Armenians and Kurds, which left them to sort out their disputes and quarrels among themselves. In many instances, Armenians chose, or were forced, to migrate to Istanbul, where there they would feel more secure. This renders the distinction between vol-untary and forced migration of Armenians blurred and vague, a product of the power struggle between the Turkish state and Kurdish landlords and between the remaining Kurds and Armenians. Such (in)formal state policies are reflected in the ways in which the state appears to either be absent or a direct actor in local politics where Kurds and Armenians battled over land and abducted girls. Nevertheless, the state created a power structure wherein Armenian rights were undermined; the state also built alliances with Kurdish landowners and tribal leaders to control Kurdish uprisings. These two factors provided a segment of the Kurdish population with an upper hand over the remaining Armenian pop-ulation in Anatolia. Because the state was not directly in control of large parts of Anatolia, it was able to maintain its control through a process of accommodation by allowing the strongest Kurdish individuals and tribes to impose their will on the rest in exchange for maintaining control over the majority of the popula-tion. In these situations, a Kurdish landlord or village head (*ağa*) usually was the middleman between the authorities and the rest of the population, be it Kurdish or Armenian.

Ara's uncle, Harut, who had killed a Kurdish man to save the abducted Armenian woman, was later given the Muslim name "Harun" and was registered on the state identity card as a Muslim. Ara was not clear whether the name change was his uncle's choice or was imposed by the state when he was issued a government identity card. When Harut/Harun visited Everek in 1992, he found that the last remaining Armenians had married with the Turkish Muslim majority. Yet the ghost of the Armenian girl that he rescued from abduction still lingered four decades later. Ara narrates:

> Since it is a small village with no hotel, it is customary that the *aǧa* would host my uncle. But this time, the *aǧa* was Kurdish. One of the remaining Armenians, married to a Turk, recognized him and told him not to stay long because the present *aǧa* was the brother of the Kurdish man whom he had killed back in 1954 to rescue the girl. She advised him also not to open the subject with anyone and not to reveal his identity.

Despite the migration of many Armenian families to Istanbul, they maintained connections with their Anatolian villages of origin. They went either to visit grandparents or the remaining members of their extended families or to seek a bride from their home villages. Ara narrates:

> I visited when I was around ten years old. That was around 1965. There were still Armenians there, and many would visit also from Istanbul. I went with one of my uncles who went back to look for a bride. At the time it was very common for people to return to find brides from their villages. But after that, none of the family members went back because by then they had all left . . . The village became populated with Kurds.
>
> Everek had no Kurds. They were living in the neighboring villages. There were only Turks and Armenians. Kurds came from neighboring villages. This happened a lot, so this was not the first time for Kurds to come. The village was small, maybe twenty or thirty houses or so, and they [Armenian families] were all intermarried. Once they were intermarried, they all become one family.

The shift in power dynamics in Anatolia has been coupled with the politicization of Armenian perception of both Kurds and Turks. Appropriating views similar to those of the Turkish state, Ara identified Kurds as people without history and land, who had been simply "living on mountains." Turks, on the other hand, were "Central Asians" and newcomers to Anatolia. Ara explained the replacement of Armenians by Kurds and Turks in Everek and the remainder of Anatolia as follows:

> In the past, Armenians outnumbered Kurds in Anatolia. And you know, Kurds have no history, because they had no land. They were nomads living on mountains, like gypsies. Kurds were moving nomads, like Turks, who came from Central Asia . . . So basically, this is how Anatolia was evacuated of Armenians.

Ara's comment frames Turks and Kurds as later arrivals to Anatolia, a view through which he situates Armenian presence as both older and more deeply rooted in the land. In such a representation, Ara explains his loss of Anatolia by reclaiming Armenian belonging to a specific geographic locale from which he has been uprooted. Ara articulates such belonging to Anatolia by speaking about the Armenian names of places, churches, monasteries, cemeteries, archaeological sites, ancient literary texts, or Armenian kingdoms in Anatolia (referring to Diyarbakır as Dikranagert, for example). Although Armenians are no longer living in Anatolia, his village had been emptied of its Armenians, and its church now stands as a mosque, Ara asserted Armenians' older and longer presence on the land, one that preceded that of Turks and Kurds. Then Ara told me that he went on a church mission in 1974, accompanying two priests who performed marriages and baptisms in villages that had no functioning churches. While he mentioned the many cities he visited during this visit, he paused at Sasun, took a deep breath, and ruminated, saying, "Ah, Sasun used to have a lot of Armenians. It was all Armenian!"

Sasun is a celebrated Armenian village and district of Anatolia. It is known for the popular epic story *David of Sasun*,[29] a national hero who fought against the "Arab"—Egyptian, to be precise—invasion of Armenia in the seventh century. Even among some people in Turkey, the people of Sasun are known for their affiliation with an Armenian identity. When I visited the office of *Agos* following the assassination of Hrant Dink, one journalist told me that upon hearing of Dink's assassination, villagers came from Sasun and slept on the sidewalk in front of the building for a couple of nights to attend the funeral. They told him: "We are Muslim, and we are proud to be so, but also proud to be Armenian. We would stand against anyone who would harm an Armenian." They represent the segment of the Sasun population that is Muslim but that affiliates with an Armenian ethnic identity—those who converted to Islam during the genocide or in the early years of the republic. Those who converted either did so because they were saved by a Kurdish village head, *ağa*, who obliged them to convert, or voluntarily converted to avoid discrimination, displacement, harassment, or stigma.

Following Sasun, Ara visited Şırnak, a city on the Syrian border, whose *ağa* was Armenian. In Şırnak, they also visited the sister of Ardash, one of the priests he was traveling with, who still lives there. I was puzzled to hear that there was still a village with an Armenian *ağa* in the southeast. Ara explained that this *ağa* was an Armenian *gavur*, meaning that he had converted to Islam, explaining that "the old Armenians who became Muslim, you see, they are called '*gavur*' [infidel]."[30] Ara went on to explain that even though Armenians convert to Islam, they do not lose their Armenianness as confessional ethnicity, as this is something that one is born into; therefore, people refer to Armenian converts to Islam as *gavur*, from the Arabic *kafir*, meaning "infidel" or "unbeliever." This practice turns religious identities in Anatolia into "racialized" categories that are biologically inherited, regardless of the current social realities or legal status of individuals. Ara explained the ambiguous situation of the Armenian converts, giving the following example:

My grandfather had an Armenian friend who stayed in Everek. He did not escape to Deir Zor with them [during the genocide]. He changed his name to Ali, which is a Muslim name. He did not change it officially with the state, but he became known by it. It was the Kurds who protected him. But since he was Armenian, even though he had a Muslim name, the Kurds still called him *gavur* [infidel]. Also, since he was not really Ali, he came to be known as "Gavur Ali." In fact, all of those who changed their identity and became Muslim stayed in Everek; conversion was what allowed them to remain and stay unnoticed.

I noticed that the name "Ali" came up a few times as Armenians spoke about those who converted to Islam. Ara explained to me that Armenians hid behind this name because it is a very common name among Kurds. Ara explained, "There are many Kurds carrying the name Ali, but *Gavur* Ali is used only for an Armenian convert to Islam." Ara remembered another *gavur* carrying the name Ali whose wife had a visible scar all around her neck. Ara explained that the scar was long, pointing with his finger on his throat and going in a semicircle around it, alluding to the act of slaughtering animals throughout Anatolia. Ara added, "It was caused when they tried to kill her during the genocide, but she survived because she was saved by Kurds who found her and protected her." Because converts never lose their Armenianness, Kurds in many instances try to match them in marriages. Knowing that this woman was also *gavur*, they married her to *Gavur* Ali. Ara concluded, "They left Everek in 1956 to Istanbul, where they live with their two sons and two daughters as openly Armenian." Ara emphasized that Istanbul was a place that permitted Armenians to be more open about who they are, partially because there was a larger concentration of non-Muslims, because the tribal vendetta code was less binding, and because the minority regime out-lined in the Lausanne Treaty was at least loosely applied there, so Armenians could have functioning communal institutions; Istanbul, unlike Anatolia, con-tinued to have functioning Armenian schools and churches.

Houri's Sasun

Houri is an Armenian from Sasun who currently lives in Istanbul. She is an active member of an Armenian church in the Gedikpaşa district of Istanbul, where we met for the first time in January 2009.[31] I arrived in the church around 11:30, and she was waiting in a room close to the gate. Churches in Istanbul usually have a security room to monitor the doors. She was warm and friendly and asked me if I would like to light a candle in the church before we spoke. When we entered the church in the middle of the Sunday liturgy, the church was almost full. The facial features and attire of the worshippers differed from those of the church-goers attending other Armenian or Rūm-Orthodox churches in Istanbul—the worshippers seemed less urban and of a lower-income strata. In other words, they looked more Anatolian than the Istanbulites in other churches.

Other Armenians had suggested that I meet Houri because she is keen on documenting the fading Armenian heritage of her village; for years, she has been recording the Armenian dialect of older Sasun women who emigrated to Istan-bul. "My own heritage is dying out and the Armenian dialect of Sasun too is slowly being forgotten," she said in a concerned tone. After losing her father, she realized that she had started losing her ties with her cultural and social past in Anatolia. This is why she started a project to document Sasun's Armenian cul-tural specificities. When I first met her, she had interviewed around fifty elderly people from different villages around Sasun. Most of the interviews were con-ducted in the local Armenian dialect, because "so many words have been forgot-ten." As an example, she told me that in this dialect, Armenians only remember the words for east and west and not for north and south. This, she explained, was mainly because of the significance of these directions in the region.

❧

The following year, in the early evening of a Ramadan day in September 2010, Houri and I met in Simit Sarayı in Beyazit. We had tea and chatted over var-ious noises—sounds from a football match, the banging sounds of *dondurma* (ice cream) being made, and later, a plethora of voices from the nearby mosques pronouncing the sunset *ezan* (call for prayer) that marked the end of a long day of fasting. Houri narrated her family's story, which reveals the local specificities of the living situation of Armenians in Anatolia after the genocide:

> Loyalty to an *ağa* was central to Armenian survival in our region; disobedience to the *ağa* could be life threatening with risk of expulsion from the region. After 1915, Armenians belonged to whoever saved them. We were lucky, we were saved by a good tribe [*aşiret*] called Şigani who are known to be one of the best because they protected their Armenians . . . they are our owners [*sahip*]. In issues of marriage, naming, and religious affiliation on identity cards, the *ağa* gets to choose the names of the newly born and who gets registered as Armenian and who as Muslim . . . etc. So, this is how Armenians were Islamized and assimilated.

Many Kurds of Anatolia had a direct involvement in carrying out the killing of Armenians during the genocide,[32] yet it is equally true that Kurds helped Armenians survive.[33] Houri explained that when Kurdish *aşiretler* protected Armenians, they also benefited from them, either through their labor or by taking Armenian girls as wives without any financial obligations to their families. In return, the Armenian girl who would marry into a Kurdish family would be able to "put pressure on the *aşiret* that kidnapped her for marriage to save the rest of her Armenian family and treat them well."

As noted earlier, the abduction of Armenian girls was a common theme in the stories I heard. Muslim girls were also kidnapped, but the abduction of Armenians by Kurds carried a different weight because of the ethnic and religious difference between the two communities. In addition, the discrepancy in power between Kurds and Armenians rendered the latter vulnerable after the republic was established, because in many instances, the Turkish state allied with Kurdish landlords (*ağalar*) in controlling the Kurdish-majority regions. It is also notable that both populations have been suppressed by the state in its efforts to govern and Turkify the region. Here, Houri offered an explanation as to why kidnappings took place:

> Armenian girls are hardworking and beautiful! When men are asked about Armenian women, they reply, "My Armenian daughter-in-law is very different than others; she adapts well and doesn't cause conflict in the family." Muslim girls also get kidnapped, but this causes problems between different tribes [*aşiretler*], and they have to pay compensation [*bedel*] to the girl's family. This is not the case for Armenian girls.

In effect, Houri emphasized that it was cheaper to kidnap an Armenian for marriage than to kidnap or marry a Kurdish girl, because the rules that governed the relationships between the Kurdish *aşiret* did not apply to Armenian women. The Kurdish *aşiret* became the *sahip* (literally owner) of the Armenians saved. (The term *sahip* connotes both ownership and possession.) Because of this ownership, the *ağa* had the right to take important decisions in Armenians' lives. Houri explained:

> Imagine an Armenian girl is engaged to an Armenian man, and for some reason, the engagement is broken. The *ağa* would claim her, saying, "Now, since she is no longer engaged, I have rights [*hakkım*] over her." Her family either gives the girl to the *ağa* to determine her future or they are obliged to leave the city, away from the influence of the *ağa*, most of the time to Istanbul.[34]

> This happened not only to unmarried girls, but to married women too. My aunt was kidnapped while her husband was in the military. She was immediately taken by her mother-in-law, and they left for Istanbul. In the 1950s, migration to Istanbul reached a peak due to the increase in incidents of Kurds kidnapping girls.

> In the late 1920s, when my grandfather went to the military police [*jandarma*] to complain about an incident, he never came back! It was reported that he was killed there. My father, who was born in 1928, became an orphan. After my grandparents died, my father was adopted by his uncle, who took him to Muş, where his [the uncle's] sister was living. She was adopted by a Muslim family in 1915 in Muş and became a Muslim. She told her brother [Houri's great-uncle] and my brother that if they were to live with her in Muş, they would have to convert to Islam. My uncle did not accept [this mandate] to convert, so they went back to Sasun. My maternal grandfather was also killed by the police in the field.

Yet it was not only the conflicts between Armenians and Kurds that promoted Armenian migration out of Anatolia. In the early period, the republican regime wanted to consolidate its power in Kurdish-majority regions through diminishing Kurdish social and political power. The violence of the Turkish state also sometimes prompted Armenians to leave for Istanbul; at other times, they were forcefully relocated by the state to other parts of the country. In the latter instances, Armenians were treated as Kurds. Houri explains:

> Seven or eight years after the Kurdish rebellion [*isyan*] of Şeyh Said [1925], the state came to tax the *ağa*, who might have been an Arab or a Kurd. See, in the

region it is difficult to know who is Arab, Turk, or Kurd. The army used to come to destroy villages, and as villagers went up the mountain in the summer, many children—Armenian and others—died because their parents put their hands on their mouths so they wouldn't cry and be heard by the soldiers.

Houri narrates how her family was forced out of Sasun as a result of the Settlement Law (İskan Kanunu) of 1934, which was meant to assimilate Kurds through forced resettlement across the country.[35]

In 1938, my family was asked to leave for İzmir. Between 1938 and 1948, there was forced migration of Kurds in areas where there had been rebellions. These policies also influenced us as Armenians, who were adopted by Kurdish *ağalar*. My father was illiterate, so to get the exact date [of his expulsion to İzmir], I asked my father if Atatürk was alive. He said that Atatürk died the year we arrived to İzmir, so this is how I knew that the family went to İzmir in 1938. While in İzmir, my family was not revealing their Armenian identity because they were considered Kurds. When I asked them if they revealed their identity, they replied, "Are you crazy?! We saw what happened to those who revealed it; they were pelted with stones."

My family went to different cities as the state was emptying the southeast. Wherever they went, they were given land and cattle. If they were [forced to] go to a poorer place, they came under the protection of the local *ağa* or the local people.

People were exiled [*sürgün edildi*] from the whole region to different parts of the country. By 1938, the state emptied the region, but the last people to leave were those living in mountainous villages like Sasun. Say, for example, if someone was missing, their family wouldn't know whether they were sent elsewhere or killed. They found out only in 1948, when the order to remain exiled [under the Settlement Law] was reversed, and people started to go back to their hometowns.

Yet some villagers never had to leave during this period, such as the Varto clan, to which Hrant Dink's wife, Rakel, belongs. Their story has many resemblances to that of Houri's Sasun, and they both ended up in the Gedikpaşa neighborhood of Istanbul. Houri explains:

Rakel Dink's family, for example, stayed on Mount Judi until they were found by Protestant missionaries. Then they brought them to the [Protestant] church here in Gedikpaşa, the one right behind us. People did not know which church or sect they belonged to, but they knew they were Armenian and Christian. When we first arrived, we attended the Protestant church. If we stayed there, we would have become Protestant. There were no churches left in Sasun; sometimes Syriac [*Süryani*] priests used to come at night and perform the rites of marriage and baptisms for Christians. My parents did not have an Armenian marriage; they were married by a *Süryani* priest in the region. Since one cannot be Christian without baptism, many parents used to suffer when an unbaptized child died, so people kept holy oil at home so that they could anoint their children.

The causes for leaving Anatolia vary among Armenians, but many point to a conflict with the Kurdish population and the refusal of the state's security system to protect Armenians in such conflicts. Like Ara's story, Houri's also indicates the difficulty of distinguishing between voluntary and forced migrations to Istanbul. Houri narrates:

My father fell ill in 1972, so obviously my mother and I became vulnerable to kidnapping. If you are living in eastern Anatolia, it always depends on whether the *ağa* is good or bad. That would determine if one would stay in the village, be forced to convert to Islam, or need to leave the village altogether. The sheikh [*şeyh*, Muslim clergyman] usually pushes the *ağa* of a village to treat Armenians badly in order to pressure them to convert to Islam. When our *ağa* treated my father well, the *şeyh* told the *ağa*, "If you treat him well, how would he convert?!"

So, a few *şeyhler* were after my father for many years to convert. Those roaming *şeyhler* have no access to homes; they cannot enter. So, they have female counterparts who are able to enter homes easily. One day, a woman came to our home and told my father that she could bring him a good-looking Muslim woman as a wife to entice him to convert. My father told her, "If you can bring me a woman more beautiful than her"—pointing at my mother—"I would!" When she looked at my mother, she said, "I can't," and left, so he never converted.

Two days later, on Sunday, I visited Houri at the church. After the liturgy, she invited me to have tea and pastry in the church hall. As an Arabic speaker, I was keen to listen to the Arabic dialect of Sasun that Houri had told me about in our previous meetings. On our way out, we went to greet Sofi, to whom I tried to speak in Arabic. She was inside, washing dishes in the kitchen, and so I greeted her in Arabic, saying *ma' essalameh* (goodbye); she did not know how to reply but smiled at me. Then she said in Turkish that she forgot Arabic since she had come to Istanbul more than twenty years ago; she had been twelve then. She left with the family, because her uncle's wife was kidnapped and killed. Then Houri said, "Yes, yes, I remember the story." Houri did not want to continue speaking about it, and the matter was immediately closed, and Sofi kept silent after Houri's comment. Sofi did not look at us again as we were leaving; she continued washing the dishes. Houri then explained to me:

People get married early so as to avoid kidnappings. Also, in the late Ottoman period, married people were less likely to be drafted to the military. My mother was engaged at the age of nine, also to avoid kidnappings.

I asked Houri if I could narrate the details of the kidnapping stories. She immediately said:

You can speak only of my family's stories! Since people gave me a hard time in using their stories, I don't see why I should not let you use mine. People get scared about making their stories known, especially the ones about kidnapping. They say that since there is a younger generation, they are worried that making their stories known would harm them. Once a claim is made on an Armenian girl [to kidnap her for marriage], then they keep harassing her even after she leaves for Istanbul. They can also harass the person to whom she is married.

Leaving Sasun was a shared predicament for many villagers. Houri said that people started leaving Sasun in the 1950s out of fear of being kidnapped, regardless of the actual frequency of kidnapping occurrences. Armenians left in significant numbers after 1965, especially after the earthquake of August 19, 1966, in the town of Varto, Muş Province. Yet the earthquake was only one factor among others that pushed Armenians to leave Sasun. Houri continued, "There had been two killings in the village that encouraged people to leave. But I don't know the details." When I asked Houri if she knew whether the state was involved in those killings, Houri was quick to say, "What state?! There is no state there. Until recently, there wasn't even electricity. The military police [*jandarma*] is the only state presence in the region." According to Houri, the governance of the region has been under military rule since the Kurdish rebellion of 1925 and, in contrast with the western parts of Turkey, the Kurdish region did not have ordinary police operating under the ministry of interior.

Mihran's Arapgir

Going westward from Sasun, Armenians present us with another set of reasons of why they left Anatolia. In a short meeting with Mihran in 2009 in his office in Istanbul, he told me about his experience in his native Arapgir:

> I come from Arapgir or Arapkir in Malatya Province. I was born in 1943. There used to be many churches in Arapgir, close to twelve churches.[36] The main church was the cathedral of the Holy Mother of God [*Surp Asdvadzadzin*]. This was partially destroyed during the genocide, and from the early republic onwards, it was used as a school. The municipality decided to sell the land and the church, and in September 1957, it was sold to a Muslim from the village named Hüseyin for 28,005 Turkish Liras. The church was then blown up with dynamite for the new owner to make use of it.[37]
>
> When I was growing up, there was no functioning church in Arapgir, as the remaining churches closed, were converted, or were destroyed. There were traveling priests who came from time to time to perform marriages and baptisms for the remaining Armenians. For example, I was baptized at the age of nine, with my brother and sister. My sister was nineteen at the time and was baptized right before she was married . . . Out of two thousand to three thousand Armenians in the village, currently [in 2008] there are maybe four Armenians left in Arapgir.

Mihran spoke of different reasons for leaving Arapgir. For him, leaving was an individual decision, but for most it was communal:

> While in Arapgir, I attended primary school. While nothing was said directly against me, teachers would hint about me being an Armenian. This happened especially when the teacher came from outside Arapgir. I decided to move to Istanbul in 1955 to attend the high school of Surp Haç Tıbrevank, an Armenian school. My parents, however, did not want me to leave.[38]

But for the majority of the people in Arapgir, it was the Settlement Law of 1934, and not the conflict with the local Kurdish population (as in Everek), that prompted people to leave in groups, as was the case with Houri's family leaving Sasun in the late 1930s. Mihran went on to tell me about other reasons that Armenians were pushed out of Anatolia through a story he had heard from someone from Yozgat:

Once I was in a meeting, and some people were talking about an elderly Armenian from Yozgat who came to Istanbul at a very early age. I think he came in the mid-1930s. Later, I found this elderly man and asked him about his story. Although he was only a couple of years old when he came, he was still able to remember. He told me that state officials came one night in their house and gave his family a week to leave their house. It looked like the state was choosing two or three families from each village and asking them to leave, so as Muslim migrants from the Balkans could be resettled in the houses left by the Armenian families who were asked to leave.

Another person from Yozgat also spoke to me of the resettlement of Balkan Muslims in place of Armenians: the state requested that Armenian families share their homes with Balkan migrants, and consequently, many Armenians *chose* to migrate to Istanbul. Such a policy, aimed at replacing the local Armenian population with Balkan Muslims, is in line with the fact that Turkish nationalists were largely Balkan Muslims who adopted and created Anatolia as a Turkish homeland after being expelled themselves from their home villages and cities in the Christianized Balkans.[39]

Returning to Arapgir, Mihran continued, "The Settlement Law [İskan Kanunu] was of course a big thing for Arapgir. The state didn't want to leave villages and areas with high concentrations of Kurds."[40] Yet, as with Ara's Everek, except for the application of the Resettlement Law, we find that the line between state-imposed, state-encouraged, and voluntary migration is thin, because the role of the state as communicated through these narratives remains unclear. Mihran concluded our meeting with this impression:

> The state definitely wanted to collect all Armenians in one place. It is known— although I still don't have the exact quotation—that one high-level state official said that it was easier to control and eliminate non-Muslims as long as they are concentrated in one place. This is why they wanted to collect all Armenians in Istanbul.

❧

The stories of Ara, Houri, and Mihran speak of multiple Anatolian Armenian experiences and indicate that every Anatolian locale had its own specificities. The stories are indicative of both variations and similarities among the experiences, depending on the region, the existing local power dynamics, and the degree and kind of state intervention in each region. These three lives, however, do not constitute a collective history shared by all or most Anatolian Armenians; nor do I suggest that the lived experiences of Anatolian Armenians are limited to those described in these stories. Rather, the stories are fragments from diverse lives that form a consetellation showing how Armenians—after being denativized conceptually in historiography and legally through Lausanne—were compelled to leave their villages yet another time, with no prospect of return.

DIVERSE LABELS FOR THE ARMENIAN CATASTROPHE

During our final meeting, Houri explained to me that the variety of experiences during the genocide produced a range of local labels to describe what happened, in contrast with the standardized legal term "genocide." Local variations in the terms adopted by different villages reflect the unique occurrences within each village; after all, people could only speak about their own specific experiences. Armenians were not annihilated uniformly; while the Turkish state policy of cleansing Anatolia of its Armenian population was systematic, the methods used varied.

Houri's village, located in the Kurdish-majority region of Anatolia, emphasized the violence they experienced through the way they named and differentiated events. This was reflected in their terminology and periodization, which marked distinct episodes of violence in their history. The villagers identify two major events, both labeled as *ferman*, a Persian word used in Ottoman Turkish to mean a decree or an edict issued by a sovereign ruler. *Ferman* was used during the Ottoman Empire for orders and edicts issued by the ruling sultan. Houri explained that the Birinci Ferman (First Decree) or Büyük Ferman (Great Decree) describe the 1915 events, during which Armenians escaped, were killed, or were taken by the local *ağa*. It is notable that labeling the 1915 genocide as *ferman* reflects the conviction that it was an order given by the government of the time. When I asked Houri about Mıgırdiç Margosyan's usage of the word *kafle* (from the Arabic *qafilah*, meaning "caravan") in his novel *Tespih Taneleri* to refer to the 1915 events, she said that *kafle* means a group of people marching. Marching is how people in the Diyarbakır region, such as Margosyan's family, would have experienced the genocide.[41] Therefore, those who use *kafle* experienced deportations and then returned in masses. The people of Sasun, however, did not experience deportations. Because Sasun is a mountainous village with harsh terrain, people were instantly killed, hid in the mountains, or were adopted by Kurds—and so they use *ferman* to speak of the instantaneous killing by a decree.[42]

The forced evacuation of Sasun in the 1930s following the 1934 Settlement Law, known as İkinci Ferman (Second Decree), is what Houri refers to as "exile." For "exile," Houri used the Turkish word *sürgün*; however, in the local dialect of Sasun, they use its Arabic equivalent, *nafii*, because the deportations of the villagers in the 1930s again were on the orders of the state.[43] Putting the forced migration of the 1930s, the Second Ferman, in a linear sequence with the first reflects the way in which Houri and others in Sasun experienced and interpreted them as being related and consequential. The people of Sasun experienced the First Ferman of 1915 (the genocide), the Second Ferman (Settlement Law), and then the kidnapping of women that followed as all ultimately leading to their exile from Sasun. For them, the Armenian catastrophe has a much longer temporality and is not limited to the legally and historically defined crime of "genocide" that took place during World War I.

These stories suggest that eastern Anatolia was subjected to a different regime than the rest of the country following the Kurdish uprising of Şeyh Said in 1925.[44] To write the Anatolian past from the vantage point of Armenians who came from three different regions of Anatolia is to contemplate the afterlives of the Armenian genocide, which challenge "genocide" as an event that brought Armenian history in Anatolia to an end. In addition, shedding light on the variety of experiences of Anatolian Armenians after 1923 produces counter-histories that contest the exclusive ethnic claims of the Turkish state to the land and population of Anatolia.

SITUATING THE ARMENIAN PAST IN ANATOLIA

The stories of Ara and Houri demonstrate that the Armenian predicament in places like Everek and Sasun was intertwined with that of the Kurds. "The Şeyh Said rebellion [*isyanı*] in 1925 affected not only the Kurds, but everyone in the region [*bölge*], including Armenians," Houri explains. Therefore, Armenian history in Anatolia cannot be told as part of the collective history of Turkey or of Armenians; rather, it is situated in local and individual experiences that are a result of the Turkish state's efforts to assimilate the Kurdish population and suppress political rebellions in the southeast. I say "local and individual," because the lives of ordinary Armenians presented here reveal the ways in which the state implemented a variety of formal, informal, and semiformal policies to control Kurds and Armenians, depending on the region and the political circumstances of the time. Consequently, attempting to construct a collectivist history is futile, and anthropologists and historians are left with only situated knowledges that are specific, local, and partial.[45]

Following the emergence of Christian Balkan nationalisms, the Ottoman Empire lost its Christian majority in those provinces. Similarly, the Republic of Turkey was established on the basis of Sunni Islam as an ethnic marker of the nation as enshrined by the Lausanne Treaty. This nationalist identification created a hierarchy among Turkey's citizens, in which those who identified themselves with Turkish culture, language, or identity assumed the privileged position. They were followed by the Alevis, who were considered Turks but were not Sunni; then the Kurds, who, as Muslims, were encouraged to assimilate into Turkishness; and finally, Armenians, who were unassimilable because their non-Muslim affiliation rendered them foreign (of a different ethnicity and race). As Ara demonstrated, in many instances, the Armenian conversion to Islam did not ensure complete assimilation into Turkishness, because the converts still carried the racialized epithet *gavur*.

It was in this historical context that the Settlement Law of 1934 aimed to alter the entire demographic makeup of Anatolia. Its measures targeted the Kurds, who resisted assimilation, and with them the Armenians, who became part of the Kurdish social fabric in places like Sasun after the genocide. The law's stated purpose was to "preserve Turkish culture [*Türk kültürü*]" (article 1); to achieve this, the law divided Turkey into three governing regions, according to the demographic makeup of each area (article 2). The first region was one with a concentration of people "belonging to Turkish culture." The second region had a population that was to be assimilated into Turkish culture. The third region, which we can understand from the law as having had a Kurdish majority, was to be emptied and residence in it was to be banned. Furthermore, the law prevented non-Turkish speakers and those who do not speak Turkish as their mother tongue (which mainly targeted the Kurds) from forming a village, a neighborhood in a city, or a craft. Finally, another measure that affected Armenians specifically, was the article that states: "Non-Muslims (*ecnebi*; literally, foreigner)[46] living in towns and cities cannot constitute more than 10 percent of the entire population. Moreover, they cannot establish separate neighborhoods" (article 11) where they would constitute a majority.[47] It was in the aftermath of this law that Houri's family as Armenians were implicated with the Kurds and forced to resettle in western Anatolia. They constituted two elements of otherness: they were non-Muslims (*ecnebi*) and part of the Kurdish tribal and sociocultural fabric.

As a result of the Turkish state's self-definition and its demographic-engineering laws, Anatolia was fragmented through a long war with the Kurdish population and emptied of its remaining Armenians. The stories presented here provide several reasons for the migration of Armenians out of Anatolia: conflict with Kurds (Everek), the abduction of Armenian girls (Everek and Sasun), the Settlement Law to concentrate the Kurdish population (Sasun and Arapgir), migration instigated by the resettlement of Balkan Muslims in Armenian homes, forcing Armenians to abandon their homes to resettle them (Yozgat), migration after the Varto earthquake of 1965 (Muş region), and migration to attend Armenian schools in Istanbul in the absence of institutions in Anatolia (Arapgir). The republican regime therefore made it almost impossible for the Armenians—whom the regime had to keep as citizens under the Lausanne Treaty—to stay in Anatolia.

The conditions of migration also differ. Ara and Houri present two cases in which Armenians left Anatolia. Ara left because the family was in conflict with the *ağa* over the abduction of an Armenian girl; Houri's family left during the Settlement Law, due to the Kurdish rebellion. The former was an individual family, while the latter was shared with the whole village, if not the entire Kurdish region. Yet upon returning to Sasun in the late 1940s, Houri's family had to leave for Istanbul in the 1970s to avoid being themselves abducted. Mihran's migration, on the other hand, was an individual decision that was neither a pattern in Arapgir nor encouraged by his family. Individual decisions to attend Surp Haç Tıbrevank school, along with the efforts of the Armenian Patriarchate to resettle Armenians in Istanbul, will be explored in more detail in chapter 4.

Even in cases that appear to be idiosyncratic and local, the role of the state in each migration case reflects the mechanisms that shaped a hierarchical system of differentiation in the early republican period, the foundation of which was set by the Lausanne Treaty. State policies allowed for the emergence of informal hierarchical relations between Kurds and Armenians. The accumulated results from formal, informal, and semiformal migrations led to the eventual migration of Armenians. The actual role of the state, and the perception of Armenians of that role, varied in the different examples discussed. The role of the state as perceived by Armenians is reflected in the way they label the course of events. First, the role of the state appears as a decree (*ferman*) experienced in Sasun. Later, Houri's story tells us that the state was only present in the southeast through military police (*jandarma*) and not through civil governance. Ara's and Houri's stories show that the state did not protect the Armenians in conflicts with the local Kurds. Finally, Houri and Mihran (through his story about Yozgat) spoke of the state as directly involved in the resettlement and movement of populations to change the demographic makeup of the Kurdish region. In their narratives, the state resettled Kurds—and Armenians, who were treated as Kurds—in the western provinces of Turkey, moving Balkan Muslims to replace Armenians. Anatolia's demographic makeup was not settled by Lausanne; rather, shifts in the region's demographic makeup continued well into the life of the republic. The various degrees of involvement of the state in Anatolia render the description and labeling of such roles a challenge: Are Armenians refugees, forced migrants, internally displaced peoples, economic migrants, or political migrants in Istanbul? The terms we use therefore must be problematized in order to contextualize the afterlives of the Armenian catastrophe.

If we compare Anatolian Armenians to the Rūm-Orthodox (Greeks) of Anatolia, we find that the latter were forced to leave, along with the Muslims of Greece, through a legally binding treaty signed at Lausanne, guaranteed by the two states and by the European powers of the time. The Armenians, by contrast, were left in the realm of the informal, without a titular nation-state to advocate for them. For this reason, Kemal Yalçın says in his travelogue, where he traced surviving Armenians in eastern Anatolia, that the search for surviving Armenians in Anatolia "isn't like the Greek [Rūm] one."[48] The task of writing a history of Armenians in Anatolia after 1923 presents many challenges, because one cannot write a narrative that applies to the majority of the remaining Armenians. Additionally, there is the question of sources and archives discussed earlier.

Such variation in experiences produced the Anatolian fragments that are situated in the different experiences, memories, and even labels to describe that past. In light of the genocidal destruction experienced by Armenians, followed by the further dispersion of the residual population that remained in Anatolia, the stories presented here give only partial knowledge of the silenced communities that no longer exist in Anatolia. However, one can still preliminarily sketch some patterns in lived experiences by juxtaposing these various fragments of situated knowledges;[49] for example, people in areas with a high concentration of Kurds had a different experience from areas that did not.

These fragmented narratives do not assume a unified or a holistic history of Armenians in Anatolia, nor do they fit neatly within a state-centered or diasporic historiographical frameworks. Rather, they expose the limits of both erasures and the structural exclusions embedded in nationalist history. As Haraway reminds us, knowledge is always partial, embodied, and situated—and the histories recounted in this chapter illustrate precisely that. They are not meant to supplement an existing historical narrative but to disrupt, unsettle, and complicate how history itself is conceived.

It was only after I heard the stories of Anatolian Armenians that I understood Kaspar's answer to my question of how Armenians stayed in Anatolia after 1915 and 1923, saying, "When you are chasing dogs or cats, after a while you will lose track of some of them; some are going to hide, others will escape. But you cannot kill every single one of them." His short answer was poignant and spoke well of the degree of arbitrariness and disposability of Armenian lives. Yet the fragmentation of Armenian histories did not end with their displacement from Anatolia. As the following chapter explores, even in Istanbul and the diaspora, Armenians encountered new forms of erasure—both from the state and within their own communities. The denativization of Anatolian Armenians continued, not only through the Turkish state's policies but also through the ways they were perceived and positioned by Armenians in Istanbul and France.

CHAPTER 4

SAVING OR DISPLACING?

Resettling Armenians in Istanbul and Paris

The tight security measures around the Armenian Patriarchate in the Kumkapı district of Istanbul resemble those of a highly secured government building or a foreign embassy: cars are not allowed into the street, and the entrance has two gates leading to a room with an X-ray security machine. As I entered and handed in my bag to be checked, I found myself in a building in a neoclassical style, newly renovated, and a garden enclosed by a high, old cement wall. The lobby appeared to be that of an official institution, decorated with many portraits of previous patriarchs who had headed it, most of whom were from the Ottoman period.

After waiting for few minutes in the reception hall, I was welcomed by Aram, a priest who held an administrative position at the patriarchate. On learning that I had spoken with Armenians considered "liberals" and at odds with the patriarchate, he passionately complained about how secular Armenians exposed the community, especially when *Agos*, the newspaper established by Hrant Dink, was publishing news and articles that were critical of the community and its leadership. The tensions he mentioned sounded similar to those that exist in wider Turkish society between the secularist and religious camps. Nonetheless, given that Armenians are a minority group categorized as "non-Muslims" in accordance with the Treaty of Lausanne, their primary link with the state continues to be through their religious affiliation as a community, with the Armenian Patriarch in Istanbul acting as a representative of the community.[1]

The secular camp believed that Dink wanted to create an alternative voice to that of the patriarchate. In their view, as long as the patriarch, a religious figurehead, continued to represent Armenians as a confessional collective and mediate with the state on their behalf, Armenians could never be full citizens of the republic. To the conservatives, however, Dink had weakened the integrity of the community. To give me an example of how Dink's activism had harmed Armenians, Aram explained that the Armenians of Malatya had started procedures to ask the state to return the confiscated church in that city, and that these efforts had been halted after Dink's assassination. In his view, Armenians now felt more vulnerable and were scared to take such an action. Aram insinuated that Dink should not have spoken freely about issues pertaining to Armenians on the pages of *Agos*. Dink, on the other hand, was unwavering in his public critique of Armenian community institutions. His motivation, as described by Gerard Libaridian, was to liberate Armenians from being exclusively defined by the state. This would require the community to rely less on its religious intuitions.[2]

Aram's critique of Dink, and secular Armenians in general, arose from his concern for the future of Armenians in Turkey. Armenians, in Aram's opinion, should maintain a low profile and channel their politics through the patriarchate. Since the foundation of the republic, some thirteen Armenian communities had remained in Anatolia, he said. With the migration of Armenians to Istanbul, churches and other community institutions became confiscated property (*mazbut vakıf*): if the number of Armenians dropped below a certain number in a given place, the state could confiscate their communal properties on the basis that there was no community to use them. Efforts to regain communal properties were therefore in vain, because Armenians had left their towns and villages to move to Istanbul and Europe. Consequently, the patriarchate in Istanbul was unable to perform liturgical services or to provide education for the residual Armenians in Anatolia.

The disappearance of Armenians from Anatolia, whether through emigration or conversion, Aram continued, "did not happen in one period; it took over ninety years for it to be completed." Yet despite their disappearance, one continues to come across incidences that reflect their silenced past. Aram highlighted that many crypto-Armenians (hidden Armenians) continue to live in Anatolia. He offered the following examples: when the patriarch visited Gaziantep, he was struck by his meeting with an Armenian convert with a Turkish name, who did not speak Armenian, but was able to recite verses in classical Armenian from a poem by Saint Nerses (he was probably referring to the famous twelfth-century theologian and poet Nerses Shnorhali). Also, when the patriarch came close to a cemetery in the city, someone approached him and asked him to say a prayer, because "many people buried here are from your folk!"—thus acknowledging that Armenians continued to live there decades after the genocide.

Aram regarded the Varto earthquake of 1966 in the Muş region as a significant turning point in the lives of Armenians in Anatolia.[3] First, it pushed more

Armenians from this region to flee to Istanbul; second, and more importantly, the patriarchate established a committee of lay people to aid the victims of the earthquake. In the beginning, he said, Armenians in Istanbul were surprised because they did not know whether there were still Armenians living in Anatolia, and if so, where and how many. But with the earthquake, Armenians in Istanbul started to see significant numbers of Anatolian immigrants to the city, who mostly spoke Kurdish and Turkish as their first language. The patriarchate's activities became increasingly confined to Istanbul as more Armenians migrated or were forced out of their cities and villages. With this continued emigration to Istanbul, Aram explained that the clergy concentrated on resettling many Armenians within the city. It offered these Anatolian immigrants accommodation and financial support until they were able to adapt to life in Istanbul or, eventually, migrate to Western Europe. Aram insinuated that because the patriarchate was unable to continue to serve them in Anatolia, it felt compelled to relocate the remaining Anatolian population rather than to risk "losing" them to cultural assimilation, either through religious conversion or through marriage into Kurdish or Turkish Muslim families. Furthermore, by encouraging the migration of Armenians, the patriarchate would seek to increase its constituency in Istanbul where the minority regime outlined in the Lausanne Treaty is at least partially applied.

It was apparent that the patriarchate was working within the framework of the minority regime established by the Lausanne Treaty, itself building on the Ottoman millet system in which the church represented the confessional community, a role that with Lausanne gained a more explicitly ethnoracial dynamic in representing Armenians. The dynamics of numerical representation in the city directly correlate with the political influence of the patriarchate; as the Armenian community's size increases, so does the patriarchate's political power. Just as the minority regime granted special rights to non-Muslim citizens, it ensured that each religious group continued to live as a community. Non-Muslim citizens did not hold citizenship rights as individuals, as was the case with Turkish Muslim citizens; instead, their citizenship rights were mediated through their confessional ethnicity. The paradox is that by empowering the patriarchate's position as the representative of Armenians before the state, the minority regime weakens individual Armenians as citizens. Such a paradox explains the tension that existed between secular Armenians, such as Hrant Dink, and the patriarchate.

The experiences of Anatolian Armenians often have not fit into the simplified narratives and rigid understandings of Armenianness and Armenian history that are widespread in Istanbul and the Armenian diaspora in France. Many cultural practices of Anatolian Armenians overlap to some degree with those of their non-Armenian neighbors. And the relations between Anatolian Armenians and their non-Armenian neighbors also have been complex: Turks and Kurds massacred Armenians, but they also helped Armenians survive. When Anatolian Armenians emigrated to Istanbul, or later to Europe, their locally inflected Armenianness was often not understood or valued by Armenians in their new communities. This chapter highlights the fact that there have been multiple and contradictory forms of Armenianness, including Islamized ones, as well as multiple and contradictory sorts of relations between Anatolian Armenians and their neighbors.[4] It also suggests that the dismissive response to Anatolian Armenians on the part of Armenians already living in Istanbul or Paris is itself denativizing. By denying Anatolian Armenians the right to articulate an experience of being Armenian that is different from the one institutionalized in Turkey or France, Armenians in Istanbul and Paris have contributed to the sense of rupture and estrangement experienced by Anatolian Armenians. This denial has deepened the denativization of Anatolian Armenians from their locally defined Armenianness.

"SAVING THE REMNANT"

In the late 1990s, a period when books began to be published and music albums produced that spoke of the Armenian presence in Anatolia, the Turkish writer Kemal Yalçın traveled across Anatolia to trace the experiences of Armenians who remained in Anatolia. He documented his impressions, interviews and accounts in *Seninle Güler Yüreğim* (translated as *You Rejoice My Heart*).[5] In this travelogue, Yalçın interviewed Zakarya, an architect from the Kayseri region. Unlike Aram, Zakarya believed that the patriarchate knew about the remaining communities in Anatolia and exerted efforts to resettle them in Istanbul as early as the 1950s, before the Varto earthquake.[6] Furthermore, according to Ara—whose story was narrated in chapter 3—such missions to Anatolia continued well into the 1970s. Ara told me that he was sent in 1974 with Ardash, a priest whom he had met while studying at the Armenian theological seminary in Jerusalem, on a mission to Anatolia.[7] "The patriarchate sent us to baptize Armenian children, and to perform church marriages for Armenians who only had civil marriages." He continued:

> Such missions though were not regular and not to the same regions. Before we left, the patriarchate gave us a list of villages where they knew there were Armenians. We started with Dikranagert [the Armenian name for Diyarbakır].

There, we hired a Kurdish driver who took us around the region. We covered some villages around Dikranagert—Muş, Sasun . . . now, when I tell you the names of these cities, I don't mean the exact cities, I also mean villages surrounding those cities. We first approach the *ağa* as we enter each village and ask his permission before we enter Armenian homes.

From Ara, we deduce that the patriarchate knew about the places where Armenians were still living and communicated with them to meet their needs whenever it was possible by sending priests to conduct religious services. Zakarya agreed with Aram that, rather than prioritizing the needs of the remaining Armenians in Anatolia, the patriarchate focused its efforts on resettling Armenian youth in Istanbul, ensuring they could attend Armenian schools, learn the language, and be safeguarded from disappearance through assimilation, which they faced if they remained in Anatolia. Zakarya explained:

> The Armenians in Istanbul were well aware of this situation in Anatolia: how many families were living in which corner of what province, how many school-aged children these families had, etc. Through some method or other, and with greater or lesser accuracy, such information was gathered and kept in Istanbul. Armed with this information, they would go every year to Anatolia and collect the school-aged children to Istanbul, in order to provide them with an education, with the younger ones being sent to the Şişli Karagözyan Armenian Orphanage, and the middle and high-school students living at [the high school of Surp Haç] Tıbrevank. With the intention of "saving the remnant," great efforts were made under the tiring conditions of the period. And the only way to "save this remnant" was education. Education and more education.[8]

It is important to emphasize that the patriarchate's efforts to "save the remnant" were driven by concerns over the assimilation of Armenians in Anatolia and the desire to strengthen its demographic and institutional base in Istanbul. Viewing education as the key to preserving Armenian identity, the patriarchate prioritized bringing school-aged children to the city, where they could attend institutions like the Şişli Karagözyan Armenian Orphanage and Tıbrevank. By focusing on education, the patriarchate sought not only to safeguard the language and culture of the remaining Armenians but also to ensure their integration into Istanbul's Armenian community. These efforts intensified in the 1950s as the migration of Armenians to the city became a deliberate strategy to counter the erasure of Armenian identity in Anatolia.

FIGURE 4.1 Students not only studied and played sports here, but also lived on campus, creating a comprehensive educational environment that combined academic, physical, and residential life for Armenian male students from Anatolia.

FIGURE 4.2 The renowned library of Surp Haç Tıbrevank, which once housed significant leftist literature in the Armenian language, smuggled from the Soviet Union into Turkey during the 1950s and 1960s. As is customary in Turkish schools, a portrait of the republic's founder, Mustafa Kemal, is prominently displayed alongside texts of his speeches. A special shelf labeled "Atatürk Kitaplığı" (the Atatürk Library) holds additional books about Atatürk and further texts of his speeches.

Zakarya and I met in Istanbul in November 2009 to talk about his memories and experience of Surp Haç Tıbrevank (the Seminary of the Holy Cross), where he attended high school. Before speaking about Tıbrevank, he highlighted its background and the reason behind its establishment in 1952. In the late Ottoman period, Zakarya explained, the Armenian Seminary at Armaş (near İzmit) was the main theological school for the education of Ottoman Armenian clergy and a pilgrimage center. Armaş was also a center of culture, arts, and literature, and housed a printing press.[9]

Even before the Ottoman period, Armenian monasteries in Anatolia traditionally acted as schools, not only for clergy but also for laypeople. Such schools had a broad curriculum, covering subjects from theology to literature, history, medicine, and philosophy. Monasteries were educational centers similar to today's universities, Zakarya explained. "They preserved and disseminated knowledge; manuscripts of geography, history, and literature were written or copied there. In monastery manuscripts, you would find all sorts of knowledge. Monks used to document whatever was around them." Armaş, however, was unique, because it was the main Armenian school and a self-governing body, as the system of monasteries had been in place long before the Ottoman Empire. Around 1915, the Armaş Seminary was destroyed—burnt and completely demolished—and its name was subsequently changed to the current Turkish name, Akmeşe. Following its destruction, the majority of its faculty and students were relocated to the Armenian Seminary in Jerusalem.

After World War I, therefore, the Armenians who remained in Turkey were left without a theological school to train clergy. Zakarya said that it was impossible to gain permission to establish a community institution, given the law that prohibits the establishment of institutions based on ethnic or religious identity—a law that runs contrary to the minority protection articles of the Lausanne Treaty. The law only allows religious institutions to exist if the institutions had been established in the Ottoman period.[10] As a result, all of the functioning Armenian schools, churches, hospitals, and orphanages were founded during the Ottoman period, which makes Tıbrevank a unique exception for Zakarya. Yet, when Tıbrevank was founded in 1952, it was not established as a purely new Armenian community foundation (*vakıf*). A previous foundation carrying the same name had existed since 1860 and was used as an orphanage during World Wars I and II. Thus, the "establishment" of Tıbrevank in 1952 was, from the perspective of the state bureaucracy, the revival of an already existing Ottoman foundation.

As Turkey entered multiparty politics in the 1950s, Armenians were able to obtain permission to open Tıbrevank because of the good relationship the community had with the ruling Demokrat Parti (DP).[11] At the time, Turkey had no Armenian seminary and the patriarchal seat was vacant, so the community advocated for the opening of a seminary, especially given that the Armenian patriarch must be of Turkish citizenship by law. Hence, it was necessary to have a theological school in Turkey that would prepare future clergy, including patriarchs and bishops.[12]

Surp Haç Tıbrevank was thus envisioned and founded by Patriarch Karekin I Haçaduryan as a *tıbrevank*, a theological seminary. Haçaduryan was elected as the Armenian Patriarch of Constantinople in 1951 by the Holy Synod, a position he occupied until his death in 1961.[13] He was a Turkish citizen from Trabzon, and hence he was known as *Trabzontsi*.[14] Many Tıbrevank graduates spoke with admiration of Haçaduryan's commitment, saying that he accepted his post on the condition that the government would approve the opening of a theological seminary. Because he had himself been a student at Armaş, the new patriarch envisioned Tıbrevank as a revival of the destroyed seminary. Furthermore, several graduates of the school told me that the successful opening of the school was partly due to the pressure exerted by the United States on the Turkish government during the Korean War (1950–1953), when Turkey supported the U.S. military by sending supporting troops to Korea, which led to the admission of Turkey into NATO in 1952.

When I met Nubar, who was both a graduate of the school and had previously held an administrative position in it, he explained that when it opened for the 1953–1954 academic year, Tıbrevank had thirty-three Anatolian pupils. Those pupils were recruited by an Armenian priest named Sahak Vartabed, who was sent by Haçaduryan to explain the mission of the school to Armenians in Anatolia.[15] Nubar was keen to demonstrate Haçaduryan's vision, which extended beyond the future of the school and seminary to have a positive impact on the entire Armenian community in Istanbul. "The patriarch did not only want to solve the problem of lack of clergy," he explained, "rather, he also saw the education of Armenians as of paramount importance for their future in Turkey." Nubar continued, saying that the patriarch's vision of the school was demonstrated when Haçaduryan expressed in the inauguration speech his hope that the pupils would "become what they want to be." The aim of the patriarch was not to prepare all students for priesthood: at one point, the school had 125 pupils, and the patriarch knew that the community did not need so many priests. Even though Surp Haç Tıbrevank was functioning like other non-Muslim minority high schools (*lise* in Turkish), the fact that it was a theological seminary (*tıbrevank*) as well, students who wished to receive ecclesiastical training had the option to stay longer and obtain it.

Meeting the graduates of Tıbrevank in Istanbul and Paris, I found a sense of pride and solidarity among them. Whenever they emigrated, they established alumni clubs. Zakarya continued:

> At Tıbrevank we shared everything, from pocket money to clothes. Perhaps this is the reason behind the leftist tendencies of its graduates as well. Tıbrevank enabled us to create wealth from our poorness; and by wealth, I don't mean money. Have you heard the expression "to become something out of nothing" [*yoktan var olmak*]? This is what Tıbrevank gave us.

Echoing Zakarya, Nubar said that many graduates continue to be proud of the school because they all came from very humble backgrounds. "We started from nothing" (*sıfırdan geldi*), which literally means "we started from point zero" and succeeded. In the same sense, Tigran, a graduate of the school and now a medical doctor said that Armenians owed who they are to Tıbrevank, saying, "If I hadn't gone to Tıbrevank, I would have remained uneducated in my village, or not even existed!"

The school was also regarded as having benefited the entire Armenian community in Turkey. As Nubar said, "[The] school might be small and simple, but it had a big effect. You can imagine how much a well-educated person can contribute to many; one person from Anatolia might have affected the lives of a thousand in Istanbul." Zakarya emphasized that Tıbrevank enriched not only the Armenians, but Turkish society at large:

> The graduates of the school contributed a lot to Turkey: its graduates became professionals, engineers, medical doctors, dentists, and lawyers. Also, important publishing houses such as Adam and Aras are owned by graduates; Mıgırdiç Margosyan, an important literary figure, was once the director of the school. There are many graduates who became successful and even important figures outside of Turkey, from bishops to university professors, and even an actor in the Royal Shakespeare Company, Kevork Malikyan, who also acted in *Midnight Express*!

The graduates of the school attributed their own professional and life achievements to the school for opening up educational opportunities for them in Istanbul and affording them the prospect of pursuing education at the city's top universities. Meanwhile, the Armenian church saw the mission of the school to be salvaging the remaining Armenians in Anatolia by moving them to the city, where they could have the same educational opportunities and institutional support as the Armenians of Istanbul.

The story of Tıbrevank has been narrated as a success that led to an Armenian cultural renaissance in Istanbul, but the efforts encouraging Armenians' migration out of their Anatolian locales came at a price. In his autobiographical novel *Tespih Taneleri* (*Prayer Beads*), the former director of the school and renowned Armenian novelist Mıgırdiç Margosyan offers a more critical perspective on the school. While it is often celebrated for providing education to Anatolian Armenians and enriching the Armenian community in Istanbul, Margosyan sheds light on the unintended consequences of its success. He expresses regret that the school, by drawing Armenian youth away from their towns and villages in Anatolia, contributed to the depopulation of Armenian communities, leaving their cities and villages even more vulnerable to erasure. In his novel, Margosyan depicts the arrival of the representative of Patriarch Haçaduryan in Anatolia to recruit Armenian male students for Tıbrevank, presenting three distinct reactions from the parents of potential students:

"Welcome, respected sir [*effendi*]. The orders of our respected patriarch are a duty for us. May Tıbrevank be blessed! However, we cannot send our sons to this school. Instead of studying there and becoming priests or *vertebed*,[16] it is better that they stay here. They will be nurtured with our values and manners [*terbiye*], will learn to master a craft [*zanaat*] and will form their own families here. Our roots [in Anatolia] have already dried out like an almond tree during *seferberlik*,[17] shall we consciously dry out our offspring by sending them to Istanbul to become priests [*vertebed*]? Would such a thing ever be possible?!"

" We have reverence for the commands of our respected patriarch because he is first and foremost our father, our spiritual leader, and therefore thinks for our best. However, we also wish to see our children grow up, get married, and form their own families. So that we can give them the names of our brothers, sisters, mothers and fathers, whom we lost during *Kafle*, so the fire of our hearts can be extinguished [*ciğerimizin ateşi sönsün*]."

" I really do not understand this! Are there no Armenian kids in Istanbul? Why are they not registering them in the school, and instead coming and taking our children? Forty years have passed since the *Kafle*. And no one ever called us or asked about us. Now is that fair?"[18]

According to Margosyan's novel, Armenian parents regarded the school as depleting the remaining Armenian population in Anatolia and not as an effort to save them. These three responses encapsulate an enduring grief over the loss of family and community experienced during the genocide, coupled with a deep yearning to rebuild what had been shattered. For these parents, the genocide was not a distant event relegated to the past but an ongoing reality that continued to shape their present and future.

The enduring impact of the genocide is further reflected in the terminology used by parents in Margosyan's novel, as they discuss their experiences and losses through localized language that reveals how Armenians experienced the genocide differently across various locales, shaped by regional contexts and specific historical circumstances. One parent employs the term *seferberlik*, a Turkish word often associated with the Armenian genocide, which essentially denotes the mobilization of troops during wartime, indirectly alluding to the Armenian killings. Another parent uses *kafle*, a Turkish term for "caravan," to describe the mass deportations of Armenians to the Syrian Desert that transpired during the genocide.[19]

Furthermore, wanting to keep their children, who carry the names of their perished family members, demonstrates the ways in which Armenians continued to live in the shadow of the genocide in Anatolia, the very landscape upon which the genocide took place. Margosyan emphasizes that the genocide was not rendered in the past, but continues in the present: Armenians were, and still are, "living in the future created by it,"[20] to use Saidya Hartman's expression for speaking about the afterlives of slavery in the United States. Through the stories of these three fictional parents, Margosyan brings to light an often-silenced aspect of Tıbrevank's history. While the school is commonly celebrated as a success story that enriched the Armenian community in Istanbul, Armenians in Anatolia perceived the patriarchate's plan to relocate their children to Istanbul as a setback. Margosyan offers a vision of the future that contrasts sharply with that of Armenian institutions in Istanbul. While the patriarchate saw urban consolidation as the path to safeguarding Armenian identity and demographic presence, Margosyan's narrative emphasizes the importance of preserving a connection to Anatolia as integral to Armenian survival and continuity. For these parents, sending their children away meant further eroding what remained of their communities, making it even more difficult to rebuild in the aftermath of destruction. Anatolian Armenians had already grappled with the repercussions of the state's failure to protect them from land seizures and the abduction of their children. With the arrival of the patriarch's representative, they now faced another attempt to promote the emigration of the new generation out of Anatolia, this time initiated by the Armenian Patriarchate.

DISMISSALS OF LOCALLY INFLECTED ARMENIANNESS IN ISTANBUL AND FRANCE

Upon their arrival in Istanbul, Armenians from Anatolia faced a certain stigma. Houri (see chapter 3), a woman from Sasun who had moved to Istanbul, had to contend with Armenians from the city who met her with dismissive attitudes, failing to regard her as Armenian:

> You miss where you come from, and it was not easy for us to stay in Sasun, and it was not easy to live in Istanbul. My mother covers her hair, for example. From our looks and lifestyle people think we are Kurds. In Istanbul, I live as a stranger to my own culture, and this culture is dying with me. My own heritage is dying, the Armenian dialect of Sasun, too, is being forgotten. Once there was an event here in the Armenian church hall, and I sang in Armenian. Then one of the organizers told the audience, "Look at our girl, she came here with no knowledge of Armenian. Now she can sing in it." Hearing this, I felt uncomfortable and replied, "I came to Istanbul with no knowledge of *Turkish*! But I did speak Armenian and Kurdish." And the guy told me, "But your Armenian [dialect of Sasun] is not really Armenian!"

Similarly, Mıgırdiç Margosyan reflected on his experience upon moving from Diyarbakır to attend one of the Armenian schools in Istanbul, saying: "The Turkish word 'Gavur' and Kurdish 'filla' have been replaced by the jeering, ridiculing words of the Armenian children in the orphanage: Hurry, come and see, Kurds have come from Anatolia."[21] This comment implies that during his time in Diyarbakır, Margosyan endured racist slurs in Turkish and Kurdish due to his Armenian identity.[22] However, upon relocating to Istanbul, he faced a different form of derogatory language when Armenians in the city, to his surprise, referred to him as a "Kurd." The prevailing perspective among Armenians who have emigrated from Anatolia is that Armenians depart southeastern Anatolia as Armenians, only to be received by the city's Armenians as Kurds; in Istanbul, they are consistently viewed as outsiders and frequently marginalized. It is worth highlighting that when Armenians in Anatolia are subjected to such slurs by both Kurds and Turks, despite the prejudice and hostility they face, their identity as Armenians is still acknowledged. However, when Armenians in Istanbul label Anatolian Armenians as Kurds, they effectively erase their Armenianness, denying them the opportunity to self-identify and express a distinct Armenian experience that deviates from the standardized and institutionalized narrative in Istanbul.

In *Tespih Taneleri*, his autobiographical novel, Margosyan also underscores the tension that exists between Anatolian Armenians and those in Istanbul through the conversation between the locals and the visiting priest, the *vertebed*: "Respected *Vertebed* . . . do not get me wrong, but we are not on very good terms with our Armenian brothers in Istanbul. If you ask me why this is the case, I would like to tell you briefly, without causing you headaches."[23] The man went on to tell the *vertebed* the story of a cloth dealer called Bezaz Anto, who went to Istanbul to buy cloth for his trade.[24] Anto decided to visit the well-known Armenian cemetery in Şişli before he returned to Diyarbakır. Entering the cemetery, he was surprised to see the caretaker (*kapacı*) well-dressed in a suit, a tie, and a hat, standing at the entrance to the cemetery, and was equally surprised by the cemetery's beauty and well-maintained appearance. He then noticed a man praying in front of a grave, so he went and prayed with him. After the prayers, he introduced himself in Armenian, but when he saw the agitation this caused the man, he introduced himself again, this time in Turkish, saying: "Brother, I am Armenian! My name is Antranig Bezazyan . . . I come from *Diyarbakır*." The man replied, "What can I do? There are many Armenians here!" The man telling the story then finished by telling the *vertebed* that in Anatolia "we are ready to die for being Armenian, and this man is telling me that he does not care about my Armenianness. Would such a thing ever be possible?!"[25] This vignette from Margosyan's novel highlights the profound disparity in the perception of Armenianness between Anatolian Armenians and those in Istanbul. For the Anatolians, maintaining their Armenian identity and staying on their land were resilient acts of survival in the face of the Turkish state's efforts to displace them and erase their history from Anatolia. In contrast, those in Istanbul were already an established community in the aftermath of the Lausanne Treaty, with community institutions and a strong demographic presence.

The stigma experienced by Anatolian Armenians endures as they relocate to France, often imposed by the Armenian diaspora there. When I first met Madame Shushan, who headed one of the Armenian culture centers in Alfortville, I asked for her help in meeting Armenians from Turkey. I had known that Armenians from Turkey send their children to local Armenian schools and local cultural centers where they can join other children in activities designed to promote the usage of the Armenian language outside the classroom. Shushan's first reaction was to express her frustration about the Armenians from Turkey. She complained that they "do not open up to strangers easily; they don't even speak to us [French Armenians]!" Shushan then explained the difficulty in meeting Armenians from Turkey, whom, to my surprise, she referred to in French as *les turcs* (the Turks), saying, "There is nothing to know! I can tell you what you need to know!" She went on, explaining, "Those *Turks* come to France, speaking only Turkish, watch Turkish television, and do not know or say anything about the genocide. When they go to church, they pray like Muslims: opening up their arms, and women cover their hair. A few weeks ago, as two women entered the church speaking Turkish, a [French-Armenian] woman had a fit, saying, "we are here [in France], so as not to hear this language again!"

Shushan labeled recent Armenian migrants from Turkey as Turks throughout our conversation, instead of using the common reference for them in France *les Arméniens de Turquie* (the Armenians of Turkey) or *Bolsahayer* to specify the Armenians from Istanbul.[26] Shushan's response wasn't an isolated incident; instead, it reflected a prevailing perspective among French Armenians with nationalist tendencies. Her criticism of recent Armenian migrants from Turkey reveals markers of belonging to the Armenian diaspora in France. Such markers include speaking Armenian and advocating for the recognition of the genocide: for many in the diaspora, both constitute the *Hay tad*, "the Armenian cause," which they believe every Armenian should advocate for. Shushan's anxiety comes from the fact that migrants from Turkey do not meet the strict criteria of belonging within this diasporic space, coupled with the tension that often exists between newcomers and older migrants.

Naming Armenians from Turkey as "Turks" is a symptom of the French Armenians' misconception of the Armenian predicament in Turkey and their experience of the afterlives of the genocide. Many Armenians from Anatolian cities and villages do not speak Armenian due to the systematic policies of the Turkish state to shut down Armenian schools and the forced immigration of Armenians from Anatolia to Istanbul. Additionally, Armenians from Turkey do not speak comfortably and publicly about the genocide, in contrast to many diasporic Armenians, due to societal and self-imposed restrictions on the topic in Turkey. Cumulatively, all these specificities of the Armenian experience in Turkey have to an extent de-Armenianized Turkish Armenians in the eyes of French Armenians like Shushan. Armenians have become outsiders both in Turkey and among diasporic Armenians. An Armenian from Istanbul once explained this dilemma by saying, "We leave Turkey as Armenians, and arrive in France as Turks!" While Armenians in Turkey are treated as a foreign minority, in the diaspora, they are often perceived as a group that has relinquished their identities and embraced the language and culture of those responsible for the genocide; consequently, they are regarded as complicit and even disloyal to the Armenian cause. Armenians in France are thus subjected to yet a third level of othering, where they leave Anatolia as Armenians, arrive in Istanbul as Kurds, and in France as Turks. But when some diasporic Armenians call them "Turks" in France, they reduce the Armenian survivors in Turkey to the very label that dispossessed them and robbed them of their lands and properties in Anatolia.

Contrary to the beliefs of certain members of the Armenian diaspora, the genocide in Anatolia is an ongoing issue that does not belong solely in the past; instead, it remains a vivid component of the daily existence of Anatolian Armenians. This was evident in the narratives of Ara and Houri in the preceding chapter and in the statements made by Margosyan's characters when the *vertebed* visited to recruit students for Tıbrevank. Due to the different political and social realities of Armenians in Turkey, Armenian migrants from Turkey relate to the genocide in a different way from diasporic Armenians. They may not be able to speak about it publicly and use it for political activism, or even to employ the term "genocide," but it is still an inseparable aspect of their lives, as well as of their family histories and social memory. Moreover, the mass extermination they endured is not solely encapsulated by the generic term "genocide," which is the conventional expression employed in international law and by Armenian institutions advocating for international recognition of the genocide. They depict the genocide using local terminology, reflecting the language prevalent in their local communities and the specific manner in which the genocide is remembered in particular regions of Anatolia. In contrast, for the diasporic institutions, the genocide happened in a different temporality (during World War I) and geography (Anatolia). It is thus receding to a distant past in a now-foreign land. Simultaneously, the Republic of Armenia, after its independence from the Soviet Union in 1991, has come to replace Anatolia as a "homeland" (a point to which I return in the next chapter).

The alienation of the diaspora from Anatolia is demonstrated in the ways in which it claims ownership of the definitive, authentic Armenian culture. However, such claims by the diasporic community do not remain unchallenged by Anatolian Armenians in France. During one of the Armenian music classes in Paris, two Armenian women were speaking about a grocery that sells ready-made Armenian dishes. One of them was recommending that the other try the *imam bayıldı*.[27] During the conversation, I overheard Ara's sister commenting on this conversation in Turkish, to a Turkish friend of mine who was visiting that day from Istanbul: "They [diasporic Armenians] think that this food is the real thing, but they only hear about those dishes from their parents or grandparents. For us [Armenians from Turkey], we cook it ourselves."

Upon learning about the dispute regarding the use of Turkish in the church, Krikor responded with a remark: "Yes, they don't want to hear *that* language! But they only know how to remember the Turkish that their own grandparents used to speak with them!" This observation underscores the diverse linguistic backgrounds among Ottoman Armenians, some of whom spoke Kurdish, Turkish, or Arabic as their mother tongue while identifying with the Armenian church, as Krikor emphasized.

Shushan pointed to the deeper anxiety that Armenians from Turkey look, behave, and sound like the enemy when she explained, "When they go to church, the *Turks* pray like Muslims: they open up their arms, and women cover their hair." Such an observation is essentialist in an Orientalist way, casting Turks and other Muslims in France as somewhat backward populations that cannot or are unwilling to adapt to the French and European ways. It is evident that when Shushan remarked on how Armenians pray "like Muslims," she associates eastern Christian practices with Islam, rendering Catholic mannerisms in France to be the acceptable way to behave like Europeans. In France, Armenians became "westerners" and the recent migrants from Turkey are expected to reeducate themselves and imitate the assimilated French Armenians. In contrast to the Armenian diasporic understanding of identities as embedded in binaries, Armenians who continued living in Anatolia and facing the continuous efforts to dispossess them from their land, history, and culture speak of complex yet fluid relationships with the local Kurds and Turks, as the next section discusses.

THE INTERTWINED COMMUNITIES OF THE PAST

Behind his cash machine in his grocery shop in Alfortville, Haig had a digitally produced colored picture of Hrant Dink surrounded with artificial yellowish roses, right below a small icon of Christ. Armenian wine, Turkish rakı, and French cognac were to be found on the right of Dink's picture, and mixed nuts from Lebanon and Turkey on the left. The shop had a plethora of products from different parts of the world from which members of the local Armenian population had originated, with Armenian, Turkish, Arabic, Greek, and Latin scripts juxtaposed.

On a usual day, Haig needed nothing more than to be asked the simple question "how are you?" to start complaining about how tired he was from the long hours of work at his shop in Alfortville. "Fatigué! Travail, travail, travail (Tired! Work, work, work); I have been awake since five in the morning," he would say with a wrinkled face. Though he was born in Sasun, his family left for Istanbul because of a land dispute with the local Kurds that turned into a conflict, as a consequence of which his sister's husband was killed. Haig's father sought the

FIGURE 4.3 Haig's grocery store in Alfortville, which serves the local Armenian community as well as multiple migrant communities from the wider Middle East and Francophone Africa who live in the area. After the assassination of Hrant Dink, Haig placed a portrait of Dink near the cash register, surrounded by flowers in memoriam. The store provides a glimpse into the Armenian world of Alfortville, offering products from Armenia, Turkey, and Lebanon, representing flavors of their countries of origin. Above Dink's portrait is an icon of Christ giving a blessing, set up in a semi-altar arrangement that overlooks the cashier. The photograph captures the blending of cultural, religious, and political elements that shapes aspects of the Armenian diasporic experience in Alfortville.

help of the *jandarma* (military police), who told him that they could not interfere in the dispute. Haig's grandfather then rented a truck (*kamyon*) and drove the entire family and their belongings to Istanbul in 1966, only three months after Haig's birth.

The majority of Haig's family left Turkey in the early 1980s. He once told me that they were unable to regain any of their property left in Sasun: "We still have the *tapu* [land deed], but what value does it have? If I go back," Haig said while pointing with his right hand to his throat, "they will kill me." Nevertheless, he would often outspokenly compare his life in France with that in Turkey, where he had more time off because he used to work only five days a week. "You see, people in the villages exchange products. Here! Look! People don't work for the value of work, but they work for *this*," he said, indicating the twenty-euro bill that I had just given him to buy my groceries.

Haig did not bear grudges against either Kurds or Turks and often blamed his predicament on "politics" and "religion," which is why he always avoided talking about both. After a few moments of silence, Haig went back to the story of their exodus from Sasun: "the day the family left Sasun, everyone was in haste. As the *kamyon* was leaving, some Kurds were throwing stones at us, while our Kurdish neighbor came after us to bid us farewell. She took me in her arms to kiss me. After leaving the village, my mother realized that they had forgotten me with our Kurdish neighbor. I was barely three months then. Driving back to the village, my parents found me in the arms of our Kurdish neighbor waiting for my parents to come back." Haig told me that the family had an intimate friendship with their Kurdish neighbors that his mother was shedding tears for having to leave them. I asked him if he would take his children to visit Sasun. He replied, "Non, c'est fini! It is finished for them, they are here now, they are French, and they are like everyone else here."

In his first novella, *Gavur Mahallesi* (*The Infidel's Quarter*), Margosyan paints a picture of the intertwined lives of people of disparate ethnic and religious groups in his early years in Diyarbakır, where communities and languages coexisted, forming one multifaceted culture in the city. The daily lives in *The Infidel's Quarter* feature Armenians, Kurds, Chaldeans, Assyrians, Jews, and Turks,[28] and the narrator himself uses Armenian, Kurdish, and Turkish interchangeably.[29] In the opening scene of the novella, Margosyan presents the intertwined nature of residents' lives when Meryem, an Armenian woman, died and Uso, the caretaker of Surp (Saint) Sarkis Church, rang church bells to announce her death. The *ezan*, the Muslim call for prayer, resonated while merging with the church bells, forming one soundscape in the city. Margosyan describes:

> Uso's unceasing church bell ringing made the Muezzin from the nearby Sheikh Matar Mosque lament "God give patience" as he remembered his duty and went to call out for prayer from atop the historical four-booted minaret.

> "Allahu ekber, Allahu ekber! . . ."
> "Ding-Dong, ding-dong"
> "Allahu! . . ."
> "DING"
> "Ekber!"
> "DONG"

When the Muezzin Nusret, whose huge nose had turned the color of tomatoes in the cold, came back down [from] the minaret, Uso was still pulling on the church bell rope with his short rotund body. He was secretly glad that Muezzein Nusret had given up and came back down the minaret. The sound of the church bell continued to ring out, ring out far away. It caused all sorts of confusion as it reached the frozen ears of every Armenian.[30]

Despite the power discrepancy in Anatolia, Margosyan in this scene hears the *ezan* and bells as weaving an auditory tapestry that reflects the city's harmony, where Uso continued ringing the bell while Muezzin Nusret was calling for the *ezan*.[31] As Margosyan paints it, the merging of the bell and the *ezan* become counterpoint; while different, they form one symphony that is unique to the city and its inhabitants.

Later, in the second chapter (titled after the neighborhood midwife "Kure Mama"), Margosyan specifies that he uses the collective plural pronoun "we" in a specific time and place, which he defines as "those born in Diyarbakır during a certain time."[32] Therefore, his collective "we" is not limited to the Armenians of the city or to Armenians elsewhere in the abstract sense of belonging, as is the case with the nationalist ideologies of states and diasporic institutions. Instead, he articulates Armenians belonging to this city as being intertwined with other communities and as being focused on a very specific environment, a locality with known neighbors and social relations. In this sense, when Anatolian Armenians open their arms in prayer and women cover their hair while in church—as Shushan complained—they resemble their Kurdish and Turkish Muslim neighbors, as well as the local Christians with whom all share the same geographies and cultural practices.

As the Armenian community's understanding of what "Armenianness" means shifted both in Istanbul and Paris, such practices came to be regarded as a contradictory form of being Armenian. Armenians in Istanbul and Paris negotiated ways to assimilate into Turkish and French societies, and in the process, the parameters of being Armenian became monolithic and homogenized. Moreover, the dispersion of Anatolian Armenians had disrupted the close connections that Armenians had maintained with both their fellow Armenians and non-Armenians. This disruption represents another facet of denativization, one that brought an end to shared locally specific traditions—cultural, religious, and linguistic traditions such as those that Margosyan depicts in his novels and those Haig discussed.

The ethnographic encounters discussed in this chapter shed light on the various ways in which tensions surface when Armenians from Anatolia come into contact with Armenians in Paris and, to a lesser extent, with those in Istanbul. This tension stems from the fact that a considerable portion of the Armenians in both cities do not have immediate personal connections to Anatolia. Instead, the Armenian language, culture, history, and even cuisine are acquired in a more abstract manner, lacking the organic transmission that often occurs within familial or community settings, because this transmission was disrupted by the genocide. Such "authentic" cultural practices are learned from books and evolve in isolation from what Ella Shohat calls, their native "geocultural landscape."[33] By contrast, those who remained in Anatolia and lived through the aftermath of the genocide have knowledge that, though ruptured, has nevertheless been sustained socially and culturally. It is important to highlight here that the tension that exists between the Armenians from Anatolia and Istanbul also speaks to another facet of the genocide. Namely, many Armenians in Istanbul trace their families to Anatolia; therefore, they were also displaced from their geocultural landscape, even though they continue to live within the borders of Turkey, the successor state of the Ottoman Empire.[34] They have additionally assimilated within the political culture of the dominant Turkish culture as means of survival, rebuilding their lives in Istanbul after the genocide.[35]

The lives of Anatolian Armenians do not correspond to how they have been imagined by the diasporic institutions or to how the Turkish state sees them. In this context, as a denativized community, the Anatolian Armenians' experiences challenge the dominant narratives created by powerful institutions aiming to homogenize their identities within nationalistic frameworks.[36] Denativization has separated Armenians from their geocultural landscape, whether they live in Istanbul or Paris. These ruptures have resulted in seemingly contradictory perceptions of social belonging for outsiders. However, for Armenians who remained in Anatolia after the genocide, these nuances continue to be an integral part of their multifaceted and complex sense of belonging, which has not been completely standardized by a state or diasporic institutions. As Armenians establish themselves in France, they are subjected to assimilation efforts in French society, yet assimilation is also, at times, self-imposed. At the same time, they are afforded privileges that are not typically extended to the descendants of refugee or migrant communities in France, a topic explored in the next chapter.

CHAPTER 5

NEW CONCEPTIONS OF BELONGING

Armenianness Reimagined in France

I n late May 2008, the Armenian community of Alfortville, celebrated the thirtieth anniversary of the 1978 establishment of the Armenian school of Surp (Saint) Mesrop in the neighborhood.[1] Alfortville has been receiving Armenian migrants since the 1920s, and in addition to the school, the city has an Armenian Culture Center, the Armenian Church of Saints Peter and Paul (established in 1929 by the first wave of Armenian refugees), a Protestant Armenian church, and a plethora of social and political clubs. In the coffeehouses that are so essential to the everyday life of the neighborhood, patrons speak a language that merges Armenian (with its western and eastern variants), Turkish, and French.

The school's celebration took place between Thursday, May 29, 2008, and Sunday, June 1, 2008, at l'Espace Culturelle d'Alfortville, a municipally owned venue for cultural events at 148 rue Paul Vaillant Couturier that is commonly called "Le 148." The celebrations commenced with a four-day exhibition of artwork by the pupils of Surp Mesrop. As with all formal events in the Armenian community, the local mayor at the time, René Rouquet, and the hierarchy of the Armenian Apostolic Church in France attended the opening. On this occasion, a representative from the Armenian embassy was also present. The omnipresent Armenian members of the mayor's team, who worked closely with him and were on his election list, facilitated the interactions between the mayor and the community.[2] At such events involving the Armenian community, the team members typically surround the mayor as he stands or walks, sit beside him during formal ceremonies, and are the first to greet him when he arrives in his black car.

The opening speaker was Sarkis Sarkisyan. An Armenian member of the mayor's team, Sarkisyan is from Istanbul, sits on the board of the Surp Mesrop School,

(a)

(b)

FIGURE 5.1 (a) Surp Mesrop School and (b) the Armenian Church of Saints Peter and Paul. The school is built on the same grounds as the church, reflecting how both institutions collaborate to foster and maintain Armenian belonging. Together with cultural centers, they work to strengthen the community through shared religious and educational initiatives. The photograph of the Armenian Church of Saints Peter and Paul was taken following a requiem mass for those who died during the genocide. The church remains a vital hub for remembrance and identity. Both stand on Komitas Street, named after the iconic Armenian priest and composer who symbolizes resilience for many diasporic Armenians, having survived the genocide and maintained Armenian liturgical music in diasporic churches.

FIGURE 5.2 The Genocide Memorial in Alfortville, featuring children carrying a single piece of cloth made by attaching the French and Armenian flags. This symbolic merging of flags represents the way Armenian institutions in Alfortville perceive their community: as Armenians fully integrated into French society. The memorial itself reflects how the Armenian community reinforces their strong connections to their adopted homeland while commemorating the genocide that took place in Anatolia during World War I.

and is active in the administration of the church. Speaking in Turkish-accented French, he emphasized the school's important role in maintaining the Armenian language in the diaspora, especially given that the school is named after Surp Mesrop, the saint who created the Armenian alphabet in 405 CE in order to translate the Bible from Syriac into Armenian. He then thanked the mayor and the people of Alfortville for the moral and financial support they provide to the school. Mayor Rouquet followed with a short speech, which he opened by saying, "Today, the twenty-ninth of May, is an important and happy day. On this day, in 1998, the French Parliament acknowledged the Armenian Genocide of 1915." The comment about the genocide came as a surprise to me and to many in the audience, who fell silent for a few seconds before breaking into fervent applause. Rouquet was himself behind the bill that publicly acknowledged the genocide in France that year. Rouquet then echoed Sarkisyan's comment about the importance of the school in preserving the Armenian language and went on to praise Armenians' contributions to all aspects of Alfortville's history and life.

The celebrations of the thirtieth anniversary of the Surp Mesrop School ended with a concert at the Pôle Culturel, the main auditorium of Alfortville. The performance of folk, classical, and nationalist Armenian songs was billed as one of the major events of the season, and only a handful of seats remained empty. Sitting in the middle row were the mayor, the Armenian archbishop of France, and the notables of the community, well dressed in dark suits and ties. The performance was by Ensemble Naïri, directed by Haïk Davtian (who is from Armenia), and included 150 participants. It was a pan-Armenian event: the participants and audience were Armenians from France, Turkey, Lebanon, Syria, Greece, and Armenia. No matter their country or territory of origin, all raised their voices in the final songs of the concert, which expressed nationalist sentiments for Yerevan, the capital of the post-Soviet Republic of Armenia. It was a (trans)national moment, with the choir and musicians from Istanbul, Aleppo, Athens, and Beirut gathered in a suburb of Paris to sing for Yerevan—which had slowly come to replace Anatolia as a "homeland," both politically and sentimentally. Most Armenian genocide survivors, of course, are descended from Armenians from Anatolia or Istanbul.

⌘

Diasporic formation involves both *roots* and *routes*, to use Paul Gilroy's pun, embracing where people come from and where they settle.[3] Forced and voluntary migration patterns often have sociohistoric roots, with migrants and refugees choosing their destinations based on geographic proximity, language and cultural ties, colonial history, and other factors. After the genocide, the establishment of the Republic of Turkey in what was Ottoman Anatolia or western Armenia rendered many Armenian survivors who returned to their towns and villages as foreign, and those who became refugees became stateless. Armenians arrived in France as *apatride*, stateless, and were left in a liminal state in both their place of origin (the homeland) and their destination (the host country). Pierre Bourdieu uses the Greek term *atopos*, meaning "of no place" or "out of place," to describe the state of the immigrant. This term, which Bourdieu originally used to describe the Algerian migrant's experience in France, could encapsulate the Armenian predicament in both Turkey and France. Bourdieu describes the state of the immigrant as "neither citizen nor foreigner, not truly on the side of the Same not really on the side of the Other, he exists within that 'bastard' place, of which Plato also speaks, on the frontier between being and social non-being.

Displaced, in the sense of being incongruous and inopportune, he is a source of embarrassment."[4]

Armenian genocide survivors have formed significant diasporic communities in Syria, Lebanon, Palestine, Greece, Cyprus, and the United States, as well as in France. However, the particularity of the French context is that it was shaped by the French colonial interests in the Near East coupled with the diplomatic treaties signed in the aftermath of World War I. French republicanism after World War I intersected with Armenian diasporic nationalism. As a result, the Armenian diaspora in France became integrated into French society in a way specific to French social and political contexts.

The remembrance rituals for the genocide in Anatolia and the collective singing for Yerevan speak to the Armenian diasporic experience in France, highlighting a shift in the Armenian relationality to their homeland. Public events such as the Surp Mesrop anniversary, by helping to situate the ways in which Armenians built new lives in France, invite us to contemplate the centrality of local political contexts in shaping diasporic belonging.[5] This chapter investigates another aspect of denativization by examining the ways in which the genocide inaugurated a process of community formation that came into being within three homogenizing national projects: Turkish nation-state building, French assimilation policies, and the development of Armenian diasporic institutions.[6] The chapter considers the different pressures that were placed on Armenians as they made their way from Anatolia to Istanbul and finally to Alfortville. In this process, Armenians were encountering and responding to the pressures of these homogenizing projects in different ways. Consequently, this chapter discusses the assimilation of the Armenian genocide survivors in France and examines the meaning of their *nativization* in France. It sees both the Armenian claim of being "native" in their host country and the vision of the Republic of Armenia as a diasporic homeland as yet another aspect of survivors' denativization from Anatolia.

As Armenians in Anatolia who did not leave immediately after the genocide continued to be cleansed and uprooted under the Turkish republican regime, the Armenians in the diaspora were being rooted in France, with the Republic of Armenia eventually replacing Anatolia as the diasporic homeland. These two processes worked in tandem to further the denativization of Armenians from Anatolia. The previous chapter shed light on the reception of Anatolian Armenians by Armenians already living in both Istanbul and Paris. It examined both the role of the Armenian Patriarchate in Istanbul in promoting their migration out of Anatolia and the ways in which Anatolian Armenians were denied their Armenianness by the Armenians in Istanbul and in the diaspora in France. Anatolian Armenians later moved to France, where many applied for refugee status and were received by the Armenian diasporic institutional structure discussed in this chapter.

Diasporic institutions redefined and homogenized Armenianness, so that in the diaspora, genocide remembrance and speaking the Armenian language became benchmarks for defining a person's Armenianness, along with thinking of the Republic of Armenia (rather than Anatolia) as a homeland after the republic's independence from the Soviet Union. This chapter examines two central factors that contributed to this redefining of Armenianness: first, the need for Armenians to assimilate into French culture because of the French republican emphasis on homogeneity; and second, the importance of genocide as a foundational and unifying event for the diaspora. The chapter demonstrates that, by assimilating in a way that their difference could not be seen as a threat, Armenians in France have been able to continue to reproduce Armenian culture in a homogenized way. It also discusses how Armenians have been able to reposition themselves as a "native" community within France, a process that, I argue, has deepened their denativization from Anatolia.

ARMENIANS IN FRANCE: FROM REFUGEES TO DIASPORA

Since the mid-nineteenth century, foreign labor has been an important supplement to the French workforce.[7] Following World War I, France was the first European country to grant residency based on labor contracts for foreign workers, which was also essential for the postwar reconstruction.[8] The French historian of immigration Gérard Noiriel argues that despite the number of migrations to France, immigrants have been conspicuously absent from the historiography of France and that "immigration [became] 'external' to past and present-day French society."[9] In the interwar period, the number of foreign residents in France tripled, surpassing the number in all other European countries before World War II and also in the United States in 1931.[10] Despite, or maybe because of, the fact that France has the longest tradition of migration of any European country,[11] migration has been seen throughout history as problematic in France since the nineteenth century, not only by the French government, which saw the presence of the migrant workers as temporary, but also by historians and sociologists in France. Immigration was cast within a gloomy narrative of misfortune and poverty that had forced the migrants to leave their homes.[12] However, from 1968 onward, an ethnic awakening developed among France's many ethnic and migrant groups. The resulting movements included not only immigrant causes such as Berber nationalism[13] and feminist demands, but also regionalist movements among France's linguistic minorities.[14]

Concepts of displaced people as migrants and refugees, and, more generally, as foreigners developed after the French Revolution and the foundation of the French Republic. The definition and practice of nationality have led governments to establish legal definitions of populations that place foreigners outside the borders of national identification, assigning them specific rights but denying them the full civil rights granted to citizens.[15] The French Revolution, Noiriel argues, added two essential elements to the French model of immigration: a passion for politics and a defense of human rights. For that reason, from the nineteenth century to World War II, France welcomed the largest number of refugees of any European country.[16]

Though much of the literature focuses on France's negative view of North African migrants, the stigma that went hand in hand with the image of the migrant was not attached solely to North African migrants; the French also initially stigmatized Armenians, seeing them as "threatened by assimilation" and engaged in a struggle to "preserve their originality."[17] As a result, Armenians were seen as a threat to French assimilation policies in the interwar period, the initial period of Armenian immigration to France. Meanwhile, the French policy of receiving immigrants and granting them rights was far from being homogeneous: there was discrepancy in the way national policies applied on the local municipal level depending on the economic and political life of each city.[18]

Immigrants in France were stratified in three types: labor migrants, colonial subjects, and stateless (*apatride*) refugees. Unlike many other migrant communities, Armenians arrived to France in the early 1920s as stateless refugees; another important legal condition for many Armenian immigrants was being unable to work.[19] Their designation of statelessness posed a challenge, because Armenians had no home country to which they could return and thus were destined to remain in France.[20] Their condition was complicated by the Turkish government's refusal to take responsibility for the refugees who had left the cities and villages of Anatolia during and after World War I,[21] banning their return after the signing of the Lausanne Treaty, as argued in chapter 2. As refugees, Armenians did not arrive with labor contracts like labor migrants. Rather, as genocide survivors, they arrived weak, skinny, orphaned, and widowed, and were encouraged to leave France.[22]

Over the course of the twentieth century, however, refugee status has benefited Armenians in France, because refugees have been regarded more favorably than migrants in pursuit of economic betterment and jobs—as if "political persecution was the only 'excuse' native Frenchmen could accept for immigration" of foreigners into France, Noiriel suggests.[23] For example, despite the relatively small number of Spanish migrants to France in 1939, scholars have devoted much more attention to this small group than to the larger group that included economic migrants. Similarly, only those Italian migrants considered to be escaping fascism were well regarded, and Armenians were perceived solely in the reflective light of Missak Manouchian, the Armenian who played an important role in the French anti-Nazi resistance—known as the "Manouchian Affair"[24] and for having survived the Armenian genocide.

By the end of World War I, most surviving Armenians had found refuge in the neighboring Arab Ottoman provinces of Syria, Aleppo, Jerusalem, and Mosul, as well as in Egypt (which ceased to be Ottoman on the eve of World War I). Outside the ex-Ottoman Arab provinces, France hosted sixty-five thousand Armenian refugees, around 30 percent of all Armenian refugees in the Near East and Europe.[25]

The mass and forced movement of the population was not unique to Ottoman Armenians. The aftermath of World War I witnessed the disintegration of the three multiethnic empires—the Romanov, Hapsburg, and Ottoman Empires.[26] The successor nation-states that emerged devised rigid classifications of populations and had clear visions of which groups constituted the *ethnos*, or the dominant group for which a state rules by minoritizing or cleansing excluded others.[27] Their narrow definitions turned millions into minorities, refugees, internally displaced persons, and other types of outsiders created by sociopolitical demographic engineering. Estimates indicate that Europe contained some 9.5 million refugees in the 1920s.[28] The refugee problem was pan-European, and France, which needed foreign labor to rebuild its economy after losing many workers during the war, was one of the highest recipients of postwar refugees, as stated earlier.[29] The successor states of the Ottoman Empire established mono-ethnic nation-states in the Balkans that were recognized by the Paris Peace Conference (1919).[30]

According to Keith David Watenpaugh, multiple factors turned Armenian genocide survivors into a stateless population during the years 1920–1922. These include the collapse of the repatriation provisions of the Treaty of Sèvres, the unsuccessful attempts to establish an independent Armenian state, and the emergence of Kemalist policies that denied Armenians the right to return to their homeland and denaturalized those residing beyond the newly established state's borders.[31] It is in this context that Armenians arrived in France as *apatride* refugees with a French travel document that stated their reason of travel as being unable to return to their homeland.[32] This French document had two possible legal implications. First, it did not allow Armenians to return to Anatolia and deprived them of all legal rights to the properties they had left behind—thus fitting with the Turkish nationalist policies and the laws newly instituted by the Turkish parliament.[33]

Second, it created a legal framework for them to stay in France, because they could not return to their country of origin, the Ottoman Empire, which had ceased to exist. The deportees were initially resettled as refugees in camps in the coastal city of Marseille, and then many moved to northward to interior cities such as Lyon, Alfortville, and Paris. At the same time, many Armenian refugees had escaped to the newly created French mandates from the territories ceded by France in the Treaty of Ankara of 1921,[34] and this treaty made their return to Anatolia from Syria and Lebanon legally and pragmatically difficult because these territories became under the control of the Turkish nationalists. France turned Armenians into citizens in the French Mandates of Lebanon in 1924.[35] By giving the refugees legal frameworks to live in the countries of their exile, the French government practically absolved the nascent Turkish state from responsibility for the predicament of the Armenian refugees and lessened the state's obligation to repatriate or compensate the Armenians who fled or were expelled from its territory during and after World War I.[36] Furthermore, after signing the Lausanne Treaty in 1924, the French government withdrew its recognition and patronage of the Armenian government-in-exile, which France had granted in 1921.[37]

With the Turkish republican regime replacing the Ottoman state, and Ottoman Armenians unable to return to their Anatolian villages, now subject to heavy-handed Turkification projects, Armenians in France were stateless; and after the demise of the Ottoman Empire, there was no country of origin to return to. Recognizing the government's discomfort with regard to Armenian statelessness, Aram Turabian, an Ottoman Armenian who emigrated to France in the 1890s and fought in the French army, wrote to French authorities in 1938 explaining the "exceptional" circumstances of Armenians in France. He notes that unlike other foreigners in France, Armenians "have neither consulate nor ambassador to defend us, we do not even have a national homeland . . . where we could seek refuge if necessary."[38] In other words, the Armenians in France, just like the Armenian delegation at the Lausanne Conference, fell through the cracks of the nation-state order, because they did not have a state to speak in their name and advocate for their rights.

THE DIASPORA'S RESPONSE TO FRENCH DEMANDS FOR ASSIMILATION

Armenians, like other immigrants in France, did not escape the French government's policies of assimilation. Even those French officials who were aware of the extermination policies that Armenians had survived did not have sympathy for or interest in Armenians' desire to preserve their language, culture, and identity. On the contrary, French officials distrusted the refugees' lack of nationality, questioned their loyalty, and wanted to subvert their ethnic distinctiveness in society.[39] Coupled with anti-refugee sentiments in France during the economic crisis of the 1930s, this relegation of Armenians to *apatride* status shaped the way they integrated into French society. Though the economic crisis limited the number of foreign workers in factories, it reduced the number of unemployed Armenians because, in the absence of foreign workers, they relied on Armenians.[40]

The French state's aspiration for assimilation and demographic homogeneity was not a new idea in French politics. In his social history of nineteenth-century France, Eugene Weber explains the ways in which modern France is built on the assimilation of the population to the culture and language of Paris. Educated urban elites sought to "civilize" and convert the rest of France using policies similar to those later implemented in the French colonies. Weber notes that peasant language and activities were regarded as inferior, "savage" in some instances,[41] just as those of the colonized peoples in North Africa or the "New World" were.[42] In the nineteenth century, French republicanism sought to homogenize the population by removing markers of distinctiveness from public visibility. For this reason, homogenization policies have been perceived as "cultural destruction" by immigrant and regionalist groups in France.[43]

The assimilation policies in France were primarily exercised through military service and schooling in the French language,[44] which was not the predominant language of France until the mid-nineteenth century.[45] In addition to education and language, *laïcité* (secularity) has been foundational in defining the French national community. Yet Etienne Balibar argues that French *laïcité* does not mean the absence of the sacred from politics and public life, but rather, the "sacralization of the state," in which the French civic state replaces Catholicism with its own rituals, such as civic rituals and national festivals.[46] Balibar's argument sheds light on why the French assimilation model calls for homogenization and simplification and, consequently, why "groups defined according to criteria of 'ethnic' or national origin have not been tolerated." However, this general statement about the French model has an important exception: when an ethnic group does not appear to have a cohesive communal ethnic identity, this lack of unity is taken by the French state to ensure its assimilation into the national community.[47]

The attitude of the French state toward language diversity reveals the same ethic. While France hesitantly signed on to the European Charter for Regional and Minority Languages (ETS No. 148) in May 1999 (it had been available for signature since November 1992), the French Government accompanied its signature with a declaration of its understanding, citing Article 1 of France's "Reservations and Declarations for Treaty No. 148", that the "aim of the Charter is not to recognize or protect minorities but to promote the European language heritage" and that the use of the term "groups" in the Charter referring to speakers of a language (as is the case with Article 7 of the Charter) "does not grant collective rights to speakers."[48] Despite signing the Charter, France has never ratified it or put it into force to date. Whether to allow a diversity of languages and cultures is a contested topic in France, and the issue has an important genealogy that sheds light on the ideology followed by the state. As far as the French state is concerned, the protection of languages is practiced for the sake of either "European heritage" or the "heritage of France" but not as a means of preserving communal identity or collective rights. It is thus treated as an issue of history, culture, and heritage that stands apart from contemporary politics and is not considered a means of future socialization of communities living within the French Republic.

The communal attributes used in the French state's discourse and policies push heterogeneous communities toward developing a homogeneous communitarian identity. It is notable that the "Algerian community" in fact includes Arabs and Berbers, and the "Muslim community" encompasses diverse migrant communities from many countries whose members have different mother tongues and cultural traditions. Although such communities may intrinsically have some level of affiliation because they come from the same state or share confessional beliefs, the French state imposes its own view of their communal affiliation, which affects these communities' efforts to negotiate a place—whether through integration and/or assimilation—in French society. The attitudes of the French state, therefore, have played a role in pushing Armenians to develop a homogeneous communitarian identity.

Armenians themselves argued that if they were to be able to stay in France, they would need to assimilate into the society, disappearing and passing unnoticed by avoiding signs of visible difference such as speaking their native language or retaining certain sociocultural customs.[49] Armenians understood that they should not show any sign of communal affiliation, especially in public. French republicanism after World War I allowed for asserting one's specific identity, but only if one did so in the private sphere, within the walls of houses and the gates of Armenian churches and community institutions.

The French requirement for assimilation has influenced the ways in which the Armenian diasporic institutions school their members and train them to value a particular way of being Armenian: one that is homogeneous. During the thirtieth anniversary celebration of Surp Mesrop that I attended in 2008, the pictures of the school's activities that were exhibited portrayed the pupils of Surp Mesrop celebrating French Catholic customs such as Santa Claus parties before December 25, although Armenian Christmas is celebrated on January 6, the same day as the celebration of the Epiphany. Mardi Gras (Ash Wednesday) and Mi-Carême (the "mid-Lent" in the third Thursday of the Catholic Lent), none of which are traditional Armenian religious and social customs, were also celebrated. The school's mission was reflected in Sarkis Sarkisyan's comment

FIGURE 5.3 The 2009 commemoration of the Armenian genocide in Paris, held beneath the emblematic Arc de Triomphe, which also serves as the Tomb of the Unknown Soldier memorial. It is one of the few commemorative events in this symbolic location that honors events occurring outside France. The ceremony simultaneously commemorates the victims of the genocide under the Ottoman Empire and the Armenian soldiers who fought and died for France, reflecting a dual purpose of remembrance.

to me when I referred to the Armenian migrants from Turkey as "Turkophone Armenians," as most of them speak Turkish as their first language. "We have no Turkophone Armenians," Sarkisyan insisted, "we only have Armenians! In the school we teach the pupils how to be Armenian and French—Armenians who are fully integrated into French society." Our conversation was then interrupted by someone who asked him a question in Armenian, at which point the two carried on a fifteen-minute-long conversation in Turkish, using only a few Armenian words. Sarkisyan's words reflected the official stance of the Armenian school, which aims to downplay the languages of their countries of origin so as to create a homogeneous Armenian constituency that thinks of itself as primarily Armenian but as being well assimilated in France.

It is within France's assimilationist policies that Sarkis Sarkisyan's assertion—that there are no Turkophone Armenians, only Armenians, and that the school's role is to cultivate pupils as both Armenians and fully integrated French citizens—takes on its full significance. An important component of "Armenian-ness" in the context of the diaspora in France—in addition to the rigid benchmarks of genocide recognition, the ability to speak Armenian, and loyalty to the Republic of Armenia—is an ability to assimilate and be French in a way that preserves homogenized aspects of being Armenian and maintains some of the cultural distinctiveness sanctioned by the diasporic institutions.

EFFORTS TO POSITION ARMENIAN AS A "REGIONAL" LANGUAGE IN FRANCE

At a community event that was part of the thirtieth anniversary celebration of Surp Mesrop, the director of the school said that language links people with their history. Language also creates a special identity for a group: "Only an Armenian can speak Armenian. When I speak Armenian in public, others immediately ask me 'Hay es?' [Are you Armenian?]." She spoke of the importance of the Armenian language to the seven hundred thousand Armenians in France, saying that Armenian is not a "foreign" language, but an integral part of France.[50] At another event that was part of the anniversary celebration—the concert that closed the celebration—the presenter who welcomed the guests made a comment in a similar vein. "We consider Armenia a province of France. Let us not forget that the last Armenian king was exiled to Paris [in 1393].[51] As there are regional languages in France, like Provençal and Breton, Armenian, too, is a regional language in France."

Comments referring to Armenian as an integral language in France along-side other regional languages might seem puzzling—but they reflect efforts by diasporic institutions to position Armenians and their language within a French political discourse around diversity that is defined by an already existing regional diversity and not the diversity formed out of immigration. In making such a claim, Armenians characterize their presence in France as part of the already existing diversity and thus separate themselves from other immigrant communities in the country. This could be partly due to the fact that Armenians could not go back to their place of origin or a homeland, while also being under a strong pressure to assimilate in France.

After the genocide, the Armenian homeland in the Ottoman Empire was emptied of its Armenian inhabitants, the land was subsumed into the Republic of Turkey, and the eastern part of Armenia became part of the Soviet Union, creating a permanent exile for Armenians—and with this exile, came the challenge of sustaining the western Armenian language. With the dispersion of survivors, Armenians adopted the languages of their host countries, which made the maintenance of Armenian as the everyday vernacular challenging. But given the historical and religious significance of the language to Armenian self-identification, Armenian retained a symbolic value and was privileged in diasporic institutions such as churches, schools, and cultural centers.[52] Such institutions assumed responsibility for Armenians' human, ideological, and fiscal resources, a role that they had played even before the genocide.[53] These institutions assumed this role anew in the complex setting of the diaspora when, in the absence of a nation-state, Armenians faced the question of who would lead.[54]

Diasporic institutions were navigating the cultural, political, and linguistic landscape of France, where language homogeneity still is a cornerstone of the "unity of the republic."[55] Article 2 of the constitution of the Fifth French Republic, adopted on October 4, 1958, states, "The language of the Republic is French."[56] In the early 1980s, France started to recognize multiplicity in its society. Terms such as "multiracial," "multicultural," "plural," and "pluricultural" were added to the official French political lexicon.[57] This shift started during the presidential campaign of François Mitterrand (in office 1981–1995), when language diversity became an important topic in political debates. In these discussions, the use of one's native language was presented as a right for France's native communities, though not for its immigrant communities. In a famous speech delivered on March 14, 1981, before his election in Lorient, Bretagne (Brittany), a region whose native population speaks Breton, Mitterrand declared:

The time has come for a law for the languages and cultures of France that recognizes their real existence. The time has come to open wide the doors of schools, radio, and television and to allow their dissemination, and to give them all the space they deserve in public life. . . .

It hurts people in their deepest self [when] one offends their language and culture. We proclaim the right to be different [le droit à la différence]. It is disgraceful that France rejects this wealth; it is the last country in Europe to deny its components basic cultural rights recognized in the international conventions to which it has acceded.[58]

The government established the National Council for Regional Languages and Cultures (le Conseil national des languages et cultures régionales) by a decree on September 23, 1985, early in Mitterrand's presidency.[59] It is notable that the council was founded before the adoption of the European Charter for Regional or Minority Languages,[60] which was proposed by the Council of Europe in May 1992. France did not sign this treaty until May 7, 1999, and the French Constitutional Council declared that the charter did not conform to the constitution of the French Republic. The prime minister at the time, Lionel Jospin, gave a speech in parliament in defense of the charter on June 23, 1999, arguing that acknowledging regional languages and cultures would not challenge the "fundamental values but recognize and perhaps also save a heritage whose diversity enriches France." He noted that ratifying the charter "does not challenge the Republic, undermine national unity, or even weaken the French language as the language of the Republic. We all live together under the same law, we are equal in rights, but we are not all identical [nous sommes égaux en droits, mais nous ne sommes pas tous identiques]."[61]

In 2001, the department responsible for the French language, la Délégation générale à la langue française, was expanded to include, in addition to French, the category of "languages of France." This change was reflected in an extension of its official name to la Délégation générale à la langue française *et aux langues de France* (DGLFLF). The DGLFLF website says that these changes aim "to mark the government's acknowledgement of the linguistic diversity of our country."[62] The DGLFLF divides the languages of France into two categories: regional languages (*langues régionales*), which are either dialects or languages that are native to particular regions of France, and nonterritorial languages (*langues non-territoriales*), which include languages that are "nonnative" to France—i.e., the languages of immigrants. Western Armenian is acknowledged within the second category,[63] while representatives of Armenian organizations in France make the case that Armenian (in its western dialect) is a regional language.

The French government has tried to accommodate European Union (EU) laws without violating the constitution. While it did not ratify the Charter for Regional and Minority Languages, in 2008, the French parliament appended article 75-1 to the constitution to provide official recognition of "regional languages" (but not non-territorial languages). The article states, "Regional languages are part of the heritage of France [Les langues régionales appartiennent au patrimoine de la France]."[64] It is notable that while France has hosted many Italian, Spanish, and Portuguese immigrants, none of those languages are recognized as non-territorial along with Arabic vernaculars, Berber, Judeo-Espagnole (Ladino), Yiddish, and western Armenian. It is notable that these non-territorial languages are languages that do not have official status in any state.[65]

Influential diasporic institutions adopted a discourse that essentially *nativized* Armenians, rendering the Armenian language a "regional" (rather than a migrant) language in France. The term "native" in English refers to aboriginal characteristics or the ability to trace ancestry to a particular place. Some institutions that represent Armenians in the political arena have used terms such as "regional" and "provincial" to anchor Armenians in France, claiming that they are part of the historic fabric of French society (unlike any other migrant or refugee group) and have been since well before World War I. Armenians thus historicize their presence in the host country to assert they were part of France before the arrival of refugees in the early 1920s and thereby reduce the sense of this influx as a problem for the French state.

Within this context, one can understand why the director of the Surp Mesrop School and the host of the music concert said that the Armenian language is "native" to France. Being refugees with no possibility of return posed a challenge for Armenians. On the one hand, host societies insisted on their assimilation, and on the other, Armenian community leaders called for a commitment to an Armenian cultural distinctiveness that expressed an awareness of their history, especially of the genocide, and that maintained usage of the Armenian language.[66] Armenians saw challenges in the efforts, imposed or self-imposed, to assimilate into French (and other host) cultures, which left Armenians with a perpetual anxiety that after this great rupture in history and exile from their homeland their identity, language, and culture might be lost through dispersion, assimilation,[67] or migration.[68] Many also saw marrying non-Armenians (*odars*)[69] as a threat that would amount to "ethnocide,"[70] because for them, such marriages would accomplish the aim of the genocide: the loss of one's consciousness of Armenian history, culture, and language.

The French state still does not officially regard western Armenian as a regional language, but starting with Mitterrand's presidency, the government has taken special measures to promote Armenian language and culture because of the specificity of the Armenian genocide and the loss of the Armenian homeland. In fact, Mitterrand was the first French president to speak publicly about the genocide, mentioning it in a speech in Vienne (Isère) in January 1984.[71] Since then, the Armenian diasporic institutions have furthered what Khatchig Tölölyan calls their "stateless power"[72] to pressure the French state to take action in two main arenas: to formally designate the Young Turks' mass annihilation policies as "genocide" and to institute measures to promote Armenian language and culture in France as a result of surviving mass annihilation.[73]

While national efforts to gain acknowledgment for non-French languages started in 2001 with the DGLFLF, regional efforts to acknowledge western Armenian began earlier. As illustrated by Aram Turabian's 1938 letter, Armenians constantly feel the need to reassert their loyalty and to remind the French state of their sacrifices for French causes. This spirit also fueled the letter written by the mayor of Alfortville to allow the use of Armenian language in schools. A proposal submitted to the French state on February 2, 1983, by the mayor of Alfortville at the time, Joseph Franceschi (in office 1965–1988), suggested using Armenian in state exams. The letter acknowledges "the efforts made in favor of respecting regional identities" and continues:

> We should not forget that there are ethnicities whose identity should be equally respected... This is the case of the important Armenian community in France. [...]
>
> A number of the survivors of what no one fails to consider the first genocide of the twentieth century have found refuge on our soil.
>
> The majority of them, as well as their descendants, have acquired French nationality. They participate actively in the life of our country, and many among them ... have in the dark hours of our history united in the resistance against the Nazi oppressor.[74]

The mayor's argument was based primarily on the Armenians' experience of genocide and their participation in French national causes. In this way, he was able to make the case for the exceptional treatment of Armenians and the western Armenian language in France. The sections in the second half of this chapter focus on how loyalty to France has paved the way for gaining acknowledgment for and the official remembrance of the Armenian genocide and, ultimately, nativizing Armenians in France.

While the discourse of diasporic institutions in France sought to nativize Armenians, it was achieved through historicizing their presence in France by highlighting key moments such as the exile of the last Armenian king to France and the fact that Armenians fought and died for French causes during the World Wars I and II. Being descendants of genocide survivors who lost their homeland permanently and had no state to go to has emphasized the reason why they needed to have a special status in France. It is in this context that the nativization of Armenians in France has worked in tandem with denativizing them from their Anatolian homeland.

THE CENTRALITY OF GENOCIDE REMEMBRANCE FOR THE DIASPORA

Scholars often divide Armenian communities into two groups: those living in the ancient homeland and those living in the widely dispersed diaspora.[75] However, the diaspora is far from monolithic, not only because of the diversity of its populations but also because of the different lands of origin and destination. Additionally, Armenians tend to differentiate between two categories within the broader diaspora: the Armenian trade colonies (*kaghutahayutiun*) that predate the genocide, which existed as early as the sixth century, and the diaspora (*spiurk*)[76] that formed in the aftermath of the genocide.[77] The genocide therefore has been described as a "founding event"[78] or "founding moment"[79] of the diaspora—making it what Veena Das calls a "critical event" that marks contemporary Armenian history and a temporal divide between what was experienced before and after the event.[80] Many Armenians idealize the time before the genocide when they were still living on their lands within a diverse Ottoman Empire, seeing the genocide as a rupture to the imperial order that Armenians were part of. The genocide and the diaspora became central to affirming and reproducing individual and communal Armenian identity[81] and are mostly regarded as unique markers for western Armenians, who lived in Ottoman Anatolia, known by many as western Armenia. By contrast, eastern Armenians—those who lived in the lands of the Russian or Persian Empires, or who later lived in Armenia, Russia, or Iran—were not the direct victims of the genocide. Of course, the distinction between these two categories is not rigid, as some genocide survivors escaped to Soviet Armenia during the genocide, and more than forty thousand genocide survivors migrated to Soviet Armenia from the Middle East, Greece, Bulgaria, and France between 1921 and 1936 (a migration that was dubbed "repatriation").[82] It has been estimated that after World War II, as many as a hundred thousand Armenians migrated to Soviet Armenia from the diaspora.[83] The main migration took place from 1945 to 1949.

The genocide and its denial became central to the contemporary Armenian experience and political engagement in the diaspora. Consequently, Armenians saw themselves as "a nation of victims," first through the violence of mass killings, then through the denial of their nationhood by the Turkish state.[84] For Armenians, the genocide was also an "equalizer" of Armenian identity within heterogeneous diasporic communities.[85] Diasporic communities are diverse not only in class, education level, and the places that members inhabit, but they also carry the political, economic, regional, and linguistic variations of their homeland. These variations naturally engender competition over semiotic and political representation, control over institutions, communal funds, and recruitment of loyal constituencies or attracting cultural producers.[86] As such, genocide forced this largely heterogeneous population of Armenians—peasants, merchants, and intellectuals from all over the Anatolian plateau and Ottoman urban centers; Apostolics, Catholics, and Protestants; speakers of Armenian, Turkish, Arabic, Kurdish, and local Armenian dialects—to live together in new cultural and geographic spaces. Diasporic institutions created new concepts of "Armenianness," taking surviving the genocide as a common denominator for the refugees in the many places of their dispersal.[87]

The meaning and understanding of the Armenian diaspora thus were transformed radically. Over time, it has ceased to be a diaspora of merchants, laborers, fortune seekers, intellectuals, and political exiles; it has become instead a nation in exile, a community of victims and descendants of survivors and refugees.[88] The Armenian self-image as a "chosen people" in the biblical sense was fused with the secular idea of being a politically repressed people.[89] In other words, the Armenian church continued to play an important part for Armenian political self-perception, thus blurring the religious–secular binary.[90] In the context of the genocide, being an Armenian in the diaspora came to mean being a survivor,[91] and remembering the genocide has become one of the two benchmarks—the other being speaking Armenian—for defining one's Armenianness.[92] In the shadow of the genocide, Armenian identity, language, and culture can no longer be taken for granted. Armenians are expected to sacrifice for the family, local community, and nation to prevent assimilation into the host culture, a phenomenon known as "white genocide." After the independence of Soviet Armenia, Armenian institutions oriented more attention toward the Republic of Armenia on behalf of its national interests in addition to advocating for genocide recognition by world governments.[93]

Many Armenian institutions in the diaspora have emphasized that Armenian identity is expressed through one's commitment to the Armenian cause (*Hay tad*), which generally implies speaking the Armenian language, supporting and sending one's children to a local Armenian school, which is usually owned by the local church, and advocating for genocide recognition among other commitments of being Armenian in diasporic setting.[94] The diasporic institutions—including churches—in France and other places in which Armenians have settled have invested in schooling as a fundamental element for political mobilization and identity creation.[95]

In her comparative study of post-genocide Armenian and Jewish lives in France, Maud Mandel argues that memories of genocide have defined how Armenians and Jews have constructed contemporary understandings of communal affiliation and group solidarity. Mandel argues that it took Armenians fifty years to turn the genocide into a public symbol of their communal life in France.[96] The slow process by which the genocide was memorialized in Armenian life could reflect the fact that Armenians were refugees "seeking to establish stable home lives, rebuild a steady family economy, learn the local language, and find lost relatives."[97] While this description is true, specific case studies from Mandel's own historical research[98] and my own fieldwork in Paris reveal that many Armenian refugees resisted assimilation and integration and even refused to learn French. An Armenian woman in her sixties told me that her mother kept most of her belongings in suitcases, while her father used to read the daily newspapers for signs that they could return to their cities and villages in Anatolia.[99] In a context in which many refugees were resisting assimilation, the genocide came to be an important unifying factor, a means of smoothing out conflicting views within the diaspora and between the diaspora and the Armenian state.

THE GENOCIDE AT ITS FIFTIETH ANNIVERSARY

The commemoration of the genocide has an important history that goes back to marking the fiftieth anniversary in 1965. In the 1960s, Soviet Armenia built a monument commemorating the genocide and another for the Armenian victory over Turkish forces in the Battle of Sardarabad (1918) in order to appease Armenian national feelings and ease tensions with the diaspora.[100] Such efforts by Soviet Armenia intensified following demonstrations in Yerevan in April 1965 for the recognition of the genocide and the Turkish denial of the 1915 events during the same period. Although the first public commemoration of the genocide was in 1919,[101] and other memorial events took place, such as in Marseille in 1927,[102] the year 1965 was a turning point. The fiftieth anniversary of 1915 shifted the focus of Armenian communities—to use Tölölyan's terms—from post-genocide exilic nationalism to diasporic transnationalism, meaning that Armenians in the aftermath of the genocide have moved from the exilic mode of survival, where their ethnic identity was central, as was the case with the first generation of refugees, to the diasporic identification that evolved as later generations forged new identities and settled permanently in new places with no prospect of return.[103] With such a shift, mobilization for the recognition of the genocide became central to the Armenian diasporic state, experience, identity, and overall raison d'être. For Armenians, Tölölyan asserts, the homeland continued to play an important role in both contexts—the exilic and the diasporic.[104]

In 1965, demands for official recognition of and recompense for the horror of the Armenian genocide exploded for several reasons. First, 1965 marked the fiftieth anniversary of the beginning of the massacres, reminding many Armenians of how long they had waited for recognition, trials, or reparations. In fact, the file of Ottoman Armenians had not been opened since the totally ignored Treaty of Sèvres of 1920, which divided Ottoman lands among European empires, granting an enclave in eastern Anatolia for the establishment of an Armenian state. In addition, the increased Russification of Soviet Armenia and assimilation of diasporic Armenians in Western Europe and North America created realities and challenges for Armenians that were different than those faced by the generation who survived the genocide. It was therefore a time of despair and of existential questioning about the future of Armenians in Soviet Armenia and the diaspora. Second, despite the Istanbul tribunal sentencing eighteen defendants for crimes against Armenians, including three Committee of Union and Progress (CUP) leaders responsible for the genocide—Talaat Paşa, Enver Paşa, and Cemal Paşa, who were sentenced in absentia and escaped to other countries—Armenians felt that justice for the crimes committed against them was not served.[105] The crimes of the Young Turk regime, the predecessor of the Turkish state, went unrecognized, unpunished, and uncompensated at a time when Turkey was a member of NATO and a crucial ally for the Western bloc during the peak of the Cold War.[106]

Tony Judt's essay on the politics of memory in Europe, "From the House of the Dead," shows that the decade of the 1960s was a turning point in the acknowledgment of the Jewish Holocaust in Europe. Before then, European leaders had been "blind to the racial specificity of Hitler's victims,"[107] and the return of Jewish survivors to their home countries and cities had largely not been welcomed by local authorities or populations in Europe.[108] The first spark of change, according to Judt, happened in 1962 in West Germany, when the teaching of history in German schools started to cover the 1933–1945 period, including the extermination of Jewish Europeans. However, according to Judt, this decision was made not to offer justice to the victims of Germany but rather to build the "health of German democracy." Before 1962, German authorities had ignored and hoped to forget the Nazi period, and acknowledgment of the Jewish victims was marginal or nonexistent.[109] Also excluded from the debate about Nazism were the remaining victims, such as the Roma, Black, and Slav populations, among others. Even today, the Roma communities continue to face exclusion, evictions, and deportations across Europe with little or no attention given to such racial violence.[110]

Also in 1965, the Soviet regime started to permit national commemorations of the genocide in public, which it had previously banned, and nearly a million Armenians demonstrated in Yerevan. Two memorials were constructed, one for the genocide and another at the spot where the ragtag Armenian army had stopped advancing in 1918 in the Battle of Sardarabad.[111] In Soviet Armenia, the acknowledgment of the genocide became a catalyst in Armenian national awakening,[112] as it was the first time the event had been publicly commemorated, and the demonstrations took on a nationalist character as the crowd shouted for justice and for restoration of lost Armenian lands.[113] The Soviet authorities allowed Armenians to have a commemoration a few kilometers from the Armenian–Turkish border, which was also a significant Cold War frontier. Although the slogans in the demonstrations were against the Turkish state (not the Soviet one), many state and Communist Party functionaries in Armenia were afterward dismissed from their posts. Among those arrested were leaders of an opposition political party in Armenia.[114]

Whether in Soviet Armenia or in the diaspora, the 1965 genocide commemorations had a symbolic meaning greater than the number of people participating might suggest. It was a time that also witnessed the emergence of a new generation of Armenians, who, according to Katchig Tölölyan, were "young people who were the first post-Genocide generation in [the] diaspora to be well educated in large numbers and versed in both Armenian and non-Armenian traditions of art, thought, and politics, the stock-taking was marked by a rejection of the anti-Soviet stance of the older leadership."[115] In the diaspora, the day launched a collective effort[116] to pressure Turkey to acknowledge the genocide and to exhort other governments to extend recognition.[117] Because of the dynamics within Armenian communities, as well as the divisions of the Cold War, the genocide and Turkey had been neglected as rallying points for diasporic political activities after 1945. A critical self-assessment started in 1965 with the fiftieth anniversary commemoration.

MARCHING TOWARD KOMITAS:
THE GENOCIDE REMEMBERED

The Armenian genocide is commemorated in Paris on April 24 each year, in remembrance of the day in 1915 when many of the Armenian intelligentsia of Istanbul were arrested and killed. In other regional communes in France, the events take place on the Sunday closest to April 24. In Paris, the events take place in three locations: the Armenian Cathedral of Saint John the Baptist, the Tomb of the Unknown Soldier (Tombe du Soldat inconnu) at the iconic Arc de Triomphe (Victory Arch) facing the Champs-Élysées, and the official Armenian genocide memorial in Paris, marked by a statue of Komitas, an Armenian priest and musician who came to France to escape the genocide and who became an icon of Armenian culture in France. I will discuss the sequence of events that took place in 2009 in order to demonstrate the centrality of the genocide commemoration for the Armenian diaspora as well as including Armenians in French history and politics.

On Friday April 24, 2009, a requiem liturgy for the victims at the Armenian cathedral in Paris inaugurated a series of events. The Armenian archbishop of France presided over the liturgy with priests and deacons from all over France. The service was attended by heads of Armenian associations in France, the Armenian Catholic bishop of Paris, and high-level diplomats from the embassy of the Republic of Armenia. The church was small for the number of attendees; many could not enter to light a candle until after the liturgy. Members of Armenian cultural and political organizations distributed flyers to the many attendees, advertising everything from summer camps in Armenia and Syria to lectures, concerts, and dance performances in Paris and around France.

Walking or driving from the church, a few hundred Armenians proceeded to the site of the Arc de Triomphe, while others went directly to the corner of George V Avenue to await the demonstration at the Turkish cultural center. The arch is emblematic in French national political culture, both because it hosts the Tomb of the Unknown Soldier (installed in 1920) and because of its grand structure and location at the beginning of the Champs-Elysées. Many important events in French history, and especially those related to the World Wars I and II, are commemorated there; many ceremonies are held honoring French soldiers killed in battle. As on all French national days, a French flag hung in the middle of the Arc de Triomphe on April 24, just above the flickering flame on the Tomb of the Unknown Soldier. Armenian demonstrators stood in front of the arch holding Armenian flags, some of which had the French flag on the reverse. In the middle of the arch and in front of the flame, war veterans carried Armenian and French

FIGURE 5.4 The Komitas statue at the genocide memorial site in Paris's 8th Arrondissement. The mayor of Paris placed a floral arrangement at the base of the statue, which was complemented by red flowers added by demonstrators. The statue of Komitas serves as the official site for commemorating the Armenian genocide in Paris.

flags with inscriptions. Military bands played solemn martial music, while French and Armenian dignitaries placed flowers on the Tomb of the Unknown Soldier. The music accompanied the guests until they left the site.

While the ceremony at the Arc de Triomphe was formal and attended by government officials, the third and final event of the day was popular and did not include French and Armenian officials. A few thousand demonstrators met at the corner of the Champs-Elysées and George V Avenue in close proximity to the Turkish cultural center. The entire route, which extended from this meeting point through rue François 1er and ended at the Komitas statue by the Seine River, was closed. The marchers shouted slogans as they made their way to the statue, and a children's drummer band played at intervals. Demonstrators held Armenian and French flags: a French flag was placed at the beginning of the march, and the demonstrators held Armenian ones. A truck with loudspeakers played music, and the masses shouted anti-Turkish slogans such as "Justice, justice pour le people Arménien!" (Justice, Justice for the Armenian people!) and "Turquie, Turquie, Assassin!" (Turkey, Turkey, Assassin). The demonstrators carried a large banner that read:

24 April 1915
ARMENIAN GENOCIDE
Today the Turkish State denies the extermination
of 1,500,000 Armenian victims in 1915.
NO to a denialist Turkey in Europe.
YES to a Europe of Human Rights.

Arriving at the Komitas statue, where an official flower arrangement sent by the mayor of Paris sat at the base, demonstrators laid red flowers around the statue, and many took pictures of their children in front of it.

At the memorial, a series of Armenian speakers repeatedly called upon the French president at the time, Nicolas Sarkozy, to fulfill his promise and approve the law passed by parliament that criminalizes the denial of the Armenian genocide. The guest speaker for the day was the head of the Kurdish associations in France, who asserted the fraternal relations between Kurds and Armenians. Despite the Kurdish role in the Armenian massacres during World War I and in their forced migration from Anatolia in republican Turkey, Kurds and Armenians sometimes treat each other with fraternity, especially in the face of the Turkish state. The Kurdish speaker described the Turkish state as being "barbaric" for its practices against its Armenian and Kurdish citizens and asserted that there is "no entry for Turkey into civilization [meaning the European Union] without acknowledging the Armenian genocide." In closing, he thanked the head of the Greek-Cypriot associations in France (who had been the guest speaker in the 2007 commemoration) and asked the public to "be vigilant!" and to "fight daily for the acknowledgement of the genocide."

It is evident from these commemoration events that the genocide defined the official Armenian diasporic experience in France. Furthermore, the spokesperson's focus on "fighting daily for the recognition of the genocide" emphasizes the role that commemorations play in making the recognition of the genocide

FIGURE 5.5 This statue of an Armenian soldier, dressed in a French military uniform, stands at the entrance to the Armenian Apostolic Cathedral of Saint John the Baptist in Paris. The French inscription reads, "1914–1918 / For the Armenian volunteers of the French army / died for France." The statue underscores how Armenian volunteers, despite being of an immigrant community, fought and died for French causes. In doing so, it firmly inscribes the Armenian legacy within French history.

a focal point for the Armenian community's collective efforts, channeling the community's commitments and resources into this issue. It also demonstrates the ways in which the genocide was turned into the primary focal point for the community's political energies and became the common denominator of being an Armenian in France. In other words, to be in the diaspora means being a genocide survivor or a descendent of one and to work on gaining acknowledgment for it. The commemoration of the genocide in France is framed within a narrative that highlights the Armenian contribution to French national causes, as the next section demonstrates.

"MORT POUR LA FRANCE": EMPHASIZING ARMENIAN LOYALTY TO FRANCE

On April 23, 1965, the French daily *Le Monde* ran an article on its first page (continued on page six) entitled "The Fiftieth Anniversary of a Tragedy: The Armenian Massacres in Turkey," written by Frédéric Feydit, a French historian and a member of the Armenian Academy of St. Lazar in Venice. This article presented two arguments for officially defining the mass annihilation of Ottoman Armenians as genocide—arguments that Armenian activists evoked in their appeals to governments in France, Canada, the United States, and the European Union. The first is a statement attributed to Adolf Hitler, in which he gave orders to his military chiefs on August 22, 1939, to exterminate people of Polish race and language (many of whom were Polish Jews). Hitler said, "Who still speaks today of the annihilation of the Armenians [Wer redet heute noch von der Vernichtung der Armenier)?" The second is a telegram that Talaat Paşa (the Ottoman minister of the interior during World War I) sent on September 15, 1915, ordering the extermination of Armenians living in Turkey.[118] In the article, Feydit emphasizes Armenian loyalty to France by stating that even though a number of them had not been granted French citizenship at the time, they died for French national causes (*mort pour la France*) during World Wars I and II.[119]

The celebration of Surp Mesrop's anniversary and the commemoration of the genocide, the two ritual events discussed in this chapter, reveal the discourse adopted by influential institutions that essentially *nativized* Armenians. The genocide anniversary activities in Paris suggest that the official commemoration of the genocide is presented as an event with an important French national context and not as an ethnic marker unique to Armenians. The Armenian diaspora in France helped to bring about this official and public commemoration of the genocide—an event that, after all, took place outside France and was only remotely related to French national history or concerns. If one strategy to nativize Armenians in France was to position Armenian as a regional language, then another was to illustrate Armenian loyalty to France by emphasizing the sacrifices of Armenians who died while serving in French armies.

Many genocide memorials in France commemorate not only the Armenians massacred by factions in the Young Turk government at the time but also the Armenians who died while fighting in French armies. In keeping with Feydit's points in his *Le Monde* article, a closer look at the Komitas statue reveals that it fulfills this dual function. An inscription on the left side reads: "Homage to Komitas, composer, musicologist, and to 1,500,000 victims of the Armenian genocide of 1915 perpetrated by the Ottoman Empire"; on the right side are the words: "For the memory of the Armenian combatants engaged voluntarily and those who resisted. Died for France [*mort pour la France*]."

This strategy was reflected during the parliamentary debate about public recognition of the genocide on May 26, 1998. The mayor of Alfortville, René Rouquet, was the rapporteur for the parliamentary foreign affairs commission (Commission des affaires étrangères). As the first speaker during the session, he presented the historic and political arguments in favor of formal recognition of the genocide. Next, Jean-Pierre Masseret, the secretary of state for war veterans (*anciens combattants*), endorsed Rouquet's position on recognition. Masseret emphasized France's role in welcoming the survivors of the 1915 "events" (*événements*) and their children. He referred to Armenians as "the French community of Armenian origin" (*la communauté française d'origine arménienne*), thereby downplaying Armenians' foreign origins and highlighting their sacrifices for the French state. The community, he said, "has given all its best to France, and it fought for freedom and human dignity, which are cardinal virtues of the Republic." He added that as the minister responsible for war veterans, he knew "the contribution that the [French] community of Armenian origin brought to this fight with the price of their own blood," and he then mentioned additional instances in French history when Armenians fought for French causes.[120]

A few months after the genocide commemoration events, I expressed my puzzlement to an Armenian friend about the inclusion of Armenian soldiers who died while fighting within the French armies.[121] Krikor was the first Armenian I met in Paris; he was from Istanbul and an activist in the leftist politics in Turkey at the peak of the anti-communist strife in the 1970s before his arrival in Paris in 1978. His remark was similar to comments I have heard from other Armenians:

Do you think that Armenians had a choice in that? Do you think it would have been possible for them to gain such acknowledgement from the French state and to construct such memorials without a mention that there are Armenians who fought and died for France? I don't think it would have been possible otherwise.[122]

Some commentators have argued that in France, "assimilation leads to the 'disappearance of foreignness.' "[123] The reluctance of the French state to acknowledge the right to express one's difference[124] has pushed Armenians to look for an alternative to the stark choice between assimilation and expression of their ethnic difference. To adapt to French social and political culture, Armenians have conformed to the French republican ethic by assimilating into French society in such a way that their difference could not be seen as an ethnic marker and hence a threat.[125] One can consider such assimilation to be a form of negotiation; Armenians were establishing belonging to their host country on their own terms.[126]

The statues of Komitas and the Armenian soldier in French military uniform represent an alternative to full assimilation: they both represent a path to integration in French society and reflect the special recognition the French state has granted to Armenians to express their cultural specificities. Armenians have expressed their difference adaptively, becoming part and parcel of France by making themselves resemble native subnational groups within France. The Armenian soldier communicates the message that Armenians, like other good French citizens, fought and died for French causes; Komitas highlights the fact that as genocide survivors, Armenians have lost their homeland and have nowhere to return to. The two statues therefore narrate Armenians' distinctiveness from other migrant groups, especially those whom the French state perceives and racializes as "unassimilable," such as North African Muslims.[127]

THE "STATELESS" POWER OF THE ARMENIAN DIASPORA

In the EU member states, the regulatory power over populations, traditionally the province of nation-states, is passed upward to supranational entities (such as EU institutions in Brussels and Strasbourg) and downward through decentralization and federalization to subnational entities (such as the Basque, Catalan, Flemish, and Scottish communities).[128] As a result of these two patterns of rescaling of state power, a larger space has been made available for diasporas, migrant communities, and native communities to exist and to express themselves subnationally, as well as to make new claims on nation-states.

Diasporas ultimately pose challenges, if not a threat, to nation-states, because as Vered Amit argues the very "construction of diasporas is fundamentally about the effort to assert and sustain very particular social boundaries across space and time, to 'make oneself at home in the world' through an avowal of membership in an ethnonational collectivity."[129] Consequently, diasporas have become both sub- and transnational communities.[130] This dual state of affiliation allows diasporas to forge identities that challenge the standardized and often rigid national borders, filial belongings, and exclusive power of the state in areas such as capital, labor, ideas, information, cultural commodities, and belonging.[131]

Given the French nation-state's antipathy to groups' self-definition according to their ethnic or national origin,[132] we might ask to what extent Armenians challenged the French order. After all, Armenians posed a threat to the French establishment when they arrived in the 1920s as *apatride*, creating their own communal associations and remaining in contact with Armenians both in the diaspora and the "homeland."[133]

In contrast to the situation of Armenians in France, Armenians in the United States arrived in a society that already had ethnic subcommunities and religious pluralism,[134] and those in Lebanon and Syria were encouraged to maintain their cultural distinctiveness.[135] In the 1950s and 1960s, however, Syria and Lebanon diverged with the rise of Arab and Syrian nationalist ideologies in Syria. Unlike Lebanon, Syria moved toward a centralized state that left narrow space for confessional representation, which confined the work of the Armenian institutions—yet such relations were relaxed in the 1970s as the government reintegrated confessional groups in a corporatist system in which such groups ensured loyalty to the state in exchange for a degree of autonomy.[136]

While most post-Ottoman nationalist movements developed their exclusive nation-states and propagated their national history and language through the schooling system and media, Armenians in the diaspora have pursued similar ends through the "stateless power" of non-state institutions.[137] The concept of stateless power positions the hegemony exercised by diasporic institutions against the misconceptions that diaspora is anti-state, open, cosmopolitan, transnational, and capable of offering flexible and multiple identities. Diasporas are not boundless, and one cannot associate their perceived openness with cosmopolitanism.[138] Diasporic scholarship therefore should not neglect the power that diasporic institutions exercise or their ability to propagate and create nationalism through their institutions.[139] Khachig Tölölyan observes that in the amassing of stateless power, the "(re)production of culture and of contesting visions of collective identity is a quotidian, persistent, and costly activity, conducted not just by a few individual aesthetic producers but also by larger groups of journalists, intellectuals, teachers, scholars, activists, artists, performers, and entertainers, some of whom are associated with . . . organizations and institutions that offer material support and make ideological claims."[140] These institutions therefore constitute "a diasporic civil society that nurtures and sustains the public sphere of debate and cultural production."[141] In this light, Tölölyan emphasizes the similarities between nation-states and diasporic institutions that are important to consider in the case of Armenians in France.

Some diasporic institutions are designed to influence political events in the host nation and dominate major communal institutions. In a Foucauldian sense, Tölölyan argues, they have both productive and prohibitive power. They exercise productive power by extending social services and producing meaning and identity through discursive means, as well as by administering pedagogy in Armenian language, national history, and folk music and dance.[142] Such reproductive measures carry within themselves prohibitions against a critical view of past events and alternative modes of being Armenian. The stigma against such expressions was most visible when imposed on Armenian migrants from Turkey, because of their Turkified or Kurdified culture, lack of knowledge of the Armenian language, or failure to articulate their Armenianness through speaking and advocating for genocide recognition.

One such institution of the Armenian diaspora in France is the Armenian church, which has played a central role in the production of Armenian identity in the diaspora. As a religious institution, its function extends beyond spiritual life, serving as a key site for the preservation of language, cultural practices, and communal solidarity. Razmik Panossian's reading of Armenian history demonstrates that the distinction between religion and secular nationalism has been blurred, as Armenian secular nationalism carries an important religious dimension. Even as Armenian national identity became increasingly secular, the church remained deeply embedded in its articulation, reinforcing a national consciousness that was both political and spiritual.[143]

Tölölyan similarly argues that in contexts where cultural and ethnic public life is restricted, religious institutions serve as alternative spaces for communal expression. Because the religious sphere remains deeply involved with language, discourse, and cultural transmission, it becomes a primary site for sustaining identity when other public forms of ethnic self-representation are unavailable or suppressed. The Armenian church, therefore, has not only provided a framework for religious belonging but has also functioned as a vital institution through which the Armenian diaspora in France—and elsewhere—has maintained its collective memory, linguistic heritage, and sense of national continuity.[144]

The ambiguous boundaries between religion, history, and language highlight an important distinction between the political and nonpolitical, especially for diasporic communities such as that of the Armenians. Thus, the Armenian school of Surp Mesrop in Alfortville takes its name from Saint Mesrop, who was both the inventor of the Armenian alphabet, and hence a national hero, and the translator of the Syriac bible into Armenian. The school stands on the same land as the church and is owned and partially managed by the church. In fact, having strong physical and administrative ties between the school and the church could be traced back to the Ottoman Empire, when the church provided a place where Armenians could exercise autonomy over their religious and family affairs. For that reason, and despite anti-religious responses during the nineteenth-century movement to secularize Armenian societies, the church continued to play important political and cultural roles that became central to the Armenian national consciousness that emerged in the nineteenth century.[145] Religion has thus been an important unifying force for Armenians, providing "the only major pan-Armenian institution."[146] According to Boghos Zekiyan, Armenians could "secularize without rejecting religious faith."[147] The current catholicos of Cilicia, Aram I, has written, "It is often quite difficult, if not impossible, in any given stand or function of the church to distinguish between faith and politics, theology and ideology. The church is a political factor par excellence in the Armenian diaspora."[148] This raises questions about the inseparability of religion and politics in the Armenian context: Is the teaching of Armenian history through religious education (in diasporic schools or in Turkey) then a cultural necessity for an officially recognized confessional ethnic community, or is it a political act? Is commemoration of the genocide victims in a church liturgy a religious act or a political one? The very question of what constitutes the political and the non-political is always complex, as acts framed as cultural or religious often carry political weight.[149]

Essentially, then, the Armenians in France have had to navigate the terrain between the French republican requirement of assimilation and the homogeneity (that took place through re-Armenianization of diasporic communities) demanded by the Armenian diasporic institutions.[150] In this context, it is vital to recall Sarkis Sarkisyan's comment about Surp Mesrop School's mission: "In the school we teach the pupils how to be Armenian and French—Armenians who are fully integrated into French society." In response to assimilation, Armenians practiced self-imposed assimilation into French culture, and in response to homogeneity, they participated in the reproduction of Armenian culture. Armenians therefore swing between visibility and invisibility, between the two extremes of assimilation and re-Armenianization—the former in public, the latter in private.[151]

Yet the distinction between the private and public spheres is blurred. Just as host countries reshape migrants, diasporic communities influence their new habitus. For example, Armenians have left many ethnic markers (*marquage ethnique*) in France, especially around communal spaces and memorials. Visible examples of Armenian ethnic distinctiveness abound in the public spaces of France:

Armenian churches (some, like the Paris cathedral on rue Jean Goujon, built in a noticeably Armenian style); schools and cultural centers carrying Armenian names written in Armenian script; monuments to genocide victims; signs over restaurants and grocery shops; Armenian toponyms on streets and gardens (for example, streets named after the Armenian capital, Yerevan [or Erevan in French] in Issy-les-Moulineaux and Valance and streets named after other Armenian places or landmarks in Gardanne, Grenoble, Avignon, and Clamart); the twinning of French cities with Armenian counterparts (Alfortville is twinned with Ashtarak); street posters and public demonstrations; graffiti in Armenian; and epitaphs in Armenian script in communal cemeteries.[152]

Armenians' visible ethnic markers are not perceived by the French state as a salient threat to the French republican ethic as is the case with headscarves and Muslim piety, because the perceived success of the Armenians as a migrant community in France is not due to their break from Armenian cultural traditions or to their adoption of French values, language, and mannerisms. Rather it is due to a "process of identity negotiation" in which Armenians have met many of the French social and professional needs for successful integration while maintaining links with their group and culture of origin.[153] I endeavor to understand the ways in which Armenians integrated in France (when returning to their Anatolian homeland became impossible) while maintaining their cultural distinctiveness by drawing on another ethnographic example, the genocide commemoration in Paris—which represents the official discourse and activism of the Armenian diasporic institutions and not necessarily the experiences and attitudes of ordinary Armenians in France.

The public events of celebrating the Surp Mesrop School and honoring the genocide memorials reveal the dynamics of negotiation between the French state and the Armenian diasporic institutions, articulated through a discourse that sets Armenians as distinct from other migrant communities by casting them native to France: the Armenian diaspora shows loyalty to France and to the French state; the state recognizes Armenians as French citizens with a special need to protect their language and culture, particularly as genocide survivors, and publicly commemorates the genocide, noting that Armenians fought for French national causes and "died for France."[154]

Celebrating the Surp Mesrop Armenian School in Alfortville was a moment in which Armenians could weave a claim of being "native" in their host country and articulate a vision of the post-Soviet Republic of Armenia as their diasporic homeland. Such a narrative is noteworthy, because through it we see the ways in which Anatolia has been replaced by Armenia as the diaspora's homeland, even though the majority of Armenians in France are descendants of Armenians who

survived the genocide in Anatolia. Anatolia was confined to a closed history, frozen in time between narratives of golden age of Armenian political and cultural
achievements and the genocide. This chapter argued that the culmination of
these forces is yet another aspect of the denativization of Armenians from Anatolia in the efforts of the Armenians in France to integrate in their host country
while supporting the only remaining part of their historical homeland that still
has Armenians living in it: the Republic of Armenia. In other words, the denativization of Armenians from Anatolia was channeled through their nativization in
France, with Armenia replacing Anatolia as a homeland.

CHAPTER 6

ENDURING DENATIVIZATION, ENDURING PRESENCE

I n the summer of 2008, I was at a concert by the Turkish pop diva Sezen Aksu. At that time, she was performing all across Turkey, including giving several concerts in Istanbul itself, to promote her newly released album *Deniz Yıldızı* (*Starfish*). One of the songs on the album was dedicated to Hrant Dink, eighteen months after his assassination in January 2007. As Aksu performed, the three-thousand-strong audience sang along with her, completely enraptured. Between songs, she spoke about tolerance, love between people, and her own diverse ethnic background in a way that normalized and celebrated the diversity within Turkey's population.

Aksu performed a song dedicated to Hrant, titled "Güvercin" (which means "dove"). This song was likely inspired by Dink's final article, published in *Agos* on the same day he was assassinated. In the article, Dink explained his feelings about being turned into a target after he was condemned under article 301 of the Turkish Penal Code for "insulting Turkishness," saying, "I may see myself as frightened as a dove, but I know that in this country people do not touch doves. Doves can live in cities, even in crowds. A little scared perhaps, but free." Dink, fully aware of his vulnerability, likened himself to a fragile dove navigating a crowded city. However, this fragility did not deter him from wielding his pen and maintaining hope that he could continue to write freely. Despite the constant death threats and legal battles he faced, his spirit remained unyielding; he didn't foresee the tragic fate that awaited him shortly after he uttered those words. Dink's hope transcended the grim political realities in Turkey.

Sezen Aksu's lyrics mourn Dink's murder, likening his spirit to a dove whose flight over the city has been tragically grounded. Istanbul is depicted as irrevocably changed by his death, the hopeful vision and vibrant life he embodied now extinguished. His lifeless body, lying on the sidewalk, transforms it into a silent witness to his violent end and a keeper of the lasting record of his uncompromising spirit. With his passing, the creative and courageous voice that once resonated through Istanbul falls silent. Through this lament, Aksu's lyrics poignantly questions whether the city can ever again be the cradle of such resilient and bold voices, or if the dreams Dink carried have perished with him.

Aksu's song and comments triggered a conversation on the unequal treatment of Armenians in Turkey among those with whom I attended the concert. One person, clearly frustrated by the conversation about Dink and the Armenians in Turkey, said, "But if Armenians are complaining and unhappy in Turkey, why don't they go back to Armenia?"

This sentiment, expressed by a university-educated Turkish acquaintance in her early forties, highlights a pervasive attitude within educated Turkish urban culture. It demonstrates a lack of awareness regarding the fact that Armenians in Turkey have historical ties to Anatolia rather than to the Republic of Armenia. The denial of the Armenian presence in educational curricula, history books, media, and public discourse—except within the context of denying the genocide and attributing blame to Armenians for their own victimization—perpetuates this ignorance. In Turkey, there is a substantial knowledge gap regarding Armenian culture, history, and religion, which we can largely attribute to deliberate efforts to erase Armenian heritage and their very existence from collective memory as well as from the Anatolian landscape.

This chapter lays out how Turkish nation-building policies have systematically silenced and erased Armenian history: renaming villages, demolishing or converting churches, denying the genocide through selective memorials, and relegating Armenians to an "ancient" or "foreign" presence. On another level, the chapter shows how Armenians respond to—and endure—this protracted dispossession by reasserting their connection to Anatolia: mapping lost hometowns, recounting family narratives, and emphasizing their culture's deep roots in the land. Speaking of denativization as *enduring* refers simultaneously to the persistent effort to sever Armenians from their historic homelands (the verb sense of "enduring") and to the lived reality of asserting presence in the face of that uprooting (the noun sense—what is endured).

Denativization has fostered the belief that "Armenians come from Armenia," leading many Turkish citizens to assume that Armenians never had a historical presence in the country.[1] This false notion became more entrenched as Armenians left Anatolia for Istanbul and later emigrated to Western Europe or North America and as many cultural and social traits specific to Anatolia—languages, dialects, and syncretic religious and cultural practices born of long periods of coexistence with non-Armenians—disappeared. Many buildings and churches were either demolished or converted to other functions: churches, for example, became mosques. Buildings and objects were divorced from their organic function in the social lives of people and became artifacts of a silenced, largely unknown past. People, too, changed names, identities, and locations.

A basic principle in the process of denativization is to deface what was not erased, silencing the past by ascribing new meanings and contexts to events rather than by eliminating those events completely. History, as Michel-Rolph Trouillot notes, is a synthesis of mentions and omissions; silences in historiography are continuously created, a process that is intrinsic to the production of knowledge about the past.[2] It is within this web of silence and reinterpretation that Anatolia is fading away from the Armenian present and Armenians from the Anatolian past. This is the cumulative impact of denativization as an ongoing process. Let us return to Ara's village, Everek, to examine the production of such silences and the ways in which denativization is an enduring process.

MY SEARCH FOR EVEREK

After the conversation with Ara over a kebab lunch in Alfortville in 2008 that I evoked in chapter 3, I sought to locate his village, Everek, on the contemporary map of Turkey. I found no trace of it. In those early months of my fieldwork, I was still learning the geography of Anatolia, and had difficulty locating the places that people told me about. The next time I saw Ara, I checked all the possible spellings of the village's name with him and then carried out further internet and map searches—and still I was unable to find it. Finally, I went back to Ara and told him that the village did not exist on the map. He was shocked and distressed, and told me in a frustrated tone in French, "Ça existe! Je l'ai visité!" (It exists! I visited it!).

I went back to the internet and ran several additional searches and finally found a site with an Armenian map of the Kayseri region with the key Armenian villages around it, published in Cairo in 1936. That site is dedicated to the Armenian heritage of the village of Efkere, and there I found the name "Everek" on the map, written in Armenian as "Էվէրէկ." I then searched for different spellings for the village name, typing it with a G instead of a K, as Armenian pronunciations use them interchangeably depending on the regional dialect. The search "Evereg, Turkey" led me to two results. The first was the Armenian Genealogy Forum,

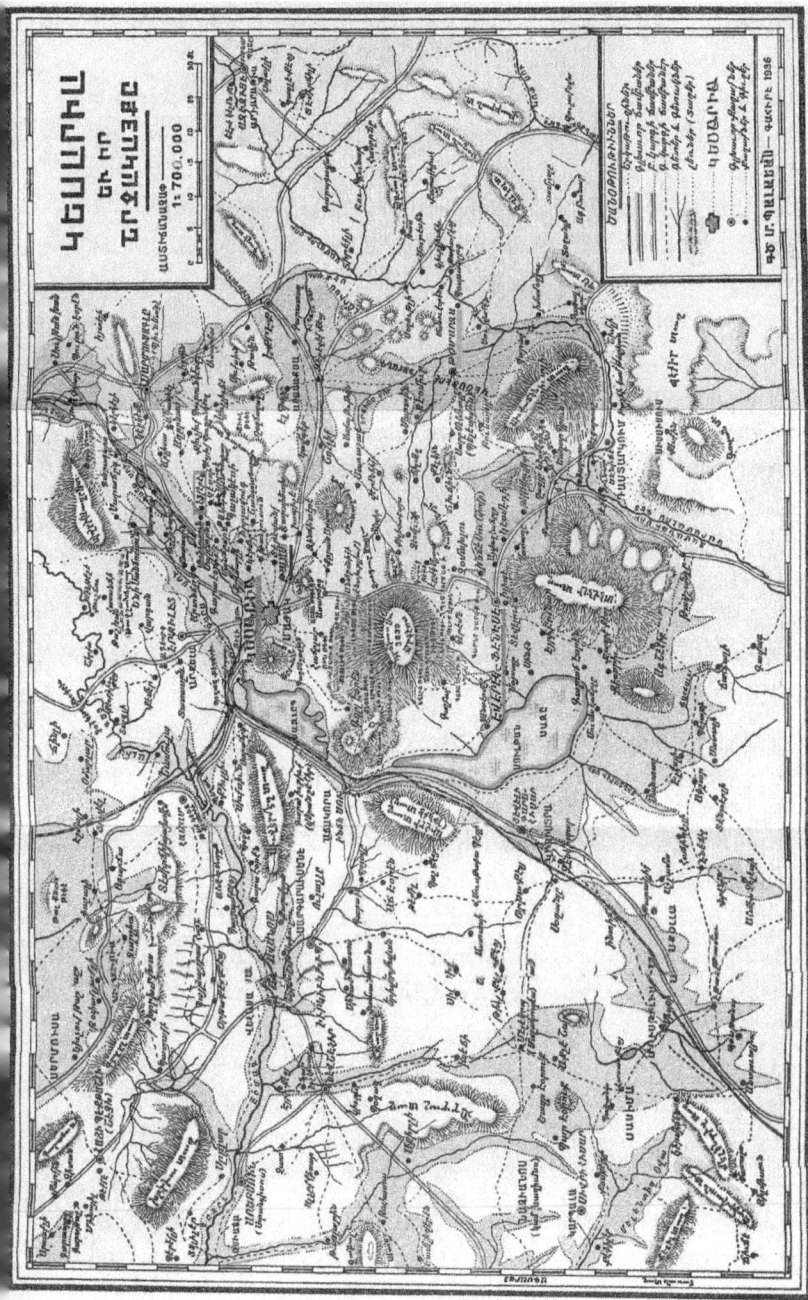

FIGURE 6.1 Armenian villages around Kayseri (Cairo, 1936). The regional capital, Kayseri—Gesaria in Armenian—is bolded and underlined near the center of the map. The sister villages Everek-Fenese are hyphenated and underlined in the lower central area. Moonjoosoon (underlined) and Efkere (boxed) are northeast of Kayseri, while Talas (underlined) lies to the southeast. Tomarza, also underlined, is east of Everek-Fenese.

Source: Reprinted with permission from OVENK.COM.

which mentioned that the city of Evereg is now called Develi, and the second was a Wikipedia article on Develi, which said that there is a two-hundred-year-old Armenian church in the "Everek quarter" of Develi.

Going back to Ara, I told him about my findings; he insisted, however, that Everek was not in Develi and that Develi was a neighboring city. As was the case in many parts of Anatolia, the republican regime has changed metonyms and expanded cities to include neighboring villages alongside other measures to Turkify the landscape and erase indicators of local non-Turkish names, entities, villages, and neighborhoods that were rendered "foreign." The same happened with the Armenian built environment. Ara added that Surp Toros (or Saint Theodoros), the Armenian church in Everek, had been converted to the Fatih Camii (a mosque). It is notable that the name that the building was given when it became a mosque was "Fatih," which is an Arabic title meaning a "conqueror" for the Muslim faith. The name evokes the Ottoman Sultan Mehmet, who was given the title "Fatih Sultan" for conquering Constantinople (Istanbul) in 1453, making what had been a part of the Christian Eastern Roman Empire the capital of a Muslim empire. The choice of this name suggests a parallel between Sultan Mehmet Fatih's conquest of Constantinople and the Turkish nationalist efforts to assert dominance over Anatolia by confiscating and appropriating Armenian properties.

Denativization continues beyond the forced migration of Armenians and the conversion of their buildings to target the bones of their dead in Everek. Toward the end of our meeting, Ara told me of another moment of destruction and displacement to his Everek. "While the church still remains as a mosque, our cemetery was demolished around 1965. Armenians were forced to pick up the remains of the Armenians buried there and remove them, taking them to Istanbul. If you go to the Armenian cemetery in Şişli, Istanbul, you will find part of the place labeled "Everek: this is where the bones of the *Everekliler* [the people of Everek] were moved to."

Ara demonstrates the ways in which the erasure of Armenian presence and memory in Everek was deliberate and extended beyond the displacement of the living. Not only were Armenians annihilated and those who remained pushed from the land, but the Turkish state also sought to displace the deceased from their final resting place. In doing so, the state sought to eliminate any visible reminders of the Armenian community's historical presence in the region. And when traces were found, they were made to speak of an ancient or a temporally unidentified past. This process aimed to deny the violence and destruction upon which the Republic of Turkey was founded and to downplay the historical existence of Armenians in Anatolia.

GENOCIDE DENIAL THROUGH A DISCOURSE OF TOLERANCE AND CALCULATED MISTRANSLATION

In a study of the renovation of the ancient church of Surp Haç (Holy Cross) on the Island of Akhtamar, near Van, which took place in 2005–2006 and was carried out by the Turkish government, political sociologist Bilgin Ayata places the concurrent efforts to renovate Armenian historical sites in Anatolia within the Turkish government discourse of neo-Ottoman multiculturalism.[3] Some foreign policy analysts have described such a shift in Turkish policies toward non-Muslims as "neo-Ottomanism," in which non-Muslim minorities are absorbed into Turkish culture and diversity and tolerance in Turkish society are said to stem from Turkey's rich Ottoman past rather than from a European ideal of tolerance.[4] By forging a new continuity with the Ottoman past, ruptured by Kemalism, neo-Ottomanism forged a link between a supposedly "tolerant" Ottoman past and the Turkish present under the Justice and Development Party (Adalet ve Kalkınma Partisi, knowns as AKP), which came to power in 2002. This narrative serves as a bridge that transcends historical periods marked by repression, genocide, and violence against non-Muslims and Kurds, spanning from the Armenian massacres of 1895 to the present day. By doing so, it seeks to absolve the Turkish state of the genocidal policies of its predecessor (given that the Turkish state is legally considered the successor to the Ottoman State, as stipulated in the Treaty of Lausanne). This narrative also seeks to absolve the Turkish state of the ongoing violence that has persisted throughout the republican era against Kurds, the remaining Armenians and their properties, as well as the denial of this violence.[5]

It is noteworthy that out of 2,538 Armenian churches, 451 monasteries, and 2,000 schools that once existed in Ottoman Anatolia before World War I, only 59 churches and 16 schools remain today, mainly in Istanbul.[6] Following Trouillot's insight that "mentions and silences are . . . counterparts of which history is the synthesis,"[7] the violent episodes against Armenians are silenced through an articulation of a discourse of tolerance and coexistence.[8] In this reading, the act of renovating the church in Akhtamar becomes a token of Turkish "tolerance" meant to systematically silence the destruction of thousands of other Armenian sites.

This selective recognition is further reinforced by the way the church of Akhtamar is represented in state-sponsored narratives, such as the September 2011 edition of Turkish Airlines' widely distributed *Skylife* magazine. In its description, the church is acknowledged as a historical monument but framed within a broader, depoliticized narrative of cultural diversity, subtly stripping it of its deep Armenian significance. By featuring Akhtamar on the cover of Turkey's national carrier magazine, the state projects an image of inclusivity and preservation while deflecting attention from the broader history of violence, destruction, and erasure. The strategic placement of the church within the national discourse serves to communicate a message of tolerance and inclusion to both citizens and tourists, while simultaneously obscuring the larger reality of the continuous efforts to destroy and redefine Armenian sites as "Anatolian"— a category that subsumes the region's diverse histories and cultures under a homogenized Turkish national framework.[9]

The Diyarbakır church of Surp Giragos (discussed in chapter 3) was also renovated, following the renovation in Akhtamar, in the context of the AKP reforms toward non-Muslim citizens. Commenting on the renovation of Surp Giragos in *Agos* on October 21, 2011, the Armenian novelist Mıgırdiç Margosyan emphasized the importance of the communal efforts to reopen the church and the solidarity it fostered among the now mostly dispersed Armenians of Diyarbakır. For him, the restoration, accomplished with the limited means of the community, becomes both a physical and symbolic act, cultivating solidarity not only among Armenians in the present but also reconnecting them with their historical and cultural roots in the city.[10]

The restoration of the church, however, did not go through without disagreements. Margosyan spoke of two opinions that emerged during the restoration of the church. The first was that there was no need to renovate it, because there was no longer a community in the city; the second emphasized that the heart of the matter was about maintaining Armenian presence, rather than about whether there were people there or not. Margosyan agreed with this second opinion, because for him, if Armenians forget and deny their history, they lose the battle of survival.[11] While Margosyan is aware that Surp Giragos is one of the thousands of churches that were destroyed or converted in the past, he believes that renovating the church—even knowing that there are no longer any Armenians to pray in it—reflects the reverence Armenians hold for both their own heritage and their ancestors. His view also projects a future of the city that includes Armenians, even if they are no longer living there, as symbolically represented by this iconic church.

Far from keeping the past alive, the renovation of Armenian sites carries another meaning, as these renovations have taken place concurrently with the Turkish state's continuous denial of the genocide. One ought to pose questions concerning the motivation behind these renovations and their relation to a neo-Ottoman discourse of diversity and tolerance. Such a shift in the Turkish government's policies and in efforts to renovate symbolic churches signifies a shift in the foundational myth of the Republic of Turkey. The Ottoman past that was once suppressed by the Kemalist ideology of the republic as being "unmodern," "regressive," and "religious" (the Kemalist republic being modern and secular) was being reinvented in the first decade of the twenty-first century by AKP ideology as a model for tolerance and pluralism that is superior to European multiculturalism.[12] At the time of the renovation of the Akhtamar and Surp Giragos churches, the AKP government's strategic aims were fourfold: improving its relationship with the Republic of Armenia; commodifying religious and heritage sites for tourism; engaging in public diplomacy to prove the long tradition of Turkish "tolerance" toward minorities; and, ultimately, countering the Armenian genocide claims.[13] Since 2010, however, Turkey witnessed the failure of the first three of these aims, with the AKP government dropping "tolerance" toward minorities from its public diplomacy strategy and with the increased violence against Kurds and civil society at large. Christian places of worship continues to be violated in Turkey, and especially in the Kurdish regions. The church of Surp Giragos, along with other churches in Diyarbakır such as those of the Armenian Catholics, Syriacs, Chaldeans, and Protestants, was confiscated in 2016, a year after the centennial of the Armenian genocide; some churches were even heavily damaged.[14] The decision, however, was reversed in 2017 after a decision of the Supreme Court of Appeals in Turkey.[15]

If a discourse of tolerance served as one strategy for genocide denial, another strategy that has helped to perpetuate denialism is the use of carefully chosen language to avoid referring directly to the genocide. Krikor spoke of how denialism is embedded in the psyche of many Turkish intellectuals and explained that the denialist discourse continues to be reproduced, disguised as acknowledgment. He gave me an example of an email exchange with a Turkish journalist who is known to be sympathetic to Armenians. In an article, the journalist used the Armenian expression *Medz Yeghern* (Great Crime) to refer to the genocide, claiming that he was employing the same expression that Armenians use. He translated the expression to the Turkish *Büyük Felaket* (Great Catastrophe). Krikor wrote to him saying that the Armenian word *yeghern* does not mean *felaket* (catastrophe/disaster) in Turkish, but rather *cürüm* (crime). Krikor continued, "I did not argue about which word he used in Turkish. I just had an issue with his mistranslation of the Armenian word. *Yeghern* means a crime and not catastrophe." The journalist's response dismissed Krikor's point on translation; he said that it was too late to call it a crime (*cürüm*), and that from now on the meaning of the word would remain "catastrophe" ("Bu saatten sonra felaket, cürüm olmaz," as he worded it in the email). Casting doubt on the sincerity of this journalist—who signed the 2008 apology campaign "I Apologize" (*Özür Diliyorum*), an initiative issued by Turkish civil society to apologize to Armenians—Krikor pointed out that he had been among the signatories of this initiative.

It is notable that the mistranslation of the Armenian term *Medz Yeghern*—to mean *catastrophe* rather than *crime* in Turkish—provided a cunning way to address Armenian suffering without squarely blaming the Turkish state as the perpetrator. Through the use of an expression rooted in Armenian language and history, it effectively removed the political charge from the genocide, evading direct implications or accusations toward the Turkish government as the sole responsible entity, consequently (intentionally or unintentionally) absolving the perpetrator of the crime. The text of the apology campaign reinforced this ambiguity by employing the Turkish term "Büyük Felaket" (Great Catastrophe) that mirrors this mistranslation by framing the events of 1915 in a way that sidesteps direct acknowledgment of genocide.

This choice of wording contributed to broader criticisms of the campaign, which many argued favored vagueness and emotional understanding over a substantive dialogue on the historical injustices committed against Armenians. In her critical examination of the campaign, Ayda Erbal highlights that within Turkish civil society and among academics and intellectuals, there has been a historical pattern of either outright denial of the Armenian genocide or complicity in denialist agendas through their silence on the issue.[16] She asserts that the Turkish apology campaign, instead of confronting the past directly, operates within a framework that informs Turkish citizens that there is a need for an apology and encourages them to empathize with the suffering of Armenians. However, the campaign avoids explicitly acknowledging the events of 1915 as a genocide. This avoidance of clear recognition, in her view, hinders meaningful and open debates on the significance of acknowledging the genocide for reconciliation.[17]

It is true that the many Turkish intellectuals, and the text of their apology, speak of the violence committed against Armenians. Yet, their written apology carefully avoids using the term "genocide," often to avoid provoking the state or facing retribution from the state or society. However, it is also true that some of the signatories have explicitly used the term "genocide" in their own writing and activism and have advocated for its recognition. Regardless of their choice of terminology, signatories faced varying degrees of risk, as the Turkish state has targeted them irrespective of whether they framed 1915 as a genocide or not.

It is also worth noting that Armenians, starting with Hagop Oshagan, have used the term "catastrophe" to speak about violence committed against Armenians during World War I, as have contemporary philosophers such as Marc Nichanian. While Nichanian employs "catastrophe" to expose the destructive element of genocide even when the evidence of genocide has been annihilated, some Turkish scholars appropriate his term to circumvent using "genocide" altogether. The use of the term "catastrophe" serves as a means to discuss an unspecified event without implicating a specific perpetrator, thus avoiding posing a challenge to the official Turkish narrative while seemingly acknowledging Armenian suffering. When Turkish liberal intellectuals and global leaders also adopt this term, it transforms into a "political tool" that can serve to obscure the crime committed against Armenians.[18] In Krikor's view, by avoiding the term "genocide," intellectuals sever the link between the crime and its perpetrators, ultimately diverting attention from the question of reparations.

Similarly, after Hrant Dink's assassination, banners reading "We are all Armenians" flooded the streets of Istanbul. While widely seen as an act of solidarity, this slogan—like the deliberate mistranslation of *Medz Yeghern*—also raises questions about whether it inadvertently obscured the structural reality of genocide denialism in Turkey. Instead of calling for an end to denialism or demanding accountability for the broader historical violence that culminated in Dink's murder, the slogan individualized the event, shifting the focus to symbolic identification rather than recognition of historical responsibility. In this sense, the assassin's act was not an isolated incident but yet another iteration of a systematic pattern of violence against Armenians, sustained through both direct repression and historical erasure. Yet the public response—however well-intended—risked further effacing the need for an explicit reckoning with Turkey's entrenched genocide denialism, which permeates both state institutions and society.

REMEMBERING WHAT WAS NOT

On Friday March 13, 2009, a month before the genocide commemoration discussed in chapter 5, I entered my Armenian language class a few minutes late. There were usually four of us students, two of whom were a retired couple. The husband's father was Armenian; his mother was French, and so was his wife. The couple had decided to learn Armenian to "connect back to the culture" of the husband's father. When I arrived to class that day, they were discussing with the teacher the news in *Direct Matin*[19] that the garden behind the Komitas statue, the genocide memorial in Paris, had been named after the Armenian capital; it would be known as Jardin d'Erevan (the Garden of Yerevan). I noted that such honors always centered on Yerevan and the Republic of Armenia, never on Armenian cities in Anatolia—a pattern explored in chapter 5, including the Ensemble Naïri concert, French street names, and other instances. Anatolia was the Armenian heartland for more than two millennia, until the genocide, and the Armenians in France are largely from Anatolia, not Armenia. "Why not

Dikranagert [Diyarbakır] instead of Yerevan?" I asked.[20] The Armenian teacher replied, "Dikranagert would honor Turkey, which even has a different name now, Diyarbakır. The Armenians who stayed in Anatolia are very few, invisible, and don't have a voice." She added that paying tribute to Armenia's capital would also be a way of honoring both the Armenian nation and the entire diaspora residing in France.

Naming the garden that houses the primary genocide memorial in Paris after the capital of the Republic of Armenia recontextualizes the historical memory of the genocide in the contemporary French Armenian context. The Garden of Yerevan thus invents a narrative that addresses the contemporary experience of Armenians in France, where they see the diaspora as rooted in the aftermath of the genocide and Armenia as their diasporic homeland, despite being descendants of survivors from Anatolia—now increasingly referred to as historic Armenia. This narrative conveys a past that did not exist, because it is being reconstructed through the lens of the present. The past is thus subjected to the gravity of the nation-state and represented in the present through the lens of contemporary politics, rewritten to be in line with present realities.

Placing the past under the influence of the nation-state has played a role in the process of denativizing Armenians from their Anatolian roots in both France and Turkey. I once told Krikor that I had noticed that two of his past concerts in France had described his music group as "from Armenia." Although the music is "Armenian," it is not characteristic of music from the Republic of Armenia, but rather represents the Armenian music of Anatolia. Krikor replied:

> Yeah, this is true. You know, in France, people ask me where I came from. I say, "Istanbul." After we have a lengthy discussion, they come back and ask me, "So how often do you go back to Yerevan?!" And this is after Armenia got its independence from the Soviet Union. Before Armenia's independence, they got confused between being Armenian and coming from Istanbul; for them, I don't come from a country that represents my ethnicity!

Selim, a Turkish friend of Krikor who was visiting from Istanbul, added, "Yes, this is a very French mode of thought. If you speak about Turkey, then everything there must be *Turkish* in the ethnic sense." We went on to discuss how the music albums of Ottoman Armenian composers I purchased in Istanbul do not label the composers as simply "Armenian" (*Ermeni*) but instead describe them as "of Armenian origin" (*Ermeni asıllı*).

Under different circumstances and for various purposes, Armenian citizens of France and of Turkey might be described not as simply Armenian but as being "of Armenian origin." The French expression *la communauté française d'origine arménienne* ("the French community of Armenian origin," used in French government documents that advocated for the genocide recognition discussed in chapter 5) and the Turkish *Ermeni asıllı* ("of Armenian origin") are synonymous labels for Armenians that relegate Armenianness to the past and not the present, diminishing its relevance in the contemporary context. At one level, the French state's stance resembles that of Turkey; both discourses exhibit assimilationist tendencies that deny or undermine extranational collective identity within each nation.

At another level, however, the Turkish republican model also erodes communal diversity to assimilate the different confessional ethnicities, particularly within domains such as Ottoman heritage. For instance, the field of Ottoman classical music boasts numerous non-Muslim contributors, but after the establishment of the republic, it was Turkified (along with other cultural and historical facets of the diverse Ottoman society), becoming simply "Turkish classical music" (*Türk sanat musiği*). In the field of architecture, Selim shared with me that the celebrated Ottoman Armenian architects, the Balyan family—known for their role in building notable Ottoman structures such as the Dolmabahçe Palace, the Çırağan Palace, the Ortaköy Mosque, and numerous Armenian churches, to mention but a few—are occasionally introduced to foreign tourists by guides either as Italian, under the name of the "Balyan*i*" family (by adding an "i" to the name), or with their Armenian identity deliberately omitted. These designations exclude Armenians from participating in shaping an aspect of what is now considered a part of Turkey's national culture. This exclusion from Turkey's contemporary identity also has had ramifications on how Armenians have been depicted in the nationalist retelling of history.

THE REPUBLIC OF ARMENIA AS AN IMAGINED HOMELAND

Criticism of Armenian diasporic institutions is common among leftist-inclined Armenian migrants from Turkey such as Krikor. As an Armenian from Istanbul, Krikor is a fierce critic of the diaspora. While he feels that, as an Armenian from Turkey, he continues to live in the aftermath of the genocide and with its consequences, diasporic Armenians, in his opinion, "are too comfortable; they have their houses and work in France, and do not want to be bothered with the past beyond genocide recognition." Such comfort renders the Turkish denial of the genocide an important factor in uniting the diverse constituencies of the

Armenian diaspora. Thus, Krikor maintains that if Turkey were to acknowledge the genocide, the diaspora would likely face a crisis, as they would have to reassess their relationship with Turkey and reconsider the foundations of their collective identity, which has long been informed by denial and the demand for recognition. For the diaspora, he said, "Turkey is kept at a distance, enclosed and limited to history books and grandparents' memories." He concludes that beyond activism for genocide recognition, Anatolia is fading away from the diaspora's present and future. Krikor's perspective is that if Turkey were to officially acknowledge the genocide, it would create more distance between Anatolia and contemporary Armenian life, reducing the region to a place of nostalgia where Armenians long for the lost golden ages in their history. It would no longer be a place of relevance for contemporary Armenian social and political realities.

During the Cold War, the Armenian diaspora in Western Europe and North America held diverse views on Armenia being a Soviet republic. Some distanced themselves due to the political climate of their host countries, while others, with more left-leaning politics, embraced it. Until Armenia's independence in 1991, Armenians were divided along the Cold War divisions between East and West.[21] After the Republic of Armenia achieved independence from the Soviet Union, the diaspora embraced it as a substitute for the lost homelands in Anatolia. The diaspora became an asset for Armenia;[22] as one French Armenian once told me, "Azerbaijan has gas; Georgia, the sea; and Armenia, the diaspora." Such links are made manifest through maps of Armenia and the tricolored flag, omnipresent at every community event from genocide memorials to church services on Easter and Christmas. For example, the photographs in an album on display at the Surp Mesrop School anniversary in 2008 (discussed in chapter 5) were of one class's field trip to Armenia, titled "Voyage en Armenie, 2004." The class was accompanied by Sarkis Sarkisyan, who worked closely with the mayor of Alfortville at the time and held an administrative position at the Armenian school. The photographs show students' visits to sites important for engendering identity formation for the Armenian diaspora: the genocide memorial in Yerevan; archaeological sites of churches and monasteries; schools, where they are shown meeting other students; national museums; and the headquarters of the Armenian Apostolic Church at the Holy See of Etchmiadzin.

As diasporic Armenians increasingly rooted themselves in France through their activism on genocide recognition, their sense of a diasporic home gradually shifted from Anatolia to the Republic of Armenia, particularly after Armenia's independence, when, like many other diaspora communities in France, they gained a titular ethnonational state. Claiming ties to Armenia is a common practice among Armenian diasporic institutions. A children's poster exhibition at the celebration of Surp Mesrop's anniversary highlights some aspects of the education that students receive at the school.

The posters depict scenes from Armenia's history and geography, teaching the children that they are part of the diaspora of the Republic of Armenia—a state that, with rare exceptions like occasional class trips, neither they nor their parents (apart from migrants from Armenia) have visited. This sense of belonging emerged before the recent increase in visits to Armenia, reflecting a shift in how the homeland is being reimagined by the diaspora. As Sossie Kasbarian argues, for many in the western Armenian diaspora, the Republic of Armenia functions as a "step-homeland" rather than a direct ancestral homeland. This relationship, shaped more by circumstance than descent, reflects the rupture of genocide and exile, forcing diasporic Armenians to negotiate between a mythical homeland and the reality of a post-Soviet nation-state. The portrayal of Armenia in these posters reinforces this shift, presenting the republic as the focal point of Armenian belonging, even for those whose ancestral roots lie in Anatolia.[23]

The republic is portrayed as a locus for a universal Armenian culture and as a homeland for Armenians. For example, one poster states in French, "Only 50 percent of Armenians live in Armenia and another 50 percent live in the diaspora." This assumption reflects the way the Republic of Armenia has been constructed as a step-homeland in the diaspora, serving as a substitute national center despite its historical disconnect from many western Armenians' places of origin. Yet, the notion that those outside Armenia are part of a diaspora is a statement that some Armenians in Turkey (whether they are from Istanbul, Anatolia, or Musa Dağ) and in parts of Syria—all part of the ancient Armenian homelands—would contest. On the posters, the sole mention of Anatolia as the homeland of their grandparents or parents is in a statement that Ottoman Armenians were loyal Ottoman subjects and that the Turks massacred Armenians during the genocide. This selective remembering further distances the Armenian past in Anatolia from the present, reinforcing the shift in diasporic consciousness from dispossession in Anatolia to an affiliation with the Armenian nation-state.

Yet Anatolia does not disappear from the diasporic imagination completely: it remains in the nostalgic imagination of the French diaspora. Madame Shushan, who heads one of the Armenian culture centers in Alfortville, has criticized Armenians in Turkey, as discussed in chapter 4. But her criticism is coupled with another discourse about their cultural and historical value in the eyes of the diaspora. Shushan explains that "for us, French-Armenians, meeting Armenians coming from Anatolia is a big thing; I am moved every time I see an Armenian from Dikranagert [Diyarbakır], as if they came from a history book. We only hear about those cities in history books."

This framing—where Anatolia is evoked as a distant, historical space rather than a lived reality—reinforces the idea that the diasporic attachment to the region is becoming symbolic. The very fact of Armenians coming from Dikranagert, the capital of an ancient Armenian kingdom east of Diyarbakır, is what interests Shushan, rather than the lived experiences of these Armenians, shaped by Turkish and Kurdish cultural influences. By privileging the classical and the ancient while disregarding contemporary complexities, this nostalgic gaze sustains a hegemonic trope that erases the ongoing histories of Armenians in Anatolia. It denies them a meaningful place within the larger diasporic trajectory, positioning them instead as relics of the past—figures who exist to fulfill an imagined ideal rather than as members of a shared and ever-changing Armenian world.[24]

The Armenian diaspora's creation of the Republic of Armenia as a symbolic homeland represents a pivotal act of reimagining their identity and connection to the land they were forced to leave. Simultaneously, the Turkish state's renovation of Armenian historical sites, such as the church of Akhtamar, while commendable in terms of preserving cultural heritage, significantly avoids addressing the violence and historical injustices that Armenians have witnessed. Instead, these restorations place Armenians on a different timeline than that of the Turkish nation-state, framing their presence as part of a distant, completed past rather than an ongoing historical and political reality. This approach is exemplified in the Turkish Airlines magazine, which features Akhtamar on its cover while presenting it within a generalized narrative of cultural diversity. By acknowledging the church as a historical site but detaching it from its specific Armenian significance, the article reinforces this temporal displacement. In doing so, the Turkish state reinforces a narrative in which Armenians belong to an antiquated, museumified history of ancient or medieval Anatolia rather than to its present or future, further marginalizing them from national memory and political recognition.[25]

These two distinct endeavors—restoration without recognition and historical framing without continuity—work together to obscure the Armenian connection to Anatolia. By emphasizing the ancient and medieval aspects of these sites, they effectively sever them from their contemporary local context, sidestepping the violence, erasure, and displacement that characterize recent Armenian history. This process encapsulates the essence of denativization, which involves erasing the contemporary presence and lived experiences of Armenians in Anatolia, leaving behind only traces of a distant and fragmented past detached from its actual history.

In essence, the Armenian diaspora's shifting homeland—from Anatolia to Armenia—and the Turkish state's selective historical renovation unintentionally converge in erasing the history of Armenians in Anatolia, effectively completing the circle of denativization by erasing the Armenian narratives from the contemporary life of the Anatolian landscape. Rather than merely preserving or erasing the past, these Turkish state and Armenian diasporic practices actively shape how ruins are made, perceived, and experienced in the present. As Ann Stoler argues, ruination is not merely the result of historical violence but an enduring, corrosive process (*to ruin* as a verb, not a static ruin) that embeds imperial debris—material, social, and psychological—into contemporary life. This framework reveals how the demolition of Armenian cemeteries and structures operates alongside the renovation of Armenian churches and state-led tourism projects, not as contradictory acts, but as dual mechanisms of ruination. That is to say, these practices reshape and control historical narratives by perpetuating erasure. The selective preservation involved in such renovations depoliticizes the past, detaching these sites from their historical and communal meanings. Together, these processes obscure the continuity of Armenian presence in Anatolia, transforming historical remnants into tools for state power and narratives control that further marginalize Armenians' contemporary connections to these spaces.[26]

PERPETUAL DISPLACEMENT

As the process of denativization unfolds in Turkey, marked by changes in place names, architectural renovations, and the apology campaign, Armenians in Istanbul continue to grapple with a sense of estrangement from their Anatolian locales. This ongoing process of Turkish nation-state formation involves the state's consistent reinforcement of its dominance by simultaneously erasing both the physical and narrative ties between Armenians and Anatolia, while actively formulating exclusive nativist claims that seek to sever Armenians' connection to their historic landscapes. The displacement of Armenians in Turkey is not merely physical; some forms of displacements have occurred without the movement of people. As the previous chapters have demonstrated, denativization also operates on the level of ideology, narrative, and perception. This process is not limited to Anatolia and Istanbul, the vicinity of the violence against Armenians, but also continue in Armenian diasporic spaces.

The denativization of Armenians has resulted in more than just their exclusion from Turkey's nation-building project. Houri's experience of leaving her native Sasun in fear of being abducted underscores a rupture in history, memory, and cultural—one that persists even among Armenians in Istanbul, where her village dialect and mannerisms marked her as an outsider. In this context, the displacement of Armenians transcends the simple Armenian–Turkish binary. Armenians in Turkey, particularly those who remained in Anatolia, have survived between the cracks of both Turkish and Armenian historiography, existing in liminal spaces that neither fully recognize. Armenian writers have described the nonphysical displacement of Armenians in Turkey in multiple ways: such as Armenians in Istanbul being themselves a "diaspora," even though they call Istanbul home; being "foreign" or an "other" at home; and being "step-citizens" of the Republic of Turkey.[27] While these expressions differ, they converge in emphasizing a significant rupture in Armenian belonging, even within the homeland itself.

Although some Armenians in Turkey do not identify as part of a diaspora, their profound longing for their ancestral Anatolian homelands mirrors the sentiments typically expressed by diasporic communities. This sentiment is particularly poignant given that the majority of Armenians in Istanbul are either displaced themselves or descendants of survivors of earlier displacements. Recognizing these deep historical and emotional ties, some scholars have described Armenians in Istanbul as a diaspora, highlighting their enduring connection to a homeland they no longer inhabit. Yet placing oneself on the Anatolian landscape is not only a diasporic practice; many Armenians in and from Istanbul continue to articulate a sense of belonging to Anatolia[28] and to trace themselves and their families to Anatolian neighborhoods, cities, and villages. Melissa Bilal describes the complex relationship that Armenians in Turkey have to Anatolia as a form of longing for home (Anatolia) while being at home (Istanbul)—a dynamic that challenges conventional definitions of diaspora. She argues that Armenians in Istanbul experience a duality of belonging and displacement, where Anatolia remains an imagined homeland deeply tied to memory and cultural identity, even as they inhabit Istanbul, which functions as an extension of that homeland. This layered relationship complicates the notion of "home," demonstrating how displacement can occur within one's perceived homeland due to historical ruptures, silences, and ongoing marginalization under the Turkish nation-state.[29]

The experience of Anatolian Armenians in Istanbul, therefore, compels us to go beyond the binary of *home* and *displacement* and to recognize how displacement operates not only through forced migration but also symbolically and discursively. Whether in Anatolia, Istanbul, or among Armenians in France, Armenians remain estranged from their homelands and histories, and Anatolia is estranged from them. The Armenian genocide is not a closed chapter in history but an ongoing process—one perpetuated through violence, erasure, and denial. And yet, this erasure has never been total. Even as some seventy-thousand Armenians officially remain in Turkey, they continue to assert their presence through storytelling, memory, and acts of refusal, unsettling the structures that seek to erase them.

ASSERTING PRESENCE

Beyond resisting erasure, Armenians engage with their past in ways that actively reframe their belonging, generating counter-histories that challenge the Turkish state's exclusive claims to nativeness. These narratives do not simply respond to denial but assert a distinct historicity, one that reclaims presence in the face of ongoing dispossession. This ongoing engagement speaks to the dual meaning of endurance—as both the persistence of denativization and the assertion of Armenian presence despite it. Consider the following three statements, which were among the many I heard from Armenians who left Turkey for France during my fieldwork there:

> When I asked Vahan which language he usually speaks at home, he said, "We speak Turkish at home; it is much easier for us. I don't know Armenian well." He then made a distinction between Turkish as the practical language that he speaks best, and Armenian, which he regretted that he does not speak, but described as his "mother tongue."
>
> Harout told me that one could learn Turkish grammar in a day or two, unlike Armenian, which requires a long time to master. He emphasized this by pointing out that a Turkish grammar book would be only few pages in length (between his almost-touching thumb and index fingers), while Armenian grammar would need volumes to explain. Harout's explanation of this was that "Armenian is an ancient language, much older than Turkish, and therefore much more complex and difficult to learn."
>
> Ani explained that Armenians lived in Anatolia before the arrival of the Turks, who came as tribal invaders from Central Asia. She asked if I had visited Anatolia, and I said, "No, not yet." "Well, when you go, you will see it for yourself! You will not find a place in Anatolia that does not have stones with Armenian inscriptions." She went on to explain that Armenian buildings and stones are much older than Turkish ones: "We lived on this land much longer than the Turks."

The reflections shared by Vahan, Harout, and Ani poignantly articulate the impact of historical and cultural forces on their personal and collective identities. Vahan's preference for speaking Turkish at home, even though he recognizes Armenian as his mother tongue, underscores both the practical challenges and the profound loss associated with the fading use of western Armenian. This situation highlights the complex relationship between identity and language within Armenian communities, where Turkish has become the practical language of daily use, at the expense of their native language. This shift occurred as Armenians were being displaced from Anatolia, leading to the loss of communal and educational institutions that facilitated language transmission. Harout's remarks about the complexity of Armenian grammar in contrast with Turkish's simplicity symbolize the linguistic challenges Armenians face: both the broader pressures to assimilate within Turkey and the difficulties of maintaining a linguistic community in the diaspora. Ani's observations emphasize the ancient Armenian presence in Anatolia, which she contrasts with the relative newness of Turkish presence; she asserts a historical connection to the land that predates and resists the ideologies that have dispossessed Armenians.

Together, these statements not only illustrate the enduring denativization of Armenians but also their active survivance through maintaining and asserting their presence in the midst of the ongoing cultural and geographic displacement. Endurance in this context is seen not just in the persistence of denativization as the afterlives of the genocide, but also in the continuous and perpetual assertions of survivance through the telling of these counter-narratives. In the face of dispossession, ethnic cleansing, and erasure, Armenians speak of belonging by placing themselves prior to the establishment of the state that dispossessed them, effectively contesting, even subverting, the Turkish state's own nativist claims over Anatolia. These Armenian voices reflect the afterlives of the genocide when they inscribe themselves into the history of the land from which they were collectively dispossessed. Such articulations of belonging are not limited to the way Armenians place themselves on maps that do not exist and are no longer recognizable. Armenians also create narratives of belonging that emphasize their presence in and connection to Anatolia, and they present this belonging as being a part of a longer temporality than that of the Turkish republic or the Ottoman Empire, as the preceding three examples demonstrated.

Similarly, when confronting the Turkish state and public, Hrant Dink articulated the Armenian experience by emphasizing the Armenian connection to Anatolia.[30] I take the following passage, from his address at the conference held at Bilgi University in September 2005, as emblematic of his articulation of the Armenian experience of dispossession. It is notable that this conference was perhaps the first public event in Turkey since World War I to discuss the Armenian predicament during the war and that it was held one year after Dink's controversial article on Sabiha Gökçen was published. At the conference, Dink said that he would "show courtesy and not name" the event (genocide) that the "Armenian people . . . dispersed across all corners of the world . . . have internalized in their minds." He explains that its "name is irrelevant for us," but that "this event, this rooting out . . . has already been perceived and internalized, and it has been inscribed in the genetic code." He further underscores Armenians' experience of this "rooting out" by focusing on the deep relationship between people and their geography:

> There is an important definition in philosophy: The relationship between a living being and the territory of the living being is precisely life itself . . . Life is the name given to that relationship. This is valid for all living beings—for plants, animals, and also human beings. A living being exists with its territory; outside its territory, it ceases to exist. If you were to take it from that territory and transport it elsewhere, even if you carried out this act by placing it on a golden tray, it would mean that you are severing its relationship with its territory, you are severing its roots. This is the definition. Yes, that is what forced deportation is . . . this is the nature of the thing you are looking at, and trying to explain . . . people who lived on these lands for four thousand years, people who had produced culture and civilization on these lands, were broken apart from the land they lived on for this or that reason, and were dispersed across all corners of the world. Those who died, those who survived, and those who were dispersed.[31]

In this text, Dink interprets Armenian history as one marked by profound disruption, characterized not only by physical displacement but also by the severing of cultural, historical, and contemporary ties to the homelands. The Armenian catastrophe includes not only the annihilation of the majority of Ottoman Armenians but also the process of displacing survivors—those who survived in Anatolia and those living in the diaspora—by severing their connection to their territory and, consequently, their identity and history. He sees Armenian belonging in Anatolia as organic, asserting that for Armenians, living outside their territories means "ceas[ing] to exist" in some sense.

In this statement, Dink challenges the narrative imposed by the Turkish state, which dispossessed Armenians, by emphasizing the devastating consequences of annihilation and forced deportation on individuals and communities: namely, the severance of the fundamental connection between people and their geography. By doing so, Dink is not merely refusing the state's version of events; by articulating a counter-narrative he is also affirming the Armenian narrative of survivance. By emphasizing an organic connection to Anatolia, Hrant Dink articulates a perspective that diverges from the nationalist project critiqued by Marc Nichanian. Nichanian specifically criticizes the nineteenth-century efforts by Armenian intellectuals to forge a homogeneous national identity through the construction of an "Armenian native" image.[32] Unlike these intellectual projects, Dink's focus is on recognizing and affirming the continuous presence of

Armenians in their homeland, in direct challenge to the Turkish state's policies to erase this presence and exclude Armenians from historical narratives through its own nativist discourse.

Throughout his speech, Dink refrains from naming the Armenian predicament as genocide, telling his audience that he is showing them "courtesy," given that the mention of genocide could amount to insulting Turkishness both in law and in effect.[33] While Dink does not explicitly name the genocide, his description of forced deportation as a severance of life from territory implicitly speaks of the policies of annihilation. He tells of a story shared collectively by Armenians in Turkey and the wider diaspora, rather than entering into the polemics of naming. Thus, he makes this history accessible for the Turkish public to hear, albeit still challenging to confront. Dink invites his Turkish audience to acknowledge and reflect upon the violent past and the painful experiences of Armenians. By sidestepping the polarizing polemics of naming, he presents the challenge of confronting the truth of the past in a manner less likely to trigger the defense mechanisms often activated by more direct accusatory language. Dink therefore embarks on an alternative to the route used by the Armenian diasporic intuitions that advocate for genocide recognition, a route that is perpetually contested by the Turkish state—namely, a debate anchored in document-based historiography about the legality of the crime of genocide.[34] Instead, Dink's narrative articulates the Armenian experience of annihilation, loss, and dispossession from their cultural and historical roots in Anatolia, which he says go back "four thousand years." Rather than engaging with assertions or denials of genocide, Dink confronts his Turkish audience as a member of a denativized community that lived in Anatolia until the genocide and that now represents less than 1 percent of the country's population, with the majority of Armenians dispersed far away from their Anatolian homelands.

By framing the issue within a broader context of the relationship between living beings and their territories, Dink extends the relevance of the Armenian predicament; he speaks on the human condition. He is seeking empathy and understanding from the Turkish public while challenging them to confront the historical realities of Armenian suffering. Dink's strategy highlights the delicate balance between pushing for recognition and navigating the sensitivities of a nation that refuses to grapple with its violent past. Ultimately, for Dink, the recognition of Armenians as human beings who are connected to a geography and history comes as a prerequisite to, and even takes priority over, the recognition of the crime of genocide.

This interpretation of the Armenian predicament by many interlocutors in Paris and Istanbul as well as through Dink's writing prompted me to employ the term "denativization" to describe the Armenian experience of annihilation and their ongoing rooting out. The controversy stirred by Dink over Gökçen's confessional ethnicity helps us to contextualize the Turkish nationalist understanding that equated being Muslim with Turkishness and to understand why it was more acceptable for Gökçen to be the daughter of Bosnian Muslims than to be a local Anatolian Armenian. While the nativist discourse in Turkish nationalism positioned Anatolia as a source of cultural and linguistic authenticity in the early republican period, it focused on this authenticity only as it pertained to Muslim populations in a racialized sense. This selective reading of history not only obscured the linguistically and religiously diverse past of the region, it also set the stage for the construction of a monolithic ethnonational narrative of national identity.

The Turkish nationalist reading of history frames Turkish nativism in a narrative that positions modern Turks as descendants of the ancient Hittites. Given that Hittites predate Hellenic and Armenian presence in Anatolia, Turkish nativist claims position the presence of contemporary Turks in Anatolia as older than that of either Greeks or Armenians. The Turkish nationalist narrative does also acknowledge that Turks have roots in Central Asia, from which they came to Anatolia as invading tribes—a component of Turkish nationalism that regards historical and cultural connections to other Turkic-speaking peoples of Central Asia. The nationalist narrative weaves the story of Hittites as Anatolian natives and the story of invading central Asians together into a single narrative. This narrative shows how Turkish nativism in Anatolia roots Turkish nationalism in an ancient past while denying this connection to the ancient past to other communities; Turkish nationalists make exclusive nativist claims to the land.

The 1990s witnessed the reemergence of the nativist debates in Turkey regarding what constitutes Turkish nativeness.[35] The term "native" in Turkish, *yerellik*, refers to land, a particular locality, but also to aspects of culture such as music, folklore, and language. The term therefore connects land to culture.[36] Such nativeness is contrasted with term *yabancilik*, which connotes foreignness or something of external origin. While this debate was overshadowed by the opposing political strands between the secularists and Islamists, there remains no consensus on the meaning of *yerellik* in Turkey. It was not uncommon for many in Turkey to regard Armenians and other non-Muslims as both *yabancilik* and *yerellik*, leading them in some instances to refer to non-Muslims as *yerli yabanciler*— "local foreigners"—a term that would distinguish them from visitors or tourists.[37] It is within this understanding that Gökçen would be considered a "native," even with parents who came from Bosnia, and that Dink's claim that she was an Anatolian Armenian would trigger the Turkish military to intervene in "defense" of Gökçen's Turkishness, ultimately leading to Dink's assassination.

Dink defines Armenians as having an organic connection to Anatolia as the place where Armenian culture and language began, thus emphasizing the "natural" connection between Anatolia and Armenians. In doing so, he articulates a counter-nativist claim that positions Armenians as having a connection to Anatolia that predates that of the Turks, in whose name Armenians were annihilated and expelled, with those who survived rendered foreign. In another political speech, Dink makes a declaration about the historical continuity and ancient roots of the Armenians in Anatolia:

> The first truth that must, before all else, be acknowledged in respect to the question of land is this: Armenians did not arrive in Anatolia post facto. According to some sources, they have been living on these lands for four thousand years, and were the continuation of a deeply-rooted civilization on these lands as a sedentary society of a productive nature . . . Armenians were among the keystones, and even driving forces of Anatolia. In other words, *it would be more in line with truth to consider them not as a nation with a claim [to] this land, but [as] the land itself.*[38]

The statement "Armenians did not arrive in Anatolia post facto" counters the often-prevalent narrative promoted by the official Turkish nationalist discourses that exclude Armenians from the local history of the region, a narrative that has been used historically to justify their political marginalization in Turkey. Dink's remark emphasizes that Armenians have been an integral part of Anatolian history since well before the establishment of modern state boundaries. Furthermore, in asserting that Armenians are "the land itself," Dink diverges from discourses on sovereignty and territoriality of ethnonationalism. He emphasizes that the connection to Anatolia is not merely territorial, but rather is also geographic—that is, deeply rooted in the cultural fabric of Armenians. This relationship implies a sense of a continuous presence and interdependence between people and their geography, which is central to Dink's argument about the catastrophic impact of the genocide and forced deportation on Armenians, both individually and collectively.

Dink's perspective in this speech challenges the conventional framework of the genocide that prevails in many diasporic circles, as well as the discourse on minority rights and multiculturalism in Turkey. The typical discourse surrounding the genocide predominantly focuses on the violence committed in the past, with less emphasis on its present or future implications. However, as a Turkish citizen, Dink addressed these historical events not merely to seek recognition from the state, but rather to advocate for a different future. He envisioned a Turkey where Armenians are recognized as full and equal citizens, moving beyond their minoritized confessional ethnicity. His approach allows for new possibilities for inclusive and equitable citizenship. Moreover, Dink critiqued the conventional approach to minority rights, which he saw as inherently exclusionary. By granting rights based on minority status, such policies do not treat Armenians as equal citizens but rather as perpetual outsiders within their own country. Additionally, the popular discourse on multiculturalism, while promoting inclusion, often glosses over historical injustices and depoliticizes the violent past.

Dink was aware of these discourses and was publicly responding to them, as his two speeches quoted indicate. Armenians are "the land itself"—but it is the Anatolian landscape without its Armenians and other non-Muslims that the Young Turk regime responsible for the genocide sought to rule. In the context of Turkish nativist claims to Anatolia and in the shadow of the genocide, Anatolia therefore continues to be central to the Armenian imaginary, both in Turkey and in the diaspora, as a homeland and a place of origin for dispossessed and dispersed Armenians. It is notable that by claiming that Armenians existed on the land for four thousand years, Dink challenged two central nationalist narratives for Armenians and Turks. First, he challenged the narrative that Armenian history is marked by Christianity and formed what Armenians say was the first Christian state in history by saying that Armenians existed as a people before Christianity. This assertion is in line with Dink's own secular politics; he refused to limit Armenians to a minority status defined by their confessional belonging to Armenian Christianity and the institution of the Armenian Apostolic Church. Second, he challenged the Turkish nationalist insistence on a superior or exclusive claim to Anatolia by pointing out that because the Armenians were on the land for so long, their presence in Anatolia predated that of the Hittites, the invented ancestors of the Turks. His remarks ultimately subvert the Turkish nativist claims that denativize Armenians.

Discourses of origins and native belonging are a double-edged sword, just as nationalism is. Such discourses are used by dispossessed populations as they counter colonial and nationalist claims, but are also employed by nation-states, leading in many instances to the dispossession, exclusion, and sometimes the annihilation of some communities from the national project—as we have seen in the Armenian case in Turkey. The Turkish state excludes Armenians using a nativist discourse, which can be countered through the long-standing Armenian presence and connection to Anatolia. This is not to equate the two discourses. The Turkish state employs nativeness to exclude Armenians, Kurds, Rūms (Greeks), and Jews from its ethnonational state project, while survivors confront the ongoing predicament of denativization by reclaiming the Armenian belonging to Anatolia and reinstating Armenians in the past and present of Anatolia as a mode of survivance. Armenians fight for their inclusion as equal citizens with historic and cultural ties to the land and not merely as a minority appealing for recognition or a modicum of tolerance.

According to Dink, the Armenian experience in its entirety can be summarized as being torn away from the geography upon which Armenians lived and produced culture for thousands of years, yet he also wants to move away from having trauma as the central plot of their history and the driving force of their self-identity. To this end, he concluded his address at the conference held at Bilgi University by telling an anecdotal story, a story that he previously related in response to a comment made by Süleyman Demirel, the former Turkish president (in office 1993–2000). Dimirel had once said that "we won't even give three pebbles to the Armenians," referring to land concessions, and Dink responded by narrating the story of Beatris, an Armenian woman from Sivas, who, after emigrating to France, continued to visit her home village. On her last visit, she passed away, and the villagers called Dink to help them locate her relatives. After Dink found her daughter and informed her of Beatris's death, the daughter traveled to the village with the aim of burying her mother in Istanbul. The daughter called Dink from there in tears, as one of the villagers told her, "She is your mother, she belongs to you, but if you ask me, let her stay here, let her be buried here . . . The water finds a way through the cracks [*su çatlağını bulur*]." Upon hearing what the villagers told Beatris's daughter, Dink broke down and said, "It was true, the water had found its crack."

This Turkish expression, *su çatlağını bulur*, speaks of a stream of water that eventually finds a "crack," a channel, that it will continue to follow after being obstructed and diverted.[39] The expression became exemplary of Beatris's fate: she was forced to leave her village, then eventually found her way back to her roots, and without intending to, ended up being buried in the same soil that she was forced to leave. Despite all the forces that pushed her into exile, she returned and ended her life in the place where she should have continued to live. The expression suggests that sooner or later, such a fate is inevitable and unstoppable: like the water, Beatris found her own way despite obstacles.

Commenting on Beatris's story, Dink concluded by addressing the public's "paranoia" about losing land: "Yes, we Armenians have our eyes on these lands, because our roots are here, but do not worry; it is not in order to take these lands away, but to come and one day be laid deep in them."[40] In this passage, Dink emphasizes the Armenian affinity for Anatolia, which is based on historical and affective connections rather than territorial ambitions. He addresses a common concern in Turkey about Armenian land claims by highlighting the importance of recognizing Armenians' deep-seated ties to Anatolia. Dink's discursive strategy aims at emphasizing that Armenians' longing to return and be interred in these lands arises from cultural, affective, and historical bonds—something that the Turkish state and society fail to recognize and systematically deny—not from desire for territorial acquisition. Through the telling of Beatris's story Dink insinuates that the fears of losing exclusive ownership or sovereignty are mainly concerns of states and nationalists, which often overshadow the human cost of realizing ethnonationalist territorial claims. He urges his Turkish interlocutors to reconsider the meaning of belonging to a land beyond nationalist exclusivities, embracing coexistence with its diverse peoples based on equal citizenship rights rather than racial or ethnic entitlements. While Demirel spoke about territoriality from the ethnonational vantage point of the state, through the telling of Beatris's story, Dink shifted the discourse of belonging to one of presence, insisting on Armenian survivance despite their physical absence.

Yet most Armenians, unlike Beatris, do not meet their desired fate. When Haig, the grocer in Alfortville who had left Sasun as a child due to conflict with local Kurds, lost his father a few years ago, he had to bury him in the local cemetery, as it was not possible to bury him in his native Sasun. Haig's eyes misted over as he told me the story of his father's gravestone, which he designed with a map of Anatolia drawn on it, on which Sasun was marked with a dot. But that was not all; Haig had also put his father's picture on the gravestone, positioned in such a way that the eyes of the portrait are directed toward the map of Anatolia, "so that he keeps looking at Sasun; you know, he wanted to be buried there, not here." Haig cannot claim his family's land in Sasun, which was confiscated by the state and distributed to local Kurds, and he remains reluctant to take his children there, even for a visit. While graves are sites of absence and silence, when visited, they still evoke stories and presences, memories and imagination.[41] Living in the afterlives of the genocide, Armenians continue to be conditioned by the presence of their dead ancestors,[42] who were forced out of the place they continue to evoke. Locating themselves on ancient maps in storytelling or on gravestones, Armenians defy denativization through the assertion of their presence.

Following the Bilgi University conference in 2005, Dink spoke of the foundational violence of the republican regime, referring to the "Armenian issue" as "the greatest of all taboos in Turkey, one that was *present at the creation of the state* and which represents the principal 'other' of Turkish national identity."[43] There have been several legal cases against writers and activists who have countered the state's narrative by speaking of such violence and by discussing the Armenian predicament on the eve of the republic's foundation.[44] The list includes Orhan Pamuk, Ragıp Zarakolu, Murat Belge, Elif Shafak, and Hrant Dink himself. Dink explained the pressing centrality of the violence perpetrated against Armenians in contemporary Turkey as one that pertains to the very foundation of the Turkish state, rather than being merely a debate over matters of democratic reforms or over gaining equal rights as a minority. This is why when Dink revealed Gökçen's Armenianness, he signaled to the state that, by recounting her story, he was scrutinizing its foundational myth. The republican regime established in the aftermath of the Ottoman imperial demise was largely created on Armenian ruins, through the systematic killing, deportation, and dispossession of Armenians, as well as the appropriation of their properties and the erasure of those who remained, either through assimilation or forced migration.

When discussing Hrant Dink's assassination with Krikor, he asked, why would a journalist, a member of a minority of less than seventy thousand persons, be regarded as a threat in a country of more than eighty million? And why else would Dink's assassin regard his killing as an accomplishment, publicly declaring that he killed the infidel? Krikor was adamant in telling me that the Armenian predicament in Turkey is not a matter of numbers, civil rights, or even genocide recognition: "Even if the few thousand remaining Armenians left Istanbul today, the 'Armenian' will continue to constitute a threat; it is not a matter of statistics or logic; it is a state of mind." For him, Hrant Dink was assassinated because he posed a challenge to the Turkish establishment and to ordinary citizens, who could not stand to hear an Armenian who refused to assimilate, emigrate, or be silenced. Dink made the suppressed Armenian narrative of dispossession heard once more, bringing to the foreground the genocide not only as an event of the past but as an ongoing structure in Turkey. And yet, even as the state attempts to suppress this history, acts of refusal continue to emerge. Krikor, like many other Armenian citizens of Turkey, has always emphasized to me that "Turkey is built on the ruins of Armenians"—a statement that, in itself, stands as a counter-history of the Turkish nation-state, exposing its foundational violence and positioning the annihilation and survivance of Armenians as new centers from which to conceive Turkish republican history.

Counter-histories do not emerge simply by exposing the destructive foundations of the Turkish nation-state, but by Armenians writing their own histories, reclaiming narratives, and asserting presence. These histories are not merely acts of remembrance; they are refusals to be erased, refusals to be confined to the past. They subvert the silences imposed by the state, challenge its denials, and insist on a history that cannot be contained within nationalist amnesia. The struggle over history is not just about what has been lost, but also about what remains, what is continually claimed, and those who refuse to disappear or be silenced. There are multiple sustained projects—both in Turkey and France—that challenge these imposed silences. These acts of refusal are not merely personal gestures of remembrance but part of larger, collective efforts that look beyond nostalgia, focusing instead on future presence.

For example, Terre et Culture ("Land and Culture"), founded in France, was the first organization to conduct on-the-ground work restoring and preserving Armenian historical structures in Turkey, Armenia, Artsakh (Nagorno-Karabakh), Syria, and Iran, ensuring that Armenian material heritage endures despite the systematic destruction of cultural sites. Collectif 2015, an outgrowth of Terre et Culture, emerged in France to mark the centennial of the genocide, challenging the foundational violence of the Turkish state by demanding recognition, restitution, and reparations, refusing to let dispossession be normalized. The organization emphasizes the need for acknowledgment of the genocide, the return of confiscated properties to the Armenian Patriarchate in Istanbul, and the payment of reparations by the Turkish state. Similarly, the Turkey Cultural Heritage Map, initiated by the Hrant Dink Foundation in Istanbul, documents thousands of Armenian, Rūm-Orthodox, Syriac, and Jewish sites across Anatolia, transforming them into interactive spaces of counter-historical storytelling. Through digital mapping, immersive media, and historical narratives, it uncovers the local history of buildings, neighborhoods, and villages, reclaiming their original names, functions, and geography—long erased by the Turkish state—by inscribing on those maps the lived experiences of non-Muslims drawn from collective memory and historical sources.

Each of these initiatives operates as an intervention against the logic of denativization—asserting that Armenians are not merely victims of historical violence but active agents in shaping their future by reclaiming both their place on the land and their presence in history.[45] This refusal to disappear echoes the struggle of Hrant Dink, who insisted that Armenians were not relics of the past but part of Turkey's living fabric, and who envisioned a future where coexistence and justice were possible, a conviction for which he paid with his life. This refusal also recalls the persistence of those who continue to demand justice despite state repression, those who return to ancestral villages to reclaim erased histories, and those who challenge the nationalist mythologies that seek to overwrite Armenian belonging. Whether through physical restoration, archival reconstruction, or digital mapping, these projects do more than counter the amnesia imposed by the Turkish state—they forge new pathways for Armenian presence, ensuring that memory is not just about preserving the past but carried forward as a claim to the future.

AN EPILOGUE OF RETURN

Kimse ilk basmaz bir toprağa	No one is the first to set foot on any soil
Sırtlanırsın geçmiş ruhları	You're always borne by souls who passed before
...	
Ölülerimle kaldım coğrafyamda	I stayed in my geography with my dead
Sen kendini inkâr ettin	Yet you denied your very self
resmî oldun, hakikatinden boşaldıkça	Turned official, emptied of truth
Hayatımla kaldım coğrafyamda	I stayed in my geography with my life
kendi tarihimi yazmaya	to write my own history

—Karin Karakaşlı, "Tarih-Coğrafya"/"History-Geography"

"Nothing that has ever happened should be regarded as lost for history," Walter Benjamin once wrote, reminding us that history is not a settled record but a constellation of fragments—scattered, silenced, waiting to be reanimated by those who refuse to forget and insist on telling their stories.[1] This book has traced the endurance of erasure, but also the endurance of presence of Armenians who have survived not only the physical destruction of genocide but also the more pervasive violence of being rendered illegible within their own geography.

And yet, despite it all, they remain. The soil remembers even when history forgets; stories find their way, even when no archive remains to hold them. The voices that once echoed through the narrow streets of Diyarbakır, Everek, Sasun, and Mardin have not fully vanished—they persist in the worn inscriptions of forgotten churches, in the names whispered between generations, in the longing that shapes the stories the living continue to tell. For those who stayed, memory is not about looking back with remorse or nostalgia but about remaining in the present and carrying themselves into the future—a way of being, woven into the fabric of their daily lives, a refusal to let absence have the last word.

It is in this space—between remembrance and silence, between presence and erasure—that poetry stands as a counterpoint to forgetting, asserting the endurance of presence and survivance. I began the book with an epigraph drawn from the poem "History-Geography" by Karin Karakaşlı.[2] Now, at the book's end, I return to her words positioning them as both a proclamation and as a mode of survivance in the face of the enduring erasures—acts of silencing, dispossession, and denial that continue to shape Armenian existence. The poem, written in Turkish, starts with a declaration that reads as an attempt to subvert nationalist claims: "No one is the first to set foot on any soil / You're always borne by souls who passed before." This assertion underscores the intertwined histories of countless peoples who have inhabited the land, rejecting singular claims to ownership and challenging the exclusive entitlement that underlies nationalist projects.

The poet then cries a solemn rebuke to the forces that seek to erase the Armenian narrative of dispossession: "I stayed in my geography with my dead / Yet you denied your very self / Turned official, emptied of truth." These words, mournful yet defiant, are a testament to the presence of Armenians who remain inextricably linked to their homeland—not through claims based on myths and artifacts or imagined by national or religious ideologies. Rather, Karakaşlı articulates an organic relationship to the geography, because for Armenians, the soil is a sanctuary where their dead are remembered and honored, and it is also the past that informs their present. In the midst of absences and silences, the emptied geography stands as a witness to the history of violence and destruction that remains denied.

The poet, an Armenian from Turkey, speaks to us across the pages, reminding us that the Anatolian soil is imbued with both Armenian lives and bones throughout history.[3] She sees a continuum between history and geography, which she hyphenates to say that despite being separate concepts, they together articulate the Armenian experiences of violence and survivance. The *history* of the genocide, displacement, erasure, and dispossession lies in—to quote Dink—"being torn away from" the *geography* of Anatolia, and vice versa. Furthermore, the annihilation of Armenians from the land and their systematic eradication from the history of Anatolia have worked in tandem, and both are inseparable from the ongoing process of, and resistance to, denativization. History-geography, therefore, are not merely adjacent or related concepts but are intertwined, shaping and being shaped by one another—and in this entanglement, they also shape the nuances of

the Armenian experience. Benjamin reminds us that history is a process of inter-
ruptions, of moments that defy the neat, teleological narratives of the victors. If
the Turkish state has tried to impose a linear, triumphant narrative that erases
the catastrophe of the Armenians, then Armenian storytelling—through poetry,
literature, memory—is an interruption, a rupture in the state's archive of denial.
Karakaşlı's words perform such a rupture. But they are also an act of survivance,
as Gerald Vizenor might argue—a way of refusing both victimhood and assimilation, of reclaiming space and meaning on Armenian terms. The poet does not
simply mourn loss; she declares her presence, transforming history-geography
into a mode of survivance.

In discussing the connection to and denativization from a place, it is crucial to distinguish between the organic bonds that local inhabitants have with
their environment and the nationalist, often abstract claims that are constructed
without direct personal or familial ties. This distinction highlights how lived
experiences and relational connections to a locality differ significantly from the
imagined and ideological constructs imposed by nationalist narratives.

I read Karin Karakaşlı's poem, along with the speeches by Hrant Dink discussed earlier, as providing critical perspectives on locality by articulating a relationship to Anatolia as an act of survivance—one that unsettles erasure, insists
on presence, and affirms belonging through memory, storytelling, and the enduring connections people maintain with their homeland. In doing so, they diverge
markedly from and also counter the nationalist portrayal of the Turkish state,
which seeks to deny these histories and sever Armenians from their geography.
Throughout the book, we heard such articulations in the way Armenians place
each other on the map of pre-genocide Anatolia; in the way Margosyan speaks
in *Gavur Mahallesi* of his belonging to Diyarbakır using a collective pronoun,
embracing not only Armenians but also other communities; and in the way Ara,
Houri, and Haig long for and remember Everek and Sasun. These connections
are deeply entrenched in direct experiences and historical continuity, cultivating
belonging and presence that are grounded in personal and familial ties to specific locales. Such expressions of connection are rooted in direct experiences and
historical continuity, offering an understanding of an identity that is articulated
through one's personal or family connection to a particular locale. Such experi-
ential relationality transcends simplistic nativist claims of nationalist projects.
In contrast, the Turkish state's discourse on Anatolia often leverages nativism to
craft a narrative that supports its nationalist agenda, forging a sense of exclusivity
and ownership that is disconnected from the personal histories and realities of its
diverse inhabitants. Such a discourse denativizes populations that do not belong
to the state's imagined confessional ethnicity.

Nationalist propositions of being the first or original inhabitants on a territory—evidenced by archeological, literary, scriptural, or other claims—are often foundational for racially exclusive, and at times annihilatory, nation-states. Such propositions are also dangerous: they have been used as a pretext for the exclusion, dispossession, and extermination of millions in modern history. Thus, while both perspectives—the Turkish nationalist perspective and that taken by critics such as Dink and Karakaşlı—involve claims to the land, they should not be conflated. Dink and Karakaşlı do not assert dominance or ownership but rather speak as the dispossessed—their articulations affirm presence. Their voices do not reinforce nationalist territoriality but rather expose its violence. By articulating their connection to Anatolia, they underscore a complex understanding of belonging, one that acknowledges multiple narratives and the deep, often invisible, ties that people have to their environments.

Reflecting on her poem in the context of a set of photographs on the emptied Anatolian landscape, Karakaşlı captures the unseen and unspoken echoes of loss and destruction that continue to haunt the Anatolian present:

[T]he Genocide of 1915 is present in the whimsical shadows, in the murmur of trees, in ruined churches and schools, in vineyards without owner and wine. We do not see the blood, nor do we witness the violent expulsions, but instead we see the ghosts who walk the roads of no return, who were given no graveyard, and we hear the lamenting song of the survivors who still long for an acknowledgement of their suffering and injustice.[4]

This visualization sets a haunting scene that resonates deeply with earlier historical traumas that Armenians faced. Just a few years before the genocide, Zabel Yessayan evocatively described the Adana region after the massacres of 1909 as a "deathly wasteland . . . [with] immense piles of ash."[5] This stark imagery not only captures the immediate desolation but also prefigures the similarly devastated landscapes of Anatolia after the genocide that would start in 1915. The ruins left behind, traces of destruction, and the emptied landscapes across Anatolia resonate with Yessayan's words, speaking of the atrocities that remain unrecognized. These sites demonstrate the capacity of geography to convey the history and trauma of a people, even—and especially—in the midst of denial. Beyond merely physical territories, these spaces are imbued with culture, history, and personal meaning. In her poem, Karakaşlı draws a contrast between *territory*, often tied to nationalism, political borders, and control, and *geography*, a realm of boundless possibilities, plural in its meanings, open to reimagining, and oriented toward multiple futures. Instead, she believes that "places and spaces absorb the energy around them" and are imbued with cultural significance that bears witness to unspoken histories.⁶ The poet here echoes Dink's reflection that Armenians desire to return to Anatolia not as conquerors or heroic founders of a state, but as children seeking solace in a cradle where their forebears lie.

In her plea, there is a warning against a denialism more insidious than that of the Turkish state: a denialism that urges Armenians to forsake the truth of their experience for a state-sanctioned rendering of the past. For to deny their experiences is to estrange themselves from their own history-geography. For Karakaşlı, time and place are inseparable, to disentangle Armenians from their past is to sever their connection to Anatolia. The opposite is also true: to sever Armenians from Anatolia is to disentangle Armenians from their past. The poet asserts that Armenian lives are etched into Anatolia both temporally and spatially in ways that refuse to be forgotten and rewritten in favor of the official nationalist version of the past.

For many Armenians in and from Turkey, the assassination of Dink was not just an act of violence against an individual but an attempt to silence an entire community; its history, culture, and experience; and ultimately to deny them a future, perpetuating the genocidal violence that runs through the very fabric of the Turkish republic. That is why her last verse—"I stayed in my geography with my life / to write my own history"—is a decisive proclamation of presence. It is a refusal to let the ongoing policies of erasure and narratives of denial, authored by the state and its apologists, claim the last word. For by being connected to their geography and among their dead, Armenians could articulate their own experiences and write their history, a history not centered on perpetrators or limited to victimhood.

As this book draws to an end, we give the final word to the poet, whose voice rises above the din of erasure and silence. These words remind us that to be Armenian in Turkey is not just a matter of historical record but a reclamation of a past and a present that cannot be untangled from the land itself. It is a declaration that despite attempts at silencing, despite the forces of assimilation or emigration, and despite the ongoing structure of denial and erasure, Armenian survivance is manifest through the very act of telling and retelling our stories. Storytelling is a refusal to yield to the pressures of forgetting and forgoing; a reclamation of a space within narratives that is intrinsic to remembering the lives lost on these lands. Ultimately, storytelling is an assertion of presence. For in the midst of perpetual loss, persistent denial, and protracted anxieties about the future, to stay on "my" geography and to write "my own" history is not just to say "I survive." It is to affirm that even in erasure, the dead bear witness, and the living keep telling their stories. For history is never settled, and to assert presence is to insist that the past cannot be dictated by those who justify or deny its crimes. As long as these stories are retold, the past remains unfinished, still waiting to be written. Each fragment of a story is a brushstroke on the canvas of history—not to complete the picture. Instead, to disrupt its supposed clarity, to add depth where erasure sought to flatten, to reveal the layers that neat histories attempt to conceal. And in this layering, in this act of storytelling, there is a return—not to a place as it once was, but to a presence that refuses to be erased.

NOTES

BEGINNINGS

1. Lerna Ekmekçioğlu describes excluding Armenians and other non-Muslims from Turkishness while also forcibly including them as paradoxical policies; see Lerna Ekmekçioğlu, "Republic of Paradox: The League of Nations Minority Protection Regime and the New Turkey's Step-Citizens," *International Journal of Middle East Studies* 46 (2014): 657–679.

2. I am here invoking Michel Löwy's understanding of Walter Benjamin's thesis VI on history; Michel Löwy, *Fire Alarm: Reading Benjamin's "On the Concept of History"* (London: Verso, 2016), 44.

3. Article 301 punishes every person who insults Turkishness and Turkish national identity. See Amnesty International, "Turkey: Article 301 Is a Threat to Freedom of Expression and Must Be Repealed Now!," EUR 44/035/2005 (Public Statement), December 1, 2005.

4. Ethnic cleansing and genocide question the legitimacy of the state, and therefore denial of violence and distortion of the history of the state's foundation is central. Ronald Grigor Suny, *"They Can Live in the Desert but Nowhere Else": A History of the Armenian Genocide* (Princeton, N.J.: Princeton University Press, 2015), 365.

5. On genocide denialism in Turkey, see Fatma Müge Gökçek, *Denial of Violence: Ottoman Past, Turkish Present, and Collective Violence Against the Armenians, 1789–2009* (Oxford: Oxford University Press, 2015).

6. The Republic of Turkey calls its Asiatic territory *Anadolu*, Anatolia, from the Greek word *Anatoli* (Ἀνατολή), meaning the "east." It is the homeland of diverse populations, including Armenians.

7. Saidiya Hartman, *Lose Your Mother: A Journey Along the Atlantic Slave Route* (New York: Farrar, Straus and Giroux, 2007), 133.

8. Harry Harootunian, *The Unspoken as Heritage: The Armenian Genocide and its Unaccounted Lives* (Durham and London: Duke University Press, 2019).

9. Audre Lorde, "The Transformation of Silence Into Language and Action," in *Sister Outsider: Essays and Speeches* (Berkeley, Calif.: Crossing, 1984), 40–44.

10. Ruth Behar, *The Vulnerable Observer: Anthropology That Breaks Your Heart* (Boston: Beacon, 1996), 2.

11. Behar, *The Vulnerable Observer*, 3.

12. Lorde, "The Transformation of Silence Into Language and Action," 41–42.

13. T. S. Eliot "Little Gidding," *Four Quartets* (New York: Harcourt, Brace and Company, 1943), 39

14. Edward W. Said, *Representations of the Intellectual* (New York: Vintage, 1996), 32.

15. See Edward W. Said, "The Future of Criticism," *MLN* 99, no. 4 (September 1984): 951–958.

INTRODUCTION

1. In the Armenian church, "Christmas" constitutes the commemoration of both the Nativity and Epiphany of Christ, celebrated together on January 6. The Armenian church is the only one that keeps the old tradition of celebrating both events on the same day. Other Eastern churches, as well as the Roman Catholic Church and the Anglican Communion, commemorate the Nativity and Epiphany on separate days, December 25 and January 6, respectively.

2. For anthropological work on Armenians in republican Turkey, particularly studies that demonstrate the ways in which past violence persists in the present, see Zerrin Özlem Biner, "Acts of Defacement, Memory of Loss: Ghostly Effects of the 'Armenian Crisis' in Mardin, Southeastern Turkey," *History and Memory* 22, no. 2 (Fall/Winter 2010): 68–95; Ayşe Parla and Ceren Özgül, "Property, Dispossession, and Citizenship in Turkey; Or, the History of the Gezi Uprising Starts in the Surp Hagop Armenian Cemetery," *Public Culture* 28, no. 3 (2016): 617–653; Alice Von Bieberstein, "Treasure/fetish/gift: hunting for 'Armenian gold' in post-genocide Turkish Kurdistan." *Subjectivity* 10 (2017), 170–189; Anoush Tamar Suni, "Palimpsests of Violence: Ruination and the Afterlives of Genocide in Anatolia," *Comparative Studies in Society and History* 65, no. 1 (January 2023): 192–218; and Umut Yıldırım, "Mulberry Affects: Ecology, Memory, and Aesthetics on the Shores of the Tigris River in the Wake of Genocide," in *War-torn Ecologies, An-Archic Fragments: Reflections from the Middle East*, ed. Umut Yıldırım, Cultural Inquiry, 27 (Berlin: ICI Berlin Press, 2023), 27–66. The growing body of historical scholarship that explores state policies of homogenization and the continued presence and experiences of Armenians in the early years of the republic, includes Uğur Ümit Üngör, *The Making of Modern Turkey: Nation and State in Eastern Anatolia, 1913–1950* (Oxford: Oxford University Press, 2011); Talin Suciyan, *The Armenians in Modern Turkey: Post-genocide Society, Politics and History* (London: IB Tauris, 2016); and Lerna Ekmekçioğlu, *Recovering Armenia: The Limits of Belonging in Post-genocide Turkey* (Stanford, Calif.: Stanford University Press, 2016).

3. Mikkel Bille, Frida Hastrup, and Tim Flohr Sørensen, "Introduction: An Anthropology of Absence," in *An Anthropology of Absence: Materializations of Transcendence and Loss*, ed. Mikkel Bille, Frida Hastrup, and Tim Flohr Sørensen (New York: Springer, 2010), 3.

4. Karin Karakaşlı "History and Geography," in Kathryn Cook, *Memory of Trees* (Heidelberg: Kehrer, 2014), 147. See also Dickran Kouymjian, "Introduction," in William Saroyan, *An Armenian Trilogy* (Fresno: California State University Press, 1986).

5. Leslie Marmon Silko, "Language and Literature from a Pueblo Indian Perspective," in *English Literature: Opening Up the Canon*, ed. Leslie A. Fielder (Baltimore, Md.: Johns Hopkins University Press, 1981), 54–72.

6. Toby Austin Locke, "Death and the Storyteller," May 4, 2017, http://tobyaustinlocke.com/death-and-the-storyteller. Hard copy in author's possession.

7. Locke, "Death and the Storyteller."

8. Numbers are approximate and contested. Mark Mazower, *Dark Continent: Europe's Twentieth Century* (New York: Vintage, 1998), 61, estimates the deaths between 800,000 and 1.3 million. Erik Zürcher, *Turkey: A Modern History* (London: IB Tauris, 1993), 120, estimates them between 600,000 and 800,000. Ronald G. Suny, *"They Can Live in the Desert but Nowhere Else": A History of the Armenian Genocide* (Princeton, N.J.: Princeton University Press, 2015), xxi, estimates the number killed "conservatively" at 600,000 to 1 million. Turkish official historians estimate the deaths as low as 200,000 (see Zürcher, *Turkey*, 120). The common Armenian estimate is 1.5 million; see Vahakn N. Dadrian, *The History of the Armenian Genocide: Ethnic Conflict from the Balkans to Anatolia to the Caucasus* (New York: Berghahn, 1995).

9. For a detailed treatment of the reasons of the Armenian genocide, see Suny, *"They Can Live in the Desert."* For a discussion that focuses on the role of religion and nationalism in the genocide, see Ronald Grigor Suny, "Writing Genocide: The Fate of the Ottoman Armenians," in *A Question of*

Genocide: Armenians and Turks at the End of the Ottoman Empire, ed. Ronald Grigor Suny, Fatma Müge Göçek, and Norman M. Naimark (New York: Oxford University Press, 2011), 15–41.

10. Suny, *"They Can Live in the Desert,"* xiv–xv.

11. Maud Mandel indicates that France received 65,000 Armenians, and that number made up approximately 30 percent of the total number of refugees. It was on this basis that I approximated the number of refugees would have been at least 200,000. See Maud S. Mandel, *In the Aftermath of Genocide: Armenians and Jews in Twentieth Century France* (Durham, N.C.: Duke University Press, 2003), 21.

12. For an example of a travel document granted to Armenians by France, see Martine Hovanessian, *Les Arméniens de leur territoirs* (Paris: Autrement, 1995), 12.

13. Hannah Arendt, *Origins of Totalitarianism* (San Diego, Calif.: Harvest, 1973), 268–269.

14. On hidden Armenians in Turkey, see Avedis Hadjian, *Secret Nation: The Hidden Armenians of Turkey* (London: IB Tauris, 2018).

15. According to the first population count since the establishment of the republic, which was in 1927, there were 64,745 Armenian speakers in Turkey (table 21, p. 31). The largest number of Armenian speakers were in Istanbul, with a total of 45,255 (table 27, p. 34), making the number of Armenian speakers in the rest of the country 19,490. The 1927 census undercounted Armenians, because it did not have religious affiliation as a category, only language spoken. This census therefore did not give the total number of Armenians, as it did not account for the Armenians who did not speak Armenian. Armenians who converted to Islam during and after the genocide were not considered ethnically Armenian, but simply "Muslim." Overall, in 1927, non-Muslims in all of Turkey made up 2.64 percent of the population and 31.14 percent of the population of Istanbul (table D, pp. 61–62). See *Umumî Nüfus Tahriri, Fesikül III, 28 Teşrinievvel 1927* (Ankara: Başvekâlet Müdevvenat Matbaası, 1929). The 1965 census, however, did the population count based on religious affiliation, showing that there were 69,526 Gregorian Armenians in Turkey (table 21, p. 227). This, however, does not account for Catholic and Protestant Armenians. See *Genel Nüfus Sayımı: Nüfusun Sosyal ve Ekonomik Nitelikleri 24 October 1965* (Ankara: TC Başbakanlık Devlet İstatistik Enstitüsü Matbaası, 1969). For a detailed treatment of the Armenians in Istanbul and Anatolia, see also Suciyan, *The Armenians in Modern Turkey*, 54–59.

16. Given the displacement of Armenians within Turkey, scholars have extended the term "diaspora" to speak of the Armenian citizens of Turkey (especially Istanbul), because they live in what became a foreign country to them; they belonged to a homeland now lost and experienced a nostalgia for the past akin to that of other diasporic communities. I employ "denativization" throughout this book to speak of both the Armenian diasporic experience outside Turkey and that of those who remained as Turkish citizens. For a discussion on the debate of whether the Armenians in Istanbul are diasporic, see Hrag Papazian, "Are Istanbul Armenians Diasporic? Unpacking the Famous Debate," in *The Armenian Diaspora and Stateless Power: Collective Identity in the Transnational 20th Century*, ed. Talar Chahinian, Sossie Kasbarian, Tsolin Nalbantian (London: IB Tauris, 2024), 232–249.

17. On how the Jews of Turkey are treated as strangers, see Marcy Brink-Danan, "Names That Show Time: Turkish Jews as 'Strangers' and the Semiotics of Reclassification, *American Anthropologist* 112, no. 3 (2010): 384–396. For a detailed case study on racialization of Jewish converts in Turkey, see Marc David Baer, *The Dönme: Jewish Converts, Muslim Revolutionaries, and Secular Turks* (Stanford, Calif.: Stanford University Press, 2009). For discussions on citizenship and belonging shaped by ethnonationalism, where religion plays a central role in defining ethnicity, see the recent work on religious conversion such as M. Kravel-Tovi, *When the State Winks: The Performance of Jewish Conversion in Israel* (New York: Columbia University Press, 2017); Esra Özyürek, *Being German, Becoming Muslim: Race, Religion, and Conversion in the New Europe* (Princeton, N.J.: Princeton University Press, 2015). On the Jews of Morocco, see A. Boum "The Plastic Eye: The Politics of Jewish Representation in Moroccan Museums," *Ethnos* 75, no. 1 (2010): 49–77.

18. For the historical context of the term *millet* in Ottoman history, see Benjamin Braude, "Foundation Myths of the Millet System," in *Christians and Jews in the Ottoman Empire*, ed. Benjamin Braude and Bernard Lewis (New York: Holmes & Meier, 1982), 1: 69–90.

19. The term "Rūm" or "Rūm-Orthodox" (pronounced like "room") has its roots in Arabic and is used in Ottoman and Modern Turkish, where it originally referred to the Eastern Roman Empire and by extension its official church, the Eastern Roman (Orthodox) Church. However, as Hellenic (Greek) nationalism began to rise in the eighteenth century, the "Rūm-Orthodox" population living in the Ottoman Empire started to be identified as Hellenes or Greeks. This shift in nomenclature led to the translation of the word "Rūm" (Roman) as "Greek." Consequently, Eastern Orthodoxy is now often referred to as "Greek" Orthodoxy, rather than the more historically accurate "Roman Ortho-doxy." In this book, I use the term "Rūm" (with the Anglicized plural "Rūms") to refer to what is commonly known as the "Greek" minority in Turkey and to denote Orthodox Christians during the Ottoman period. The term "Greek" is reserved for citizens of Greece, the Hellenic Republic.

20. The primary doctrinal divergence between Chalcedonian and non-Chalcedonian Christianity cen-ters on their interpretation of the nature of Jesus Christ. Chalcedonian Christians, which encompass Roman Catholics, Eastern Roman Orthodox, and the Anglican Communion, among others, assert that Jesus Christ is simultaneously fully divine and fully human, embodying two distinct natures and two wills that coexist within a single person. This theological doctrine was established at the Fourth Ecumenical Council at Chalcedon in 451 CE. In contrast, non-Chalcedonian Christians, compris-ing the Armenian, Coptic, Syriac, and Ethiopian Churches, maintain that Jesus Christ possesses a unified, composite nature and will, representing both divinity and humanity. In summary, Chalce-donian doctrine emphasizes the duality of Christ's nature, while the non-Chalcedonian traditions emphasize the unity of his nature.

21. Mark Mazower, *The Balkans: A Short History* (New York: Modern Library, 2002), 73.

22. For an examination of how the labels "Turk" and "Muslim" became conflated beginning in the nine-teenth-century Ottoman Empire and continuing into the Republic of Turkey, see Howard Eissen-stat, "Metaphors of Race and Discourse of Nation: Racial Theory and the Beginning of Nationalism in the Turkish Republic," in *Race and Nation: Ethnic Systems in the Modern World*, ed. Paul Spickard (New York: Routledge, 2005), 239–256.

23. Sebouh Aslanian argues that the racialization of Armenians has an earlier genealogy starting in the mid-nineteenth century. Being an Armenian shifted from a premodern concept of *azg* ("nation" in Armenian) to the modern *azgut'iwn* ("nationality"). This transformation was marked by a change in how Armenians perceived their collectivity, particularly in relation to the Armenian Apostolic Church and its doctrinal differences with other Christian confessions, notably Roman Catholicism and Eastern Roman Orthodoxy. In the premodern understanding of nationhood, the Armenian *azg* was closely tied to the confessional bounds of the Armenian Apostolic Church, thus excluding Armenian Catholics and Protestants (who later formed two separate millets in Ottoman adminis-tration). In the latter half of the nineteenth century, *azg* underwent a transformation, evolving into *azgut'iwn*, signifying nationality in the European secular sense. See Sebouh David Aslanian, *Early Modernity and Mobility: Port Cities and the Printers Across the Armenian Diaspora, 1512–1800* (New Haven, Conn.: Yale University Press, 2023), 365, 376–377.

24. Baer, *The Dönme*, xi.

25. Baer, *The Dönme*, 238–239.

26. Ayşe Parla, *Precarious Hope: Migration and the Limits of Belonging in Turkey* (Stanford, Calif.: Stan-ford University Press, 2019), 6–7.

27. Aslanian, *Early Modernity and Mobility*, 365, 376–377, speaks of deconfessionalization of Arme-nians. Gil Anidjar, *Semites: Race, Religion, Literature* (Stanford, Calif.: Stanford University Press, 2008), 19–20, speaks of the detheologization of Jews in Germany under the Nazi regime.

28. Aslanian goes further to argue that this transformation also carried a territorial dimension, imbuing the lands of the premodern *azg* with political significance, effectively giving rise to an Armenian identity characterized by modern concepts of race and ethnicity, with a specific national language firmly rooted in the land—a confluence that together constituted the elements of nationality. Aslanian, *Early Modernity and Mobility*, 377.

29. Ekmekçioğlu, *Recovering Armenia*, 97.

30. Paul A. Silverstein, "Immigrant Racialization and the New Savage Slot: Race, Migration, and Immigration in the New Europe," *Annual Review of Anthropology* 34 (2005): 364.

31. Racialized confessionalism operates in a manner akin to the historical perception of biological differences among "races," a perception that, despite lacking scientific grounds, played a pivotal role in establishing and legitimating racist hierarchies. Both concepts rely on the perception of intrinsic differences to legitimize systems of power and exclusion and establish racial supremacy of one group over others. I thank Michael Pifer for providing me with the insightful analogy between racialized confessionalism and the historical perception of biological differences.

32. Sebouh Aslanian, in *Early Modernity and Mobility*, speaks about Armenians as a "confessional nation" to emphasize the role of the Armenian Apostolic Church in maintaining a sense of a communal identity among the Armenian diaspora that transcends geographic boundaries and unifies the dispersed Armenian community. "Confessional ethnicity," on the other hand, describes the interplay between religious affiliation and ethnic identity in the late Ottoman period leading into the establishment of Turkey in 1923.

33. On the experience of the conversion of Islamicized Armenians "back" to Christianity, see Ceren Özgül, "Legally Armenian: Tolerance, Conversion, and Name Change in Turkish Courts," *Comparative Studies in Society and History* 25, no. 3 (2014): 622–649. Özgül demonstrates that while the converts could become Christian, they could not be recognized as Armenian.

34. Marc Nichanian, *The Historiographic Perversion* (New York: Columbia University Press, 2009), 7.

35. Nichanian, *The Historiographic Perversion*, 7.

36. Nichanian, *The Historiographic Perversion*, 7, 15. Nichanian differentiates between generic names for events, such as "genocide" and emblematic names such as "Auschwitz" for the Holocaust and "1915" for the Armenian genocide.

37. Raphael Lemkin, *Axis Rule in Occupied Europe* (Clark, N.J.: Lawbook Exchange, 2005). Chapter 9 discusses the term "genocide," which Lemkin describes as "a new term and conception for destruction of nations" (79).

38. On Lemkin and the Armenian genocide, see Steven L. Jacobs, "Raphael Lemkin and the Armenian Genocide," in *Looking Backward, Moving Forward: Confronting the Armenian Genocide*, ed. Richard G. Hovanisian (Routledge, 2003).

39. Vartan Matiossian, *The Politics of Naming the Genocide: Language, History, and "Medz Yeghern"* (London: IB Tauris, 2022), 56. Matiossian uses *tseghasbanutyun* in eastern Armenian phonetics, the Library of Congress transliteration is *ts'eghaspanut'iwn*, and it is pronounced in western Armenian as *tseghasbanutiwn*.

40. Matiossian, *The Politics of Naming the Genocide*, 56–57; Mardiros Sarian [Martiros Sarean], *Fē d'agombli ew Astutsoy tēm paterazm: Polis, Nurē Ōsmaniyēi mēj It't'ihatakanneru gaghtni oroshumnerē: Hayots' bnajnjman sharzhaṛit'neru masin* [Fait accompli and war against God. The secret decisions of the Unionists taken at Nuri Osmaniye, Constantinople: On the motives of the Armenian extermination] (Paris, [1933?]), 4. Sarian's reference is from an article written by Kéram Kévonian, "I. Introduction," Union internationale des organisations terre et culture website, https://www.collectif2015.org/en/Chapitre-1-Introduction.aspx, last visited June 30, 2022.

41. Marc Nichanian, "Catastrophic Mourning," in *Loss: The Politics of Mourning*, ed. David L. Eng and David Kazanjian (Berkeley: University of California Press, 2002), 101.

42. David Kazanjian and Marc Nichanian, "Between Genocide and Catastrophe," in Eng and Kazanjian, *Loss*, 133.

43. Nichanian, *The Historiographic Perversion*, 123.

44. Kazanjian and Nichanian, "Between Genocide and Catastrophe," 133.

45. One of the Armenian terms for the genocide is *Medz Yeghern*, often translated in Turkish as *Büyük Felaket*, or "Great Catastrophe," rather than "Great Crime" as the Armenian *Yeghern* indicates; Catastrophe is *Aghed*. For a discussion on the ways in which translations are manipulated to silence and deny the Armenian genocide in Turkey, see Nazan Maksudyan, "Walls of Silence: Translating the Armenian Genocide Into Turkish and Self-Censorship," *Critique* 37, no. 4 (November 2009): 635–649; and Matiossian, *The Politics of Naming the Genocide*, chap. 5. I return to this point in chapter 6 to discuss the usage of *Yeghern* as a denialist strategy in Turkey.

46. Ella Shohat explores the differentiation of North African Jews from Muslims, wherein Jews were perceived as "whiter" and more civilized within an Orientalist framework. She describes this as a process of "de-indigenizing" the Jew, whereby the image of the indigenous is set against European conceptions, aiming to dissociate local Jews from their Arab and Muslim sociocultural contexts. In the context of Turkish nationalism, Armenians have been denativized, reinforcing the notion that the Muslim Turk is the native and thus forging an exclusive claim to the land from which Armenians and other non-Muslims are excluded. Thus, while North African Jews were racially differentiated to align more closely with European colonial powers, enhancing their perceived status yet alienating them from their Muslim neighbors, Armenians in Turkey were denativized and actively erased from the national narrative to reinforce an exclusive Turkish identity. Both processes show how state and colonial projects manipulate minority identities for political ends. Ella Shohat, "On Orientalist Genealogies: The Split Arab/Jew Figure Revisited," in *The Arab and Jewish Questions: Geographies of Engagement in Palestine and Beyond*, ed. Bashir Bashir and Leila Farsakh (New York: Columbia University Press, 2020), 89–121.

47. William Dalrymple, *From the Holy Mountain: A Journey in the Shadow of Byzantium* (London: HarperCollins, 1997), 87. For more details on the destruction and neglect of Armenian buildings in Turkey, see Dalrymple, *From the Holy Mountain*, 83–88, and Tessa Hofmann, "Armenians in Turkey Today: A Critical Assessment of the Situation of the Armenian Minority in the Turkish Republic" (Brussels: The EU Office of Armenian Associations of Europe, 2002), 39–42.

48. Nancy Rose Hunt, *A Nervous State: Violence, Remedies, and Reverie in Colonial Congo* (Durham, N.C.: Duke University Press, 2016), contrasts the singular *aftermath* to the numerous *afterlives*, which I borrow here to highlight the multiple afterlives of the Armenian genocide.

49. Here I am invoking Edward Said, who sees the struggle between Palestinians and Zionism as one between a presence (that of Palestinians on the land) and an interpretation (that of the Zionist narrative that denies the presence of Palestinians). Edward W. Said, *The Question of Palestine* (New York: Vintage, 1978), 8–9.

50. Edward W. Said, *Culture and Imperialism* (New York: Vintage, 1994), 61. For a detailed treatment of Edward Said's methodology in Armenian and post-Ottoman studies, see Hakem Al-Rustom, "Between Anatolia and the Balkans: Tracing Armenians in a Post-Ottoman Order," in *An Armenian Mediterranean: Word and Worlds in Motion*, ed. Kathryn Babayan and Michael Pifer (Palgrave).

51. Zerrin Özlem Biner, *States of Dispossession: Violence and Precarious Coexistence in Southeast Turkey* (Philadelphia: University of Pennsylvania Press, 2020); David Leupold, *Embattled Dreamlands: The Politics of Contesting Armenian, Kurdish and Turkish Memory* (London: Routledge, 2020).

52. For moving beyond categorical binaries as a decolonizing method, see Linda Tuhiwai Smith, *Decolonizing Methodologies: Research and Indigenous Peoples* (London: Zed, 1999), 27.

53. The term "denativization" does not reinforce the nineteenth-century construction of the "native" by Armenian intellectuals, a construction that was critiqued by Marc Nichanian in *Mourning Philology*. Through the reading of literary texts, Nichanian shows how the "Armenian" was invented as a native

to create a distinct Armenian national identity rooted in an ancient past. The invention of the native entails, in Nichanian's words, an "auto-ethnographic project" whereby the creation of a modern notion of Armenianness is rooted in the past and constructed through archeological, philological, and ethnographic methods to establish a continuous narrative of Armenianness that was ancient and awaiting discovery in nineteenth century. See the introduction and chapter 2 of Marc Nichanian, *Mourning Philology: Art and Religion at the Margins of the Ottoman Empire*, trans. G. M. Gohsgarian and Jeff Fort (New York: Fordham University Press, 2014). As Helen Makhdoumian argues, Nichanian here is working within postcolonial studies, not critical Indigenous studies or settler colonial studies. See Helen Makhdoumian, "Armenian Studies in Conversation with Critical Indigenous Studies and Settler Colonial Studies: An Invitation," *Journal of the Society for Armenian Studies* 29 (2023): 6–8.

54. Patrick Wolfe, "Settler Colonialism and the Elimination of the Native," *Journal of Genocide Research* 8, no. 4 (2006): 387–409. On seeing the genocide and its denial as forming the structure of the Turkish state, see Talin Suciyan, "Armenian Genocide and its Denial: A Comprehensive Tool of Supremacism?" in *Denial of Genocides in the Twenty-First Century*, ed. Bedross der Matossian (Lincoln, NE: University of Nebraska Press, 2023).

55. Such periodization usually starts from the Europeanization process, the Tanzimat in the late Ottoman Empire, passing through the Hamidian massacres (1894–96), the Young Turk revolution (1908), the Adana massacres (1909), the genocide (1915–1918), post–World War I (1918–1923), the formation of diasporic communities (post-genocide onward), and the post-Soviet Republic of Armenian (1991 onward). Recently, scholars have paid attention to the Armenians who remained in Turkey since 1923.

56. Bedross Der Matossian, "Contending Trends in the Armenian Historiography of the Late Ottoman Empire: Inclusion vs. Exclusion," *New Perspectives on Turkey* 53 (November 2015): 175, indicates that the three phases of violence, namely the Hamidian massacres, the Adana massacres, and the Armenian genocide dominate the majority of the work written on Ottoman Armenians.

57. Bedross Der Matossian, in *The Horrors of Adana: Revolution and Violence in the Early Twentieth Century* (Stanford, Calif.: Stanford University Press, 2022), 4, presents these reasons to critique the positioning the Adana massacres as leading to the genocide.

58. This phonetic spelling uses the Library of Congress transliterated system. In western Armenian phonetics, it would be pronounced *"Averagnerun mech."*

59. Nichanian, "Catastrophic Mourning," 101.

60. Nichanian, "Catastrophic Mourning," 101.

61. Zabel Yessayan, preface to *In the Ruins: The 1909 Massacres of Armenians in Adana, Turkey* trans. G. M. Goshgarian (Boston: AIWA, 2016), 3–4.

62. Bedross Der Matossian, *Shattered Dreams of Revolution From Liberty to Violence in the Late Ottoman Empire* (Stanford, Calif.: Stanford University Press, 2014).

63. Der Matossian, *The Horrors of Adana*, 3–4, argues that the Adana massacres were not a "dress rehearsal" for the Armenian genocide.

64. Gerard J. Libaridian, "The Ultimate Repression: The Genocide of the Armenians, 1915–1917," in *Genocide and the Modern Age: Etiology and Case Studies of Mass Death*, ed. Isidor Wallimann and Michael N. Dobkowski (Syracuse, N.Y.: Syracuse University Press, 2000), 210.

65. In this context, Armenians were rendered what Giorgio Agamben calls *homo sacer* (the sacred man), who is unprotected by the law and whose killing does not constitute a homicide. For a reading of Essayan's *In the Ruins* through Agamben's concept of *homo sacer*, see Maral Aktokmakyan Erdoğan, "If This Is Life: Rethinking the Modern Subject Through the Aporia of Biopolitics" (PhD diss., Boğazici University, Istanbul, 2016), chap. 2. The Ottoman government at the time failed to prosecute the perpetrators of the massacres; see Der Matossian, *The Horrors of Adana*, chap. 8.

66. Patrick Wolfe, in "Settler Colonialism and the Elimination of the Native," argues that settler colonialism has both strives for destruction of native societies as well as builds new colonial societies in their place. I apply this idea by thinking of the constructive and destructive aspects of nation-states.

67. Mahmood Mamdani, *Neither Settler nor Native: The Making and Unmaking of Permanent Minorities* (Cambridge, Mass.: Harvard University Press, 2020).

68. In his survey of the Armenian genocide, Ronald Suny makes the gesture reading the Armenian predicament in light of other populations who face homogenization yet "refuse to disappear." Suny, *"They Can Live in the Desert,"* 365.

69. Achille Mbembe has theorized such state policies as "necropolitics," wherein state sovereignty is enshrined by its capacity to determine who may live and who must die. Achille Mbembe, "Necropolitics," *Public Culture* 15, no. 1 (2003), 11.

70. Suny, *"They Can Live in the Desert,"* 352.

71. For multidirectionality as a method of approaching memories of violence, see Michael Rothberg, *Multidirectional Memory: Remembering the Holocaust in the Age of Decolonization* (Stanford, Calif.: Stanford University Press, 2009), 7–12. Here I am particularly thinking through Rothberg's discussion of how W. E. B. Du Bois understood his African-American experience of racism by visiting the Nazi ghetto in Warsaw in 1952 (Rothberg, chap. 4).

72. Arendt, *Origins of Totalitarianism*, 293. Quoted in the context of historical disasters by Gil Anidjar, "On the Political History of Destruction," *ReOrient* 4, no. 2 (2019): 150.

73. Saidiya Hartman, *Lose Your Mother: A Journey Along the Atlantic Slave Route* (New York: Farrar, Straus and Giroux, 2007), 5.

74. Hartman, *Lose Your Mother*, 6. See also Orlando Patterson, *Slavery and Social Death: A Comparative Study* (Cambridge, Mass.: Harvard University Press, 1982).

75. In speaking about her grandmother who was sexually abused during the genocide, Susanne Khardalian said she "was alive but she was a walking corpse." See "Grandma's Tattoos," *Al-Jazeera*. On sexual violence during the genocide, see Matthias Bjørnlund, "'A Fate Worse Than Dying': Sexual Violence During the Armenian Genocide," in *Brutality and Desire: War and Sexuality in Europe's Twentieth Century*, ed. Dagmar Herzog ([place of publication?]: Palgrave Macmillan, 2010). Uğur Ümit Üngör, "Orphans, Converts, and Prostitutes: Social Consequences of War and Persecution in the Ottoman Empire, 1914–1923," *War in History* 19, no. 2 (2012): 173–192. Elyse Semerdjian, *Remnants: Embodied Archives of the Armenian Genocide* (Stanford, Calif.: Stanford University Press, 2023).

76. David L. Eng and David Kazanjian, "Introduction: Mourning Remains" in End and Kazanjian, *Loss*, 2.

77. Nichanian, "Catastrophic Mourning," 101.

78. Nichanian, "Catastrophic Mourning," 101.

79. Eng and Kazajian, *Loss*, 6.

80. Zabel Yessayan, *In the Ruins: The 1909 Massacres of Armenians in Adana, Turkey* trans. G. M. Goshgarian (Boston: AIWA, 2016), 11. The Armenian *mēj* (pronounced *"mech"* in western Armenian) means "in" or "among." *Awerak* (pronounced *"averag"* in Western Armenian), which means "ruins," can also figuratively mean "ruined people" according to the famous dictionary of Step'an Malkhaseants'. See Step'an Malkhaseants', *Hayerēn bats'atrakan baṛaran*, Vol. 1 (Yerevan: Haykakan SSṚ Petakan Hratarakch'ut'iwn, 1944), 296. I am grateful to Michael Pifer for bringing this figurative meaning to my attention.

81. This is the approach that Eng and Kazajian develop in their introduction to *Loss*.

82. The republican regime in Turkey is seen by Orientalist historians such as Bernard Lewis as a unique secular moment in Muslim history. See Hakem Al-Rustom, "Internal Orientalism and the Nation-State Order: Turkey, Armenians, and the Writing of History," *ARIEL: A Review of International English Literature* 51, no. 4 (2020): 1–31.

83. Patterson, *Slavery and Social Death*, 38.

84. Jared Sexton, "The Social Life of Social Death: On Afro-pessimism and Black Optimism," *InTensions Journal* 5 (Fall/Winter 2011).

85. Gerald Vizenor, "Aesthetics of Survivance," in *Native Liberty: Natural Reason and Cultural Survivance* (Lincoln: University of Nebraska Press, 2009), 85–86.

86. Vizenor, "Aesthetics of Survivance," 85.

87. On the application of Vizenor's survivance in the Armenian context see Helen Makhdoumian, "Connected Memoryscapes of Silence in Micheline Aharonian Marcom's *Draining the Sea*," *Modern Fiction Studies* 66, no. 2 (2020): 301–324; also Keith David Watenpaugh, "Kill the Armenian/ Indian; Save the Turk/Man: Carceral Humanitarianism, the Transfer of Children and a Comparative History of Indigenous Genocide," *Journal of the Society for Armenian Studies* 29 (2022): 1–33.

88. Vizenor, "Aesthetics of Survivance," 85.

89. Eng and Kazajian, *Loss*, 6.

90. Yael Navaro's work on occupied northern Cyprus in *The Make-Believe Space: Affective Geography in a Postwar Polity* (Durham, N.C.: Duke University Press, 2012).

91. See for example Biner, *States of Dispossession*; on the way Armenian genocide is present through practice of treasure hunting in Turkish Kurdistan, see von Bieberstein, "Treasure/Fetish/Gift;" Suni, "Palimpsests of Violence;" for an exploration of the persistent yet publicly unacknowledged violence against Armenians in southeast Turkey—what Michael Taussig terms "public secrecy"—see Biner, "Acts of Defacement, Memory of Loss;" on the emergence of stories about the destroyed Armenian cemetery that was replaced by Gezi Park in Istanbul during the 2013 anti-state demonstrations, see Parla and Özgül, "Property, Dispossession, and Citizenship in Turkey."

92. Ann Laura Stoler, ed., *Imperial Debris: On Ruins and Ruination* (Durham, N.C.: Duke University Press, 2013).

93. Ann Laura Stoler, " 'The Rot Remains': From Ruins to Ruination," in *Imperial Debris: On Ruins and Ruination*, ed. Ann Laura Stoler (Durham, N.C.: Duke University Press, 2013), 24.

94. For an analysis of how the denial of the Armenian genocide is situated within an Orientalist discourse that glorifies rather than condemns the Turkish state, see Al-Rustom, "Internal Orientalism and the Nation-State Order."

95. Walter Benjamin, "Theses on the Philosophy of History," thesis IX in *Illuminations: Essays and Reflections*, trans. Harry Zohn (New York: Schocken, 1969), 257.

96. Patrick Wolfe, in "Settler Colonialism and the Elimination of the Native," argues that settler colonialism is not an event but a structure that continues after an event of conquest has ended.

97. Dan Mellamphy and Nandita Biswas Mellamphy, "What's the 'Matter' with Materialism? Walter Benjamin and the New Janitocracy," *Janus Head* 11, no. 1 (2009): 172.

98. Suciyan, "Armenian Genocide and its Denial," 67. For a detailed history of the Turkish state denial of violence against Armenians, see Fatma Müge Göçek, *Denial of Violence: Ottoman Past, Turkish Present and the Collective Violence Against Armenians, 1789–2009* (New York: Oxford University Press, 2015).

99. Kazanjian and Nichanian, "Between Genocide and Catastrophe," 128. On the way the Armenian genocide was meant to "envisage a future in which Armenians never existed" see Suciyan, "Armenian Genocide and its Denial," 66.

100. See Arendt, *Origins of Totalitarianism*; Hartman, *Lose Your Mother*.

101. Marlene Schäfers, "Afterlives: An Introduction," Allegra Lab: Anthropology for Radical Optimism, May 2020, https://allegralaboratory.net/afterlives-introduction, visited February 17, 2024).

102. Avery F. Gordon, *Ghostly Matters: Haunting and the Sociological Imagination* (Minneapolis: University of Minnesota Press, 2008), 7–8, 195. I am grateful to Zerrin Özlem Biner for introducing me to this text. Marlene Schäfers brings Gordon's work to explain afterlives as "endings with an 'after.' " Schäfers, "Afterlives: An Introduction."

103. Some of the recent work in history and anthropology includes: Jordanna Beilkin, *The Afterlife of Empire* (Oakland: University of California Press, 2012); Gastón Gordillo, *Rubble: The Aftermath of Destruction* (Durham, N.C.: Duke University Press, 2014); Alice Wilson, *Afterlives of Revolution: Everyday Counterhistories in Southern Oman* (Stanford, Calif.: Stanford University Press, 2023); Leyla Amzi-Erdoğdular, *The Afterlife of Ottoman Europe: Muslims in Habsburg Bosnia Herzegovina*

(Stanford, Calif.: Stanford University Press, 2024). In the Armenian context in Turkey, see Çiçek İlengiz, "Magical Afterlives in Post-genocidal Turkey," Allegra Lab: Anthropology for Radical Optimism, May 2020, https://allegralaboratory.net/magical-afterlives-in-post-genocidal-turkey, visited May 6, 2024; Suni, "Palimpsests of Violence." In the Armenian context in Armenia, see Ayşenur Korkmaz, "Crafted Presence: The Afterlives of the Armenian Genocide in Armenia" (PhD diss., University of Amsterdam, Amsterdam, 2022).

104. Walter Benjamin, "The Task of The Translator," in *Illuminations: Essays and Reflections*, trans. Harry Zohn (New York: Schocken, 1985), 71; quoted by Gordillo, *Rubble*, 20–21.

105. Michel-Rolph Trouillot, *Silencing the Past: Power and the Production of History* (Boston: Beacon, 1995), chap. 3. This notion of Armenians in Turkey being unthinkable in Turkish and Armenian historical narratives is further developed in chapter 1. It applies Trouillot's arguments on the Haitian Revolution to the Armenian context.

106. For an analysis on how the Turkish official narrative blames Armenians for their predicament, see Fatma Ulgen, "Reading Mustafa Kemal Atatürk on the Armenian Genocide of 1915," *Patterns of Prejudice* 44, no. 4 (2010), 369–391.

107. Most recently, Turkish president Recep Tayyip Erdoğan used this term in 2020, and it was widely understood that he was referring to Armenians. An Armenian member of the Turkish parliament, Garo Paylan, reacted to Erdogan's usage of the term, saying, "*Kılıç artığı* [leftovers of the sword] was invented to refer to orphans, like my paternal grandmother, who survived the Armenian Genocide." *Ermeni Haber Ajansi*, May 6, 2020, https://www.ermenihaber.am/tr/news/2020/05/06/Garo-Paylan-Erdo%C4%9Fan/182720, last accessed December 21, 2022.

108. Ohannes Kılıçdağı, "Yine mi 'kılıç artığı'?," *Agos*, May 8, 2020, http://www.agos.com.tr/tr/yazi/24005/yine-mi-kilic-artigi.

109. On the production of silence in historical narratives, I am guided by Trouillot, *Silencing the Past*, chap. 2.

110. Vizenor, "Aesthetics of Survivance," 85.

111. The destroyed and renovated Armenian buildings are discussed later in chap. 6. The term "surviving objects" of the Armenian genocide was developed by Heghnar Zeitlian Watenpaugh, *The Missing Page: The Modern Life of a Medieval Manuscript from Genocide to Justice* (Stanford, Calif.: Stanford University Press, 2019).

112. On refusal and the exercise of intellectual sovereignty, I build on Audra Simpson, "On Ethnographic Refusal: Indigeneity, 'Voice' and Colonial Citizenship," *Junctures*, no. 9 (December 2007): 67–80.

113. Simpson, "On Ethnographic Refusal."

114. Simpson, "On Ethnographic Refusal." See also, *Mohawk Interruptus: Political Life Across the Borders of Settler States* (Durham, N.C.: Duke University Press, 2014).

115. Simpson, "On Ethnographic Refusal," 67–68.

116. Walter Benjamin, "Theses on the Philosophy of History," in *Illuminations: Essays and Reflections*, trans. Harry Zohn (New York: Schocken, 1969), 71.

117. I engage with Jacques Derrida's notion of "afterlife of survival" from "Archive Fever: A Freudian Impression," *Diacritics* 25, no. 2 (Summer 1995): 41, through the interpretive lens provided by Vizenor, "Aesthetics of Survivance," 103. Vizenor reinterprets Derrida's concept, substituting "survival" with "survivance," a modification I adopt here to frame the agency in the Armenian historical experience.

118. Locke, "Death and the Storyteller." In his essay "The Storyteller," Walter Benjamin states that "the storyteller has borrowed his authority from death."

119. Gordillo, *Rubble*, 6.

120. Yael Navaro, "The Aftermath of Mass Violence: A Negative Methodology," *Annual Review of Anthropology* 49 (2020): 162.

121.   Locke, "Death and the Storyteller." See also Navaro, "The Aftermath of Mass Violence."

122.   In a commentary on Walter Benjamin's essay "The Storyteller," Uwe Steiner speaks of the communi-
       cation of experience as no longer belonging to the individual, rather to the collective." Uwe Steiner,
       Walter Benjamin: An Introduction to His Work and Thought, trans. Michael Winkler (Chicago: Uni-
       versity of Chicago Press), 131.

123.   Navaro, "The Aftermath of Mass Violence," 161–173.

124.   Article II of the "Convention on the Prevention and Punishment of the Crime of Genocide"
       defines genocide as the "intent to destroy, in whole or in part, a national, ethnical, racial or religious
       group."

125.   Marc Nichanian, ed., *Writers of Disaster*: *Armenian Literature in the Twentieth Century*, vol. 1, *The
       National Revolution* (London: Gomidas Institute, 2002), 13–14. Yael Navaro develops the concept
       of negative methodology in her study of ethnographies examining the aftermath of violence, build-
       ing on Nichanian's work; see Navaro, "The Aftermath of Mass Violence,"163.

126.   Walter Benjamin rejects historicism, which is the possibility that one could know the past the way it
       really was, in thesis VI, "Theses on the Philosophy of History." Commenting on Benjamin, Michel
       Löwy, *Fire Alarm: Reading Benjamin's 'On the Concept of History'* (London: Verso, 2016), 5, states:
       "For revolutionary Romanticism the aim is not a return to the past, but a detour through the past on
       the way to a utopian future."

127.   Mandel, *In the Aftermath of Genocide*, 21.

128.   Whenever a place has a more than one name, I provide the local name followed by the official name
       recognized by the Turkish state.

1. KILLING THE INFIDEL:
ARMENIAN ERASURES AS TURKEY'S COUNTER-HISTORIES

1.   For the "deep state" in Turkey, see Başak Ertür, "The Conspiracy Archive: Turkey's Deep State on
     Trial," in *Law, Violence, Memory: Uncovering the Counter-Archive*, ed. Stewart Motha and Honni
     van Rijswijk (Abingdon, UK: Routledge, 2016), 177–194. See also Yael Navaro, *Faces of the State:
     Secularism and Public Life in Turkey* (Princeton, N.J.: Princeton University Press, 2002).

2.   For the larger context of the 1955 Istanbul pogroms, see Dilek Güven, "Riots Against the Non-Mus-
     lims of Turkey: 6/7 September 1955 in the Context of Demographic Engineering," *European Journal
     of Turkish Studies: Social Sciences on Contemporary Turkey* 12 (2011).

3.   Hrant Dink, "A Dove Skittishness in My Soul," first published in *Agos*, English translation posted
     on the Turkish site *Bianet*, January 22, 2007, https://bianet.org/english/politics/90552-a-doves
     -skittishness-in-my-soul, accessed March 16, 2022.

4.   Echoing Benjamin's "Theses on the Philosophy of History," thesis V in *Illuminations: Essays and
     Reflections*, trans. Harry Zohn (New York: Schocken, 1969), 255.

5.   For news coverage, see Fiachara Gibbons, "He Believed His Love for His Country Would Save Him,"
     The Guardian (London), January 22, 2007; Amberin Zaman, "Turkish Journalist Who Spoke up for
     Armenians Is Shot Dead in the Street," *Daily Telegraph* (London), January 20, 2007.

6.   "Fury After Police Pictured Posing with Dink Murder Suspect," *The Guardian*, February 3, 2007,
     https://www.theguardian.com/world/2007/feb/03/turkey.international, accessed May 12, 2021.

7.   Navaro, *Faces of the State*, chap. 6, speaks of the cult of Mustafa Kemal and his continuous "appari-
     tions" throughout the republic's history who comes to rescue the nation from its internal and exter-
     nal enemies.

8.   Catherine Gallagher and Stephen Greenblatt, *Practicing New Historicism* (Chicago and London:
     The University of Chicago Press, 2000), 52.

9. Here I am invoking Edward Said's "intertwined histories and overlapping territories" that he discusses as a methodology for decolonization. Edward Said, *Culture and Imperialism* (New York: Vintage, 1993), 18, 61.

10. Fatma Ulgen, "'Sabiha Gökçen's 80-Year-Old Secret': Kemalist Nation Formation and the Ottoman Armenians" (PhD diss., University of California San Diego, 2010), 110.

11. Before the abolition of Ottoman honorific titles, Mustafa Kemal was known as "Paşa," an honorary title used for army officers, ministers, and governors. Following the Turkish victory in the War of Independence, he was also given the title "Gazi" (Ottoman-Turkish from Arabic that means "conqueror" or "warrior," usually for the sake of Islam). In the early republican years, Mustafa Kemal was known by the combined titled Gazi Paşa.

12. All the details of Gökçen's meeting with Kemal are summarized from Ayşe Gül Altınay, *The Myth of the Military Nation: Militarism, Gender, and Education in Turkey* (New York: Palgrave Macmillan, 2004), 35–36.

13. For a treatment of this myth in the construction of Turkish historiography, see Altınay, *The Myth of the Military Nation*, chap. 1.

14. Quoted from Gökçen's memoirs and used in the same context by Altınay, *The Myth of the Military Nation*, 40.

15. Ersin Kalkan, "Sabiha Gökçen mi Hatun Sebilciyan mı" [Sabiha Gökçen or Hatun Sebilciyan?], *Hürriyet*, February 21, 2004, https://www.hurriyet.com.tr/gundem/sabiha-gokcen-mi-hatun-sebilciyan-mi-204257.

16. Text in English is from a website dedicated the Hrant Dink Memorial Lecture at Boğaziçi University, http://hrantdinkmemoriallecture.boun.edu.tr/index.php/en/hrant-dink, accessed May 12, 2021.

17. "11-Month Prison Sentence for 'Gul Is Armenian' Comment," *Armenian Weekly*, November 6, 2010, https://armenianweekly.com/2010/11/06/11-month-sentence, last visited December 9, 2019.

18. This was during a joint TV program for the presidential candidates between two Turkish television networks, NTV and Star TV, in early August 2014. See "Erdoğan: Afedersin Ermeni Diyen Oldu" *Bianet*, August 6, 2014 https://m.bianet.org/bianet/toplum/157616-erdogan-afedersin-ermeni-diyen-oldu, accessed November 24, 2024.

19. Examples of these are in the life stories of the grandchildren of converted Armenians complied in Ayşe Gül Altınay and Fethiye Çetin, *The Grandchildren: The Hidden Legacy of the "Lost" Armenians in Turkey* (New Brunswick, N.J.: Transaction, 2014).

20. In a study on the connection between the Turkish denial of the Armenian genocide and the formation of the Turkish nation, Fatma Ulgen suggests that questioning Gökçen's parentage is a delicate matter that touches on the very foundation of the Turkish state. See Ulgen, "'Sabiha Gökçen's 80-Year-Old Secret.'"

21. Ulgen, "'Sabiha Gökçen's 80-Year-Old Secret.'"

22. Ronald Grigor Suny, "Constructing Primordialism: Old Histories for New Nation," *Journal of Modern History* 73 (December 2001): 870.

23. Fatma Müge Göçek, *Denial of Violence: Ottoman Past, Turkish Present and the Collective Violence Against Armenians, 1789–2009* (New York: Oxford University Press, 2015), 8–9.

24. Michel-Rolph Trouillot, *Silencing the Past: Power and the Production of History* (Boston: Beacon, 1995).

25. Benjamin, "Theses on the Philosophy of History," thesis VII, 256.

26. Michael Löwy, *Fire Alarm: Reading Benjamin's "On the Concept of History"* (London: Verso, 2016), 54.

27. Benjamin, "Theses on the Philosophy of History," thesis VII, 256.

28. Banu Karaca offers this reading of Benjamin's thesis VII by extending the meaning of the German noun *Überlieferung* ("the manner in which it is transmitted"), "to lore, to stories about the past—often triumphalist in nature—and to the ways in which they are told, retold, and passed on from one generation to another," and not just "the mere transfer of ownership," as the English translation

is rendered. Banu Karaca, "Art, Dispossession, and Imaginations of Historical Justice: Thinking with the Works of Maria Eichhorn and Dilek Winchester," *Critical Times* 3, no. 2 (August 2020), 225–226.

29. Edward W. Said, *The Question of Palestine* (New York: Verso, 1979), xxxv.

30. The essay is part of Said's *The Question of Palestine*, 56–114.

31. Said, *The Question of Palestine*, 54.

32. Ella Shohat, "Sephardim in Israel: Zionism from the Standpoint of Its Jewish Victims," *Social Text*, no. 19/20 (Autumn 1988): 1.

33. Hans-Lukas Kieser, *Iskalanmış Barış Doğu Vilayetleri'nde Misyonerlik, Etnik Kimlik ve Devlet 1839–1938* (Istanbul: İletişim Yayınları), 27–28. Quoted in the context of the exclusion of violence against Armenians in Turkish historiography in Talin Suciyan, *The Armenians in Modern Turkey: Post-genocide Society, Politics, and History* (London: IB Tauris, 2016), 10.

34. For a discussion on how historical narratives are constructed, often with omissions, to serve the purposes of nation-building and the maintenance of national identities, see Suny, "Constructing Primordialism."

35. Trouillot describes four "crucial moments" as fact creation or the gathering of sources, the assembling of archives, the formation of historical narratives from the retrieved archives, and finally the retrospective significance of the narrated history. Trouillot, *Silencing the Past*, 26. Altınay and Türkyılmaz, "Unraveling Layers of Silencing" apply Trouillot's framework to explain the silencing of converted Armenian women in historiography.

36. Frederik Le Roy, "Ragpickers and Leftover Performances: Walter Benjamin's Philosophy of the Historical Leftover," *Performance Research* 22, no. 8 (2017): 130.

37. Le Roy, "Ragpickers and Leftover Performances," 130.

38. Le Roy, "Ragpickers and Leftover Performances," 130.

39. Toni Morrison, 1998 interview with Jana Wendt on ABC (Australia), for a program called "Uncensored." Available at https://www.youtube.com/watch?v=DQomMjII22I.

40. See, for example, the story of Mehmet: "I found out that my grandmother was Armenian while doing my military service," in Altınay and Çetin, *The Grandchildren*, 71–74.

41. Tetsuo Kogawa "Trash-Art in the Age of Digital Ash," 1999, https://anarchy.translocal.jp/non-japanese /19990808trash-art.html, last visited March 15, 2022.

42. For a discussion on the failure to prosecute the perpetrators of Adana Massacres of 1909, see Bedross Der Matossian, *The Horrors of Adana: Revolution and Violence in the Early Twentieth Century* (Stanford, Calif.: Stanford University Press, 2022), chaps. 7, 8.

43. On the gendered nature of the genocide, see Ayşe Gül Altınay, "Unravelling Layers of Silencing: Where Are the Converted Armenians?," in Altınay and Çetin, *The Grandchildren*; Lerna Ekmekçioğlu, *Recovering Armenia: The Limits of Belonging in Post-genocide Turkey* (Stanford, Calif.: Stanford University Press, 2016), 9–14.

44. On sexual violence during the genocide, see Matthias Bjørnlund, "'A Fate Worse Than Dying': Sexual Violence During the Armenian Genocide," in *Brutality and Desire: War and Sexuality in Europe's Twentieth Century*, ed. Dagmar Herzog (New York: Palgrave Macmillan, 2010); Uğur Ümit Üngör, "Orphans, Converts, and Prostitutes: Social Consequences of War and Persecution in the Ottoman Empire, 1914–1923," *War in History* 19, no. 2 (2012): 173–192.

45. On violence against Alevi Kurds and the Dersim massacres, see Zeynep Türkyilmaz, "On Dersim and the Banality of Evil: The Diary of Yusuf Kenan Akım," in *TRAFO—Blog for Transregional Research*, January 5, 2021, https://trafo.hypotheses.org/26069; Cevat Dargin, "'An Oasis of Humanity Within the Damned Empire': The Armenian Question in Dersim in State-Making in Dersim Across Empire and Nation-State (1878–1938) (PhD diss., Princeton University, 2021).

46. For a study on the centrality of the military in Turkish nationalism, see Altınay, *The Myth of the Military Nation*.

47. For the information about the Dersim operation and Gökçen's quote, see Ulgen, "Sabiha Gökçen's 80-Year-Old Secret": Kemalist Nation Formation and the Ottoman Armenians," 113–114. Ulgen sites "Turkish Paradox," *New York Times*, June 20, 1937, which mentions that the casualties were 5,000 lives. In 2011, the Turkish president, Recep Tayyip Erdoğan (then the prime minister) apologized for the bombardment of Dersim. The number killed in the apology campaign was 13,000. See "Turkey PM Erdogan Apologizes for 1930s Kurdish Killings," *BBC News*, November 23, 2011, https://www.bbc.com/news/world-europe-15857429, accessed April 4, 2021.

48. The apology for the Dersim massacres that Erdoğan issued in 2011 when he was prime minister has been read largely as a way to pretend reconciliation with the past to silence discussion of the ongoing violence against the Kurds in Turkey. See Bilgin Ayata and Serra Hakyemez, "The AKP's Engagement with Turkey's Past Crimes: An Analysis of Erdogan's 'Dersim Apology,'" *Dialectical Anthropology* 37, no. 1 (March 2013): 131–143.

49. For example, Herzig, Edmund and Marina Kurkchiyan, *The Armenians: Past and Present in the Making of National Identity* (New York: Routledge, 2005), give the following sequence of chapters in their edited volume: "Genocide and Independence 1914–21"; "Soviet Armenia 1921–91"; "Armenians in the Diaspora." Two other works present the same sequence: Christopher Walker, *Armenia: The Survival of a Nation* (New York: St. Martin's Press, 1980), places the chapter "The Death of Turkish Armenia" right before a discussion of the Republic of Armenia. Ronald Grigor Suny, *Looking Toward Ararat: Armenia in Modern History* (Bloomington: Indiana University Press, 1993), discusses the Republic of Armenia and the diaspora right after the chapter on the genocide. Razmik Panossian, *The Armenians: From Kings and Priests to Merchants and Commissars* (New York: Columbia University Press, 2006), follows a similar chronology of events, leaving out Armenians who remained in Istanbul and Anatolia after the genocide. Earlier works, exemplified by the prominent historian Arshag Alboyadjian (1879–1962), who wrote several volumes on the history of Armenians in the Ottoman eastern provinces, have each ended on the destruction of Armenians in each locale during the genocide. For a short treatment on Alboyadjian's work, see Bedross Der Matossian, "Contending Trends in the Armenian Historiography of the Late Ottoman Empire: Inclusion vs. Exclusion," *New Perspectives on Turkey* 53 (November 2015): 176–177.

50. Two historical works that focus solely on the Armenians in Turkey are worth noting here: Suciyan, *The Armenians in Modern Turkey*; Ekmekçioğlu, *Recovering Armenia*. On the hidden and converted Armenian survivors in Turkey, see Avedis Hadjian, *Secret Nation: The Hidden Armenians of Turkey* (London: IB Tauris, 2018).

51. For a discussion on the silences around the converted Armenians during and in the aftermath of the genocide, see Ayşe Gül Altınay and Yektan Türkyılmaz, "Unraveling Layers of Silencing: Converted Armenian Survivors of 1915," in *Untold Histories of the Middle East: Recovering Voices from the 19th and 20th Centuries*, ed. Amy Singer, Christoph Neumann, and Selçuk Akşin Somel (New York: Routledge, 2010). For stories of children of converted Armenians, see Altınay and Çetin, *The Grandchildren*.

52. Nicolas Argenti, "Introduction: The Presence of the Past in the Era of the Nation-State," *Social Analysis* 61, no. 1 (Spring 2017): 2.

53. Kerem Öktem, *Angry Nation: Turkey Since 1989* (New York: Zed, 2011), 145. For an analysis of the official state narrative of history, see Altınay, *The Myth of Military Nation*; Fatma Ulgen's discussion of Mustafa Kemal's *Nutuk* (Great Speech), which became the foundation for Turkish history in school textbooks and official discourses, Fatma Ulgen, "Reading Mustafa Kemal Atatürk on the Armenian Genocide of 1915," *Patterns of Prejudice* 44, no. 4 (2010), 369–391

54. Altınay, *The Myth of Military Nation*, 18–19.

55. Trouillot, *Silencing the Past*, 27.

56. For a discussion about the ways in which the Armenian survivors in Turkey have been considered part of the dead, see Altınay and Türkyılmaz, "Unraveling Layers of Silencing."

57. Trouillot, *Silencing the Past*, chap. 2.

58. Ulgen, "Reading Mustafa Kemal Atatürk on the Armenian Genocide of 1915."

59. Ulgen, "Reading Mustafa Kemal Atatürk on the Armenian Genocide of 1915," 385.

60. Ulgen, "Reading Mustafa Kemal Atatürk on the Armenian Genocide of 1915," 385.

61. This passage from Kemal's *Nutuk* is quoted from Ulgen, "Reading Mustafa Kemal Atatürk on the Armenian Genocide of 1915," 387.

62. This argument is an extension of Trouillot's discussion on "Sans Souci," in *Silencing the Past*, chap. 2.

63. Altınay and Türkyılmaz, "Unraveling Layers of Silencing."

64. Trouillot, *Silencing the Past*, chap. 3. For a critique of Trouillot, see Vivaldi Jean-Marie, "Kant and Trouillot on the Unthinkability of the Haitian Revolution," *A Critical Journal of Black Politics, Culture, and Society* 15, no. 3 (2013): 241–257. I am grateful to Omid Tofighian for bringing this critique to my attention.

65. Refer to endnote 49 above for examples where the genocide has been positioned as a finality in Armenian historiography.

66. For example, works by recent historians include Talin Suciyan, *The Armenians in Modern Turkey: Post-Genocide Society, Politics and History* (London: IB Tauris, 2016); Lerna Ekmekçioğlu, *Recovering Armenia: The Limits of Belonging in Post-Genocide Turkey* (Stanford, Calif.: Stanford University Press, 2016); Ari Sekeryan, "The Armenians in the Ottoman Empire After the First World War (1918–1923)" (PhD diss., Hertford College, University of Oxford, 2018).

67. Argenti, "Introduction: The Presence of the Past in the Era of the Nation-State," 4. Argenti also argues that anthropology has adopted the Enlightenment viewpoint in considering the nation-state as "the natural endpoint of a universal process of state formation."

68. Bernard Lewis, *The Emergence of Modern Turkey* (Oxford: Oxford University Press, 1961); Erik Zürcher, *Turkey: A Modern History* (London: IB Tauris, 1993). It is notable that in the first edition of his book, Lewis speaks of the "Armenian holocaust." His stance has gradually shifted to a more denialist stance. For a discussion on Lewis's denialism, see Hakem Al-Rustom, "Internal Orientalism and the Nation-State Order: Turkey, Armenians, and the Writing of History," *ARIEL: A Review of International English Literature* 51, no. 4 (2020), 1–31.

69. For a discussion on the representation of Armenians in Turkish nationalist historiography, see Ulgen, "Reading Mustafa Kemal Atatürk on the Armenian Genocide of 1915," 385, where she offers a discourse analysis of Mustafa Kemal's *Nutuk* (Great Speech), which became the foundation for Turkish history in school textbooks and official discourses.

70. On the post-Ottoman as an analytical framework see Argenti, "The Presence of the Past in the Era of the Nation-State," and Rebecca Bryant, "Everyday Coexistence in the Post-Ottoman Space," in *Post-Ottoman Coexistence: Sharing Space in the Shadow of Conflict*, ed. Rebecca Bryant (Berghahn, 2016), 1–39.

71. Deniz Yonucu and Talin Suciyan, "From the Ottoman Empire to Post-1923: The Catastrophe as Seen by the Angel of History," *Critical Times* 3, no. 2 (August 2020): 306.

72. For seeing modern states as projects of destruction, see Charles Tilly, "War Making and State Making as Organized Crime," in *Bringing the State Back In*, ed. Peter Evans, Dietrich Rueschemeyer, and Theda Skocpol (Cambridge: Cambridge University Press, 1985); Michael Mann, *The Dark Side of Democracy* (Cambridge: Cambridge University Press, 2012).

73. Here I am referring to the two most commonly read books on Turkey: Bernard Lewis, *The Emergence of Modern Turkey*; Zürcher, *Turkey: A Modern History*.

74. Bernard Lewis quoted in Marc Nichanian, *The Historiographic Perversion* (New York: Columbia University Press, 2009), 20, from Lewis's response published in *Le Monde*, January 1, 1994. For an

analysis of the ways in which Lewis denies the genocide within an Orientalist framework that sees the formation of the Turkish state as a success story, see Hakem Al-Rustom "Internal Orientalism and the Nation-State Order: Turkey, Armenians, and the Writing of History" *ARIEL: A Review of International English Literature* 51, no. 4 (2020).

75. Nichanian, *The Historiographic Perversion*, 20

76. Zürcher, *Turkey*.

77. Zürcher, *Turkey*, 336–337.

78. Erik Zürcher "The Role of Historians of Turkey in the Study of Armenian Genocide," *REPAIR: Armeno-Turkish Platform*, June 3, 2015, https://repairfuture.net/index.php/en/armenian-genocide-recognition-and-reparations-other-standpoint/the-role-of-historians-of-turkey-in-the-study-of-armenian-genocide, accessed October 26, 2024.

79. I say that the law was "mostly" applied to non-Muslims, because the text of the law itself did not specify a particular group. The law, however, was applied mainly to non-Muslim citizens. For a comprehensive study on this tax law, see Rıfat N. Bali, *The 'Varlık Vergisi' Affair: A Study on Its Legacy from Selected Documents* (Istanbul: Isis Press, 2005).

80. Kemal Yalçın, *You Rejoice My Heart*, trans. Paul Bessemer (Tekeyan Cultural Association, 2007), 86.

81. Yalçın, *You Rejoice My Heart*, 36.

82. Ali Bayramoğlu, "Foreword," in *Sounds of Silence*, ed. Freda Balancar, trans. Nur Deriş and Ali Ottoman (Istanbul: Hrant Dink Foundation, 2012), 2.

83. Melissa Bilal, "The Lost Lullaby and Other Stories About Being an Armenian in Turkey," *New Perspectives on Turkey* 34 (Spring 2006): 69, 73,

84. Carolyn K. Steedman, *Dust: The Archive and Cultural History* (New Brunswick, N.J.: Rutgers University Press, 2001), 68.

85. Gil Anidjar, "Against History" in Marc Nichanian *The Historiographic Perversion*, trans. Gil Anidjar (New York: Columbia University Press, 2009), 129.

86. Jacques Derrida, "Archive Fever: A Freudian Impression," *Diacritics* 25, no. 2 (Summer 1995): 10

87. Trouillot, *Silencing the Past*, 5.

88. Öktem, *Angry Nation*, 84.

89. Catharina Dufft, *Turkish Literature and Cultural Memory: "Multiculturalism" as a Literary Theme After 1980* (Wiesbaden, Germany: Harrassowitz, 2009).

90. See Bilal, "The Lost Lullaby."

91. To date, five volumes were published in this series, the first subtitled "Turkey's Armenians Speak," and each of the subsequent volumes is dedicated to oral testimonies of Armenians from a specific city: Diyarbakır, Ankara, Izmit, and Kayseri.

92. Ekmekçioğlu, *Recovering Armenia*; Suciyan, *The Armenians in Modern Turkey*.

93. "Gökçen Ermeni'ydi" [Gökçen was Armenian]. *Hürriyet*, February 22, 2004. https://www.hurriyet.com.tr/gundem/gokcen-ermeni-ydi-204371, accessed March 16, 2022.

94. For a concise treatment of how Mustafa Kemal articulated the exclusion of Armenians from the Turkish nationalist project prior to the establishment of the republic, see Ulgen, "Reading Mustafa Kemal Atatürk on the Armenian Genocide of 1915."

95. Nichanian, "Between Genocide and Catastrophe," 133.

96. Selçuk Akşin Somel, Christoph K. Neumann and Amy Singer, "Introduction: Re-sounding silent voices" in *Untold Histories of the Middle East: Recovering Voices from the 19th and 20th Centuries*, ed. Amy Singer, Christoph Neumann, and Selçuk Akşin Somel (New York: Routledge, 2010), 13.

97. Marc David Baer, *Sultanic Saviors and Tolerant Turks Writing Ottoman Jewish History, Denying the Armenian Genocide* (Bloomington: Indiana University Press, 2020), 244.

98. Hartman, "Venus in Two Acts," 4.

99. Benjamin's "Theses on the Philosophy of History," thesis VI, p. 255.

2. MINORITIZED BY LAW:
LAUSANNE AS A TREATY OF COUNTER-SOVEREIGNTY

1. Onur Yıldırım, *Diplomacy and Displacement: Reconsidering the Turco-Greek Exchange of Populations, 1922–1934* (London: Routledge, 2006), 17. Yildirim also states that in the official Greek historiography, Lausanne was seen as a tragedy for bringing all Greek national aspirations to an end with the failed invasion of Asia Minor.

2. Richard G. Hovannisian, *The Republic of Armenia*, Volume 4, *Between Crescent and Sickle: Partition and Sovietization* (Oakland: University of California Press, 1996), 403. And this quote was the volume's only reference to the Lausanne Treaty.

3. As mentioned in chap. 1, the periodization of Armenian history continues in either the diaspora or Soviet Armenia after the genocide and Ottoman demise, but not in Turkey. In this narrative, the Lausanne Treaty is marked as the end for Ottoman Armenian history.

4. Uğur Ümit Üngör, "Orphans, Converts, and Prostitutes: Social Consequences of War and Persecution in the Ottoman Empire, 1914–1923," *War in History* 19, no. 2: 173–192.

5. Zabel Yessayan, *In the Ruins: The 1909 Massacres of Armenians in Adana, Turkey*, trans. G. M. Goshgarian (Boston: AIWA, 2016), 3–4.

6. Hannah Arendt, speaking of the state of survival of Jewish refugees after World War II, in *The Origin of Totalitarianism* (1958), 293. Cited in the context of disasters by Gil Anidjar, "On the Political History of Destruction," *ReOrient* 4, no. 2 (2019): 150.

7. Manu Vimalassery [Karuka], "Counter-sovereignty," *Journal of Nineteenth-Century Americanists* 2, no. 1 (Spring 2014): 142.

8. I am grateful to Rana Barakat for bringing this to my attention.

9. Vimalassery, "Counter-sovereignty," 142.

10. Quoted in Stanley Michalak, *A Primer in Power Politics* (Wilmington, Del.: SR Books, 2001), 208, from "Turkish Efficiency in Starving Armenia," *Literary Digest* (May 17, 1919), 32

11. Erik Zürcher, "The Late Ottoman Empire as Laboratory of Demographic Engineering," A paper presented at Le Regioni Multilingui Come Faglia e Motore della Storia Europea Nel XIX–XX Secolo, Naples, September 16–18 2008, 9. For the expulsion of Balkan Muslims, see Justin McCarthy, *Death and Exile: The Ethnic Cleansing of Ottoman Muslims, 1821–1922* (Princeton, N.J.: Darwin Press, 2005). McCarthy is an apologist for the Turkish state and supports the official version of history, which denies the Armenian genocide.

12. During the War of Independence, the de facto ruler of the Ottoman Empire was the provisional government of the Grand National Assembly of Turkey—TBMM (established in 1920), known as the Ankara government. Turkish nationalists and revolutionaries constituted this government, which took control from the Istanbul imperial government during the war.

13. Erik Zürcher, *Turkey: A Modern History* (London: IB Tauris, 1993), 155–156.

14. Ronald Grigor Suny, *"They Can Live in the Desert but Nowhere Else": A History of the Armenian Genocide* (Princeton, N.J.: Princeton University Press, 2015), 176.

15. "Amasya Tamimi," in *Milli Egemenlik Belgeleri* (Ankara: TBMM Kütüphane ve Arşiv Hizmetleri Başkanlığı, 2015), 9–14. A summary of the Amasya Circular in English is available in Stanford J. Shaw and Ezel Kural Shaw, *History of the Ottoman Empire and Modern Turkey*, Vol. 2, *Reform, Revolution, and Republic: The Rise of Modern Turkey* (Cambridge: Cambridge University Press), 343–344.

16. "Erzurum Kongresi Beyannamesi," in *Milli Egemenlik Belgeleri* (Ankara: TBMM Kütüphane ve Arşiv Hizmetleri Başkanlığı, 2015), 15–25. A summary in English of the Erzurum Congress is available in Shaw and Shaw, *History of the Ottoman Empire and Modern Turkey*, 344–345.

17. "Sivas Kongresi Beyannamesi," in *Milli Egemenlik Belgeleri* (Ankara: TBMM Kütüphane ve Arşiv Hizmetleri Başkanlığı, 2015), 26–31. See also, Erik Zürcher, *The Young Turk Legacy and Nation Building: From the Ottoman Empire to Atatürk's Turkey* (London: IB Tauris, 2010), 200.

18. Zürcher, *Turkey*, 157.

19. In the speech, *Nutuk*, Kemal was also emphasizing the fourth article of the Sivas Congress. See Kemal Atatürk, *Nutuk, Cilt: I, 1919–1920* (Istanbul: Milli Eğitim Basimevi, 1970), 244–245.

20. "Misak-ı Milli Beyannamesi," in *Milli Egemenlik Belgeleri* (Ankara: TBMM Kütüphane ve Arşiv Hizmetleri Başkanlığı, 2015), 32–38; Zürcher, *Turkey*, 144.

21. Zürcher, *Turkey*, 144.

22. Ayşe Gül Altınay, *The Myth of the Military Nation: Militarism, Gender, and Education in Turkey* (New York: Palgrave Macmillan, 2004), 19.

23. As paraphrased by Zürcher, *Turkey*, 144.

24. For a discussion of the ways in which the War of Independence was Turkified and Mustafa Kemal's vision of how the diverse Ottoman Muslim populations constituted one nation, see Altınay *The Myth of the Military Nation*, 18–20. Altınay also comments that the discourse about the diverse Muslim elements as a distinct ethnic group was transformed into a uniquely Turkish nationalist one starting in the 1930s.

25. For the invention of Turkishness by the Kemalist elites in the early republican years, see Fatma Ulgen, " 'Sabiha Gökçen's 80-Year-Old Secret': Kemalist Nation Formation and the Ottoman Armenians" (PhD diss., University of California San Diego, 2010).

26. Lerna Ekmekçioğlu, "Republic of Paradox: The League of Nations Minority Protection Regime and the New Turkey's Step-Citizens," *International Journal of Middle East Studies* 46, no. 4 (November 2014): 662.

27. Marc David Baer, *The Dönme: Jewish Converts, Muslim Revolutionaries, and Secular Turks* (Stanford, Calif.: Stanford University Press, 2009).

28. Mark Mazower, *Dark Continent: Europe's Twentieth Century* (New York: Vintage 1998), 42.

29. Jane K. Cowan, "The Success of Failure? Minority Supervision at the League of Nations," in *Paths to International Justice: Social and Legal Perspectives*, ed. Marie-Benedict Dembour and Tobias Kelly (Cambridge: Cambridge University Press, 2007), 31.

30. Cowan, "The Success of Failure?," 31.

31. Umut Özsu, *Formalizing Displacement: International Law and Population Transfers* (Oxford University Press, 2015), 73.

32. Jane K. Cowan, "Who's Afraid of Violent Language? Honour, Sovereignty and Claims-Making in the League of Nations," *Anthropological Theory* 3, no. 3 (2003): 271–279; Cowan, "The Success of Failure?"

33. Cowan, "The Success of Failure?," 33.

34. Cowan, "The Success of Failure?," 34.

35. Cowan, "The Success of Failure?," 33; Cowan, "Who's Afraid of Violent Language?," 287.

36. The Ankara government gained recognition through the signing of treaties during the Turkish War of Independence, most notably the Treaty of Moscow with Russia (1921); the Treaty of Kars with Russia, Armenia, Georgia, and Azerbaijan (1921); and the Treaty of Ankara with France (1921); ending with the Lausanne Treaty that was signed with France, Britain, Italy, Japan, Greece, Romania, and the Kingdom of Serbs, Croats, and Slovenes leading to the establishment of the Republic of Turkey (1923).

37. Zürcher, *Turkey*, 141, 152.

38. Michelle Tusan, *The Last Treaty: Lausanne and the End of the First World War in the Middle East* (Cambridge: Cambridge University Press, 2023), 204–205.

39. Yıldırım, *Diplomacy and Displacement*, 53.

40. Yıldırım, *Diplomacy and Displacement*, 54.

41. For the text of the Treaty of Alexandropol, see "Türkiye-Ermenistan Barış Andlaşması, Gümrü (Alexandropol), 2 Aralık 1920," in *Türkiye'nin Siyasal Andlaşmaları, I. cilt (1920–1945)*, ed. İsmail Soysal (Ankara: Türk Tarih Kurumu, 2000), 19–23. An English translation of the treaty is posted at https://www.deutscharmenischegesellschaft.de/wp-content/uploads/2011/01/Vertrag-von-Alexandropol-2.-Dezember-1920.pdf.

42. "Türkiye-Sovyet Rusya Dostluk ve Kardeşlik Andlaşması, Moskova, 16 Mart 1921," in İsmail Soysal, *Türkiye'nin Siyasal Andlaşmaları*, 32–38. The English translation quoted here is from https://www.deutscharmenischegesellschaft.de/wp-content/uploads/2011/01/Vertrag-von-Moskau-16.-März-1921.pdf.

43. As stated earlier, the land concession for an Armenian state under the Treaty of Sèvres was renounced by the short-lived Republic of Armenia (May 1918–December 1920) under the Treaty of Alexandropol of December 2, 1920.

44. The borders defined in article 8 are largely the current Syrian–Turkish border but without the Sanjak of Alexandretta. The area of the Sanjak was later ceded by France to Turkey in 1939 and became the Hatay Province. For the text of the agreement, see *Dispatch from His Majesty's Ambassador at Paris, Enclosing the Franco-Turkish Agreement signed at Angora on October 20, 1921* (London: His Majesty's Stationery Office), 2–3.

45. Great Britain, Foreign Office, *Turkey, No. 1 (1923) Lausanne Conference on Near Eastern Affairs, 1922–1923, Records of Proceedings and Draft Terms of Peace* (London: His Majesty's Stationery Office, 1923), 178–179.

46. Nesim Şeker, "Demographic Engineering in the Late Ottoman Empire and the Armenians," *Middle East Studies* 43, no. 3 (2007): 471.

47. For a history of the first Armenian survivors' arrival and settlement in France, see Maud Mandel, *In The Aftermath of Genocide: Armenians and Jews in Twentieth-Century France* (Durham, N.C.: Duke University Press, 2003).

48. Ronald Grigor Suny, *Looking Toward Ararat: Armenia in Modern History* (Bloomington: Indiana University Press, 1993), 219; Tsolin Nalbantian, *Armenians Beyond Diaspora: Making Lebanon Their Own* (Edinburgh University Press, 2020), 3, 6. On the Armenians in post-genocide Syria and Lebanon, see also Nicola Migliorino, *(Re)constructing Armenia in Lebanon and Syria: Ethno-cultural Diversity and the State in the Aftermath of a Refugee Crisis* (New York: Berghahn, 2008).

49. Donald Bloxham, *The Great Game of Genocide: Imperialism, Nationalism, and the Destruction of the Ottoman Armenians* (Oxford: Oxford University Press, 2005), 172.

50. Tsolin Nalbantian, *Armenians Beyond Diaspora: Making Lebanon their Own* (Edinburgh: Edinburgh University Press, 2019), 21.

51. Yıldırım, *Diplomacy and Displacement*, 38. Yıldırım discusses two dominant concerns in the writings on Lausanne, the first exemplified by Briton C. Busch, who focuses on settling Britain's policy in the Near East, and the second, in which Harry N. Howard considers Lausanne from the standpoint of American interests as pertains to the question of the Dardanelles and Bosphorus Straits (38). On the other hand, the concerned states, namely Turkey and Greece, have limited their evaluation of the conference to national concerns of demographic homogeneity, territorial sovereignty (9–10), and, for Turkey, abolishing the economic concessions granted to Christians and Europeans under the capitulatory regime established during the Ottoman Empire (63).

52. Renée Hirschon, "The Consequences of the Lausanne Convention," in *Crossing the Aegean: An Appraisal of the 1923 Compulsory Population Exchange Between Greece and Turkey*, ed. Renée Hirschon (New York: Berghahn, 2003), 14–15; Zürcher, "The Late Ottoman Empire as Laboratory of demographic Engineering," 12. The Orthodox Turks (Karamanli) were forced to leave in return for the Orthodox Patriarchate and the Greek-speaking Orthodox population of Istanbul remaining.

53. It is commonly understood that the Turkish delegation regarded almost all non-Muslim millets as non-Turks; see Renée Hirschon, "'Unmixing Peoples' in the Aegean Region," in *Crossing the Aegean: An Appraisal of the 1923 Compulsory Population Exchange Between Greece and Turkey*, ed. Renée Hirschon (New York: Berghahn, 2003), 8; however, it is important to highlight that members of the Turkish-speaking Orthodox population of Cappadocia (known as Karamanliler in Turkish, Karamanlides in Greek) were treated as "Turks" and referred to by İsmet Paşa at the Conference as "Orthodox Turks." This was because they spoke and practiced Orthodox Christianity in Turkish.

Furthermore, only communities that self-identified with a nation-state project were referred to in French as "les nationalités," i.e., the national minorities; see Jane K. Cowan, "The Supervised State," *Identities* 14 no. 5(2007), 548. The Turkish delegation was thus prepared to retain them on the ground that they were "Turks" and "they had never asked for special treatment differing in any respect from their Moslem compatriots"; Telegraph No. 50, in *Lozan Teleğrafları (1922–1923)*, Vol. 1, ed. Bilal Şimşir (Ankara: T.T.K. Basımevi, 1990), 143. Also, Great Britain, Foreign Office, *Turkey, No. 1 (1923) Lausanne Conference on Near Eastern Affairs, 1922–1923*, 208. See also Yıldırım, *Diplomacy and Displacement*, 61–62, 75–76.

54. Jews, however, were not regarded as a threat by the Turkish nationalists like the Armenians and the Rūms, because they were not seen as making territorial claims or collaborating with European powers. Ekmekçioğlu, "Republic of Paradox," 659.

55. The Greek state systematically hellenized its Slavic-speaking citizens who were also Orthodox Christians. See Anastasia Karakasidou, *Fields of Wheat, Hills of Blood: Passages to Nationhood in Greek Macedonia, 1870–1990* (Chicago: University of Chicago Press, 1997).

56. Faruk Birtek, "Greek Bull in China Shop of Ottoman 'Great Illusion': Greece in the Making of Modern Turkey," in *Citizenship and the Nation-State in Greece and Turkey*, ed. Faruk Birtek and Thalia Dragonas, Social and Historical Studies on Greece and Turkey Series (London: Routledge, 2005), 40–41.

57. For an in-depth study of the Young Turk revolution, see Bedross Der Matossian, *Shattered Dreams of Revolution: From Liberty to Violence in the Late Ottoman Empire* (Stanford, Calif.: Stanford University Press, 2014).

58. Fatma Müge Göçek, "The Politics of History and Memory: A Multidimensional Analysis of the Lausanne Peace Conference (1922–23)," in *Histories of the Modern Middle East: New Directions*, ed. H. Erdem, I. Gershoni, and U. Wokoeck (New York: Lynne Rienner, 2002), 211–212, 216, 218.

59. Göçek, "The Politics of History and Memory," 213. A selection of these telegrams is available in Bilal Şimşir, ed., *Lozan Teleğrafları (1922–1923)*, 2 Vols. (Ankara: T.T.K. Basımevi, 1990).

60. Yıldırım, *Diplomacy and Displacement*, 33.

61. Rıza Nur, *Dr. Rıza Nur'un Lozan Hatırları* (Istanbul: Boğaziçi Yayınları, 1992), 3: 1044–1045. Passages from Nur's memoirs were translated with the help of Sinem Adar.

62. Ekmekçioğlu, "Republic of Paradox," 668–670.

63. To speak of the paradox of how the secular republic divided its population along religious lines, Lerna Ekmekçioğlu uses the term "secular dhimmitude," where secular refers to the Kemalist state project and "dhimmitude," from the Arabic term *dhimmi*, a historical term that refers to non-Muslims who lived and were protected under Muslim rule. Dhimmitude therefore works as a "legal instrument of political marginalization *and* inclusion" Lerna Ekmekçioğlu, *Recovering Armenia: The Limits of Belonging in Post-genocide Turkey* (Stanford, Calif.: Stanford University Press, 2016), 108–109 (emphasis in original).

64. Yıldırım, *Diplomacy and Displacement*, 74. Based on the following Lausanne telegram: "From İsmet Paşa to Hey'et-i Vekile Riyaseti, 26 Teşrin-i Sâni 1338 [November 26, 1922]," in Şimşir, *Lozan Teleğrafları*, Vol. 1, 131–132.

65. For an in-depth treatment of the confiscation of Armenian properties in Anatolia, see Nevzat Onaran, *Emvâli Metrûke Olayı: Osmanlı'da ve Cumhuriyette Ermeni ve Rum Mallarının Türkleştirilmesi* (İstanbul: Belge Yayınları, 2010); Uğur Ümit Üngör and Mehmet Polatel, *Confiscation and Destruction: The Young Turk Seizure of Armenian Property* (Bloomsbury, 2011); Ellinor Morack, *The Dowry of the State? The Politics of Abandoned Property and the Population Exchange in Turkey, 1921–1945* (University of Bamberg Press, 2017).

66. For a discussion of these laws, see Morack, *The Dowry of the State?* For the Law of April 20, 1922, see pages 169-177. For the law of April 1923, see 225. Regarding prohibiting the return of Armenians before the conclusion of the Lausanne conference, see pages 195–196.

67. Taner Akçam and Umit Kurt, *The Spirit of the Laws: The Plunder of Wealth in the Armanian Genocide*, trans. Aram Arkun (New York and Oxford: Berghahn, 2015), chap. 6.

68. Nur's letter was published in French in *Journal de Genève*, December 27, 1922. Text reproduced in "26 Kânun-ı Evvel 1338 Raporudur" [Report of December 26, 1922] in Şimşir, *Lozan Teleğrafları*, Vol. 1, 282–283. Nur argued that if the conference accepted Armenian representatives as legitimate participants, it should also recognize other stateless delegates seeking political representation. Nur wrote, "If the principle of hearing all private individuals claiming to be delegates of their respective nations were accepted, the delegates of the government of the Grand National Assembly of Turkey would have the honor of proposing, on the same basis, the admission and hearing of delegations from the populations of Egypt, Palestine, Syria, Iraq, India, Tunisia, Tripolitania, the Muslim minorities of Yugoslavia, Romania, Bulgaria, and Greece, as well as the delegates of Ireland, who continuously appeal to them to have their just and legitimate demands heard at the conference."

69. Mark Mazower, "Minorities and the League of Nations in Interwar Europe," *Daedalus* 126 (1997): 53.

70. "26 Kânun-ı Evvel 1338 Raporudur" [Report of December 26, 1922] in Şimşir, *Lozan Teleğrafları*, Vol. 1, 281–283.

71. Mazower, "Minorities and the League of Nations," 53.

72. Yıldırım, *Diplomacy and Displacement*, 74.

73. Marashlian, "Finishing the Genocide," 136.

74. "From İsmet to Hey'et-i Vekile Riyasetine, 25 Teşrin-i Sâni 1338 [November 25, 1922]," in Şimşir, *Lozan Teleğrafları*, Vol. 1, 124–125 (emphasis added).

75. Yıldırım, *Diplomacy and Displacement*, 54, based on "From İsmet to Hey'et-i Vekile Riyasetine, 13 Kânun-ı Evvel 1338 [December 13, 1922]," in Şimşir, *Lozan Teleğrafları*, Vol. 1, 213–214.

76. Yıldırım, *Diplomacy and Displacement*, 62. Based on the following telegrams in Şimşir, *Lozan Teleğrafları*, Vol. 1: "From İsmet Paşa to Hey'et-i Vekile Riyaseti, 22 Teşrin-i Sâni 1338 [November 1922]," 122–123; "From İsmet Paşa to Hey'et-i Vekile Riyaseti, 25 Teşrin-i Sâni 1338 [November 1922]," 125; "From İsmet Paşa to Hey'et-i Vekile Riyaseti, 25 Teşrin-I Sâni 1338 [November 1922]," 129.

77. Levon Marashlian, "Finishing the Genocide: Cleansing Turkey of Armenian Survivors, 1920–1923," in *Remembrance and Denial: The Case of the Armenian Genocide*, ed. Richard G. Hovannisian (Detroit, Mich.: Wayne State University Press, 1999), 122–124.

78. Yıldırım, *Diplomacy and Displacement*, 74.

79. "From İsmet Paşa to Hey'et-i Vekile Riyaseti, 6 Kânun-i evvel 1338 [December 6, 1922]," in Şimşir, *Lozan Teleğrafları*, Vol. 1, 172.

80. Temuçin F. Ertan, "Lozan Konferans'ında Ermeni Sorunu," *KÖK Sosyal ve Stratejik Araştırmalar Dergisi* 2, no. 2 (2000): 213.

81. Ertan, "Lozan Konferans'ında Ermeni Sorunu," 216.

82. "From İsmet to Hey'et-i Vekile Riyaseti, 6 Kânun-ı Evvel 1338 [December 6, 1922]," in Şimşir, *Lozan Teleğrafları*, 172. Yıldırım, *Diplomacy and Displacement*, 233n75, notes that the reference to the Armenians in this telegram is mainly to those in Istanbul.

83. "From Hüseyin Rauf to İsmet Paşa, 7 Kânun-ı evvel 1338 [December 7, 1922]," Şimşir, *Lozan Teleğrafları*, Vol. 1, 174.

84. Hirschon, "'Unmixing Peoples' in the Aegean Region," 7; Mazower, "Minorities and the League of Nations in Interwar Europe," 56; Cowan, "The Success of Failure?," 33; Cowan, "Who's Afraid of Violent Language?," 287.

85. Yıldırım, *Diplomacy and Displacement*, 61.

86. This would have replicated the restrictions on non-Muslim millets in the Ottoman Empire, until the Tanzimat reforms of the nineteenth century that introduced the practice of Ottoman citizenship wherein non-Muslims started to serve in the Ottoman army.

87. Great Britain, Foreign Office, *Turkey, No. 1 (1923) Lausanne Conference on Near Eastern Affairs, 1922–1923*, 209.

88. Nur, *Dr. Rıza Nur'un Lozan Hatırları*, 3: 1046, 1049–1050.

89. Göçek, "The Politics of History and Memory," 220.

90. Taner Akçam, *From Empire to Republic: Turkish Nationalism and the Armenian Genocide* (London: Zed Books, 2004), 181.

91. Akçam, *From Empire to Republic*, 181.

92. Özsu, *Formalizing Displacement*, chap. 3.

93. Yıldırım, *Diplomacy and Displacement*, 75.

94. According to the historian Fuat Dündar, *Modern Türkiye'nin Şifresi: İttihat ve Terakki'nin Etnisite Mühendisliği (1913–1918)* (İstanbul: İletişim Yayınları, 2008).

95. Erik Zürcher, "How Europeans Adopted Anatolia and Created Turkey," *European Review* 13, no. 3 (2005): 379–394.

96. Zürcher, "The Late Ottoman Empire as Laboratory of Demographic Engineering," 12.

97. See, for example, the text of the Erzurum Congress (1919) that referred to the Muslim elements (*anasır-ı İslamiye*) in article 1, Christian elements (*anasır-ı Hıristiyaniyeye*) in article 3, and non-Muslim elements (*anasır-ı gayr-ı Müslimenin*) in article 5. "Erzurum Kongresi Beyannamesi," in *Milli Egemenlik Belgeleri* (Ankara: TBMM Kütüphane ve Arşiv Hizmetleri Başkanlığı, 2015), 20. The same with Sivas Congress articles 1 and 4 in *Milli Egemenlik Belgeleri*, 28.

98. Özsu, *Formalizing Displacement*, 71–83.

99. On the confiscated Armenian properties, see Uğur Ümit Üngör and Mehmet Polatel, *Confiscation and Destruction: The Young Turk Seizure of Armenian Property* (London and New York: Bloomsbury Academic, 2011).

100. Mazower, "Minorities and the League of Nations in Interwar Europe," 48.

101. Hirschon, "The Consequences of the Lausanne Convention," 14–15.

102. Ayhan Aktar, "Homogenising the Nation, Turkifying the Economy: The Turkish Experience of Population Exchange Reconsidered," in *Crossing the Aegean: An Appraisal of the 1923 Compulsory Population Exchange Between Greece and Turkey*, ed. Renée Hirschon (New York: Berghahn, 2003), 80.

103. Hirschon, "The Consequences of the Lausanne Convention," 17.

104. Bedross Der Matossian, "The Taboo Within the Taboo: The Fate of 'Armenian Capital' at the End of the Ottoman Empire," *European Journal of Turkish Studies*, October 6, 2011, http://ejts.revues.org/index4411.html; https://doi.org/10.4000/ejts.4411; see also Morack, *The Dowry of the State?*

105. Çağlar Keyder, "The Consequences of the Exchange of Populations for Turkey," *Crossing the Aegean: An Appraisal of the 1923 Compulsory Population Exchange Between Greece and Turkey*, ed. Renée Hirschon (New York: Berghahn, 2003), 45.

106. Fatma Müge Göçek, "Reconstructing the Turkish Historiography on the Armenian Deaths and Massacres of 1915," *Confronting the Armenian Genocide: Looking Backward, Moving Forward*, ed. Richard Hovannisian (New York: Routledge, 2017), 215.

107. Keyder, "The Consequences of the Exchange of Populations for Turkey," 45. The creation of a Muslim bourgeoisie was central to the political aims of the Young Turk regime, as Çağlar Keyder argues in chap. 3 of *State and Class in Turkey: A Study in Capitalist Development* (London and New York: Verso, 1987). See also Ayhan Aktar, "Economic Nationalism in Turkey: The Formative Years, 1912–1925," *Boğaziçi Journal, Review of Social and Administrative Studies* 10, nos. 1–2 (1996): 281.

108. Michael Barutciski, "Lausanne Revisited: Population Exchanges in International Law and Policy," *Crossing the Aegean: An Appraisal of the 1923 Compulsory Population Exchange Between Greece and Turkey*, ed. Renée Hirschon (New York: Berghahn, 2003), 24. See also Keyder, "The Consequences of the Exchange of Populations for Turkey," 40.

109. "Treaty of Peace, Signed at Lausanne, July 24, 1923," *League of Nations Treaty Series: Publication of Treaties and International Engagements Registered with the Secretariat of the League of Nations*, Vol. 28, 33 (emphasis added), https://treaties.un.org/doc/publication/unts/lon/volume%2028/v28.pdf.

110. Rıfat N. Bali, *The 'Varlık Vergisi' Affair: A Study on Its Legacy from Selected Documents* (Istanbul: Isis Press, 2005).

111. Dilek Güven, *Cumhuriyet Dönemi Azınlık Politikaları Bağlamında 6–7 Eylül Olayları* (İstanbul: İletişim Yayınları, 2006); see also, Dilek Güven, "Riots Against the Non-Muslims of Turkey: 6/7 September 1955 in the Context of Demographic Engineering," *European Journal of Turkish Studies* 12 (2011), https://journals.openedition.org/ejts/4538.

112. Ekmekçioğlu, *Recovering Armenia*, 69.

113. Ekmekçioğlu, *Recovering Armenia*, chap. 3.

114. Gabriel Goltz, "The Non-Muslim Minorities and Reform in Turkey," *Turkey Beyond Nationalism: Towards Post-nationalist Identities* (London: IB Tauris, 2006), 179–180.

115. For a genealogy of the long history of denying violence against Armenians in the late Ottoman period through the Republic of Turkey, see Fatma Müge Gökçek, *Denial of Violence: Ottoman Past, Turkish Present, and Collective Violence Against the Armenians, 1789–2009* (Oxford: Oxford University Press, 2015).

116. Quoted in Kans-Lukas Keiser, ed. *Turkey Beyond Nationalism: Towards Post-nationalist Identities* (London: IB Tauris, 2006), ix.

117. For a study on the ways in which Kemal's speech became foundational for the Turkish nationalist historiography, see Fatma Ülgen, "Reading Mustafa Kemal Atatürk on the Armenian Genocide of 1915," *Patterns of Prejudice* 44, no. 4 (2010): 369–391.

118. Fatma Ulgen, " 'Sabiha Gökcen's 80-Year-Old Secret.'" This point is explored in chap. 2.

3. ANATOLIAN FRAGMENTS:
THE LIFE STORIES OF THREE SURVIVORS

1. On the way the Armenian genocide and Kurdish struggle are intertwined and the way both have left marks on Diyarbakır, see Serap Ruken Şengül, "Broken (His)tories Inside Restored Walls: Kurds, Armenians and the Cultural Politics of Reconstruction in Urban Diyarbakir, Turkey" (PhD diss., University of Texas at Austin, 2014).

2. Giragos is the Armenian version of the Greek saint name Kyriakos, meaning "he who belongs to the Lord."

3. The church of Surp Giragos was renovated by the Surp Giragos Armenian Foundation with the help of the Diyarbakır, Kurdish-controlled municipality and reopened for worship in 2011. In 2016, the Turkish state expropriated the church along with 6,300 plots of land by an "urgent expropriation" decision taken by the cabinet. See "Surp Giragos Armenian Church Among Expropriated Properties in Diyarbakır," *Armenian Weekly*, March 28, 2016. Also, Pinar Tremblay, "Why the Turkish Government Seized This Armenian Church," *Al-Monitor*, April 8, 2016.

4. "Armenian Church in Diyarbakır Reopens After 7 Years," *Hürriyet Daily News*, May 9, 2022, https://www.hurriyetdailynews.com/armenian-church-in-diyarbakir-reopens-after-7-years-173604, accessed October 5, 2023.

5. Hannah Arendt, *The Origins of Totalitarianism* (San Diego, CA: Harcourt Brace, 1976), 163.

6. Julia Kristeva, *Hannah Arendt: Life Is a Narrative* (Toronto: University of Toronto Press, 2001), 34.

7. Quoted in Kristeva, *Hannah Arendt*, 4, 37. Arendt here quotes Isak Dinesen.

8. Veena Das, *Critical Events: An Anthropological Perspective on Contemporary India* (Delhi: Oxford University Press, 1997).

9. Walter Benjamin, "Theses on the Philosophy of History," thesis VIII, in *Illuminations: Essays and Reflections*, trans. Harry Zohn (New York: Schocken, 1969), 257.

10. Donna Haraway, "Situated Knowledges: The Science Question in Feminism and the Privilege of Partial Perspective," *Feminist Studies* 14, no. 3 (1998): 575–599.

11. James Clifford, "Introduction: Partial Truths," in *Writing Culture: The Poetics and Politics of Ethnography*, ed. James Clifford and George E. Marcus (Berkeley: University of California Press, 1986).

12. Haraway, "Situated Knowledges."

13. Haraway, "Situated Knowledges," 584.

14. David Arnold and Stuart Blackburn, *Telling Lives in India: Biography, Autobiography, and Life History* (Bloomington: Indiana University Press, 2004), 5.

15. Matei Candea, *Corsican Fragments: Difference, Knowledge, and Fieldwork* (Bloomington: Indiana University Press, 2010).

16. Here I am invoking Walter Benjamin's anti-historicist view of history: "To articulate the past historically does not mean to recognize it 'the way it really was' (Ranke). It means to seize hold of a memory as it flashes up at a moment of danger." Walter Benjamin, "Theses on the Philosophy of History," thesis VI, in *Illuminations: Essays and Reflections*, trans. Harry Zoh (New York: Schocken, 1969), 255.

17. Arnold and Blackburn, *Telling Lives in India*, 3.

18. Later in the chapter, I present the ways in which the genocide is remembered and labeled differently depending on the experience of the local population.

19. Eric Hirsch and Charles Stewart, "Introduction: Ethnographies of Historicity," *History and Anthropology* 16, no. 3 (September 2005): 266.

20. I am here employing Melissa Bilal's observation that lullabies that she studied are both autobiographical and historical. Melissa Bilal, "The Lost Lullaby and Other Stories About Being an Armenian in Turkey," *New Perspectives on Turkey* 34 (Spring 2006): 72.

21. See Introduction and Chapter 1 on Benjamin's view of history as an assemblage of fragments and "flashes" that disrupt official narratives.

22. Leyla Neyzi, "Oral History and Memory Studies in Turkey," *Turkey's Engagement with Modernity: Conflict and Change in the Twentieth Century*, ed. Celia Kerslake, Kerem Öktem, and Philip Robins (New York: Palgrave Macmillan, 2010), 445.

23. Kayseri is the Arabic and Turkish name for Caesarea of Cappadocia. It was an important center for Christian theological education. It is especially known for the three fourth-century theologians known as the Cappadocian Fathers (St. Basil the Great, St. Gregory of Nyssa, and St. Gregory Nazianzus) revered by all churches, East and West. The Armenian saint, Gregory the Illuminator (ca. 257–ca. 331), who is famous for "baptizing" the Armenian king and nation in 301, was raised and received his theological education there.

24. Harry Harootunian, *The Unspoken as Heritage: The Armenian Genocide and Its Unaccounted Lives* (Durham, N.C.: Duke University Press, 2019).

25. Selim Deringil, " 'The Armenian Question Is Finally Closed': Mass Conversions of the Armenians in Anatolia During the Hamidian Massacres of 1895–1897," *Comparative Studies in Society and History* 51, no. 2 (2009): 359–361.

26. Lerna Ekmekçioğlu, "A Climate for Abduction, a Climate for Redemption: The Politics of Inclusion During and After the Armenian Genocide," *Comparative Studies in Society and History* 55, no. 4 (2013): 525–526. For sexual violence and rape as policy during the Armenian genocide, see Katherine Derderian, "Common Fate, Different Experience: Gender-Specific Aspects of the Armenian Genocide, 1915–1917," *Holocaust and Genocide Studies* 19 (2005): 1–25.

27. Wadie Jwaideh, *The Kurdish National Movement: Its Origins and Development* (Syracuse, N.Y.: Syracuse University Press, 2006), 45–46.

28. It is notable that Anatolian Kurds see Armenians as close enough to be abducted and incorporated into their families, which is a relation that exists in other contexts such as the "cross cousinage" in Tunisian–Italian relations discussed by Naor Ben-Yehoyada, *The Mediterranean Incarnate: Region Formation between Sicily and Tunisia since World War II* (Chicago: University of Chicago Press, 2017).

29. In Armenian, *Sasuntsi Davit*.

30. *Gavur* is used also by Muslims in the southeast to identify Muslims who are known to have Armenian ancestry, especially if the ancestry is traced back to an Armenian male.

31. Information provided in this chapter also represents a cumulative account of my other encounters with Houri on September 3 and 5, 2010, in Istanbul.

32. Ronald Grigor Suny, *"They Can Live in the Desert but Nowhere Else": A History of the Armenian Genocide* (Princeton University Press), 283, all of chap. 9.

33. Suny, *"They Can Live in the Desert but Nowhere Else,"* 322. The most notable case of Kurdish protection of Armenians is in the Kurdish Alevi city of Dersim. For an in-depth study on the Dersim case, see Cevat Dargin, "'An Oasis of Humanity Within the Damned Empire': The Armenian Question in Dersim in State-Making in Dersim Across Empire and Nation-State (1878–1938) (PhD diss., Princeton University, 2021), 286–325.

34. On marriage patterns in Kurdish societies, see Jwaideh, *The Kurdish National Movement*, 45–46, and refer to the earlier discussion on abduction in Ara's narrative.

35. The Settlement Law (no. 2510) of 1934 categorized Turkey's populations into three groups and divided the countries into three zones, as I will explain later in the chapter. The context that Bahri speaks about here was when she, as an Armenian, was deported along with the Kurds to the western parts of Turkey (Zone 2). For the details of this law, see Joost Jongerden, *The Settlement Issue in Turkey and the Kurds: An Analysis of Spatial Policies, Modernity and War* (Leiden: Brill, 2007), 175–178.

36. Churches in the Arapgir district are listed in Khazhak Drampyan, "Arapgir Kaza: Churches, Monasteries and Holy Sites," trans. Hrant Gadarigian, Houshamadyan website, https://www.houshamadyan.org/mapottomanempire/vilayetofmamuratulazizharput/kaza-of-arapgir/religion/churches-and-monasteries.html, accessed May 12, 2021.

37. This story was verified with actual dates and numbers from an article in Turkish published on the internet by Murat Bebiroğlu, an Armenian from Arapgir who wrote an account about his visit to his hometown. Murat Bebiroğlu, "Arapkir 2008," *HyeTert*, October 24, 2008, https://hyetert.org/2008/10/25/arapkir-2008, accessed October 8, 2023.

38. I elaborate on the issue of leaving Anatolia for Istanbul to attend Armenian schools in chapter 4.

39. Erik J. Zürcher, "How Europeans Adopted Anatolia and Created Turkey," *European Review* 13, no. 3 (2005): 379–394.

40. According to an estimate, non-Turkish speakers living on Turkey's southern borders were not allowed to occupy 20 percent of the land. Jongerden, *The Settlement Issue in Turkey and the Kurds*, 177.

41. Mıgırdiç Margosyan, *Tespih Taneleri* (Istanbul: Aras, 2006). Chapter 4 discusses the term *kafle* in Margosyan's novel in the context of the efforts of the Armenian Patriarchate in Istanbul to take Armenian male children to educate them in an Armenian school in the city.

42. Syriac Christians of the same region also use *ferman*, or the Syriac term *sayfo*, meaning "sword." I am grateful to Bedross Der Matossian for bringing the commonalities and differences in terms used by Syriacs and Armenians to my attention. For the Syriac genocide, *sayfo*, see David Daunt, Naures Atto, and Soner O. Barthoma, *Let Them Not Return: Sayfo—The Genocide Against the Assyrian, Syriac, and Chaldean Christians in the Ottoman Empire* (New York: Berghahn, 2017).

43. For a treatment on the ways in which the memories and labels of the Armenian genocide vary across ethnoreligious communities in Mardin, see Zerrin Özlem Biner, "Acts of Defacement, Memory of Loss: Ghostly Effects of the 'Armenian Crisis' in Mardin, Southeastern Turkey," *History and Memory* 22, no. 2 (2010): 68–94.

44. Kerem Öktem, *Angry Nation: Turkey Since 1989* (New York: Zed, 2011), 84–85, 120, states that southeastern Anatolia was ruled by an emergency state, whereas western Anatolia was under a democratic polity of state institutions. This preliminary finding is also in line with other studies. See, for example, Murat Yüksel's sociological study on demographic engineering policies and the effects of the resettlement law on Dersim in the 1930s and 1940s; Murat Yüksel, "Forced Migration and the Politics of Internal Displacement in the Making of Modern Turkey: The Case of Dersim, 1937–1947"

(PhD diss., Department of Sociology, Columbia University, 2008). See also Lerna Ekmekçioğlu's historical study that gives evidence that Armenians were escaping Anatolia to Istanbul around the same time; Lerna Ekmekçioğlu, *Recovering Armenia: The Limits of Belonging in Post-genocide Turkey* (Stanford, Calif.: Stanford University Press, 2016). More comparative research on Kurds and Armenians in Anatolia, on the one hand, and Rūm-Orthodox (Greeks) and Armenians in Istanbul, on the other, is still needed to substantiate this claim.

45.   Haraway, "Situated Knowledges."

46.   I have translated the word *ecnebi* in article 11 to mean "non-Muslim" rather than the literal meaning "foreigner" for two reasons: First, Anatolia did not have the number of foreign citizens needed to form as much as 10 percent of a city or a region, as article 11 indicates. Second, scholars like Rıfat Bali demonstrate that many of the laws issued in the 1920s and 1930s stipulating that employees of a certain job should be "Turkish," which practically meant Muslim, was designed to purge non-Muslim citizens of Turkey from certain professions and replace them with Muslims; see Rıfat N. Bali, *The "Varlık Vergisi" Affair: A Study on Its Legacy from Selected Documents* (Istanbul: Isis Press, 2005).

47.   For an in-depth study of the settlement laws in Turkey, see Jongerden, *The Settlement Issue in Turkey and the Kurds*; Yüksel, "Forced Migration and the Politics of Internal Displacement in the Making of Modern Turkey."

48.   Yalçın, *You Rejoice My Heart*, 36.

49.   Haraway, "Situated Knowledges."

4. SAVING OR DISPLACING?
RESETTLING ARMENIANS IN ISTANBUL AND PARIS

1.   For the tension between the secular and religious camps among the Armenians in Istanbul, see Hratch Tchilingirian, "The 'Other' Citizens: Armenians in Turkey Between Isolation and (Dis) Integration," *Journal of the Society for Armenian Studies* 25 (2016): 129.

2.   Dink was adamant about secularizing the Armenians of Istanbul; see Gerard Libaridian's introduction to Tube Çandar, *Hrant Dink: An Armenian Voice of the Voiceless in Turkey*, trans. Maureen Freely (New Brunswick, N.J.: Transaction, 2016), xx.

3.   The earthquake hit on August 19, 1966, and measured 6.9 on the Richter scale.

4.   The book does not delve into the subject of Islamicized Armenians. For an exploration of this topic, see Ayşe Gül Altınay and Fethiye Çetin, *The Grandchildren: The Hidden Legacy of the "Lost" Armenians in Turkey* (New Brunswick, N.J.: Transaction, 2014); Avedis Hadjian, *Secret Nation: The Hidden Armenians of Turkey* (London: IB Tauris, 2018).

5.   Yalçın's book was published in English as *You Rejoice My Heart* (2007). His travels in Anatolia began in July 1998. The book was initially published in Turkish in December 2000, but the publisher then informed Yalçın that "because of a warning from on high, we won't be able to distribute your book." The book was destroyed in June 2002 by order of Istanbul's thirteenth public notary and was later published in Germany in 2003 (see the preface to the second Turkish edition in the 2007 English translation). In 2006, the book was published by Birzamanlar, a progressive publishing house in Istanbul that has published many books documenting Armenian and other communities' history of Anatolia, including Osman Köker's *100 Yıl Önce Türkiye'de Ermeniler: Orlando Carlo Calumeno Koleksiyonu'ndan Kartpostallarla* [Armenians in Turkey 100 years ago: with the postcards from the collection of Orlando Carlo Calumeno] in 2005.

6.   Yalçın, *You Rejoice My Heart*, 206. Armenian emigration from Anatolia continued after the genocide and throughout the life of the republic. For example, Istanbul hosted refugee camps for the Armenian victims of the Settlement Law of the 1930s; see Lerna Ekmekçioğlu, *Recovering*

Armenia: The Limits of Belonging in Post-genocide Turkey (Stanford, Calif.: Stanford University Press, 2016).

7. The Armenian Patriarchate of Jerusalem enlisted Armenians from Anatolia to join their seminary and receive training to become priests. I am grateful to Bedross Der Matossian for providing this information.

8. Yalçın *You Rejoice My Heart*, 206. *Tıbrevank* in Armenian means a theological seminary. It carried that name because its students had the option to continue theological education after they finished high school.

9. The seminary was financed by Gerabded Balyan, a member of the famous Balyan family of Ottoman Armenian architects, Alyson Wharton, *The Architects of Ottoman Constantinople: The Balyan Family and the History of Ottoman Architecture* (London and New York: I. B. Tauris, 2015), 56–57. The grassroot Armenian organization "Land and Culture" lists the Armaş Monastery as one of the 100 exemplary Armenian national assets. See asset number 78 on https://www.collectif2015.org/en /Projects.aspx (accessed November 3, 2024).

10. Article 101 of the Turkish Civil Law states: "Formation of a foundation contrary to the characteristics of the Republic defined by the Constitution, Constitutional rules, laws, ethics, national integrity and national interest, or with the aim of supporting a distinctive race or community, is restricted." This law runs contrary to article 40 of the Lausanne Treaty, which stipulates that non-Muslims in Turkey "shall have an equal right to establish, manage and control at their own expense, any charitable, religious and social institutions, any schools and other establishments for instruction and education, with the right to use their own language and to exercise their own religion freely therein."

11. The DP came to power in 1950 and was overthrown by a military coup in May 1961.

12. I was unable to verify whether this practice is inscribed in national law or in Istanbul municipal regulations or is merely a customary practice.

13. Turkish spelling is employed throughout the text; the name in Armenian is Գարեգին Խաչատուրեան and could also be written in English as Karekin Khachadurian.

14. *-tsi* is a suffix in Armenian that is added after the name of a city or region to identify one's belonging to that place, *Trabzontsi* thus means "of Trabzon."

15. *Vertebed* or *Vartabed* is the title of an unmarried priest in the Armenian Church. It could be translated into English as "reverend."

16. Margosyan frequently employs the vernacular pronunciation of words in his writing, and in this particular context, *Vertebed* is the local pronunciation used.

17. The word *seferberlik* does not translate readily. It literary means "mobilization for the war," but in this context the speaker means the genocide.

18. Mıgırdiç Margosyan, *Tespih Taneleri* [Prayer beads] (Istanbul: Aras, 2006), 177–178. These passages were translated by Sinem Adar.

19. For *Kafle*, refer to chapter 3 for a discussion on the local variations in referring to the Armenian genocide.

20. Saidiya Hartman, *Lose Your Mother: A Journey Along the Atlantic Slave Route* (New York: Farrar, Straus and Giroux, 2007), 133.

21. Mıgırdiç Margosyan, *Biletimiz İstanbul'a Kesildi* [Our ticket is for Istanbul] (Istanbul: Aras, 1998), 31. Quoted and translated by Burçin Erol, "How Other Is the 'Other': Mıgırdiç Margosyan's Gavur Mahallesi (1988/1992 TR) (Christian Quarter), Söyle Margos Nerelisen? (1995) (Tell Me Margos Where are You from?), Biletimiz İstanbul'a Kesildi (1998) (Our Ticket is for İstanbul)," *HÜTAD: Hacettepe Üniversitesi Türkiyat Araştırmaları Dergisi* 1 (2004): 185.

22. Although *gavur* is consistently used as a derogatory term for Armenians in Turkish, the Kurdish term *filla* can have varying connotations, sometimes neutrally referring to Armenians and at other times serving as a slur, depending on the context. I am grateful to Cevat Dargin for bringing this to my attention.

23. Mıgırdiç Margosyan, *Tespih Taneleri* [Prayer beads] (Istanbul: Aras, 2006), 179.

24. *Bezaz*, Kurdish for "cloth dealer," hence his Armenian surname Bezazyan.

25. Mıgırdiç Margosyan, *Tespih Taneleri*, 179. In Turkish: "Yaa, Vertebed hezretleri . . . Bız Haylığ içün canımızi veriyığh, adam diyi ki, bahan ne senin Haylığından! Heç bele bi şe olır!?" The Turkish used in this quote, as in many passages of Margosyan's novel, is not standard Turkish but a transliteration of the local Turkish vernacular. As the transliteration indicates, local Armenians use throat sounds that are common in eastern and southeastern Anatolia and use the Armenian *Hay* to refer to themselves, rather the Turkish equivalent *Ermeni* even though they are speaking in Turkish.

26. *Bolsahayer* in Armenian refers to Armenians (*Hayer*) coming from Bolis, the Armenian name for Istanbul, hence the combined *Bolsahayer*. For a detailed treatment of this designation, see Ekmekçioğlu, *Recovering Armenia*, 1–2. Bolis is the Armenian name for Istanbul; it derives from the Greek phrase *is tan poli*, meaning "into the city," from which the Turkish İstanbul is derived.

27. *İmam bayıldı*, literally, "the imam fainted," is an aubergine dish stuffed with garlic, onion, and tomatoes and sometimes also minced meat. It is one of the numerous dishes shared by western Armenians, Kurds, Turks, Greeks, Bulgarians, Iranians, and Levantine Arabs.

28. Alparslan Nas, "Between National and Minor Literature in Turkey: Modes of Resistance in the Works of Mehmed Uzun and Mıgırdiç Margosyan" (MA thesis, Cultural Studies, Sabancı University, Istanbul, 2011), 29–30.

29. The usage of Armenian, Kurdish, and Turkish interchangeably is prominent in the opening scene of the chapter titled "How Happy Are the Poor," in which the narrator counts in the three languages. Mıgırdiç Margosyan, *Gavur Mahallesi* [The infidel's quarter], trans. Matthew Chovanec (London: Gomidas Institute; Istanbul: Aras, 2017), 31–33.

30. Margosyan, *Gavur Mahallesi*, 2–3.

31. Alparslan Nas argues that Margosyan "does not emphasize a kind of a power imbalance in-between particular communities" in the city, nor does he focus on the image of the Turk as perpetrator. See Alparslan Nas, "Between National and Minor Literature in Turkey," 29–30.

32. Margosyan, *Gavur Mahallesi*, 7–8.

33. Here I borrow Ella Shohat's description of the predicament of Arab Jews in Israel, especially Iraqi Jews. Ella Shohat, *Taboo Memories, Diasporic Voices* (Durham, N.C.: Duke University Press, 2006), 204.

34. To explore Armenians' sense of displacement in Istanbul and their enduring longing for Anatolia, refer to Melissa Bilal, "Longing for Home at Home," *Thamyris/Intersecting*, no. 13 (2006): 55–66.

35. For a discussion on the ways in which Istanbul's Armenians adapted to the Kemalist nationalism, see Ekmekçioğlu, *Recovering Armenia*, chap. 4.

36. Nicholas B. Dirks, "Is Vice Versa? Historical Anthropologies and Anthropological Histories," in *The Historic Turn in the Human Sciences*, ed. Terrence J. McDonald (Ann Arbor: University of Michigan Press, 1996), 24.

5. NEW CONCEPTIONS OF BELONGING: ARMENIANNESS REIMAGINED IN FRANCE

1.   Between 1978 and the mid-1980s, Alfortville witnessed a large migration of Armenians from Turkey. For instance, in 1985, 40 percent of the parents of pupils at Surp Mesrop School were migrants from Turkey and were Turkish-speaking Armenians, some with basic knowledge of Armenian. In 2008, around 35 percent of the pupils' parents were migrants from Turkey, the largest group of parents by country of origin. See Seven Ananian, *30 Ans Ecole Bilingue Saint Mesrop, Alfortville 1978–2008* (Collection Alfortville-Mémoires, 2008).

2. In mayoral elections, candidates present the teams they would work with if elected, often highlighting their team members on their election posters. During the 2008 municipality elections, candidates from all parties had Armenians on their lists. While the ruling Union pour un Mouvement Populaire (UMP) candidate was himself Armenian, the majority of Armenians voted for René Rouquet, who was in office between 1988 and 2012.

3. Paul Gilroy, *The Black Atlantic: Modernity and Double Consciousness* (London: Verso, 1993). I am thankful to Melissa Bilal for bringing this point to my attention in the context of the Armenian diaspora.

4. Pierre Bourdieu, "Preface," in Abdelmalek Sayad, *The Suffering of the Immigrant* (Cambridge: Polity Press, 2004), xiv.

5. For the significance of the politics of locality in shaping diasporas, see Susanne Schwalgin, "Why Locality Matters: Diaspora Consciousness and Sedentariness in the Armenian Diaspora in Greece," in *Diaspora, Identity, and Religion: New Directions in Theory and Research*, ed. Waltraud Kokot, Khachig Tölölyan, and Carolin Alfonso (Oxon: Routledge, 2004).

6. Armenian diasporic institutions are the social and community organizations of the survivors of the genocide who were not allowed to return to Anatolia. Before France recognized the Soviet Union, the Armenian delegation in France, which was also present at the Lausanne Conference but was denied participation (discussed in chapter 2), functioned as the Armenian government-in-exile. For a historical overview, see Khatchig Tölölyan, "Exile Governments in the Armenian Polity," in *Governments-in-Exile in Contemporary World Politics*, ed. Yossi Shain (London: Routledge, 1991), 166–187.

7. Mary Dewhurst Lewis, *The Boundaries of the Republic: Migrant Rights and the Limits of Universalism in France, 1918–1940* (Stanford, Calif.: Stanford University Press, 2007), 1.

8. Lewis, *The Boundaries of the Republic*, 3–4.

9. Gérard Noiriel, *The French Melting Pot: Immigration, Citizenship, and National Identity* (Minneapolis: University of Minnesota Press, 1996), 27, 30.

10. Lewis, *The Boundaries of the Republic*, 1.

11. According to the National Museum of Immigration History in Paris, immigration to France started in the second half of the nineteenth century, making France the oldest country to receive immigrants in Europe. See Mustapha Harzoune, "Since When Has France Been a Land of Immigration?," Musée national de l'histoire de l'immigration, Paris, 2022, https://www.histoire-immigration.fr/en/migration, accessed March 18, 2024.

12. The literature on the North African migrants in France, for example, invokes themes such as uprootedness, solitude, and even madness; Noiriel, *The French Melting Pot*, 27. In addition, French politicians have frequently assigned negative labels to immigration: Michel Poniatowski equated it with "occupation," thereby marking the immigrant as an enemy, while President Valéry Giscard d'Estaing (in office 1974–1981) called it an "invasion," casting the immigrant as a barbarian. See Riva Kastoryano, *Negotiating Identities: States and Immigrants in France and Germany* (Princeton, N.J.: Princeton University Press, 2002), 17.

13. For the development of Berber nationalism in France, see Paul Silverstein, *Algeria in France: Transpolitics, Race, and Nation* (Bloomington: Indiana University Press, 2004).

14. Noiriel, *The French Melting Pot*, 27.

15. Noiriel, *The French Melting Pot*, 27.

16. Its reception of migrants and refugees then continued until the 1970s, when France welcomed 1 immigrant for every 1,000 inhabitants, a rate equaled only by the United States. At one point, France had a higher proportion of people born outside its national borders than did the United States. Elsewhere in Europe, the Federal Republic of Germany hosted 0.05 immigrant per 1,000 inhabitants, while Britain and Sweden each received 0.03 immigrant per 1,000 inhabitants, according to Noiriel, *The French Melting Pot*, 258–259.

17. Noiriel, *The French Melting Pot*, 28, quoted from Yves Ternon, *La cause arménienne* (Paris: Seuil, 1983).

18. Lewis, *The Boundaries of the Republic*, 10. In her study, Lewis compares the different ways migrants were received in the cities of Lyon and Marseille.

19. Lewis, *The Boundaries of the Republic*, 22.

20. Similarly, stateless Armenian refugees in Greece were regarded as a threat and were not granted Greek citizenship until 1968. This negative reception of refugees in Greece was shared by the Rūm-Orthodox refugees, who were considered to be of Greek ethnicity and who arrived in Greece from Anatolia following the exchange of populations stipulated by the Lausanne Treaty. See Schwalgin, "Why Locality Matters," 79–80; Renée Hirschon, *Heirs of the Greek Catastrophe: The Social Life of Asia Minor Refugees in Piraeus* (New York: Berghahn, 1998).

21. Maud Mandel, *In the Aftermath of Genocide: Armenians and Jews in Twentieth-Century France* (Durham, N.C.: Duke University Press, 2003), 32, 51, 224–225; Levon Marashlian, "Finishing the Genocide: Cleansing Turkey of Armenian Survivors, 1920–1923" in *Remembrance and Denial: The Case of the Armenian Genocide*, ed. Richard G. Hovannisian (Detroit: Wayne State University Press, 1998), 113–145.

22. Lewis, *The Boundaries of the Republic*, 22–23.

23. Noiriel, *The French Melting Pot*, 260.

24. Noiriel, *The French Melting Pot*, 260.

25. Mandel, *In the Aftermath of Genocide*, 21.

26. Michael Mann, *The Dark Side of Democracy: Explaining Ethnic Cleansing* (Cambridge: Cambridge University Press, 2005), 62.

27. Mann, *The Dark Side of Democracy*, makes a distinction between the inclusion/exclusion of people in a democracy: the more inclusive *demos* (democracy) and the exclusive *ethnos* (ruling ethnic group).

28. Mandel, *In the Aftermath of Genocide*, 19.

29. Mandel, *In the Aftermath of Genocide*, 20. Mandel's historic comparison shows that France also hosted the largest number of Jewish refugees after World War II.

30. Nation-states such as Greece and Bulgaria narrowly defined themselves by a trinitarian vision of an ethnicity, a language, and a national linguistic church. Following the defeat of Germany and its Ottoman ally in the war, the winning powers forced the Ottoman Empire to sign the Treaty of Sèvres in 1920, designed to achieve the old European imperial dream of dividing the Ottoman territories among themselves; see Erik Zürcher, *Turkey: A Modern History* (London: IB Tauris, 1993), 141, 152.

31. Keith David Watenpaugh, "Between Communal Survival and National Aspiration: Armenian Genocide Refugees, the League of Nations, and the Practices of Interwar Humanitarianism," *Humanity*, Summer 2014, 168.

32. A copy of the French travel document given to Armenians is featured in Martine Hovanessian, *Les Arméniens et leurs territoires* (Paris: Autrement, 1995). The document states: "But de son voyage: il ne peut pas retourner."

33. The possible return of Armenian refugees to Anatolia was hindered by the Ankara government, which issued the following laws that affected the Armenian presence in Anatolia: a law confiscating the property of the Armenians who had left the Cilicia region (April 20, 1922); a law extending the confiscation to all Armenians, whatever their motives for leaving or the date of their departure from Anatolia (April 25, 1923); and a law prohibiting the return of Armenians to Cilicia and the eastern provinces (September 1923, article 2).

34. Ronald Grigor Suny, *Looking Toward Ararat: Armenia in Modern History* (Bloomington: Indiana University Press, 1993), 219.

35. Tsolin Nalbantian, *Armenians Beyond Diaspora: Making Lebanon Their Own* (Edinburgh: Edinburgh University Press, 2020), 3.

36. In his study on the Armenians of Syria and Lebanon, Migliorino contextualizes their postwar resettlement in the two states, where the French Mandate authorities granted them various degree

of cultural autonomy in the 1920s. Such autonomy facilitated the "(re)construction of a new, post-Genocide Armenian world in the Levant" through a constitution that included them in the parliamentary system in both countries. Capitalizing on such autonomy, the refugees established institutions (political parties, associations, schools, media, etc.) that enabled both the preservation and development of Armenian culture in the host states; see Nicola Migliorino, *(Re)constructing Armenia in Lebanon and Syria: Ethno-cultural Diversity and the State in the Aftermath of a Refugee Crisis* (New York: Berghahn, 2008), chap. 2.

37. Tölölyan, "Exile Governments in the Armenian Polity," 181.

38. Quoted in Mandel, *In the Aftermath of Genocide*, 19, 22. Like Turabian, who described Armenians' special status as migrants, Sayad (the sociologist of Algerian migration to France par excellence) considers the Algerian migration to France "une immigration exemplaire" (an exemplary immigration)—a case without parallel, exceptional because of Algeria's colonial history and experience with settler colonialism and because of the uprooting of Algerian labor to work in French industrial and agrarian production. In this context, he goes so far as to see the Algerian experience as carrying the truth of all other migrations. Sayad, *The Suffering of the Immigrant*, 63.

39. Mandel, *In the Aftermath of Genocide*, 21–22.

40. S. Andesian and M. Hovanessian, "L'arménien: Langue rescapée d'un génocide," in *Vingt-Cinq Communutés Linguistique de la France*, Tome 2, *Les langues*, ed. Geneviève Vermès (Paris: L'Harmattan, 1998), 67.

41. Eugene Weber, *Peasants Into Frenchmen: The Modernization of Rural France, 1880–1914* (Stanford, Calif.: Stanford University Press, 1976), chap. 1.

42. Weber, *Peasants Into Frenchmen*, chap. 6.

43. Silverstein, *Algeria in France*, 234–235.

44. Weber, *Peasants Into Frenchmen*, chaps, 17, 18.

45. Weber, *Peasants Into Frenchmen*, chap. 6.

46. Quoted in Silverstein, *Algeria in France*, 143.

47. Noiriel, *The French Melting Pot*, 259–260. In the recent controversy in France about Muslim women wearing headscarves, the headscarf is seen as problematic because the French state does not see the wearing of a headscarf as an individual right that is guaranteed under the nation's commitment to personal freedoms and choices. Rather, the headscarf is considered a marker of an extranational communal identity based on religious affiliation, which the French state considers a challenge to the principle of the republic's indivisibility. See John R. Bowen, *Why The French Don't Like Headscarves: Islam, the State, and Public Space* (Princeton, N.J.: Princeton University Press, 2007), chap. 7; Noiriel, *The French Melting Pot*, 259–260. Additionally, see article 1 of the French Constitution, which states: "France shall be an indivisible, secular, democratic and social Republic." Further, Silverstein, *Algeria in France*, 144, argues that wearing headscarves in French public schools represents an infiltration of an ideology that does not know the separation of faith from politics. Thus, the public expression of Islamic religiosity is considered to be a political statement by a community, not a personal one.

48. For the text of the European Charter for Regional or Minority Languages (ETS No. 148, see https://www.coe.int/en/web/conventions/full-list?module=treaty-detail, accessed Oct 31, 2024. For the French Government "Reservations and Declarations for Treaty No. 148" see https://www.coe.int/en/web/conventions/full-list?module=declarations-by-treaty&numSte=148&codeNature =10&codePays=FRA, accessed Oct 31, 2024).

49. Mandel, *In the Aftermath of Genocide*, 96–103.

50. Various studies give a much lower number. Khachig Tölölyan, "The Role of the Armenian Apostolic Church in the Diaspora," *Armenian Review* 41, no. 1–161 (Spring 1988): 55–68, estimates that there are 250,000 Armenians in France. Andesian and Hovanessian, "L'arménien: Langue rescapée d'un génocide," 61, estimate 300,000.

51. The last Armenian kingdom in Cilicia fell in 1375, and its last king lived in exile in Paris in 1393.

52. In his study of post-Holocaust Yiddish, Jeffrey Shandler speaks of Yiddish as a "postvernacular" language, with a symbolic value. He states that "Yiddish is its semiotic hierarchy; unlike vernacular language use, in the postvernacular mode the language's secondary, symbolic level of meaning is always privileged over its primary level." He argues that the symbolic position of Yiddish for Jewish speakers is similar to the languages of other communities who struggle to maintain a language in the context of challenging social, political, and cultural forces—communities such as Ainu, Irish, and Navajo, and, I would add, western Armenians. Jeffrey Shandler, *Adventures in Yiddishland: Postvernacular Language and Culture* (Oakland: University of California Press, 2008), 22–23.

53. Tölölyan, "Exile Governments in the Armenian Polity," 181.

54. Tölölyan, "Exile Governments in the Armenian Polity," 180.

55. See Weber, *Peasants Into Frenchmen*. The unity of the French Republic is expressed by "republican civic nationalism" according to Riva Kastoryano, *Negotiating Identities: States and Immigrants in France and Germany* (Princeton, N.J.: Princeton University Press 2002), 27, in which acknowledging or reinforcing the diversity of languages becomes a threat to the unity of the republic.

56. The French text states: "La langue de la République est le français"; see La Constitution du 4 octobre 1958, Conseil constitutionnel website, https://www.conseil-constitutionnel.fr/le-bloc -de-constitutionnalite/texte-integral-de-la-constitution-du-4-octobre-1958-en-vigueur, accessed July 27, 2023.

57. Kastoryano, *Negotiating Identities*, 26.

58. Translated by the author. I was unable to find a complete text of this speech, and the two sections quoted here come from two independent documents. A portion of the speech was on a website that supports African cultures: www.africultures.com/php/index.php?nav=article&no=3448, accessed May 11, 2021.

59. "Decret 85–1006 du 23 septembre 1985 portant création du Conseil national des langues et cultures regionales," *Journal Officiel de la République Française*, September 25, 1985, 11046.

60. The complete text of the charter is available as "Details of Treaty No.148," European Charter for Regional or Minority Languages (ETS No. 148), Council of Europe Treaty Office website, http:// conventions.coe.int/Treaty/EN/Treaties/Html/148.htm, accessed May 11, 2021.

61. Translated by the author. For the full text of the speech, see "Déclaration de M. Lionel Jospin, Premier ministre, en réponse à une question sur la décision du Conseil constitutionnel sur la charte européenne des langues régionales, à l'Assemblée nationale le 23 juin 1999," Vie publique website, https://www.vie-publique.fr/discours/199491-declaration-de-m-lionel-jospin-premier-ministre-en -reponse-une-ques, accessed June 30, 2022.

62. As indicated in the English section of the DGLFLF site: www.dglf.culture.gouv.fr, accessed May 11, 2021.

63. The French Ministry of Culture distinguishes between the French language, which holds privileged official status, and the "Languages of France." The latter is divided into two categories. The first category includes "regional languages" such as Alsacien, Basque, Breton, Catalan, Corse, Western Flemish, Francique Mosellan, Francoprovençal, and the languages d'oïl (including Franc-Comtois, Walloon, Champenois, Picard, Norman, Gallo, Poitevin, Saintongeais, Lorrain, and Bourguignon-Morvandiau), as well as the dialects of Occitan (Gascon, Languedocien, Provençal, Auvergnat, Limousin, and Vivaro-Alpin). The second category consists of "non-territorial languages", which are not native to France but brought by immigrant communities. These include Arabic vernaculars, Western Armenian, Berber, Judeo-Spanish (Ladino), Romani, and Yiddish. Listed on https://www.culture .gouv.fr/Thematiques/langue-francaise-et-langues-de-france/Agir-pour-les-langues/Promouvoir -les-langues-de-France, accessed Oct 31, 2024.

64. Loi constitutionnelle de modernisation des institutions de la Vème République [the Constitutional Law for the modernisation of institutions of the Fifth Republic], ratified on July 23, 2008.

65. While Modern Standard Arabic has official status in many states, Arabic vernaculars do not. The same applies to Armenian: eastern Armenian has official status in the Republic of Armenia; western Armenian does not.

66. Razmik Panossian, *The Armenians: From Kings and Priests to Merchants and Commissars* (New York: Columbia University Press, 2006), 296–299, argues that Armenians had an easier time *integrating* in their host societies by maintaining their identity in the Middle East (namely, in Syria and Lebanon); they were able to foster consciousness of Armenian language, history, and culture through schooling. *Assimilation*, on the other hand, refers to losing cultural distinctiveness by adopting the language and sociocultural norms of the host society.

67. Panossian, *The Armenians*, 236–238.

68. See Susan Paul Pattie, *Faith in History: Armenians Rebuilding Community* (Washington, D.C.: Smithsonian Institution Press, 1997), chap. 7.

69. Pattie, *Faith in History*, 169–170; Anny Bakalian, *American Armenians: From Being to Feeling Armenian* (New Brunswick, N.J.: Transaction, 2011), 393.

70. Anahide Ter-Minassian, "Les Arméniens de France," *Les Temps Modernes* 504–506 (July–September 1988): 232; Schwalgin, "Why Locality Matters," 72; Ulf Björklund, "Armenia Remembered and Remade: Evolving Issues in a Diaspora," *Ethnos* 85 (3–4): 342.

71. Mitterrand said: "It is not possible to erase the traces of genocide that hit you. These must be inscribed in human memory." Assemblée Nationale, "Reconnaissance du Génocide Arménien," *Journal Officiel de la République Française*, Séance du 29 Mai 1998, Paris, France, 3.

72. Khatchig Tölölyan defines "stateless power" as "a form of power that is both productive and prohibitive and that operates even in those diasporic social formations where personal voluntarism and not communal compulsion is, or appears to be, the general rule." Khachig Tölölyan, "Elites and Institutions in the Armenian Transnation," *Diaspora* 9, no. 1 (2001): 111–112.

73. Mitterrand took other positive measures to aid migrants, including the legalization of illegal immigrants. He also supported immigrants' associations with the aim of building a stronger and more diverse civil society in France. Silverstein, *Algeria in France*, 132, 240.

74. Quoted in Ananian, *30 Ans Ecole Bilingue Saint Mesrop*, 32–33.

75. Levon Avdoyan, "The Past as Future: Armenian History and Present Politics," *Armenian Forum: A Journal of Contemporary Affairs*, no. 1 (Spring 1998): 2.

76. The word "diaspora" and its Armenian equivalent *spiurk* share the Indo-European root *s-p-r* from which words such as "spore," "sperm," "spread," and "disperse" also derive. Khachig Tölölyan, "Rethinking Diaspora(s): Stateless Power in the Transnational Moment," *Diaspora* 5, no. 1 (1996): 10.

77. Björklund, "Armenia Remembered and Remade," 338.

78. Anahide Ter-Minassian, "Les Arménien de Paris depuis 1945," in *Le Paris de étrangers depuis 1945*, ed. Antoines Marès and Pierre Miza (Paris: Sorbonne, 1994), 220.

79. Panossian, *The Armenians*, 242.

80. Veena Das, *Critical Events: An Anthropological Perspective on Contemporary India* (Delhi: Oxford University Press, 1997).

81. Cihan Tuğal, "Memories of Violence, Memories of Nation: The 1915 Massacres and the Construction of Armenian Identity," in *The Politics of Public Memory in Turkey*, ed. Esra Özyürek (Syracuse, N.Y.: Syracuse University Press, 2007), 148.

82. For a treatment of the Armenian migrants to Soviet Armenia and problematization of the concept of "repatriation" to Armenia, see Susan Paul Pattie, "From the Centers to the Periphery: 'Repatriation' to an Armenian Homeland in the Twentieth Century," in *Homecomings: Unsettling Paths of Return*, ed. Fran Markowitz and Andres H. Stefansson (Lanham, Md.: Lexington, 2004). For details of the how Lebanese Armenian understood repatriation, see Tsolin Nalbantian, *Armenians Beyond Diaspora: Making Lebanon Their Own* (Edinburgh University Press, 2020), chap. 2.

83. Björklund, "Armenia Remembered and Remade," 341.

84. Panossian, *The Armenians*, 236.
85. Gerard J. Libaridian, "The Changing Armenian Self-Image in the Ottoman Empire: *Rayahs* and Revolutionaries," in *The Armenian Image in History and Literature*, ed. Richard G. Hovannisian (Los Angeles: Undena, 1981), 158.
86. Tölölyan, "Rethinking *Diaspora*(s)," 4.
87. Panossian, *The Armenians*, 292; Suny, *Looking Toward Ararat*, 218.
88. Before the genocide, Marseille and Paris had Armenian merchants and intellectuals, called colonies. In 1910, their number in France was around two thousand. See Andesian and Hovanessian, "L'arménien: Langue rescapée d'un genocide," 66.
89. Panossian, *The Armenians*, 199–200.
90. Panossian, *The Armenians*, 200, explains the blurring of the religious–secular binary by saying that "some priests became national liberation fighters, and secular fighters received the blessings of priests."
91. Panossian, *The Armenians*, 228, 236.
92. For a comparative study of the role the genocide plays in forming the Armenian identity in the United States, see Bakalian, *American Armenians*, 347–360; for a comparative study of this role in Greece, see Schwalgin, "Why Locality Matters," 84.
93. Schwalgin, "Why Locality Matters," 84.
94. Pattie, *Faith in History*, 11, 22–23.
95. Panossian, *The Armenians*, 297–299. Similarly, Breton cultural belonging in France was mediated by the church through the schooling system; see Silverstein, *Algeria in France*, 59. On the important role of schooling in the lives of Armenians in the diaspora, see the case of the Melkonian School in Cyprus and the reaction its closure provoked in Sossie Kasbarian, "Whose Space, Whose Interests? Clashes Within Armenian Diasporic Civil Society," *Armenian Review* 51, nos. 1–4 (2009): 81–109.
96. Mandel, *In the Aftermath of Genocide*, 7.
97. Mandel argues the experience for post-Holocaust French Jewry was different from that of the Armenians, because the former did not have "to build a communal structure from the ground up." Mandel, *In the Aftermath of Genocide*, 8.
98. Mandel, *In the Aftermath of Genocide*, 35–37.
99. Cf. Suny, *Looking Toward Ararat*, 219.
100. Suny, *Looking Toward Ararat*, 227.
101. Panossian, *The Armenians*, 237.
102. Mandel, *In the Aftermath of Genocide*, 8, 213.
103. Tölölyan, "Elites and Institutions in the Armenian Transnation," 107–136. In a different context to the shift from the ethnic to the diasporic, Bakalian, *American Armenians*, 393–394, differentiates between "traditional Armenianness" and "symbolic Armenianness." The former refers to those born in the Middle East and Soviet bloc who learned the Armenian language and were raised in an Armenian (sub)culture in their home societies. The latter, on the other hand, refers to the Armenianness of those born in the diaspora (for example, in the United States, the focus of Bakalian's study) for whom the symbolic identity is a matter of choice and does not necessarily mean that they know the language or were raised in an Armenian milieu.
104. Khachig Tölölyan, "Beyond the Homeland: From Exilic Nationalism to Diasporic Transnationalism," *The Call of the Homeland: Diaspora Nationalisms, Past and Present*, ed. Allon Gal, Athena S. Leoussi, and Anthony D. Smith, IJS Studies in Judaica (Leiden: Brill, 2010), 36.
105. For a treatment of these trials, see Vahakn N. Dadrian and Taner Akçam, *Judgment at Istanbul: The Armenian Genocide Trials* (New York: Berghahn, 2011).
106. Björklund, "Armenia Remembered and Remade," 346.
107. Tony Judt, *Postwar: A History of Europe Since 1945* (New York: Penguin, 2005), 805.
108. Judt, *Postwar*, 804–810.

109. The Armenian question in Turkey moved in the opposite direction, because the Kemalist regime that founded the Republic of Turkey was regarded as a continuation of the Young Turk regime that had been responsible for the genocide. Eric Zürcher, for example, considers the period to be from 1908 to 1950, a periodization that includes the genocide as the "Young Turk era." See also Fatma Ülgen, "Reading Mustafa Kemal Atatürk on the Armenian Genocide of 1915," *Patterns of Prejudice* 44, no. 4 (2010): 369–391, for the centrality of blaming Armenians for the violence they were subjected to, as asserted by Mustafa Kemal, the founder of the republic. Generally, the Turkish discourse on Armenians has either cast Armenians as casualties of war (as a means of denying the premeditated nature of the annihilation, which would define the massacres as genocide under international law) or blamed the Armenian victims for committing treason against their own Ottoman state at the time of the war. Björklund, "Armenia Remembered and Remade," 346.

110. "Human Rights on the Margins: Roma in Europe," Amnesty International, https://www.amnesty.org.uk/files/roma_in_europe_briefing.pdf. accessed Oct 31, 2024.

111. Tölölyan explains the significance of these two Armenian memorials by comparing them with their Jewish equivalents in Israel: the Yad Vashem Holocaust memorial and the Masada; Tölölyan, "Elites and Institutions in the Armenian Transnation," 122. The difference, however, is that the Yad Vashem stands very close to the ruins of Deir Yasin, one of the first Palestinian villages to be destroyed and its population expelled by the Zionist forces on April 9, 1948, weeks before the establishment of the State of Israel on May 15, 1948.

112. Ter-Minassian, "Les Arménien de Paris depuis 1945," 220.

113. Björklund, "Armenia Remembered and Remade," 344.

114. Ter-Minassian, "Les Arménien de Paris depuis 1945," 220.

115. Tölölyan, "Elites and Institutions in the Armenian Transnation," 121.

116. Björklund, "Armenia Remembered and Remade," 344, says that it was an awakening in the diaspora. There is evidence that the genocide has been commemorated since the 1920s, so perhaps it is more accurate to say that it was the beginning of a collective effort, as many organizations and communities around France have taken actions to ensure that the genocide would not be forgotten.

117. Björklund, "Armenia Remembered and Remade," 344.

118. Frédéric Feydit, "Un tragique cinquantenaire: Le massacre des arméniens en Turquie," *Le Monde*, April 23, 1965, 1, 6.

119. Feydit, "Un tragique cinquantenaire," 1, 6.

120. Assemblée Nationale, "Reconnaissance du Génocide Arménien," 3–4.

121. It is worth noting that this is not unique to the Armenians in France. The Armenian Genocide memorial in Jerusalem is built in the Armenian cemetery of the occupied Old City both as a genocide memorial and for the Armenian Legion that assisted the French and the British in winning the Battle of Arara in September 1918. I am grateful to Bedross Der Matossian for providing me with this comparative context.

122. Similarly, a mosque was constructed in Paris to honor the twenty-six thousand Algerian colonial subjects who died for France during World War I; Silverstein, *Algeria in France*, 131.

123. Kastoryano, *Negotiating Identities*, 30, quoting Jacqueline Costa-Lascoux.

124. Tölölyan, "Rethinking *Diaspora*(s)," 26.

125. Andesian and Hovanessian, "L'arménien: Langue rescapée d'un genocide," 60–61, say that Armenians are considered the most integrated foreign community in French social life. See also the examples in Mandel's study *In the Aftermath of Genocide* and Martine Hovanessian's description of the settlement of the first Armenian refugees in France in *Les Arméniens et leurs territoires*.

126. Susan Paul Pattie, "New Homeland for an Old Diaspora," in *Homelands and Diasporas: Holy Lands and Other Places*, ed. André Levy and Alex Weingrod (Stanford, Calif.: Stanford University Press, 2004), 50.

127. See chapter 2 in Silverstein's ethnography *Algeria in France* on the Berber/Arab divide and the perception by the French political elites and policy-makers of their relative ability to assimilate.

128. Tölölyan, "Rethinking *Diaspora*(s)," 3–36.

129. Vered Amit, "Armenian and Other Diasporas: Trying to Reconcile the Irreconcilable," in *British Subjects: An Anthropology of Britain*, ed. Nigel Rapport (Oxford: Berg, 2002), 264. In countries where pluralism is tolerated, such as the United States, or where pluralism is part of the state structure, such as Syria, Lebanon, and Canada, diasporas do not pose a perceived threat, as is the case with countries that do not allow extranational collectivities, such as France.

130. Tölölyan, "Rethinking *Diaspora*(s)," 26.

131. Tölölyan, "Rethinking *Diaspora*(s)," 4.

132. Noiriel, *The French Melting Pot*, 259–260.

133. Unlike North African labor migrants (who are Muslim), both Armenian and Jewish communities are perceived to have integrated successfully into French society since the genocide, with their members rising to influential financial and political positions. Meanwhile, both Armenians and Jews have emphasized their ethnic specificities in very noticeable ways: maintaining separate languages, schools, places of worship, and social clubs. For a comparative study on the Armenians and Jews in France, see Mandel, *In the Aftermath of Genocide*.

134. Bakalian, *American Armenians*, 393–394.

135. Migliorino, *(Re)constructing Armenia in Lebanon and Syria*.

136. See Migliorino, *(Re)constructing Armenia in Lebanon and Syria*, chap. 4.

137. On the "stateless power" of diasporic institutions, see Tölölyan, "Elites and Institutions in the Armenian Transnation," 111–112.

138. Amit, "Armenian and Other Diasporas," 264.

139. Tölölyan, "Rethinking *Diaspora*(s)," 7–8.

140. Tölölyan, "Rethinking *Diaspora*(s)," 4–5.

141. Tölölyan, "Rethinking *Diaspora*(s)," 5.

142. Tölölyan, "Rethinking *Diaspora*(s)," 27.

143. Panossian, *The Armenians*, 197–200.

144. Tölölyan, "Rethinking *Diaspora*(s)," 18, 23. Such antipathy toward migrant communities' expression of their cultural and ethnic identities is clear in France, which received many migrant communities. Similarly, Armenians are unable to teach history in their schools in Turkey. History is taught as part of religious education and language for religious and liturgical functions. Turkey's non-Muslims are not allowed to perform their ritual prayers (not necessarily sermons) in Turkish but are expected to use their ethno-liturgical language: Greek for the Rūm-Orthodox, Ladino and Hebrew for Jews, and Armenian for Armenians.

145. Panossian, *The Armenians*, 198.

146. Panossian, *The Armenians*, 194.

147. Quoted in Panossian, *The Armenians*, 198–199.

148. Quoted in Panossian, *The Armenians*, 199, from Aram Keshishian, *The Witness of the Armenian Church in a Diaspora Situation:Problems, Perspectives, Prospects* (New York: Prelacy of the Armenian Apostolic Church of America, 1978), 42. The Armenian church and various nationalist groups in the diaspora have disagreed about how to interpret Armenian national belonging; see, for example, Panossian, *The Armenians*, 294.

149. Tölölyan, "Elites and Institutions in the Armenian Transnation," 127–128.

150. Ter-Minassian, "Les Arménien de Paris depuis 1945," 211.

151. This perspective of balancing integration and assimilation in the host society is shared in other Armenian diasporic communities. For example, at the Armenian Assembly National Conference in 2004, the president of the pan-diasporic Armenian General Benevolent Union said the following about Armenian hyphenated identity: "Being Armenian-American does not mean that they are 50

percent Armenian and 50 percent American. No—it means that they are 100 percent Americans, who feel a strong and full commitment to their Armenian identity" (quoted in Kasbarian, "Whose Space, Whose Interests?," 87).

152. Ter-Minassian, "Les Arménien de Paris depuis 1945," 211.

153. Andesian and Hovanessian, "L'arménien: Langue rescapée d'un genocide," 69. For an understanding of the process by which the attitude of the Armenian diaspora in Cyprus has shifted to an integrationist approach, see Sossie Kasbarian, "The Armenian Community in Cyprus at the Beginning of the 21st Century: From Insecurity to Integration," in *The Minorities of Cyprus: Development Patterns and the Identity of Internal-Excl*usion, ed. A. Varnavas, N. Coureas, and M. Elia (Newcastle upon Tyne: Cambridge Scholars Publishing, 2009).

154. For this reason, the way in which Armenians, or any other migrant group, appeal to the politics of French society tells us about France itself and sheds light on how migrants experience and adapt to France's specific political culture.

6. ENDURING DENATIVIZATION, ENDURING PRESENCE

1. Melissa Bilal, "The Lost Lullaby and Other Stories About Being an Armenian in Turkey," *New Perspectives on Turkey* 34 (Spring 2006): 82.

2. Michel-Rolph Trouillot, *Silencing the Past: Power and the Production of History* (Boston: Beacon Press, 1995), 48.

3. Armenian pronunciation of the name is "Sourp Khatch." The Turkified name of the island's name is Akdamar (white vine). For analysis of the names, refer to Bilgin Ayata, "Tolerance as a European Norm or an Ottoman Practice? An Analysis of Turkish Public Debates on the (Re)Opening of an Armenian Church in the Context of Turkey's EU Candidacy and Neo-Ottoman Revival" (working paper no. 41, Kolleg-Forschergruppe: The Tranformative Power of Europe, Freie Universität Berlin, July 2012), 10.

4. Ayata, "Tolerance as a European Norm," 18.

5. On the ways in which liberal and multicultural discourses in Turkey speak about the culture production of Armenians in a way that supresses the history of violence they are subjected to, see Bilal, "The Lost Lullaby."

6. Ayata, "Tolerance as a European Norm," 10.

7. Trouillot, *Silencing the Past*, 48.

8. Bilal, "The Lost Lullaby."

9. The detailed article on Eastern Anatolia including the church of Akhtamar is Baha Yılmaz, "Balm to Farhad's Heart: Eastern Anatolia" trans. Ahmet Sel. *Skylife*, Issue 338 (September 2011), 78–89. The church at Akhtamar is also featured on the cover of this same issue.

10. Mıgırdiç Margosyan, "Diyarbakır'ın geçmişini tüm Türkiye'ye tanıtan Mıgırdiç Margosyan: 'Tarihinizi İnkar Ederseniz Bitersiniz'" ["Mıgırdiç Margosyan, Who Introduced Diyarbakır's Past to All of Turkey: 'If You Deny Your History, You Will End'"] *Agos*, October 21, 2011.

11. Margosyan, in "Diyarbakır'ın geçmişini tüm Türkiye'ye tanıtan Mıgırdiç Margosyan: 'Tarihinizi İnkar Ederseniz Bitersiniz'" writes, "Orada tarihi geçmişinizi ayakta tutmanızdır. Tarihinizi unutup inkar ederseniz, bu sizi bitirir," which literally means "If you forget and deny your history, it will be your undoing."

12. Ayata, "Tolerance as a European Norm," 8.

13. Ayata, "Tolerance as a European Norm," 15.

14. In 2016, the Turkish state expropriated the church along with 6,300 plots of land by an "urgent expropriation" decision taken by the cabinet. "Surp Giragos Armenian Church Among Expropriated

Properties in Diyarbakir," *Armenian Weekly*, March 28, 2016. See also, Ceylan Yaginsu, "Turkey's Seizure of Churches and Land Alarms Armenians," *New York Times*, April 23, 2016; Pinar Tremblay, "Why the Turkish Government Seized This Armenian Church," *Al-Monitor*, April 8, 2016.

15. "Expropriation of Surp Giragos Armenian Church Suspended," *Armenian Weekly*, April 6, 2017.

16. Ayda Erbal, "Mea Culpas, Negotiations, Apologias: Revisiting the 'Apology' of Turkish Intellectuals," in *Reconciliation, Civil Society, and the Politics of Memory: Transnational Initiatives in the 20th and 21st Century*, ed. Birgit Schwelling (Bielefeld: Transcript Verlag, 2012), 52.

17. Erbal, "Mea Culpas, Negotiations, Apologias," 93.

18. Erbal, "Mea Culpas, Negotiations, Apologias," 88.

19. *Direct Matin* is a free and popular newspaper published on weekday mornings in Paris and distributed in the Metro stations. The article we discussed was "Un coin d'Arménie dans le 8e" [An Armenian corner in the 8th Arrondissement], *Direct Matin*, no. 429, March 13, 2009. The event was attended by the famous singer Charles Aznavour, the Armenian ambassador to Paris Edward Nalbandian, the mayor of Paris Bertrand Delanoë, and the Armenian ambassador to Bucharest Hamlet Gasparia, see *Nouvelles d'Aremenie*, no. 151 (April 2009), 91.

20. Bolis is the Armenian name for Istanbul; Dikranagert is the Armenian name for an area very close to the modern Diyarbakır, a predominantly Kurdish city in southeastern Turkey. The city was founded by Armenia's King Dikran—hence the name Dikranagert (Dikran's city).

21. Ronald Grigor Suny, *Looking Toward Ararat: Armenia in Modern History* (Bloomington: Indiana University Press, 1993), 216.

22. Gerard Libaridian, *Modern Armenia: People, Nation, State* (New Brunswick, N.J.: Transaction, 2004), 297.

23. Sossie Kasbarian, "The Myth and Reality of 'Return'—Diaspora in the 'Homeland,'" *Diaspora* 18, no. 3 (2009): 358–381.

24. Such a trope was in full force in the eighteenth and nineteenth centuries, when interest in Hebraic language and culture in Europe was divorced from Jewish people living at the time. By the same token, interest in the ancient histories and languages of the "Orient" carried no interest in the way "Oriental" people were living at the time. For a treatment of this trope in representing otherness, see Hakem Al-Rustom, "Returning to the Question of Europe: From the Standpoint of the Defeated," in *The Arab and Jewish Questions: Geographies of Engagement in Palestine and Beyond*, ed. Bashir Bashir and Leila Farsah (New York: Columbia University Press, 2020), 129–130.

25. I further develop this argument in a work-in-progress article titled "Temporal Erasure: Armenian Heritage and National Narratives in Turkey," where I examine how the Turkish state's restoration of Armenian heritage sites repositions Armenians within an antiquated ("ancient" and "medieval") past, placing them on a different temporality than that of the Turkish nation-state—a process I call "temporal denativization." Suciyan, "Armenian Genocide and its Denial," 87 argues that the decision to annihilate Armenians reconstructed a past–present–future in which Armenians had "never existed" in that geography.

26. Ann Laura Stoler, "'The Rot Remains': From Ruins to Ruination," in *Imperial Debris: On Ruins and Ruination*, ed. Ann Laura Stoler (Durham, N.C.: Duke University Press, 2013), 9–10.

27. On the experience of displacement of the Armenians in Istanbul, see Melissa Bilal, "Longing for Home at Home," *Thamyris/Intersecting*, no. 13 (2006): 55–66. On the debate on whether that Armenians of Istanbul are a diaspora, see Hrag Papazian, "Are Istanbul Armenians Diasporic? Unpacking the famous debate" in *The Armenian Diaspora and Stateless Power: Collective Identity in the Transnational 20th Century*, ed. Talar Chahinian, Sossie Kasbarian and Tsolin Nalbantian (London: I. B. Tauris, 2023). On Armenians being "the other citizens" in Turkey, see Hratch Tchilingirian, "The 'Other' Citizens: Armenians in Turkey Between Isolation and (Dis)integration" *Journal of the Society for Armenian Studies*, no. 25 (2016): 123–155. On Armenians being step-citizens of Turkey, see Lerna Ekmekçioğlu, "Republic of paradox: The league of nation minority protection regime and the

new Turkey's step-citizens" *International Journal of Middle East Studies*, no.46:4 (November 2014): 657–679.

28. Melissa Bilal speaks of the ways in which Armenians who emigrated from Anatolia to Istanbul consider Istanbul as a "home" because they perceive it as an extension to Anatolia. Many Armenians want to remain in Istanbul to preserve the Armenian heritage in Anatolia. See Bilal, "Longing for Home at Home."

29. Bilal, "Longing for Home at Home," 58.

30. He did so in three critical texts: The first is Dink's address to a meeting held by the Commission for European Union Harmonization and Foreign Affairs Commission of the Turkish Parliament (April 5, 2005), the second is his address at the conference on Armenians during the last years of the Ottoman Empire that took place at Bilgi University in Istanbul on September 24–25, 2005 titled "Ottoman Armenians During the Decline of the Empire: Issues of Scientific Responsibility and Democracy," and the third is the report he prepared for the Turkish Economic and Social Studies Foundation (TESEV) regarding the future of Turkey-Armenia relations (2006). The three texts were published posthumously in Turkish, and the English translation quoted in this book appeared in Hrant Dink, *Two Close Peoples, Two Distant Neigbours*, trans. Nazım Hikmet Richard Dikbaş (Istanbul: Hrant Dink Foundation, 2014).

31. Dink's paper at the Bilgi University conference was delivered on September 25, 2005 and the text was published in Dink's posthumous book *Two Close Peoples, Two Distant Neighbours*, 98 (ellipses in original).

32. Marc Nichanian, *Mourning Philology: Art and Religion at the Margins of the Ottoman Empire*, trans. G. M. Gohsgarian and Jeff Fort (New York: Fordham University Press, 2014). For a discussion of Nichanian's critique of the auto-ethnographic project of Armenian intellectuals in the nineteenth century, see the introduction to this book.

33. Several Turkish intellectuals have been tried under article 301 of the Turkish penal code for "insulting Turkishness" by referring to Armenian killings during World War I as genocide. Dink himself faced two trials under article 301 and was found guilty of insulting Turkishness. Dink was making the case for an Armenian narrative, as well as taking to these public forums to defend himself from such accusations.

34. Focusing on experience and not evidence-based historiography, Dink takes a similar path to that of Marc Nichanian, who argues that the essence of genocide is the denial of the crime and prefers to use "catastrophe" instead. See Marc Nichanian, "Catastrophic Mourning," in *Loss: The Politics of Mourning*, ed. David Eng and David Kazanjian (Berkeley: University of California Press, 2002), 133. More recently, Harry Harootunian, in his autobiography *The Unspoken as Heritage* (Durham, N.C.: Duke University Press, 2019), 4, makes a similar claim by saying that the Armenian genocide or any mass murder "is [not] reducible to mobilizing more historical evidence to support one or another interpretation" and that history could not address questions of memory and experience the victims lived through.

35. Yael Navaro, *Faces of the State: Secularism and Public Life in Turkey* (Princeton, N.J.: Princeton University Press, 2002), 20.

36. Navaro, *Faces of the State*, 20.

37. Or "indigenous foreigners," a term used in Turkish courts to refer to the non-Muslim citizens of Turkey. See Heghnar Zeitlian Watenpaugh, "Preserving the Medieval City of Ani: Cultural Heritage Between Contest and Reconciliation," *Journal of the Society of Architectural Historians* 73, no. 4 (December 2014): 530. See also, "Minority Foundations in Turkey: An Evaluation of Their Legal Problems," Human Rights Agenda Association website, https://en.rightsagenda.org/minority -foundations-in-turkey-an-evaluation-of-their-legal-problems, accessed October 22, 2023.

38. Dink, *Two Close Peoples, Two Distant Neigbours*, 33 (emphasis added).

39. The interpretation of the Turkish expression "the water found its crack" and its meaning in Dink's context is developed here in conversation with Zerrin Özlem Biner and Altuğ Yilmaz.

40. Dink, *Two Close Peoples, Two Distant Neigbours*, 101–102.

41. Engseng Ho, *The Graves of Tarim: Geneology and Mobility Across the Indian Ocean* (Berkeley: University of California Press, 2006), 8.

42. Toby Austin Locke, "Death and the Storyteller," May 4, 2017 http://tobyaustinlocke.com/death -and-the-storyteller, accessed March 28, 2021. In this article, Locke comments on the centrality of death for Walter Benjamin's storyteller.

43. Hrant Dink, "The Water Finds Its Crack: An Armenian in Turkey," *Open Democracy*, January 19, 2012, https://www.opendemocracy.net/en/europe_turkey_armenia_3118jsp, accessed March 19, 2024 (emphasis added).

44. Dink, "The Water Finds Its Crack."

45. Helen Makhdoumian has framed such acts of reclamation as forms of survivance. Rather than solely engaging in acts of remembrance, these initiatives enact a refusal to disappear and a future-oriented engagement with history, ensuring that Armenian presence endures beyond nationalist erasures, Helen Makhdoumian, "Connected Memoryscapes of Silence in Micheline Aharonian Marcom's *Draining the Sea*," *Modern Fiction Studies* 66, no. 2 (2020): 301–324.

AN EPILOGUE OF RETURN

1. Walter Benjamin "Theses on the Philosophy of History," thesis III in *Illuminations: Essays and Reflections*, trans. Harry Zohn, (New York: Schocken Books, 1969), 254.

2. Karin Karakaşlı, "Tarih-Coğrafya"/"History-Geography," trans. Canan Marasligil, Poetry Translation Workshop, https://www.poetrytranslation.org/poems/history-geography/original, last accessed May 4, 2024.

3. In his poem "Ozone Journal," Peter Balakian speaks of his experience of excavating Armenian bones from northern Syria; see Peter Balakian, *Ozone Journal* (Chicago: University of Chicago Press, 2015), 29–30. Elyse Semerdjian sees the bones buried in mass graves in the Syrian Desert as the "embodied archive" of the Armenian genocide. See Semerdjian, *Remnants: Embodied Archives of the Armenian Genocide* (Stanford, Calif.: Stanford University Press, 2023).

4. Karin Karakaşlı, "History and Geography," in Kathryn Cook, *Memory of Trees* (Kehrer Verlag, 2014), 147.

5. Zabel Yessayan, *In the Ruins: The 1909 Massacres of Armenians in Adana, Turkey* (Boston: Armenian International Woman's Association (AIWA Press), 2016), 11.

6. Karakaşlı, "History and Geography," 147.

INDEX

Page numbers in *italics* refer to illustrations.

GPSR Authorized Representative: Easy Access System Europe, Mustamäe tee 50, 10621 Tallinn, Estonia, gpsr.requests@easproject.com